Substantive Protection under Investment Treaties

Substantive Protection under Investment Treaties provides the first systematic analysis of the consequences of the substantive protections that investment treaties provide to foreign investors. It proposes a new framework for identifying and evaluating the costs and benefits of differing levels of investment treaty protection and uses this framework to evaluate the levels of protection for foreign investors implied by different interpretations of the fair and equitable treatment and indirect expropriation provisions of investment treaties.

The author examines the arguments and assumptions of both supporters and critics of investment treaties, seeks to test whether they are coherent and borne out by evidence and concludes that the 'economic' justifications for investment treaty protections are much weaker than is generally assumed. As such, the 'economic' objectives of investment treaties are not necessarily in tension with other 'non-economic' objectives. These findings have important implications for the drafting and interpretation of investment treaties.

JONATHAN BONNITCHA is a senior lawyer in the Australian government's Office of International Law and a visiting fellow in international investment law and policy at the Australian National University, Canberra.

CAMBRIDGE STUDIES IN INTERNATIONAL AND COMPARATIVE LAW

Established in 1946, this series produces high quality scholarship in the fields of public and private international law and comparative law. Although these are distinct legal sub-disciplines, developments since 1946 confirm their interrelations.

Comparative law is increasingly used as a tool in the making of law at national, regional and international levels. Private international law is now often affected by international conventions, and the issues faced by classical conflicts rules are frequently dealt with by substantive harmonisation of law under international auspices. Mixed international arbitrations, especially those involving state economic activity, raise mixed questions of public and private international law, while in many fields (such as the protection of human rights and democratic standards, investment guarantees and international criminal law) international and national systems interact. National constitutional arrangements relating to 'foreign affairs', and to the implementation of international norms, are a focus of attention.

The series welcomes works of a theoretical or interdisciplinary character, and those focusing on the new approaches to international or comparative law or conflicts of law. Studies of particular institutions or problems are equally welcome, as are translations of the best work published in other languages.

General Editors   James Crawford SC FBA
                   Whewell Professor of International Law, Faculty of Law,
                   University of Cambridge
                   John S. Bell FBA
                   Professor of Law, Faculty of Law, University of Cambridge

A list of books in the series can be found at the end of this volume.

Substantive Protection under Investment Treaties

A Legal and Economic Analysis

Jonathan Bonnitcha

CAMBRIDGE
UNIVERSITY PRESS

CAMBRIDGE
UNIVERSITY PRESS

University Printing House, Cambridge CB2 8BS, United Kingdom

Cambridge University Press is part of the University of Cambridge.

It furthers the University's mission by disseminating knowledge in the pursuit of education, learning and research at the highest international levels of excellence.

www.cambridge.org
Information on this title: www.cambridge.org/9781107042414

© Jonathan Bonnitcha 2014

First published 2014

Printed in the United Kingdom by Clays, St Ives plc

A catalogue record for this publication is available from the British Library

Library of Congress Cataloguing in Publication data

ISBN 978-1-107-04241-4 Hardback

for Emily

Contents

Acknowledgements

Writing a book is an individual project, but one that relies on the assistance and support of others. This book is the final product of research spanning seven years. During that time, I've run up a huge debt, both professional and personal, to friends and colleagues who've supported and encouraged me. There are a number of people I would like acknowledge, without whose support I could not have completed this work.

This book draws on my doctoral dissertation, completed at the University of Oxford in 2012. My study at Oxford was funded by the Rhodes Trust. Without this generous support, the project would not have gotten off the ground.

I'm indebted to my supervisor at Oxford, Professor Christopher McCrudden, who first sparked my interest in investment treaties. He provided insightful comments and criticism on drafts as my research progressed and invaluable support and guidance in the final stages leading up to submission. His own work has had an enormous influence on my thinking, which I have only begun to fully appreciate after leaving Oxford.

I'm grateful to the examiners of my Oxford MPhil dissertation, Professor James Crawford and Professor Dan Sarooshi, who encouraged me to pursue a doctoral project of ambition and scope, and to my DPhil examiners, Professor Rob Howse and Professor Vaughan Lowe, who encouraged me to be bolder in setting out the implications of my arguments. The comments of all four have helped me clarify and strengthen the arguments contained in this book.

The project of converting my dissertation into a full-length monograph was made possible by a Postdoctoral Fellowship at the London School of Economics (LSE) funded by the UK Economic and Social Research Council (ESRC). The Fellowship provided the time and, crucially, the intellectual distance, for me to refine and develop some of the ideas presented in my dissertation. For this, I am hugely grateful to the ESRC. At LSE, I benefited from conversations with many members of the faculty. In particular, I'm grateful for the support and guidance of my mentor, Andrew Lang, and for the energy and intellectual curiosity of Jan Kleinheisterkamp.

I'd also like to record my thanks to all those at Cambridge University Press, who helped see this project smoothly through from proposal to final product, especially Finola O'Sullivan, Elizabeth Spicer and Richard Woodham. Two anonymous reviewers provided generous comments and helpful suggestions about how the proposal might be improved. My sincere thanks to both.

My special thanks go to the team at the Australian Government's Office of International Law, particularly Mark Jennings and John Atwood, for the flexible work arrangements that allowed me to finalise the manuscript of this book while continuing to work at the coal face of investment treaty arbitration. I'm also grateful to the Crawford School of Public Policy at the Australian National University, particularly Peter Drysdale and Stephen Howes, who provided me with the Visiting Fellowship that supported the final stages of the preparation of the manuscript. Toby Hanson, Caroline Henckels, Zoe Hutchinson, Jonathan Ketcheson, Anthea Roberts and Esme Shirlow read various chapters of the final draft. I'm immensely grateful to each of them for the comments and criticisms that they provided at a crucial stage.

Over the past years, I've had the privilege of collaborating with some of the most exciting young academics working on investment treaties. My discussions with Emma Aisbett, Lauge Poulsen, Michael Waibel and Jason Yackee have had a huge influence on my own thinking. I've also benefited from discussions with a range of friends and colleagues about the ideas contained in this book. I'd like to acknowledge and thank Walid Ben Hamida, Nathalie Bernasconi, Chester Brown, Jansen Calamita, Tony Cole, Marie-Claire Cordinnier Segger, Lorenzo Cotula, Antony Crockett, Caroline Foster, Susan Franck, Michael Feutrill, Jonathan Gass, Markus Gehring, Jarrod Hepburn, Ben Juratowitch, Daniel Kalderimis, Vidya Kumar, Jurgen Kurtz, Toby Landau, Rae Lindsay, Andrew Lodder, Julie Maupin, Robert McCorquodale, Rebecca Mendelson, Kate Miles, Alex Mills, Peter Muchlinski, Federico Ortino, Martins Paparinskis, Jan Paulsson, Nicolas Perrone, Luke-Eric Peterson, Georgios Petrochilos, Michele Potesta, Jen Robinson, Fiona Roughley, Jeswald Salacuse, Aruna Sathanapally, Stephan Schill, David Schneiderman, Audley Sheppard, Muthucumaraswamy Sornarajah, Christian Tams, Celine Tan, Kyla Tienhaara, Chris Thomas, Todd Tucker, Valentina Vadi, Anne van Aaken, Gus van

Harten and Sam Wordsworth, all of whom have contributed to the development of the ideas contained in this book in different ways. I'm looking forward to continuing the conversation.

In sum, many individuals and institutions have contributed in different ways to this work. However, the views expressed here, including any errors or omissions, are mine alone and do not necessarily reflect the views of any other institution or person.

Finally, throughout the last seven years I've been sustained by the support and encouragement of friends and family. It would be impossible to list everyone who has tolerated my preoccupation with international investment law with good humour. Suffice it to mention one and to thank others in person. The wonderful Emily Speers Mears has helped me stay sane from the beginning to end of this project. In the process she has developed an impressive, if unwanted, expertise in international investment law. This book is dedicated to her; I promise to be better conversation now that it's done.

JONATHAN BONNITCHA

Abbreviations

ASEAN	Association of South East Asian Nations
BIT	bilateral investment treaty
CAFTA	Dominican Republic-Central America-United States of America Free Trade Agreement
COMESA	Common Market for Eastern and Southern Africa
DTT	double taxation treaty
ECHR	European Convention on Human Rights
ECT	Energy Charter Treaty
ECtHR	European Court of Human Rights
EU	European Union
FCN	Friendship, Commerce and Navigation Treaty
FDI	foreign direct investment
FET	fair and equitable treatment
FIC	Chilean Foreign Investment Commission
FTA	free trade agreement
FTC	Free Trade Commission of the North American Free Trade Agreements
ICJ	International Court of Justice
ICSID	International Center for the Settlement of Investment Disputes
IMS	customary international law minimum standard for the treatment of aliens
ITO	International Trade Organization
MFN	most favoured nation
NAFTA	North American Free Trade Agreement
OECD	Organization for Economic Cooperation and Development
PCIJ	Permanent Court of International Justice
PMRA	Canadian Pest Management Regulatory Agency

RCEP	Regional Comprehensive Economic Partnership
RIAA	Reports of International Arbitral Awards
TPP	TransPacific Partnership
TTIP	TransAtlantic Trade and Investment Partnership
UN	United Nations
UNCITRAL	United Nations Commission on International Trade Law
UNCTAD	United Nations Commission on Trade and Development
UNGA	United Nations General Assembly
US	United States of America
VAT	value added tax
VCLT	Vienna Convention on the Law of Treaties
WTO	World Trade Organization

Arbitral awards and cases

Cases

Investor-state arbitral awards

Other arbitral awards

Treaties

UN documents

1 Introduction

Investment treaties grant a range of generous rights to foreign investors. These include both substantive rights, such as the right to 'fair and equitable' treatment (FET) and the right to be compensated for the expropriation of their investments, and procedural rights – notably, the right to bring a claim that these substantive rights have been breached to investor-state arbitration. Since the late 1990s, there has been a rapid growth in the number of investors bringing claims under investment treaties to investor-state arbitration. Relying on the substantive rights conferred by investment treaties, investors have challenged a range of regulatory measures taken by host states, including measures to regulate the use of pesticides, the discharge of pollutants, the sale of tobacco products and the (non-)grant of medical patents. Investors have also challenged the decisions of national courts and the allocation of financial risks and returns in investment projects. Claims regularly run into the billions of dollars and involve tens of millions of dollars in legal costs. Not all these claims have been successful. Some have succeeded, some have failed and some result in settlement agreements involving concessions by one or both parties. But the amount of money at stake and the fact that foreign investors are able to frame viable claims against such a broad range of government conduct has raised questions about whether investment treaties grant overly expansive rights.

At the same time, investment treaties promise to spur the economic development of the states that are party to them and, perhaps more ambitiously, to stimulate the spread of 'good governance'. If the grant of robust substantive rights to foreign investors were necessary to realise these benefits, any associated costs might be justified. In any case, it is impossible to reach an informed view about whether the substantive protections commonly found in investment treaties are justified without examining the benefits of conferring such rights on foreign investors.

This book provides a systematic analysis of the costs and benefits of the substantive protections that investment treaties provide to foreign investors. The purpose of this inquiry is to determine whether investment treaties should provide more or less protection than they currently do. I take the arguments of both supporters and critics seriously and seek to test whether they are coherent and borne out by evidence. The book concludes with a range of recommendations for reform of the investment treaty system.

1.1 A brief history of investment treaties

While international law has long been concerned with the protection of foreign-owned property,[1] the proliferation of treaties placing obligations on host states with respect to foreign investment is a more recent phenomenon. The modern era of investment treaties is often dated from the signing of the first bilateral investment treaty (BIT) between Germany and Pakistan in 1959.[2] Yet it was not until 1969, with the BIT between Italy and Chad, that investment treaties began to grant foreign investors the right to bring disputes with the host state directly to investor-state arbitration.[3] The grant of this unprecedented procedural right to foreign investors laid the basis for the transformation of the field of international investment law by making treaties directly enforceable.[4] However, it was only after the first investor-state arbitration, more than two decades later, that the full implications of the BIT movement began to become clear.[5] In the meantime, the negotiation and ratification of BITs accelerated through the 1980s and 1990s, before continuing at a slower pace during the early twenty-first century.

There are now more than 2800 BITs, with nearly every state having signed at least one.[6] Roughly three-quarters of these BITs have entered

---

[1] Miles, *The Origins of International Investment Law: Empire, the Environment and the Safeguarding of Capital* (2013), p. 2.

[2] E.g., Dolzer and Schreuer, *Principles of International Investment Law* (2nd edn, 2012), p. 6.

[3] Yackee, 'Conceptual Difficulties in the Empirical Study of Bilateral Investment Treaties' (2008) 33 *Brooklyn Journal of International Law*, p. 430.

[4] Paulsson 'Arbitration without Privity' (1995) 10 *ICSID Review – Foreign Investment Law Journal*, p. 233.

[5] *Asian Agricultural Products v. Republic of Sri Lanka*, Final Award, 27 June 1990.

[6] UNCTAD, *World Investment Report 2013* (2013), p. 101.

into force.[7] While most early BITs were signed between a developed and a developing country,[8] BITs between developing countries are increasingly common.[9] Notwithstanding the number of BITs and the array of states involved, there is considerable uniformity in their structure and wording. Two features common to the majority of BITs are particularly important to the present inquiry. The first is that they provide a common set of substantive legal protections to foreign investment. Each signatory state is typically required to provide foreign investment from the other signatory state with FET, national treatment and compensation in the event of expropriation of the investment.[10] The second feature, as already noted, is that they allow foreign investors to bring claims that the host state has breached these protections directly to investor-state arbitration.[11] If an arbitral tribunal determines that a host state has breached the applicable BIT, it will invariably award the investor-claimant compensation for the loss it suffered as a result of the breach. Such awards are readily enforceable.[12]

Whereas all the early investment treaties were bilateral, the 1990s saw the beginnings of a shift towards the negotiation of investment treaties with a broader regional or sectoral scope. Examples of regional investment treaties include the Association of South East Asian Nations (ASEAN) Comprehensive Investment Agreement, the Common Market for Eastern and Southern Africa (COMESA) Investment Agreement and the Japan-China-Korea Trilateral Investment treaty.[13] Similarly, the Energy Charter Treaty

---

[7] UNCTAD, 'The Entry into Force of Bilateral Investment Treaties (BITs)' (2006), *International Investment Agreements Monitor*, p. 2.

[8] Dolzer, 'The Impact of International Investment Treaties on Domestic Administrative Law' (2006) 37 *International Law and Politics*, p. 955.

[9] UNCTAD, *South–South Cooperation in International Investment Agreements* (2007), p. 6.

[10] UNCTAD, *Development Implications of International Investment Agreements* (2007), p. 2; Ryan, 'Meeting Expectations: Assessing the Long-term Legitimacy and Stability of International Investment Law' (2008) 29 *University of Pennsylvania Journal of International Law*, p. 732.

[11] UNCTAD, *International Investment Agreements: Key Issues*, Vol. 1 (2004), p. 19.

[12] Arbitral awards are enforceable in the courts of states that have signed the Convention on the Settlement of Investment Disputes between States and Nationals of other States (18 March 1965; hereafter, ICSID Convention), art. 54, if the tribunal is convened under the ICSID Convention or the courts of the states that have signed the Convention on the Recognition and Enforcement of Foreign Arbitral Awards (10 Jan 1958; hereafter, New York Convention), art. III, if the tribunal is convened under any other set of procedural rules, such as the United Nations Commission on International Trade Law (UNCITRAL) rules or the rules of the International Center for the Settlement of Investment Disputes (ICSID) Additional Facility.

[13] ASEAN Comprehensive Investment Agreement (26 February 2009; hereafter, ASEAN Comprehensive Investment Agreement); Common Market for Eastern and Southern

(ECT), the most important sectoral investment treaty, confers legal protection on investments made by investors of a signatory state in the energy sector of any of the other fifty-one signatory states.[14] Increasingly, bilateral and regional free trade agreements (FTAs) also contain investment chapters modelled on BITs. The most well known of these treaties is the North American Free Trade Agreement (NAFTA),[15] but there are many others. At the time of going to press, it was envisaged that all three 'mega-regional' FTAs under negotiation – the TransPacific Partnership (TPP), the Regional Comprehensive Economic Partnership (RCEP) and the TransAtlantic Trade and Investment Partnership (TTIP) – would include investment chapters.[16]

This book concerns the full set of treaties that place substantive obligations on host states relating to the protection of foreign investment and provide for compulsory investor-state arbitration of claims that those protections have been breached. For convenience, the term 'investment treaty' is used throughout to refer to such treaties, but it is important to be clear that the analysis applies equally to the investment protection provisions contained in FTAs. Consistent with this terminology, the term 'investment treaty protections' is used to refer to the substantive obligations relating to the protection of foreign investment whether found in BITs, regional or sectoral investment treaties or FTAs.

1.2 The scope of the inquiry

This is a book about investment treaties, but it does not attempt to answer all the policy and legal questions raised by these agreements. It does not chart the history of investment treaties in detail, nor does it seek to determine whether states fully understood the implications of the treaties that they signed. It does not ask whether investor-state arbitration is an appropriate way of resolving disputes arising from the exercise of governmental authority (although the findings may have implications for this question). Instead, the inquiry seeks to determine the level of protection that investment treaties should provide to foreign investment. As well as being of academic interest, this question confronts policymakers every time they negotiate an investment treaty. The contribution

Africa Common Investment Area Agreement (23 May 2007; hereafter, COMESA Investment Agreement); Japan-Korea-China Trilateral Investment Treaty (13 May 2012).

[14] The Energy Charter Treaty (17 December 1994; hereafter, ECT), art. 13(1).

[15] North American Free Trade Agreement (17 December 1992; hereafter, NAFTA).

[16] UNCTAD, 'The Rise of Regionalism in International Investment Policymaking: Consolidation or Complexity?' (2013), IIA Issue Notes, p. 1.

of this book is both that it provides a rigorous and systematic methodology for answering this question and that, through the application of this methodology, it offers a set of answers to this question.

The methodology proposed in this book involves a comparison between the costs and benefits of adopting different levels of investment protection. In other words, the methodology is consequentialist. In Chapter 3, I develop a framework for conceptualising, identifying and evaluating the consequences of providing differing levels of protection in investment treaties. This framework is then applied to some of the most contentious issues in debate about investment treaties – questions about the level of protection that should be provided through FET and expropriation provisions. Chapters 4 and 5 review existing arbitral jurisprudence on the interpretation of the FET and indirect expropriation provisions of investment treaties. These chapters identify several different understandings of the extent of protection provided to foreign investment, which are then sketched as levels of protection that might, in future, be adopted and applied consistently. Chapter 6 uses the framework to evaluate each of these levels of protection.

The following paragraphs explain the scope of the inquiry more precisely. As will become clear, the task of evaluating variations in the drafting of every investment treaty protection (not to mention the omission of existing protections and their replacement with entirely new provisions) would require a work several times the length of this volume. Through a detailed engagement with the FET and expropriation provisions of investment treaties, I demonstrate how the framework developed in Chapter 3 could be applied to evaluate a much broader range of options.

1.2.1 The evaluation of levels of protection derived from existing arbitral jurisprudence

In this book, I evaluate a range of levels of protection derived from arbitral jurisprudence interpreting the FET and indirect expropriation provisions of existing investment treaties. These levels of protection constitute a set of options that states, in the drafting of future treaties or by the amendment of existing ones, might adopt. The primary justification for evaluating options derived from existing jurisprudence is that the options to be evaluated must themselves be defined with some degree of precision. Existing investment treaty protections are drafted in unusually vague terms, and their meaning has primarily been fleshed out through the process of interpretation and application by arbitral tribunals.[17] The question of whether investment treaties should contain provisions requiring 'fair and equitable treatment' cannot sensibly be answered without first providing a more precise articulation of the extent of protection that such provisions provide.

There is a second justification for evaluating options derived from existing jurisprudence, one that relates to the practicalities of treaty revision. Insofar as this book is addressed to policy-makers, existing state practice suggests a preference for the revision and clarification of existing standards, rather than the replacement of existing standards by new standards with no basis in current treaty practice.[18] Of course, it remains open to states to include whatever provisions on which they agree in future investment treaties. And I do not intend to foreclose the possibility, or desirability, of more radical changes to investment treaties. My claim is simply that the broad disagreement about the level of protection that is provided by existing provisions offers a useful entry point to the wider debate about how much protection investment treaties should provide. The evaluation of options derived from existing jurisprudence also means that the analysis is relevant to arbitrators and lawyers tasked with the interpretation of treaties as they are currently drafted.

1.2.2 The prospective evaluation of legal rules

Chapters 4 and 5 show that decisions interpreting provisions of existing investment treaties do not define a level of protection that is applied consistently in all disputes. The review of existing decisions identifies several different understandings of the level of protection provided by existing treaties, each of which defines a level of protection that could be adopted and applied consistently in the future. Thus, the inquiry in this book has two important characteristics. The first is that it concerns the evaluation of a set of *prospective* options, each of which would entail a degree of certainty about the level of protection provided to foreign investment. The second is that it concerns the evaluation of different

---

[17] Schill, *The Multilateralization of International Investment Law* (2009), p. 355; Bjorklund, 'Investment Treaty Arbitral Decisions as Jurisprudence Constante', in Picker, Bunn and Arner (eds), International Economic Law: The State and Future of the Discipline (2008), p. 277.

[18] US Model Bilateral Investment Treaty (2012; hereafter, US 2012 Model BIT), annex B; Canada Model Foreign Investment Protection Agreement (2004; hereafter, Canada Model FIPA), annex B.13(1); Colombia Model Bilateral Investment treaty (2007), art. III(4).

possible *legal rules*,[19] as opposed to an analysis of whether particular past disputes should have been resolved in favour of the host state or the investor.

These two characteristics of the options under consideration have implications for the range of costs and benefits that must be taken into account. The inquiry must consider the implications of the proposed rule for the full range of situations covered by the rule, including its impact on the behaviour of actors in situations that do not ultimately result in legal disputes. For example, the inquiry must consider whether adopting a high level of protection for foreign investors would encourage greater foreign investment and whether it would increase 'regulatory chill'.

1.2.3 Exceptions to substantive protections

Two additional parameters should be acknowledged, both of which relate to the extent of substantive protection provided by investment treaties. I do not consider the role that general exceptions in investment treaties play in qualifying states' obligations or the role that the public international law doctrine of necessity plays in precluding wrongfulness of breaches of investment treaties that occur in emergency situations. I have excluded general exceptions on the grounds that only a handful of investment treaties contain such provisions.[20] I have excluded the doctrine of necessity on the basis that this doctrine is applicable only in a narrow set of emergency situations.[21] Nevertheless, it would be relatively straightforward to use the framework developed in Chapter 3 to evaluate the costs and benefits of including exceptions to various levels of substantive protection.

---

[19] Some commentators have distinguished 'legal rules' from 'legal standards', arguing that 'rules' are defined with a greater precision than 'standards', e.g., Ortino, 'Refining the Content and Role of Investment "Rules" and "Standards": A New Approach to International Investment Treaty Making' (2013) 28 *ICSID Review*, p. 153. In this book, I do not adopt this distinction. Variation in the precision with which a rule/standard is drafted is a matter of degree. In the context of debate about investment treaty protections, there is little value in attempting to determine the point at which an increasingly imprecise 'rule' could be said to become a 'standard'. For this reason, I use the term 'legal rules' on the understanding that such rules may be drafted with varying degrees of precision.

[20] Newcombe, 'General Exceptions in International Investment Agreements' in Cordonier Segger, Gehring and Newcombe (eds), Sustainable Development in World Investment Law (2011), p. 358.

[21] International Law Commission, *Draft Articles of the International Law Commission* art. 25.

1.2.4 Evaluation from a general, impartial perspective

Chapter 6 evaluates each of the levels of protection identified in Chapters 4 and 5 from a general, impartial perspective. By 'general', I mean that different levels of protection are evaluated on the basis that they would be included in a range of investment treaties involving many differently situated states. This general perspective contrasts with the perspective one would adopt when determining the level of protection that should be provided by one particular investment treaty, considered in isolation. In such an exercise, the specific characteristics of the state parties to the treaty under consideration would assume greater importance. By 'impartial', I mean that all the costs and benefits associated with a given level of protection are considered. This impartial perspective differs from the self-interested perspective of a given actor (for example, a particular state), where the focus would be limited to the costs and benefits that affect the actor in question.

There are several justifications for the 'general' perspective adopted in this book. The first concerns the practicalities of the negotiation and application of investment treaties. Most existing state practice is driven by model investment treaties – template negotiating positions devised by a state and then offered to several other states.[22] This practice is unsurprising. Tailoring the level of protection provided by each individual investment treaty to the particular characteristics of the partner state(s) in question would complicate efforts to negotiate and comply with investment treaties enormously. As such, views about the level of protection that should be provided across treaties involving many differently situated states drive existing treaty practice.

The second justification is that at the time a state negotiates an investment treaty, it cannot predict with certainty the types of investments that will qualify for protection under the treaty during the period it remains in force or the range of regulatory actions that the state may wish to adopt during this period. This is not to say that states are unable to make any predictions about the future of a given investment relationship. When negotiating with the Democratic Republic of Congo, the United States may be able to predict that it is likely to remain a net capital exporter over the coming decades. My point is that it would be unwise to evaluate the terms of any prospective investment treaty solely through the lens of

---

[22] Salacuse, *The Law of Investment Treaties* (2010), pp. 12–13; Schill, *The Multilateralization of International Investment Law*, p. 89; Dolzer and Schreuer, *Principles of International Investment Law* (2nd edn), p. 8.

the investment relationship between the states at the time the treaty is signed. If a state is to bind itself with respect to an uncertain range of regulatory actions that may affect an uncertain set of future investments, it makes sense to reflect in more general terms on the merits of offering investment protection.

Two more justifications flow from the structure of investment treaties themselves. Many investment treaties contain most favoured nation (MFN) clauses.[23] An MFN clause allows foreign investors covered by one investment treaty to rely on higher levels of protection conferred by another treaty.[24] For this reason, states will need to consider the possibility that an unusually high level of protection offered in any given investment treaty may become generalised by being made available to foreign investment covered by another investment treaty. Moreover, several investment treaties have been interpreted as providing protection to investors of the corporate nationality of the home state.[25] For this reason, states will need to consider the possibility that the level of protection offered under any given investment treaty will become generalised by being made available to investors that structure investments through corporate intermediaries in the 'home' state.[26]

A final justification is of a different character, as it concerns the relationship of this book to existing academic debate. The vast majority of academic writing treats the existing network of investment treaties as a single field of academic inquiry.[27] More than one commentator has described this network as constituting a 'regime';[28] another has argued that, in many respects, these treaties 'function analogously to a truly multilateral system'.[29] Without going so far as to endorse these claims, it is clear that the academic literature regards the set of existing investment treaties as raising common legal and policy issues. I share this premise.

The justifications for the 'impartial' perspective adopted in this book are less numerous but equally compelling. The primary justification is

---

[23] Schill, *The Multilateralization of International Investment Law*, p. 140.
[24] Newcombe and Paradell, *Law and Practice of Investment Treaties: Standards of Treatment* (2009), p. 255; *MTD* v. *Chile*, Award, para. 104; *Bayindir* v. *Pakistan*, Award, para. 157.
[25] *CME* v. *Czech Republic*, Partial Award, para. 6; *Tokios Tokeles* v. *Ukraine*, Decision on Jurisdiction, para. 38.
[26] Schill, *The Multilateralization of International Investment Law*, p. 199.
[27] E.g., Dolzer and Schreuer, *Principles of International Investment Law* (2nd edn); Salacuse, *The Law of Investment Treaties*, p. 5.
[28] Ratner, 'Regulatory Takings in Institutional Context: Beyond the Fear of Fragmented International Law' (2008) 102 *American Journal of International Law*, p. 517.
[29] Schill, *The Multilateralization of International Investment Law*, p. 15.

normative: legal rules should not be evaluated solely on the extent to which they benefit one actor; all costs and benefits should be considered. These premises are foundational in scholarship concerned with the normative evaluation of legal rules.[30] The majority of existing scholarship on investment treaties also appears to take these premises as given – for example, they underpin scholarship arguing that investment treaties should balance competing interests.[31]

There are also important pragmatic justifications for adopting an impartial perspective. An impartial perspective approximates the shared perspective of the states that are party to any investment treaty. For this reason, consensual negotiations between well-informed state parties should converge towards mutually beneficial levels of protection that maximise net benefits overall. Moreover, arbitral tribunals are obliged to interpret investment treaties in light of the shared purpose of the treaty parties, as embodied in the treaty.[32] Thus, the impartial perspective adopted in this book is practically relevant to both the negotiation and interpretation of investment treaties.

A further justification concerns the perspective of states that are both sources and recipients of foreign investment. Even when negotiating a single BIT, the self-interest of such states will tend towards levels of protection that are desirable from an impartial perspective. The current trend towards multilateralism amplifies this effect. From the perspective of any one state, a multilateral investment treaty is more likely to cover relationships with both states with which it is a net capital importer and a net capital exporter. As Alvarez has argued:

> More countries than ever before are, like the PRC [People's Republic of China] and the United States, capital exporters as well as capital importers. The position of such countries in the investment regime might be said to approximate that of the individual in John Rawls' 'original position', that is, someone who is placed behind a veil of ignorance and does not know the social or economic position she occupies within society and is therefore incentivized to articulate principles of justice that are fair to all.[33]

The impartial perspective adopted in this book is akin to that of an 'original position' analysis in that it is not addressed to the self-interest of a particular state.

---

[30] E.g., Calabresi, *The Costs of Accidents: A Legal and Economic Analysis* (1970), pp. 24–33.
[31] See Section 2.5.   [32] See Section 7.3.1.1.
[33] Alvarez, 'The Once and Future Foreign Investment Regime' in Arsanjani et al. (eds), *Looking to the Future: Essays in Honor of Michael Reisman* (2010), p. 634.

Although this book evaluates different levels of protection primarily from a general, impartial perspective, the framework developed in Chapter 3 has a broader range of potential application. Chapter 3 identifies several ways in which the consequences of a given level of protection are likely to vary with the characteristics of the states in question.[34] It also shows how the self-interested perspectives of the different parties to a given treaty may diverge, particularly if investment flows between the countries are highly asymmetric.[35] As such, the framework could also be used to derive specific conclusions about the level of protection that a particular investment treaty should provide from the self-interested perspective of a particular state.[36] Nevertheless, for all the reasons explained earlier, the conclusions derived from a general and impartial perspective in Chapter 6 should be the point of departure for any discussion about the level of protection any particular investment treaty should provide.

1.3 Outline of the argument

The remainder of the book is organised as follows. Chapter 2 examines the justifications and criticisms of investment treaties raised in the existing literature in so far as they relate to the level of substantive protection that these treaties provide. The chapter argues that existing debate about investment treaties is relatively immature, in that both proponents and critics pay little attention to the normative and causal assumptions on which their arguments are based. To clarify the structure of existing debate, this chapter seeks to articulate the methodological underpinnings of existing debate and the normative premises on which various justifications and criticisms implicitly rely.

Two central claims emerge from this review. The first is that debate about the level of substantive protection provided by investment treaties seldom stems from fundamental disagreement about which objectives are desirable. Both critics and supporters appear to agree that the same set of objectives is desirable – improvements in economic efficiency, the realisation of human rights, environmental conservation, greater foreign direct investment (FDI) flows and greater respect for the rule of law. The second claim is that differences in opinion about the level of protection that investment treaties should provide stem primarily from embedded causal assumptions about the likely consequences of differing levels of

---

[34] E.g., Section 3.4.7; Section 3.7.7.   [35] See Section 3.5.2.   [36] See Section 7.2.3.

protection – for example, assumptions about whether investment treaties discourage states from taking legitimate regulatory measures to protect human rights and the environment. To a lesser extent, differences in opinion about the level of protection that investment treaties should provide also stem from disagreement about how competing objectives should be prioritised. However, this chapter argues that questions of 'balancing' can only sensibly be addressed after the objectives that need to be balanced have been specified and the causal assumptions that give rise to the supposed tension between competing objectives have been examined.

Together, the conclusions of Chapter 2 suggest that debate about the substantive protection that investment treaties provide should be more focused on articulating and examining underlying causal assumptions. The set of objectives that emerge from the critique of the existing literature provide a framework to structure a causal inquiry of this sort. In concluding, Chapter 2 argues that the consequences of investment treaty protections can be divided into five categories: their effect on efficiency, on the distribution of economic costs and benefits, on flows of FDI into host states, on the realisation of human rights and environmental conservation in host states and on respect for the rule of law in host states.

Chapter 3 of the book constitutes the analytical core of the work. It adopts the framework that emerges from Chapter 2. Within this framework, Chapter 3 examines the causal assumptions implicit in existing debate about investment treaties, reflects on whether assumptions are based on internally coherent models that link cause to supposed effect and tests the predictions and the assumptions on which they are based against available evidence. This process is dialectical. Causal assumptions from the existing literature are used to frame the empirical inquiry and suggest plausible hypotheses. These hypotheses are tested against available evidence. The insights of this examination are then used to propose further, more refined hypotheses about the likely impact of given levels of protection. From this analysis, Chapter 3 derives a set of inferences about the likely consequences of providing different levels of investment treaty protection.

In evaluating, testing and refining the causal assumptions implicit in existing debate, Chapter 3 necessarily relies on a set of assumptions of its own. The book's approach to theory and evidence is influenced by the New Haven school of law and economics. This approach is reflected both in the framework used to structure the inquiry[37] and in assumptions about the

---

[37] Calabresi and Melamed, 'Property Rules, Liability Rules, and Inalienability: One View of the Cathedral' (1972) 85 *Harvard Law Review*, p. 1102.

way actors' behaviour is affected by incentives. The assumption that actors tend to minimise the costs and maximise the benefits of their actions is common to most economic approaches, but in the New Haven approach this assumption is simply a first approximation – a useful starting point for causal theorising that may need to be modified or abandoned depending on whether it is consistent with observed behaviour of a particular actor. The chapter reflects on the validity of this, and other, underlying assumptions.

Through this analysis, Chapter 3 draws several inferences about the likely consequences of investment treaty protections. These conclusions are highly nuanced. However, one of the central conclusions of this chapter is that 'economic' objectives of investment treaties – efficiency and the attraction of FDI – are not necessarily in tension with 'non-economic' objectives, such as the realisation of human rights. This is because the economic justifications for investment treaties are weaker than is generally supposed. Protections that are more favourable to the interests of foreign investors are not, self-evidently, associated with net economic benefits.

In Chapters 4 and 5 of the book, the focus of the inquiry shifts to the level of protection currently provided by investment treaties. In these chapters the book covers similar territory to other studies of investment treaty law. However, these chapters differ from existing commentary on investment law in that they analyse the structure of reasoning used by arbitral tribunals rather than whether tribunals employ common terminology (for example, terms like 'transparency', 'legitimate expectations' and 'reasonableness'). This approach yields important insights. For example, although many tribunals agree that the FET standard protects an investor's 'legitimate expectations', tribunals have reached markedly different conclusions concerning the criteria by which protected expectations should be distinguished from expectations that are not protected by the FET standard. The chapters argue that tribunals have interpreted the FET and indirect expropriation provisions of investment treaties in several distinct ways and that each of these distinct interpretations exhibits a degree of internal coherence. Each interpretation is outlined as a level of protection that is both a doctrinally plausible interpretation of existing provisions and a model level of protection that could explicitly be adopted in the drafting of future investment treaties.

Chapter 6 evaluates the alternative levels of protection identified in Chapters 4 and 5. In doing so, this chapter applies the conclusions about the consequences of adopting differing levels of protection that emerge from Chapter 3. The analysis suggests that lower levels of protection are generally preferable to higher levels of protection. The analysis also leads to several more specific conclusions. For example, insofar as government conduct affects the interests of investors, this chapter draws attention to the distinction between the impact of government conduct on the legal entitlements of an investor and the impact of conduct on the economic value of the investment. This chapter argues that levels of protection in which a state's liability turns on the degree of interference with the legal entitlements of the investor are generally preferable to levels of protection in which a state's liability turns on the impact of the state's conduct on the value of the investment. A second specific conclusion is that several tribunals have interpreted investment treaties in ways for which there is *no* coherent normative justification. This conclusion raises a series of further questions about the wisdom of drafting investment treaty protections in vague language that confers a high degree of interpretative discretion on arbitral tribunals.

Chapter 7 considers the implications of the findings of Chapter 6 for the interpretation and drafting of investment treaties. This chapter provides a set of recommendations to states about how the drafting of the substantive protections of new investment treaties should be modified to maximise the benefits and minimise the costs associated with the grant of such rights. This chapter also argues that states are entitled to amend investment treaties prospectively, regardless of the impact such amendment has on foreign investors. Given that some arbitral tribunals are interpreting the substantive protections of existing treaties in ways for which there is no coherent normative justification, amending and redrafting the protections of investment treaties should be a matter of priority.

Chapter 7 also examines the implications of the analysis for the interpretation of existing treaties. My argument here is more cautious. On one hand, when interpreting a treaty, tribunals cannot completely disregard the text of a treaty provision, in favour of policy arguments about the level of protection that should be provided. On the other hand, even under a strictly formalist application of the Vienna Convention of the Law of Treaties, interpretation requires attention to a treaty's 'object and purpose'. I contend that the analysis in Chapters 2 and 3 sheds light on the way in which an investment treaty's object and purpose should be understood and on how that understanding of object and purpose should influence the interpretative exercise. Moreover, the reality is that the interpretation of treaties is never entirely divorced from latent assumptions about the objectives of the treaty and the consequences of adopting a given interpretation. This is particularly the case with the substantive protections of investment treaties, which are drafted in unusually vague terms. In providing a detailed and systematic examination of the extent to which differing levels of protections are likely to advance different objectives, the conclusions of the book are also relevant to the process of treaty interpretation.

2   The structure of existing debate

2.1 Introduction

This chapter examines the justifications and criticisms of investment treaties that are raised in the existing literature. In doing so, it articulates the normative and causal assumptions on which existing arguments are based. This exposition is useful in itself. Greater clarity about the underpinnings of existing arguments can shed new light on a range of debates about investment treaties. In the context of this book, this chapter performs two more specific functions. First, it shows that debate about the level of substantive protection provided by investment treaties seldom stems from fundamental disagreement about which objectives are desirable. Second, it shows that the most disagreement about how much protection investment treaties should provide stems from assumptions, often unarticulated, about the consequences of providing various levels of protection. These observations form the foundation of the framework developed in Chapter 3.

This chapter is structured as follows. Section 2.2 examines social scientific literature that seeks to explain the existence and content of investment treaties. It argues that the basic assumption in this literature is that the objective of investment treaties is to provide economic benefits to states that are party to them. Sections 2.3, 2.4 and 2.5 review normative debate about investment treaties. Section 2.3 reviews criticisms of investment treaties; Section 2.4 considers justifications for investment treaties; and Section 2.5 examines appeals for 'balance' in debate. Each section seeks to identify the methodologies being used and to articulate the normative and causal assumptions made in the course of argument. Section 2.6 concludes that debate about investment treaties can usefully be framed in consequentialist terms. It proposes a synthesis of the normative

16

premises that underpin debate about investment treaty protections, which can be used as a framework to organise such a consequentialist inquiry.

2.2 Assumptions and premises in social scientific scholarship on investment treaties

There is a substantial body of scholarship that draws on methodologies from political science, economics and international relations to propose and test explanatory theories about investment treaties. This section does not attempt to provide a full review of this literature. Rather, it attempts to show that characterisation of the objectives of investment treaties, and assessment of their effectiveness in realising these objectives, are central concerns in this scholarship. Scholarship focusing on these questions embodies a shared belief that investment treaties are intended to achieve instrumental, economic aims – the attraction of foreign direct investment (FDI) and the creation of net economic benefits.

2.2.1 'Rational actor' theories explaining why states sign investment treaties

A theoretical body of literature seeks to explain why developing states sign bilateral investment treaty (BITs).[1] In this literature, there is a particular focus on the apparent paradox that developing countries signed BITs containing rules for the protection of foreign investment while simultaneously rejecting identical rules in multilateral forums.[2] The methodological basis for this scholarship is the premise that states are unitary actors and that, in signing treaties, they act in their own interests. The majority of contributions to this literature rely on the further assumption that states are capable of rationally and accurately identifying their own interests – that they are rational actors.[3] These premises about the

---

[1] This literature focuses on BITs; however, its insights are applicable to the multilateral context.

[2] Elkins, Guzman and Simmons, 'Competing for Capital', (2006) 60 International Organization p. 841; Montt, *State Liability in Investment Treaty Arbitration* (2009), p. 112; Bubb and Rose-Ackerman, 'BITs and Bargains: Strategic Aspects of Bilateral and Multilateral Regulation of Foreign Investment' (2007) 27 *International Review of Law and Economics*, p. 307; Morin and Gagné, 'What Can Best Explain the Prevalance of Bilateralism in the Investment Regime?' (2007) 36 *Journal of International Political Economy*, p. 67.

[3] Guzman, 'Why LDCs Sign Treaties That Hurt Them: Explaining the Popularity of Bilateral Investment Treaties' (1998) 38 *Virginia Journal of International Law*, p. 669.

institutional and behavioural characteristics of states are generally assumed rather than proved.

Two more recent contributions challenge the assumption that states act rationally. Yackee argues that the acceptance of certain ideas among policy-makers – that BITs increase inflows of FDI and that FDI is necessary for economic development – rather than the accuracy of these ideas, explains states' behaviour.[4] Poulsen and Aisbett argue that states behave 'predictably irrationally' in the sense that states with no direct experience of investment treaty claims tend to suffer from optimism bias when assessing the costs and benefits of entering into investment treaties.[5]

The prevailing view in explanatory theories of BITs, including Yackee's and Poulsen and Aisbett's, is that capital-importing states sign BITs in an attempt to increase inflow of FDI.[6] These scholars also agree that, were it not for increased FDI, BITs would be contrary to capital-importing states self-interest because they limit states' ability to 'advance and protect their national interests'.[7] Given the central role of FDI in explanations for the existence of investment treaties, a number of studies have sought to investigate whether BITs are effective in attracting FDI.[8]

2.2.2 Theories explaining the content of investment treaties

A separate stream of scholarship attempts to explain the particular mix of provisions included in typical BITs. Vandevelde is a key figure in this

---

[4] Yackee, 'Are BITs Such a Bright Idea? Exploring the Ideational Basis of Investment treaty Enthusiasm' (2005) 12 *University of California Davis Journal of International Law and Policy*, p. 202; Alvarez 'The Once and Future Foreign Investment Regime' in Arsanjani et al. (eds), *Looking to the Future: Essays in Honor of Michael Reisman* (2010) pp. 619–622.

[5] Poulsen and Aisbett, 'When the Claim Hits: Bilateral Investment Treaties and Bounded Rational Learning' (2013) 65 *World Politics*, p. 301.

[6] Yackee, 'Are BITs Such a Bright Idea?', p. 202; Poulsen and Aisbett, 'When the Claim Hits', p. 302; Guzman, 'Why LDCs Sign Treaties that Hurt Them', p. 670; Bubb and Rose-Ackerman, 'BITs and Bargains', p. 302; Salacuse and Sullivan, 'Do BITs Really Work?: An Evaluation of Bilateral Investment Treaties and Their Grand Bargain' in Sauvant and Sachs (eds), *The Effect of Treaties on Foreign Direct Investment: Bilateral Investment Treaties, Double Taxation Treaties and Investment Flows* (2009), p. 120; Sornarajah, *The International Law on Foreign Investment* (3rd edn, 2010), p. 186; Bonilla and Castro, 'A Law-and-Economics Analysis of International Investment Agreements' (2006) [online]; van Harten, 'Private Authority and Transnational Governance: The Contours of the International System of Investor Protection' (2005) 12 *Review of International Political Economy*, p. 609.

[7] Salacuse and Sullivan, 'Do BITs Really Work?', p. 120. Similarly, Guzman, 'Why LDCs Sign Treaties That Hurt Them', p. 670; Bubb and Rose-Ackerman, 'BITs and Bargains', p. 302; Sornarajah, *The International Law on Foreign Investment*, p. 186.

[8] E.g., Buthe and Milner, 'Bilateral Investment Treaties and Foreign Direct Investment: A Political Analysis' in Sauvant and Sachs (eds), *The Effect of Treaties on Foreign Direct Investment: Bilateral Investment Treaties, Double Taxation Treaties and Investment Flows* (2009), p. 193.

literature. His argument begins by distinguishing liberal economic theory from nationalist economic theory.[9] In his view, liberal economic theory is the theory that free markets provide the most efficient means to allocate goods, services and investment flows.[10] This theory might, more precisely, be identified as neo-classical economic theory. He contrasts this with the theory of economic nationalism, a relatively open collection of interventionist theoretical responses to neo-classical economics based on the view that 'a state's economic policy should serve its political policy'.[11]

Vandevelde argues that BITs do not reflect economic liberalism in two key respects. First, economic liberalism calls for competitive equality between all investors, yet BITs provide one group of foreign investors with a set of legal rights beyond those provided to local investors and foreign investors from countries not covered by a BIT.[12] Second, economic liberalism calls for unrestricted investment flows. However, BITs focus on the post-establishment rights of investment and allow states the discretion to exclude foreign investors[13] (although more recent US, Canadian and Japanese BITs do provide a right to pre-establishment national treatment).[14] On the strength of these two arguments, Vandevelde suggests that BITs are better explained by the theories of interventionism and their associated political considerations than a theory of economic liberalism.[15]

A distinct body of social scientific scholarship uses neo-classical economic theory to determine whether investment treaty protections are likely to generate net economic benefits in the states that sign them (that is, to increase economic efficiency).[16] This work has its intellectual roots

---

[9] Vandevelde, 'The Political Economy of a Bilateral Investment Treaty' (1998) 92 *American Journal of International Law*, p. 621.

[10] Ibid., p. 624.

[11] Ibid., p. 622; Vandevelde, 'The Economics of Bilateral Investment Treaties' (2000) 41 *Harvard International Law Journal*, p. 476.

[12] Vandevelde, 'The Political Economy of a Bilateral Investment Treaty', p. 630; also, Stiglitz, 'Regulating Multinational Corporations: Towards Principles of Cross-Border Legal Frameworks in a Globalized World Balancing Rights with Responsibilities' (2008) 23 *American University International Law Review*, p. 549; Lowe, 'Changing Dimensions of International Investment Law', (2007) [online], p. 48.

[13] Vandevelde, 'The Economics of Bilateral Investment Treaties', p. 493.

[14] Dolzer and Schreuer, *Principles of International Investment Law* (2nd edn, 2012), p. 81.

[15] Vandevelde, 'The Political Economy of a Bilateral Investment Treaty', p. 634. For a more recent argument to the same effect, see Lester, 'Liberalization or Litigation? Time to Rethink the International Investment Regime' (2013) *Policy Analysis* [online], p. 10.

[16] E.g., Aisbett, Karp and McAusland, 'Police Powers, Regulatory Taking and the Efficient Compensation of Domestic and Foreign Investors' (2010) 86 *The Economic Record* 367; van

in economic analyses of similar legal rules in domestic legal systems.[17] Its concern is to understand the economic consequences of investment treaty protections, rather than to explain their existence. In doing so, this literature brings greater rigour and specificity to Vandevelde's discussion of the implications of neo-classical economic theory for the design of international legal rules.

2.2.3 Summary of social scientific scholarship

The preceding discussion provides a brief overview of relevant social scientific scholarship on investment treaties. There is no need to resolve debates within this scholarship at this stage. For present purposes, it is sufficient to note that the majority of this literature attributes states' behaviour to their interest in attracting FDI. If one accepts that FDI flows have normative value, then it follows that explanatory theory and evidence examining the relationship between investment treaties and FDI is relevant to normative debate about investment treaty protections.

Vandevelde's explanation of investment treaties' content is also relevant to normative debate. Indeed, he follows his own explanatory arguments to normative conclusions, relying on the premise that economic liberalism (neo-classical economics and its focus on the maximisation of economic efficiency) should be the basis for investment policy.[18] On these grounds, he recommends that the pre-establishment rights of foreign investors should be strengthened and post-establishment protections should be weakened.[19] Similar arguments are put on a firmer theoretical footing in economic analyses of investment treaty protections. The normative conclusions of this literature stem from the premise that legal rules should be evaluated on the basis of whether they increase economic efficiency.[20]

Aaken, 'International Investment Law between Commitment and Flexibility: A Contract Theory Analysis' (2009) 12 *Journal of International Economic Law*, pp. 509, 537.

[17] E.g., Blume, Rubinfeld and Shapiro, 'The Taking of Land: When Should Compensation Be Paid?' (1984) 99 *The Quarterly Journal of Economics*.

[18] Vandevelde, 'The Political Economy of a Bilateral Investment Treaty', p. 635.

[19] Vandevelde, 'The Economics of Bilateral Investment Treaties', p. 499; similarly Lester, 'Liberalization or Litigation', p. 10.

[20] Bonnitcha and Aisbett, 'An Economic Analysis of Substantive Protections Provided by Investment Treaties' in Sauvant, *Yearbook on International Investment Law & Policy 2011-2012* (2013), p. 683.

2.3 Criticisms of investment treaties

This section examines normative criticisms of investment treaties and investment treaty protections. It identifies six strands of critique in the existing literature.[21] The discussion of each strand of critique seeks to articulate the methodology being used in the literature and to identify the normative and causal assumptions on which existing arguments are based.

2.3.1 Historical methodology and critique

Critiques of investment treaties often rely on historical methodology to highlight the role that political power has played in the development of international investment law.[22] This form of inquiry examines the historical context in which treaties, arbitrations and other legal events occurred to provide explanations for them.[23] Historical inquiry usually continues to conclusions that challenge the legitimacy of international investment law. These claims rely on the implicit normative premise that law should not merely reflect the interests of the powerful. These conclusions are sometimes linked to wider critiques of international economic relations.[24]

Historical methodology illustrates how consensual arrangements can be legally effective, yet normatively questionable. For example, the observation that conditions attached to the grant of US foreign aid were responsible for Costa Rica accepting the jurisdiction of an ICSID tribunal in *Santa Elena v. Costa Rica* raises questions about whether the agreement to arbitrate the claim was in Costa Rica's interests.[25] Historical methodology also provides some evidence for the claim that the US and European states promoted customary international law on investment to further their own

---

[21] For an alternate catalogue of normative objections, see, Atik, 'Repenser NAFTA Chapter 11: A Catalogue of Legitimacy Critiques' (2003) 3 *Asper Review of International Business and Trade Law*, p. 215.

[22] Sornarajah, 'Power and Justice: Third World Resistance in International Law' (2006) 10 *Singapore Year Book of International Law*, p. 31; Miles, *The Origins of International Investment Law: Empire, the Environment and the Safeguarding of Capital* (2013), chp. 1.

[23] E.g., Muchlinski, 'The Rise and Fall of the Multilateral Agreement on Investment: Where Now?' (2000) 34 *The International Lawyer*.

[24] E.g., Blackwood and McBride, 'Investment as the Achilles Heel of Globalisation?: The Ongoing Conflict between the Rights of Capital and the Rights of States' (2006) 25 *Policy and Society*, p. 63.

[25] *Santa Elena v. Costa Rica*, Final Award, para. 25; Helms Amendment 22 USC (1994) sec. 2378a.

interests.[26] This supports a related doctrinal critique of the development of customary international law of investment, which requires that *opinio juris*, rather than self-interest or coercion, guide state practice for it to have legal character.[27]

That said, the vast number of investment treaties makes generalisation from specific historical experiences difficult. The hypothesis that BITs are imposed on developing countries by more powerful developed countries does not adequately account for the enormous diversity of bilateral relationships covered by near-identical BITs;[28] in particular, it appears inconsistent with the rapid growth of BITs between pairs of developing countries.[29] In the context of this book, there is a more specific limitation of historical scholarship. In focusing on the way that legal rules and institutions were established, historical scholarship raises important questions about whether given legal rules are justified. However, historical methodology is less well suited to answering the questions it raises. Criticisms of an existing rule's provenance do not provide grounds for choosing between various alternatives to that rule.

2.3.2 Comparative methodology and critique

Another body of scholarship on investment treaties is grounded in comparative methodology. Comparative methodology is applied both at a micro-level of individual legal rules and a macro-level of legal systems and institutions.[30] Micro-level comparative scholarship on investment treaties compares treaty provisions to legal rules that perform the same function in other legal systems. The majority of micro-level comparative scholarship compares indirect expropriation under investment treaties to US regulatory taking jurisprudence.[31] Other contributions include

---

[26] Sornarajah, *The International Law on Foreign Investment*, pp. 37–8.

[27] Wouters, Duquez and Hachez, 'International Investment Law: The Perpetual Search for Consensus' in de Schutter, Swinnen and Wouters (eds), *Foreign Direct Investment and Human Development: The Law and Economics of International Investment Agreements* (2013), pp. 36–7.

[28] Cf. Blackwood and McBride, 'Investment as the Achilles Heel of Globalisation?', p. 44.

[29] Alvarez, 'Review: *Investment Treaty Arbitration and Public Law* by Gus van Harten' (2008) 102 *American Journal of International Law*, p. 913. The spread of BITs between developing countries is documented in UNCTAD, *South-South Investment Agreements Proliferating*, p. 1.

[30] This distinction between micro and macro comparative scholarship has been drawn by others, including Zweigert and Kotz, *Introduction to Comparative Law* (2nd edn, 1998), p. 4, and, in the context of investment treaties, Vadi 'Critical Comparisons: the Role of Comparative Law in Investment treaty Arbitration' (2010) 39 *Denver Journal of International Law and Policy*, p. 82.

[31] E.g., Stanley, 'Keeping Big Brother out of Our Backyard: Regulatory Takings as Defined in International Law and Compared to American Fifth Amendment Jurisprudence'

comparisons between the indirect expropriation jurisprudence of arbitral tribunals and that of the European Court of Human Rights (ECthR);[32] comparisons between the national treatment jurisprudence of arbitral tribunals and that of the World Trade Organization (WTO);[33] and Kantor's argument that certain decisions interpreting the fair and equitable treatment standard resemble the pre-1934 US constitutional doctrinal of substantive due process.[34]

Micro-level comparative scholarship follows a relatively settled pattern of comparison and contrast to arrive at a set of observations about the differences and similarities between the legal rules under examination. This process often informs subsequent normative conclusions; however, a set of observations about similarities and differences is not sufficient grounds for normative judgement. Although there is intuitive appeal to the claim that investment treaties should not confer greater protection on private property than is common in domestic legal systems, an argument made most forcefully by Montt,[35] without recourse to extra-legal

(2001) 15 *Emory International Law Review*; Shenkman, 'Could Principles of Fifth Amendment Takings Jurisprudence Be Helpful in Analyzing Regulatory Expropriation Claims under International Law?' (2002) 11 *New York University Environmental Law Journal*; Sampliner, 'Arbitration of Expropriation Cases under U.S. Investment Treaties – A Threat to Democracy of the Dog That Didn't Bark' (2003) 18 *ICSID Review – FILJ*, p. 11; Lowe, 'Regulation or Expropriation?' (2002) 55 *Current Legal Problems*, p. 461; Appleton, 'Regulatory Takings: The International Law Perspective' (2002) 11 *New York University Environmental Law Journal*, p. 36; Graham, 'Regulatory Takings, Supernational Treatment, and the Multilateral Agreement on Investment: Issues Raised by Nongovernmental Organizations' (1998) 31 *Cornell International Law Journal*, p. 604.

[32] E.g., Mountfield, 'Regulatory Expropriations in Europe: The Approach of the European Court of Human Rights' (2002) 11 *New York University Environmental Law Journal*; Ruiz Fabri, 'The Approach Taken by the European Court of Human Rights to the Assessment of Compensation for "Regulatory Expropriations" of the Property of Foreign Investors' (2002) 11 *New York University Environmental Law Journal*; Kriebaum, 'Regulatory Takings: Balancing the Interests of the Investor and the State' (2007) 8 *Journal of World Investment and Trade*, p. 730; Wälde and Kolo, 'Environmental Regulation, Investment Protection and 'Regulatory Taking' in International Law' (2001) 50 *International and Comparative Law Quarterly*, p. 824.

[33] Kurtz, 'The Use and Abuse of WTO Law in Investor-State Arbitration: Competition and Its Discontents' (2009) 20 *European Journal of International Law*, pp. 752–5; Ortino, 'From "Non-discrimination" to "Reasonableness": A Paradigm Shift in International Economic Law?' (2005) [online].

[34] Kantor, 'Fair and Equitable Treatment: Echoes of FDR's Court-packing Plan in the International Law Approach Towards Regulatory Expropriation' (2006) 5 *The Law and Practice of International Courts and Tribunals*.

[35] Montt, *State Liability in Investment Treaty Arbitration*, p. 22:
It is shocking to consider that a United States investor may lose a case against its government in the United States Supreme Court, a German investor may lose the same case in the *Bundesverfassungsgericht* (Constitutional Court), and a French

normative criteria, the assertion does not withstand scrutiny. For this comparative argument to avoid circularity, the possibility that domestic legal systems confer unjustifiably inadequate protection on private property must be taken seriously.[36] (Montt avoids this circularity by referring back to the normative arguments that justify the level of protection provided in domestic systems.)

Macro-level comparative scholarship argues that international investment law – as a system of institutions, procedural rules and substantive rules – is analogous to some other body of law. There are three key strands within this literature: one arguing that international investment law is analogous to domestic constitutional law; a second arguing that it is analogous to domestic administrative or public law; and a third arguing that international investment law shares characteristics of several different legal regimes.[37] For present purposes, the third strand is less relevant because it is more focused on clarifying the similarities and differences between international investment law and other legal regimes than using these observations as a basis for criticism or justification of international investment law.[38]

The definitive work comparing investment treaties to public law is Van Harten's *Investment Treaty Arbitration and Public Law*. Van Harten asserts that international investment law is analogous to domestic public law in that it allows individuals to seek redress for a state's improper exercise of regulatory powers.[39] Because of this similarity in function, Van Harten argues that adjudication under investment treaties should conform to public law norms of accountability, openness, coherence and independence.[40] Van Harten also argues that the substantive rules of investment treaties should be interpreted to incorporate principles of deference to state judgement akin to principles of deference in domestic administrative law.[41] These

---

investor may lose it in the *Conseil d'État*, but, nevertheless, that any of them may win it against a Sri Lanka or Bolivia on the basis of such open-ended BIT principles as no expropriation without compensation or FET.

[36] Ibid., p. 166.

[37] Leeks, 'The Relationship Between Bilateral Investment treaty Arbitration and the Wider Corpus of International Law: The ICSID Approach' (2007) 65 *University of Toronto Faculty of Law Review*, p. 3; Marjosola, 'Public/Private Conflict in Investment Treaty Arbitration – a Study on Umbrella Clauses' (2009) *Helsinki Law Review*, p. 104.

[38] E.g., Roberts, 'Clash of Paradigms: The Actors and Analogies Shaping the Investment Treaty System' (2013) 107 *American Journal of International Law*, p. 94; Paparinskis, 'Analogies and Other Regimes of International Law' in Douglas, Pauwely and Viñuales (eds), *The Foundations of International Investment Law: Bringing Theory into Practice* (2014), p. 12.

[39] Van Harten, *Investment Treaty Arbitration and Public Law* (2007), p. 67.   [40] Ibid., p. 152.

[41] Ibid., p. 144.

arguments are developed in greater detail in a subsequent monograph, *Sovereign Choices and Sovereign Constraints*,[42] but van Harten's primary critique remains focused on the institutions and procedural rules governing investment treaty arbitration.[43]

Poirier also argues for deference, without relying so heavily on the public law analogy.[44] He contends that legal regimes embody negotiated social settlements that balance the interests of property protection against the interests advanced through government regulation. These social settlements are legitimately renegotiated by the polity governed by them from time to time.[45] This justifies the claim that investment treaties should defer to the balance struck between the protection of property rights and regulatory prerogatives within a given state. On this basis, he suggests that investment disputes should be litigated in national courts, with international arbitration available to review whether these proceedings were tainted by discrimination only after local remedies have been exhausted.[46] Recognising that this institutional reform is impractical, he argues that the second-best solution would be an appellate mechanism to review arbitration decisions,[47] thereby reaching normative conclusions similar to Van Harten's.

Schneiderman uses the comparison of investment treaties to domestic constitutional law as a basis for critique. He establishes the analogy to constitutional law by arguing that 'investment rules can be viewed as a set of binding, irrevocable constraints designed to insulate economic policy from majoritarian politics.'[48] In Schneiderman's view, constitutional rules should provide only the minimum legal basis necessary for societal dispute resolution.[49] This justifies his normative conclusion, a complete rejection of investment treaties in favour of national statutory alternatives.[50]

Critiques based on comparisons of investment treaties to public law and constitutional law are united by a common norm: that international legal adjudication should show a degree of deference to judgements made in the domestic political sphere. Constitutional critiques generally rely

---

[42] Van Harten, *Sovereign Choices and Sovereign Constraints: Judicial Restraint in Investment Treaty Arbitration* (2013), pp. 3–5.

[43] Ibid., p. 6; Van Harten, *Investment Treaty Arbitration and Public Law*, p. 151.

[44] Poirier, 'The NAFTA Chapter 11 Expropriation Debate through the Eyes of a Property Theorist' (2003) 33 *Environmental Law*, p. 918.

[45] Ibid., p. 858.   [46] Ibid., p. 919.   [47] Ibid., p. 924.

[48] Schneiderman, *Constitutionalizing Economic Globalization: Investment Rules and Democracy's Promise* (2008), p. 3.

[49] Ibid., p. 236.   [50] Ibid., p. 232.

on a stronger formulation of the principle of deference – thus, Schneiderman rejects any international review of governmental measures affecting foreign investors. Public law critiques propose a weaker principle of deference, one that would allow international review of governmental measures provided that institutions of adjudication and review possessed the characteristics of domestic courts exercising powers of judicial review. Both sets of critiques are primarily directed to the institutional structure of adjudication and review established by investment treaties.

Deference might also be invoked as a norm to evaluate alternative levels of substantive protection.[51] Montt has made this argument, relying on the comparative justification that domestic courts show a high degree of deference to governmental measures that do not entail the total destruction of property rights.[52] To the extent that this comparative methodology has a normative basis, it is through the incorporation of normative arguments about the appropriate level of deference to the exercise of public power from domestic law.[53] This engages a rich and sophisticated literature which spans constitutional theory, public law and, more recently in the United Kingdom, human rights review. A full assessment of this literature is beyond the scope of this book. Nevertheless, four basic justifications for deference in a domestic context can be identified. A brief assessment of these justifications shows that the case for treating the principle of deference to domestic political judgements as a *primary* norm that investment treaties should promote is less compelling than it might initially appear.

Democratic legitimacy is the foundation of many arguments for judicial deference.[54] A simplified version of this argument is that judges are not elected, so courts should defer to substantive value judgements made by elected officials and those exercising authority delegated by elected officials.[55] This argument has less force in the context of investment

---

[51] An argument for deference to host states in the interpretation and application of exceptions to investment treaty protections is made in Burke-White and von Staden, 'Private Litigation in a Public Sphere: The Standard of Review in Investor-State Arbitrations' (2010) 35 *Yale Journal of International Law*, p. 297.

[52] Montt, *State Liability in Investment Treaty Arbitration*, pp. 22, 229.   [53] Ibid., p. 166.

[54] Ibid., p. 227; Dyzenhaus, 'The Politics of Deference: Judicial Review and Democracy' in Taggart (ed), *The Province of Administrative Law* (1997), p. 305; Waldron, 'The Core of the Case against Judicial Review' (2006) 115 *The Yale Law Journal*, p. 1361; King, *Judging Social Rights* (2012), p. 153; *International Transport Roth GmbH* v. *Secretary of State for the Home Department* (2003) QB 728, paras. 81–7.

[55] Tremblay, 'The Legitimacy of Judicial Review: The Limits of Dialogue between Courts and Legislatures' (2005) 3 *International Journal of Constitutional Law*, p. 619; similarly, Choudhury, 'Recapturing Public Power: Is Investment Arbitration's Engagement of the

treaties because many of the states bound by them are not democratic.[56] Any general case for deference to public decision-making in the interpretation of investment treaty protections cannot be premised on the assumption that public decision-making is necessarily democratic.

A second, closely related, argument for deference in public law is based on the recognition that certain policy choices require the reconciliation of competing interests and values.[57] The argument is that, insofar as trade-offs between different values must necessarily be made, they are better made by decision-makers that are 'more closely acquainted with local issues, sensitivities and traditions.'[58] However, this reluctance to intrude into the merits of policy choices is based on the presumption that granting a public law remedy would invalidate the value judgement made by the decision maker, circumscribing the scope of its policy choice.[59] The situation under an investment treaty is different. The remedies awarded in investor-state arbitration do not invalidate a state's policy choice; they allow a state to maintain its preferred policy and compensate the foreign investor.[60]

A third argument for deference is that primary decision-makers have greater expertise in determining relevant facts and in assessing the likely consequences of various policy options under consideration.[61] This argument does not purport to offer a general justification for deference to primary decision-makers. Rather, arguments for deference based on institutional expertise are both consequentialist and contextual in character; they concern the practical implications of different institutions' relative abilities to gather and evaluate factual information on particular questions.[62] Consequentialist, expertise-based justifications for deference

Public Interest Contributing to the Democratic Deficit?' (2008) 41 *Vanderbilt Journal of Transnational Law*, p. 782.

[56] Alvarez, 'Review: *Investment Treaty Arbitration and Public Law* by Gus van Harten', p. 913.

[57] Edley, *Administrative Law* (1990), p. 34.

[58] Henckels, 'Balancing Investment Protection and the Public Interest: The Role of the Standard of Review and the Importance of Deference in Investor-State Arbitration' (2013) 4 *Journal of International Dispute Settlement*, p. 205; similarly, Poirier, 'The NAFTA Chapter 11 Expropriation Debate through the Eyes of a Property Theorist', p. 858.

[59] *Associated Provincial Picture Houses* v. *Wednesbury Corporation* (1948) 1 KB 223.

[60] Schill, *The Multilateralization of International Investment Law* (2009), p. 250; for more detailed discussion, see Section 3.3.

[61] Burke-White and von Staden, 'Private Litigation in a Public Sphere', p. 329; Henckels 'Indirect Expropriation and the Right to Regulate: Revisiting Proportionality Analysis and the Standard of Review in Investment Treaty Arbitration' (2012) 15 *Journal of International Economic Law*, p. 244.

[62] Henckels, 'Balancing Investment Protection and the Public Interest', p. 211.

may be relevant to an inquiry into the level of protection that investment treaties should provide. For example, arbitral tribunals are relatively well-placed to determine whether an environmental measure has deprived a foreign investor of its rights in an investment but less well placed to determine whether other policy measures would have been equally effective in achieving the same environmental objectives. I explore these issues and their implications in greater detail in Chapter 3.

Fourth, as a question of comparative scholarship, the degree of deference (if any) that judges in domestic courts show to the substantive judgements made in the political sphere varies significantly. One of the grounds on which it varies is the extent to which the normative justification for judicial review rests on the protection of private rights, as opposed to the promotion of reasoned public decision-making. Thus, in judicial review of the exercise of public power under the Equal Protection Clause of the Fourteenth Amendment, the US Supreme Court usually applies the deferential standard of rational basis review.[63] However, in cases in which the exercise of public power infringes a 'fundamental right' or involves the use of a 'suspect classification', the Court applies the less deferential standard of strict scrutiny.[64] This illustrates that deference to public power is not necessarily a normative premise. Rather, normative premises about the interests that should be protected by judicial review entail conclusions about the appropriate degree of deference.

This fourth issue is illustrated by the fact that the comparisons between investment treaties and domestic public law are also used as a foundation for arguments for *less* deference: the claim that the protections of investment treaties should provide greater certainty as to the extent of investors' rights.[65] In making this argument, Sanders draws on the work of Hayek, who argues that legal rules protecting private rights from interference by the state should be clear and certain because governments are capable of exploiting their power over individuals.[66]

In a similar vein, there are scholars who accept the analogy of international investment law to constitutional law but arrive at different

---

[63] *United States* v. *Carolene Products Company* 504 US 144 (1938) 152.

[64] *Skinner* v. *State of Oklahoma, ex. rel. Williamson* 316 US 535 (1942) 541; *Korematsu* v. *United States* 323 US 214 (1944) 216.

[65] Sanders, 'Of All Things Made in America Why Are We Exporting the *Penn Central* Test?' (2010) 30 *Northwestern Journal of International Law and Business*, p. 372. Epstein, *Takings*, p. 148, developing a similar argument at great length, in the context of the US 5th Amendment.

[66] Sanders, 'Of All Things Made in America Why Are We Exporting the *Penn Central* Test?' p. 372.

normative conclusions to Schneiderman. Schill, for example, accepts that international investment law does possess a threshold level of legitimacy as a constitutional system.[67] He argues that international investment law should mirror the level of deference that domestic legal systems provide when balancing the same private rights and public interests.[68] Thus, while accepting the same underlying constitutional analogy,[69] he advocates a view that is significantly less deferential than Schneiderman's. Petersmann goes still further, implying that the constitutional character of investment treaties is sufficient to demonstrate their legitimacy.[70] He argues that the substantive and procedural rules of investment treaties should draw more heavily on the 'constitutional principles' that protect individuals' fundamental rights in international economic law and human rights law, a position that appears to downplay the need for deference to decisions made in the political sphere.[71]

There is no need to resolve these debates among proponents of comparative methodology. The purpose of this review is simply to show that comparative methodology is, foremost, a descriptive methodology.[72] Comparative claims describe, with attention to certain features, the similarities and differences of the legal phenomena compared. Moving from comparative observations to normative conclusions requires a set of normative criteria by which the compared subjects should be evaluated. The difference between Van Harten's and Sanders' arguments illustrates that relying on a different set of normative premises will lead to different normative conclusions, notwithstanding a shared set of observations about the similarities between given legal regimes. To the extent that comparative scholarship is relevant to normative debate about the level of protection that investment treaties should provide, it raises the question of

---

[67] Schill, *The Multilateralization of International Investment Law*, p. 373.
[68] Schill, 'Deference in Investment Treaty Arbitration: Re-Conceptualising the Standard of Review' (2012) 3 *Journal of International Dispute Settlement*, p. 31.
[69] Although Schill sometimes uses the term 'public law', it is clear that he is referring primarily to domestic constitutional law, not domestic administrative law, see, e.g., ibid., p. 23.
[70] Petersmann, 'Human Rights, Constitutionalism, and 'Public Reason' in Investor-State Arbitration' in Binder et al. (eds), *International Investment Law for the 21st Century* (2009), p. 883.
[71] Petersmann, 'Constitutional Theories of International Economic Adjudication and Investor-State Arbitration' in Dupuy, Francioni and Petersmann (eds), *Human Rights in International Investment Law and Arbitration* (2009), p. 193.
[72] Cf. Maupin 'Public and Private in International Investment Law' (2014) 54 *Virginia Journal of International Law* (forthcoming), pp. 47–8, arguing that comparative claims entail normative conclusions.

the appropriate level of deference to the judgements made in the domestic political sphere. This section argues that the question of deference to government decision-makers is better understood as a conclusion that follows from premises about the primary norms that law should promote than as a primary norm itself.

2.3.3 Razian rule of law norms as a basis for critique

Another critique of investment treaties relies directly on principles that relate to desirable formal characteristics of law and of legal institutions that apply the law. These principles – that the judiciary should be independent, courts open and accessible and natural justice observed and that the law should be prospective, open and clear and relatively stable – can all be rationalised as components of Raz's conception of the rule of law.[73] A different conception of the rule of law, one that also speaks to the substantive content of law, is sometimes invoked as a justification for investment treaties.[74] There is no need to determine which is the 'correct' conception of the rule of law. Instead, grouping institutional, procedural and formal critiques together under the Razian banner, while addressing the substantive norms raised by other scholars separately, is a way of clarifying existing arguments in the literature that use the phrase 'the rule of law' to mean different things.[75]

Scholarship relying on Razian rule of law principles is predominantly concerned with the institution of investor-state arbitration.[76] Critics have argued that the institution of investor-state arbitration is neither open nor independent and that it fails to meet the requirements of the rule of law.[77] A more specific iteration of this critique is that arbitrators, as an epistemic community, have an interest in expanding the system of investor protection and so tend to interpret treaty standards broadly.[78]

---

[73] Raz, 'The Rule of Law and Its Virtue' (1977) 93 *The Law Quarterly Review*, p. 202.

[74] Vandevelde, *Bilateral Investment Treaties: History, Policy and Interpretation* (2010), p. 2; see Section 2.4.3.

[75] Similarly, Craig, 'Formal and Substantive Conceptions of the Rule of Law: An Analytical Framework' (1997) Public Law, p. 487.

[76] van Harten, 'Perceived Bias in Investment Treaty Arbitration' in Waibel et al. (eds), *The Backlash against Investment Arbitration: Perceptions and Reality* (2010), p. 434.

[77] Sornarajah, 'The Neo-Liberal Agenda in Investment Arbitration: Its Rise, Retreat and Impact on State Sovereignty' in Shan, Simons and Singh (eds), *Redefining Sovereignty in International Economic Law* (2008), p. 215.

[78] Corporate Observatory Europe and the Transnational Institute, *Profiting from Injustice*, [online], p. 35; Sornarajah, 'The Neo-Liberal Agenda in Investment Arbitration', p. 218; van Harten, *Investment Treaty Arbitration and Public Law*, p. 152.

This second hypothesis is plausible; however, to credibly test it, an anthropological and sociological inquiry into the opinions and motivations of arbitrators would be necessary.[79]

A distinct body of scholarship considers the relationship between the investment treaties and the degree of respect for the rule of law in the states that are party to them. In an early contribution, Crawford endorsed a Razian understanding of the rule of law[80] and argued that the role of investment treaties was to 'reinforce, and on occasion to institute, the rule of law internally' within states.[81] A second strand of arbitral and scholarly discussion focuses on legal questions arising from corruption, which is a specific and serious contravention of the rule of law.[82] The shared premise in these discussions is that discouraging corruption is an important policy objective.[83] More recently, other scholars have used social scientific methodologies to examine empirically whether investment treaties do reinforce and support respect for the rule of law.[84] The findings are mixed. For present purposes, however, the key point is that this literature is based on an agreed premise that greater respect for the rule of law in domestic legal systems would be desirable.

2.3.4 Sovereignty as a basis for critique

The norm that the sovereignty of states should be respected is often invoked to critique the substantive content of investment treaties.[85] The meaning of sovereignty is not explored in detail in this literature, but

---

[79] Shackelford, 'Investment Treaty Arbitration and Public Law, by Gus van Harten' (2008) 44 *Stanford Journal of International Law*, p. 218.
[80] Crawford, 'International Law and the Rule of Law' (2003) 24 *Adelaide Law Review*, p. 4.
[81] Ibid., p. 8; similarly Schill, 'Fair and Equitable Treatment, the Rule of Law, and Comparative Public Law' in Schill (ed), *International Investment Law and Comparative Public Law* (2010), p. 182.
[82] Raz, 'The Rule of Law and Its Virtue', p. 195.
[83] *Siag v. Egypt*, Dissenting Opinion of Professor Francisco Orrego Vicuña, pp. 4–5; Kulick, *Global Public Interest in International Investment Law* (2012), p. 332; Bishop, 'Toward a More Flexible Approach to the International Legal Consequences of Corruption' (2010) 25 *ICSID Review*, p. 65.
[84] Ginsburg, 'International Substitutes for Domestic Institutions: Bilateral Investment Treaties and Governance' (2005) 25 *International Review of Law and Economics*, p. 121; Franck, 'Foreign Direct Investment, Investment Treaty Arbitration, and the Rule of Law' (2007) 19 *Global Business and Development Law Journal*, p. 365.
[85] Shan, 'Calvo Doctrine, State Sovereignty and the Changing Landscape of International Law' in Shan, Simons and Singh (eds), *Redefining Sovereignty in International Economic Law* (2008), p. 311; Sornarajah, 'The Neo-Liberal Agenda in Investment Arbitration', p. 205; Chung, 'The Lopsided International Investment Law Regime and Its Effect on the Future of Investor-State Arbitration' (2007) 47 *Virginia Journal of International Law*, p. 963; Cheng,

it appears to refer to a state's entitlement to exercise power within its territory, subject only to the constraints of its own laws.[86] The use of this unqualified conception of sovereignty as a basis for normative critique is problematic. It is self-evident that investment treaties place limits on host states' sovereignty, in the sense that they require states to compensate investors for otherwise permissible exercises of governmental power. The same could be said for any rule of international law.[87]

Most scholars recognise that, despite its rhetorical appeal, an unqualified norm of sovereignty is not a coherent basis for normative critique.[88] The more coherent objection is that investment treaties interfere with states' ability, in practice, to implement certain desirable policies within their territory.[89] These arguments are often articulated through the language of a sovereign's 'right to regulate'.[90] For example, Muchlinski argues that investment treaties should respect a state's 'right to regulate for legitimate policy purposes', while accepting the legitimacy of restrictions on sovereignty that prevent 'abuses of power which impact adversely on investors'.[91] Disagreement about the extent of legitimate interference with sovereignty can then only be resolved by recourse to norms other than sovereignty: debate about whether the benefits of investment treaties are sufficient to justify the added difficulty and expense to a state in pursuing certain policies.[92] Engagement with this debate, in turn,

'Power, Authority and International Investment Law' (2005) 20 *American University International Law Review*, p. 507.

[86] E.g., Choudhury, 'Recapturing Public Power', p. 777.

[87] Wälde, 'Interpreting Investment Treaties: Experiences and Examples' in Binder et al. (eds), *International Investment Law for the 21st Century* (2009), p. 735.

[88] This argument is made succinctly in Lowe, 'Sovereignty and International Economic Law' in Shan, Simons and Singh (eds), *Redefining Sovereignty in International Economic Law* (2008), p. 79.

[89] Yannaca-Small, '"Indirect Expropriation" and the "Right to Regulate" in International Investment Law' (2004) [online], p. 2; Waincymer, 'Balancing Property Rights and Human Rights in Expropriation' in Dupuy, Francioni and Petersmann (eds), *Human Rights in International Investment Law and Arbitration* (2009), p. 307; Paulsson, 'Indirect Expropriation: Is the Right to Regulate at Risk?' (2005) [online], p. 3. Here, I rely on the understanding of sovereignty proposed in Howse, 'Sovereignty, Lost and Found' in Shan, Simons and Singh (eds), *Redefining Sovereignty in International Economic Law* (2008), p. 61.

[90] Mann H, 'The Right of States to Regulate and International Investment Law' (2002) [online], p. 5; Spears, 'The Quest for Policy Space in a New Generation of International Investment Agreements' (2010) 13 *Journal of International Economic Law*, p. 1042.

[91] Muchlinski, 'Policy Issues' in Muchlinski, Ortino and Schreuer (eds), *The Oxford Handbook of International Investment Law* (2008), p. 14.

[92] Hamilton and Rochwerger, 'Trade and Investment', p. 21; Ryan, 'Meeting Expectations', p. 761; Karl, 'International Investment Arbitration', p. 244.

requires consideration of empirical questions about the extent to which investment treaties discourage or prevent states from pursuing specific policies.

There is a wider body of literature that discusses the concept of sovereignty that is not commonly referred to in debates about investment treaties. It is worth noting that the conclusion of the previous paragraph – that a sovereignty-based critique is only coherent to the extent that it relies on norms other than an appeal to states' entitlement to exercise unrestricted power within their own territory – is consistent with this wider literature. Recent contributions from Jackson and Sarooshi both argue that the normative value of sovereignty rests on the extent to which it embodies other, prior, norms. In Jackson's view, a normatively justifiable conception of sovereignty should reflect a 'pragmatic functionalism' about whether given regulatory powers should be exercised at the national or an international level.[93] In Sarooshi's view, sovereignty retains normative force to the extent it can be justified by norms of 'legitimacy, autonomy, self-determination, freedom, accountability, security and equality'.[94]

2.3.5 Human rights norms as a basis for critique

Many recent critiques of investment treaties are based on human rights norms.[95] Human rights are raised in a number of different contexts in debate, including in critique of the institution of investor-state arbitration. Human rights norms also provide a link to doctrinal arguments about the proper interpretation of existing investment treaties because human rights norms are embodied legally in human rights law.[96] This book is specifically concerned with the role of human rights norms as criteria to evaluate the level of substantive protection provided by

---

[93] Jackson, 'Sovereignty-Modern', p. 801.
[94] Sarooshi, 'The Essentially Contested Nature of the Concept of Sovereignty', p. 1115.
[95] Hamilton and Rochwerger, 'Trade and Investment: Foreign Direct Investment Through Bilateral and Multilateral Treaties' (2005) 18 *New York International Law Review*, p. 45; Schreiber, 'Realizing the Right to Water in International Investment Law: An Interdisciplinary Approach to BIT Obligations' (2008) 48 *Natural Resources Journal*; Suda, 'The Effect of Bilateral Investment Treaties on Human Rights Enforcement and Realization' (2005) [online]; Brower CH, 'NAFTA's Investment Chapter: Initial Thoughts about Second-Generation Rights' (2003) 36 *Vanderbilt Journal of Transnational Law*; Peterson and Gray, *International Human Rights in Bilateral Investment Treaties and in Investment Treaty Arbitration* (2003), p. 22.
[96] Harrison, 'Human Rights Arguments in *Amicus Curiae* Submissions' in Dupuy, Francioni and Petersmann (eds), *Human Rights in International Investment Law and Arbitration* (2009), p. 413; Kulick, *Global Public Interest*, pp. 269–71.

investment treaties. To reach this scholarship, it is first necessary to distinguish doctrinal debate about the relevance of human rights law to the application and interpretation of investment treaties.

There are two scenarios in which human rights law might, arguably, be relevant in the resolution of a claim that a state has breached an investment treaty protection: a state's human rights obligations could displace an inconsistent obligation under an investment treaty, or a state's human rights obligations could be invoked to assist in the interpretation of the scope of a state's obligations under an investment treaty. The former situation is unlikely. If two rules of international law are inconsistent, one will displace the other, according to the principles of *lex specialis* and *lex posterior*.[97] Inconsistency does not arise by virtue of the fact that the two rules apply to the same conduct simultaneously. State conduct in a given field is regularly subject to obligations arising from different sources, and these 'multiple obligations regulating the same conduct are perfectly capable of coexistence'.[98] It must be impossible for a state to comply simultaneously with its investment treaty obligations and human rights obligations for them to be inconsistent in the doctrinal sense.[99]

It is difficult to imagine a situation in which a state's human rights and investment treaty obligations would be doctrinally inconsistent.[100] Consider, for example, a situation in which an investor that has been awarded an exclusive water concession significantly increases the price

---

[97] Crawford, 'Continuity and Discontinuity in International Dispute Settlement' in Binder et al. (eds), *International Investment Law for the 21st Century* (2009), p. 816.

[98] Ibid., p. 816; similarly, Study Group of the International Law Commission, *Fragmentation of International Law* (2006), para. 4:

> The principle of harmonization. It is a generally accepted principle that when several [legal] norms bear on a single issue they should, to the extent possible, be interpreted so as to give rise to a single set of compatible obligations.

[99] Hirsch, 'Interactions between Investment and Non-Investment Obligations' in Muchlinski, Ortino and Schreuer (eds), *The Oxford Handbook of International Investment Law* (2008), p. 174; Wierzbowski and Gubrynowicz, 'Conflict of Norms Stemming from Intra-EU BITs and EU Legal Obligations: Some Remarks on Possible Solutions' in Binder et al. (eds), *International Investment Law for the 21st Century* (2009), p. 546.

[100] Waincymer, 'Balancing Property Rights and Human Rights in Expropriation' in Dupuy, Francioni and Petersmann (eds), *Human Rights in International Investment Law and Arbitration* (2009), p. 308; Vadi, 'Reconciling Public Health and Investor Rights: The Case of Tobacco' in Dupuy, Francioni and Petersmann (eds), *Human Rights in International Investment Law and Arbitration* (2009), p. 485; Suda, 'The Effect of Bilateral Investment Treaties on Human Rights Enforcement and Realization', fn. 420; Kulick, *Global Public Interest*, p. 306.

of water.[101] To satisfy its obligation to ensure that residents have affordable access to water,[102] the state could have written a universal access obligation into the original concession contract, thereby avoiding any potential conflict with its obligations under the investment treaty.[103] Alternatively, the state could intervene *ex post* by subsidising the supply of water to ensure affordable access, without affecting the price charged by the investor, or it could simply expropriate the concession and compensate the investor.[104] There may be a number of policy reasons why each of these solutions is unsatisfactory, but this serves to emphasise that many of the concerns about the potential inconsistency between investment treaties and human rights are consequentialist in character.

The improbability of a state's human rights and investment treaty obligations being inconsistent means that most doctrinal scholarship focuses on the role of international human rights law in investment treaty interpretation.[105] The starting point for an inquiry is Article 31(3)(c) of the Vienna Convention of the Law of Treaties (VCLT); the threshold question is whether a human rights instrument ratified by all the parties to the investment treaty in question is a 'relevant rule of international law applicable in the relations between the parties'.[106] Even if human rights obligations meet this requirement, there remains a difficult doctrinal question of the weight to be given to human rights law in the process of interpreting investment treaties.[107] An alternative approach in doctrinal investigation of the role of human rights obligations in investment treaty interpretation relies on inductive methodology. It involves the compilation and classification of references to human rights law and cases in international investment arbitrations.[108]

---

[101] Kriebaum, 'Privatizing Human Rights: The Interface between International Investment Protection and Human Rights' (2006) 3 *Transnational Dispute Management*, p. 6.

[102] General Comment No. 15 'The Right to Water' (2002) E/C.12/2002/11, paras. 26–7.

[103] Simma, 'Foreign Investment Arbitration: A Place for Human Rights?' (2011) 60 *International and Comparative Law Quarterly*, p. 595.

[104] *Suez and Vivendi; AWG Group v. Argentina*, Decision on Liability, para. 262.

[105] Simma and Kill, 'Harmonizing Investment Protection and International Human Rights: First Steps Towards a Methodology' in Binder et al. (eds), *International Investment Law for the 21st Century* (2009), p. 691.

[106] Vienna Convention on the Law of Treaties (VCLT) (23 May 1969).

[107] McLachlan, 'The Principle of Systemic Integration and Article 31(3)(c) of the Vienna Convention' (2005) 54 *International and Comparative Law Quarterly*, p. 310.

[108] E.g., Reiner and Schreuer, 'Human Rights and International Investment Arbitration', in Dupuy, Francioni and Petersmann (eds), *Human Rights in International Investment Law and Arbitration* (2009), p. 88; Hirsch, 'Investment Tribunals and Human Rights', p. 99;

A distinct strand of scholarship criticises investment treaties on the grounds that they jeopardise the realisation of human rights norms *in practice*. This scholarship may refer to human rights instruments in the elucidation of human rights norms, but the argument does not depend on these norms having a legal character.[109] The most common methodology is case-study – either actual or hypothetical – which illustrates the consequences of an investment treaty protections being applied in a given factual scenario. Common criticisms of investment treaties are that investors may 'challenge human rights inspired measures';[110] that investment treaties 'have the potential to restrict state capacity to regulate in the public interest in the sphere of human rights';[111] and that investment law may cause 'regulatory chill' of measures that are effective in realising human rights.[112]

This failure to distinguish between different types of claims leads to confusion in the 'debate' on human rights and investment law. The most strident human rights critiques of investment treaties are based on consequentialist arguments, even when these critiques invoke the legal character of human rights.[113] The central claim in this literature is that limitations placed on the state by investment treaties have negative consequences for the realisation of human rights. On the other side, the principal set of responses is that investment treaties and human rights law are not antagonistic: because there is no doctrinal inconsistency between them;[114] because human rights jurisprudence is sometimes used to interpret investment treaties;[115] and because state conduct which violates an

---

Peterson, *Human Rights and Bilateral Investment Treaties: Mapping the Role of Human Rights Law within Investor-State Arbitration* (2009), p. 21.

[109] Suda, 'The Effect of Bilateral Investment Treaties on Human Rights Enforcement and Realization', fn. 214.

[110] Peterson and Gray, *International Human Rights in Bilateral Investment Treaties and in Investment treaty Arbitration*, p. 23.

[111] Suda, 'The Effect of Bilateral Investment Treaties on Human Rights Enforcement and Realization', fn. 19.

[112] High Commissioner for Human Rights, *Economic, Social and Cultural Rights: Human Rights, Trade and Investment* (2003), p. 21; Van Harten and Loughlin, 'Investment Treaty Arbitration as a Species of Global Administrative Law' (2006) 17 *European Journal of International Law*, p. 131.

[113] Mann H, 'International Investment Agreements, Business and Human Rights' (2008), p. 15.

[114] Fry, 'International Human Rights Law in Investment Arbitration: Evidence of International Law's Unity' (2007) 18 *Duke Journal of Comparative and International Law*, p. 100.

[115] Ibid., p. 83.

investor's human rights may also constitute a breach of an investment treaty.[116] Thus framed, the two sides of the debate do not join issue. It is possible for all the doctrinal claims about the relationship between investment treaties and human rights law to be correct and also for investment treaties to have the consequence of jeopardising the realisation of human rights.

This review of existing critiques of investment treaties on human rights grounds leads to three conclusions. First, some scholars criticise investment treaties for interfering with the realisation of human rights. This criticism is not answered by the claim that investment treaties are consistent with international human rights law. Second, to the extent that human rights norms provide a basis for critique of investment treaty protections, they rely on implicit causal assumptions about the likely consequences of a given protections for the realisation of human rights. The argument is not that investment treaty protections directly interfere with the human rights of individuals in host states – investment treaties govern the relationship between foreign investors and host states, not the relationship between foreign investors and individuals – but that the *effect* of investment treaty protections is to discourage states from taking effective steps to realise human rights in practice.[117] Third, there is little disagreement in this literature about the particular norms that fall within the set of human rights norms, nor dissent from the premise that the realisation of these norms would be desirable.

2.3.6 *Environmental norms as a basis for critique*

Environmental norms – that natural resources, ecosystems and biodiversity have intrinsic normative value and should be conserved – are another basis for critique of investment treaties. The structure of argument in this literature is relatively clear and so can be summarised succinctly. The basic argument is that investment treaties threaten host states' ability to enact environmental measures. The argument relies on the implicit causal assumption that investment treaties discourage decision-makers in host states from introducing environmental regulations because they require host states to compensate foreign investors when environmental

---

[116] Newcombe and Paradell, *Law and Practice of Investment Treaties: Standards of Treatment* (2009), p. 273.

[117] Krommendijk and Morijn, 'Proportional by What Measure(s)? Balancing Investor Interests and Human Rights by Way of Applying the Proportionality Principle in Investor-State Arbitration' in Dupuy, Francioni and Petersmann (eds), *Human Rights in International Investment Law and Arbitration* (2009), p. 423.

measures affect their interests and, further, because they create uncertainty about the scope of non-compensable regulatory activity.[118] These concerns are both based on a form of consequential reasoning. They are potentially relevant to the evaluation of investment treaties protections because they are linked to the scope of legal protection provided by investment treaties.

A related critique of investment treaties is grounded in the concept of sustainable development. In the literature on investment treaties, the concept is usually defined as 'development that meets the needs of the present without compromising the ability of future generations to meet their own needs'.[119] This definition provides clarity on the meaning of 'sustainability' – a specific form of inter-generational equity – without shedding much light on the concept of 'development' that is subject to the constraint of sustainability. In practice, the phrase 'sustainable development' functions either as a portmanteau for a collection of incommensurable norms that include environmental conservation, economic growth, realisation of human rights and distributive justice;[120] an interstitial principle – a secondary norm governing the balancing of competing primary norms such as these;[121] or as both a portmanteau and an interstitial norm.[122] Critiques of investment treaties that rely on the concept

[118] Been and Beauvais, 'The Global Fifth Amendment? NAFTA's Investment Protections and the Misguided Quest for an International "Regulatory Takings" Doctrine' (2003) 78 *New York University Law Review*, p. 132; Tienhaara, *The Expropriation of Environmental Governance: Protecting Foreign Investors at the Expense of Public Policy* (2009), p. 276; Wagner, 'International Investment, Expropriation and Environmental Protection' (1999) 29 *Golden Gate University Law Review*, p. 467.

[119] Spears, 'The Quest for Policy Space in a New Generation of International Investment Agreements', p. 1067; Cordonier Segger and Newcombe, 'An Integrated Agenda for Sustainable Development in International Investment Law' in Cordonier Segger, Gehring and Newcombe (eds), *Sustainable Development in World Investment Law* (2011), p. 105, both citing Bruntland Report of the World Commission on Environment and Development, Our Common Future, Annex, UN Doc A/42/427 (1987).

[120] Mayeda, 'Sustainable International Investment Agreements: Challenges and Solutions for Developing Countries' in Cordonier Segger, Gehring and Newcombe (eds), *Sustainable Development in World Investment Law* (2011), p. 542.

[121] Spears, 'The Quest for Policy Space in a New Generation of International Investment Agreements', p. 1070, citing, Lowe, 'Sustainable Development and Unsustainable Arguments' in Boyle and Freestone (eds), *International Law and Sustainable Development: Past Achievements and Future Challenges* (1999), p. 31.

[122] Cordonier Segger and Newcombe, 'An Integrated Agenda for Sustainable Development in International Investment Law', p. 104, citing *New Delhi Declaration on Principle of International Law Relating to Sustainable Development*, ILA Resolution 3/2002, Annex, UN Doc A/57/329 (2002).

of sustainable development tend to invoke both understandings of sustainable development: their criticism is that the economic benefits that flow from investment treaties are insufficient to justify their other consequences, articulated in terms of environmental, distributive justice or human rights norms.[123]

While acknowledging the concerns that underpin these criticisms of investment treaties, there is no need to add sustainable development to the set of primary norms capable of justifying a preference between different levels of investment treaty protection. To the extent that sustainable development functions as a portmanteau of other primary norms, these norms can be examined with greater precision if they are identified specifically. To the extent that sustainable development operates as a secondary, or interstitial, norm, its significance is examined subsequently.[124]

2.4 Justifications for investment treaties and investment treaty protections

This section examines justifications of investment treaties and investment treaty protections. Leaving potential 'economic' justifications for investment treaties to one side,[125] it identifies three strands of justification in the existing literature. The discussion of each strand seeks to articulate the methodology being used in the literature and the normative and causal assumptions that underpin it.

2.4.1 Realisation of treaties' purpose as a basis for justification

A wide range of contributions in the existing literature refer to investment treaties' purpose in the course of argument. Discussions of purpose raise two sets of issues: how investment treaties' purpose should be characterised and the significance of investment treaties' purpose in wider argument. As already noted, the prevailing view in social scientific literature is that developing states sign investment treaties for the purpose of attracting FDI.[126] In this literature, a treaty's purpose is invoked as an *explanation* for states' decision to sign that treaty.

---

[123] Mayeda, 'Sustainable International Investment Agreements', p. 772; Cordonier Segger and Kent, 'Promoting Sustainable Investment through International Law' in Cordonier Segger, Gehring and Newcombe (eds), *Sustainable Development in World Investment Law* (2011), p. 772; cf. Newcombe, 'Sustainable Development and Investment Treaty Law', p. 359.
[124] See Section 2.5.   [125] See Section 2.2.   [126] See Section 2.2.1.

In contrast, within doctrinal literature there is a lively debate about how investment treaties' purpose should be characterised (including debate of whether it is appropriate to characterise all investment treaties as having the same purpose). It is undisputed, in this debate, that the significance of an investment treaty's purpose is that Article 31(1) of the VCLT requires a treaty's provisions to be interpreted 'in the light of its object and purpose.'[127] A central issue in this debate is the level of generality with which investment treaties' purpose should be characterised. Because investment treaties confer legal protection on foreign investment, one view is that the purpose of investment treaties is simply to protect foreign investment.[128] A broader view is that the purpose of investment treaties is the protection and promotion of foreign investment – the protection of investment being the specific means by which investment treaties promote investment.[129] Other scholars argue for more general understanding of investment treaties' purpose. According to these views, the promotion of foreign investment is not an end in itself; rather, the purpose of investment treaties is to promote economic growth, sustainable development or some other ultimate objective by encouraging foreign investment.[130]

At this stage in the inquiry, I bracket the questions of how the 'object and purpose' of existing investment treaties should be characterised and how a treaty's purpose, once identified, should be incorporated into the legal reasoning of arbitral tribunals. I return to these questions in Chapter 7. At this point, I advance a different type of claim, one which concerns the relevance of existing investment treaties' purpose (however characterised) for debates about the level of protection that investment treaties should provide in the future. The claim is that the purpose of an existing treaty – as reflected in its terms – should not be the sole criterion

---

[127] VCLT, art. 31(1).

[128] Alvarez and Khamsi, 'The Argentine Crisis and Foreign Investors' in Sauvant (ed), *Yearbook on International Investment Law and Policy 2008–2009* (2009), p. 412; *Pope & Talbot v. Canada*, Award on the Merits of Phase 2, para. 116.

[129] Salacuse, *The Law of Investment Treaties* (2010), p. 109; Schill, 'Multilateralizing Investment Treaties through Most-Favored-Nation Clauses' (2009) 27 *Berkley Journal of International Law*, p. 549; Claussen, 'The Casualty of Investor Protection in Times of Economic Crisis' (2009) 118 *Yale Law Journal*, p. 1554; *SGS v. Philippines*, Decision on Objections to Jurisdiction, para. 116.

[130] Brower CH, 'Obstacles and Pathways to Consideration of the Public Interest in Investment Treaty Disputes' in Sauvant (ed), *Yearbook on International Investment Law & Policy* (2009), p. 274; Ortino, ''The Investment Treaty System as Judicial Review: Some Remarks on Its Nature, Scope and Standards' (2012) [online], p. 5; *Saluka v. Czech Republic*, Partial Award, para. 300; *Plama v. Bulgaria*, Award, para. 167.

by which new provisions that might be included in existing or future treaties are evaluated.[131] This is for several reasons. First, there may be questions about whether a treaty's purpose is a justifiable objective.[132] Second, a treaty's proximate purpose may constitute a well-intentioned, yet misguided, attempt to achieve some higher order objective. Third, a treaty may cause unjustifiable harm to other interests in the pursuit of a narrow, albeit desirable, purpose. Each of these situations illustrates why assertions about the purpose of existing treaties cannot be conclusive of debate about the criteria that should be used to evaluate provisions that might be included in future treaties.

2.4.2 Consent as a basis for justification

The fact that states have consented to investment treaties by ratifying them makes them authoritative sources of international legal obligations. However, consent is sometimes also deployed as a norm to justify the desirability of investment treaties.[133] The two assumptions underlying this norm seem to be, first, that states would only consent to investment treaties if it were in their interests to do so and, second, that any treaty that is in the interests of all the parties to it is, by definition, desirable (regardless of its impact on those that are not a party to it). Accepting consent as the sole basis for normative judgement would entail the conclusion that any freely accepted treaty provision is, by definition, justified and desirable.

Consent is a weak basis for normative judgements about investment treaties. Historical scholarship offers examples of situations in which a state's consent is legally effective, yet motivated by pressures unrelated to the content of the treaty.[134] Moreover, the link between consent and self-interest is based on the assumption that national bureaucracies are sufficiently well resourced to determine whether a set of legal arrangements accords with the national self-interest.[135] Those who rely on consent as a norm do not establish the validity of this assumption. Recent

---

[131] Cf. Ratner, 'Regulatory Takings in Institutional Context: Beyond the Fear of Fragmented International Law' (2008) 102 *American Journal of International Law*, pp. 520–4.

[132] Finnis, 'The Truth in Legal Positivism' in George (ed), *The Autonomy of Law* (1996); Hart, *The Concept of Law* (2nd edn, 1994), p. 184.

[133] Price, 'Private Party vs Government, Investor-State Dispute Settlement: Frankenstein or Safety Valve' (2000) 26 *Canada United States Law Journal*, p. 113.

[134] See Section 2.3.1.

[135] Van Harten, 'Five Justifications for Investment Treaties: A Critical Discussion' (2010) 2 *Trade, Law and Development*, p. 19.

scholarship by Poulsen and Aisbett suggests that it is not correct, at least insofar as bureaucracies of developing countries are concerned.[136] Both observations demonstrate that consent does not necessarily correspond to self-interest.

In the context of this book, there is a further, more significant limitation of consent as a norm. Taken at their highest, consent-based arguments might be capable of justifying existing investment treaties and their provisions. However, invoking states' consent offers little assistance in evaluating the relative desirability of alternative provisions that states might agree to adopt in future treaties.

2.4.3 Norms of good governance as a basis for justification

In Section 2.3.3, I showed that a formal conception of the rule of law, which approximates Raz's conception of the rule of law, forms the basis for critiques of investment treaty arbitration. The rule of law is also invoked as a justification for investment treaties and for the substantive protections contained in them. In justifications of investment treaties, 'the rule of law' is used to describe two different bundles of norms, both of which go beyond the Razian norms examined earlier in the chapter. The first set of norms is somewhat opaque but seems to reflect a belief that that the resolution of investment disputes by legal adjudication, rather than by negotiation or political pressure, is more consistent with the rule of law.[137] This premise might provide justification for compulsory investor-state arbitration, but it does not provide a criterion for evaluating different provisions defining the level of substantive legal protection to be applied in investor-state arbitration. In justifications for investment treaties, the second way that the rule of law is used is to refer to a particular set of substantive and procedural principles that govern the exercise of public power.

---

[136] Poulsen and Aisbett, 'When the Claim Hits' p. 301; Poulsen, 'Bounded Rationality and the Diffusion of Modern Investment Treaties' (2013) 57 *International Studies Quarterly*, p. 12; Vis-Dunbar and Poulsen, 'Reflections on Pakistan's Investment-Treaty Program after 50 Years: An Interview with the Former Attorney General of Pakistan, Makhdoom Ali Khan' (2009) [online]; similarly, *Wintershall Aktiengesellschaft* v. *Argentina*, Award, para. 85.

[137] Sampliner, 'Arbitration of Expropriation Cases under U.S. Investment Treaties – A Threat to Democracy of the Dog That Didn't Bark' (2003) 18 *ICSID Review – FILJ*, p. 41; UNCTAD, *Development Implications of International Investment Agreements* (2007), p. 5; Paulsson, 'Indirect Expropriation', p. 2; Vandevelde, *Bilateral Investment Treaties*, p. 119; Brower CN and Steven, 'Who Then Should Judge?: Developing the International Rule of Law under NAFTA Chapter 11' (2001) 2 *Chicago Journal of International Law*, p. 202.

This bundle of norms includes, but goes beyond, Razian rule of law norms. A number of scholars have advanced this argument.[138] The most comprehensive statement of this argument is made in a recent book by Vandevelde. Vandevelde argues that the principles of reasonableness, security (of property and contract), non-discrimination, transparency and due process are elements of the rule of law.[139] Although Vandevelde describes these norms are components of the rule of law, it is useful to label them 'good governance' norms to distinguish them from the more limited Razian conception of the rule of law. Much of his book comprises doctrinal argument, which attempts to show that the substantive terms of BITs, and decisions interpreting and applying those terms, can be rationalised as a coherent reflection of these good governance principles.[140] His argument also has a strong normative element. He contends that these principles have 'intrinsic worth' that would justify the existence of BITs, even if BITs are unsuccessful in achieving their instrumental, economic objectives.[141]

The initial difficulty with Vandevelde's argument is the assertion that the five norms that he identifies have 'intrinsic worth'. This assertion is arguable, but Vandevelde offers little by way of argument to support it. His collective justification for the five norms is exclusively instrumental: that they are components of 'liberal legalism', which, in turn, is associated with economic growth.[142] To the extent that he does justify his choice of norms individually, security (of property and contract) rests exclusively on instrumental grounds,[143] whereas non-discrimination and transparency rest primarily on instrumental grounds.[144] There is no inconsistency in suggesting that a given norm may have both intrinsic and instrumental value. However, to the extent that the desirability of a norm rests on its instrumental value, it requires empirical justification – demonstration

---

[138] See Dolzer, 'The Impact of International Investment Treaties on Domestic Administrative Law' (2006) 37 *International Law and Politics*, p. 971; Wälde and Weiler, 'Investment Arbitration under the Energy Charter Treaty: Towards a Global Code of Conduct for Economic Regulation' (2004) 1 *Transnational Dispute Management*, p. 10; Schill, 'Fair and Equitable Treatment, the Rule of Law, and Comparative Public Law', p. 159; Brower CN and Schill, 'Is Arbitration a Threat or a Boon to the Legitimacy of International Investment Law?' (2009) 50 *Chicago Journal of International Law*, p. 487.
[139] Vandevelde, *Bilateral Investment Treaties*, p. 2.   [140] Ibid., p. 12.   [141] Ibid., p. 119.
[142] Ibid., p. 114; similarly, Schill, 'Fair and Equitable Treatment, the Rule of Law, and Comparative Public Law', p. 176.
[143] Vandevelde, *Bilateral Investment Treaties*, p. 78.   [144] Ibid., pp. 337, 397.

that compliance with norm in the circumstances in question leads to desirable consequences (in this case, economic benefits).

Although Vandevelde does not provide a justification for intrinsic value of the security of property, it is worth pausing at this point to ask whether there is any coherent justification for his view. Waldron has usefully divided philosophical justifications for the protection of property rights into libertarian and Hegelian arguments. It seems unlikely that the Hegelian view – that the intrinsic value of the protection of property rights stems from property-ownership's role in the ethical development of the individual – could justify the protection of investment property owned by foreign-domiciled corporations.[145] On the other hand, libertarian theories of distributive justice, which are based on the entitlement to property justly acquired – might provide justification for the view that the security of foreign investment has intrinsic normative value.

A second difficulty with Vandevelde's argument relates specifically to the concept of reasonableness on which he relies. He contends that it is intrinsically desirable for a government's conduct to be rational, in the sense of being 'reasonably related to a legitimate host-state regulatory objective.'[146] This conception of reasonableness comprises two component norms: that government should pursue legitimate objectives and that, in the pursuit of legitimate objectives, government conduct should satisfy the criterion of means-ends rationality. The latter norm is uncontroversial. A government is more likely to be effective in realising a normatively desirable objective if its conduct has some plausible causal connection to the realisation of that objective – that is, if its conduct satisfies the criterion of means-ends rationality.[147] The former component norm – that government should pursue legitimate objectives – presupposes some account of the criteria by which legitimate objectives are identified. Vandevelde does not attempt to provide such an account. To the extent that such an account is implicit in his writing, it is through the suggestion that 'politically motivated' conduct does not pursue a

---

[145] Waldron, *The Right to Private Property* (1990), p. 351, discussing the Hegelian justification for property rights and comparing it to the libertarian view.
[146] Vandevelde, *Bilateral Investment Treaties*, p. 109.
[147] The principle that *administrative* conduct should satisfy the criterion of means-ends rationality can also be justified by a formal conception of the rule of law; see Hickman, 'The Reasonableness Principle: Reassessing its Place in the Public Sphere' (2004) 63 *Cambridge Law Journal*, p. 170. The underlying norm is that the exercise of conferrals of discretion should be circumscribed by clear and stable rules, such as the principle that discretionary authority only be exercised for the purposes for which it was conferred: see Raz, 'The Rule of Law and Its Virtue', p. 200. This rationale does not apply to legislative conduct.

legitimate objective.[148] Although this position is arguable, it is not self-evident that it is intrinsically undesirable for a government to be motivated by political pressure; indeed, many democratic political theories imply the opposite.[149]

A final qualification to Vandevelde's argument is that reasonableness, non-discrimination, transparency and due process all belong to a class of norms that relate to the exercise of government power. However, investment treaty protections are not enforced by institutions that are capable of directly constraining the exercise of public power. An arbitral tribunal's finding that a governmental measure has breached an investment treaty triggers an obligation to pay compensation to the investor, not an order invalidating or annulling the measure.[150] Accordingly, the argument that investment treaty protections can be justified by good governance norms depends on an implicit causal assumption – that such legal rules have the consequence of encouraging governments to exercise power in a certain way.

This critique of Vandevelde's norms of good governance informs four conclusions that are relevant to this book. The first is that his assertion that the security of property is intrinsically desirable depends, presumably, on an unarticulated libertarian theory of distributive justice. The second is that his conception of reasonableness cannot substitute for an account of the primary norms by which the impact of investment treaty protections on government conduct should be evaluated. The third is that the norm that government conduct should satisfy the criterion of means-ends rationality is a specific iteration of a more general principle: that the realisation of primary norms is desirable. The fourth is that his conception of reasonableness, along with norms of non-discrimination, transparency and due process, relies on implicit causal assumptions about the impact of investment treaty protections on government conduct.

2.5 The role of secondary norms in debate about investment treaties

A final set of norms is invoked by both critics and supporters of investment treaties. These norms – balance, sustainable development (in its

---

[148] Vandevelde, 'A Unified Theory of Fair and Equitable Treatment' (2010) 43 *International Law and Politics*, p. 59.

[149] Sen, *Development as Freedom* (1999), p. 182.

[150] Schill, 'Fair and Equitable Treatment, the Rule of Law, and Comparative Public Law', p. 170; see Section 3.3.

interstitial sense) and proportionality – all relate to the reconciliation of competing, incommensurable objectives. They are secondary norms that mediate between primary norms. A brief survey of references to these norms illustrates that they are relied on in a variety of different contexts, often to justify very different conclusions.

The first context in which balance is invoked is debate about the competing interests of the host state and the home state. Vandevelde, for example, argues that BITs are formally balanced, because both parties take on equal obligations under the treaty, but are often unbalanced in practice, because one state is more commonly a recipient of foreign investment than the other.[151] A second debate concerns the balance between the interests of the host state and the interests of foreign investors, as reflected in the architecture of investment treaties. One common criticism is that investment treaties are unbalanced because they confer benefits on foreign investors without imposing any duties on them.[152] A third issue relates to the institution of investor-state arbitration. Critics imply that arbitrators, many of whom have professional backgrounds in commercial law, are unlikely to bring a balanced perspective to the resolution of disputes.[153] Although these debates do not directly relate to the level of substantive protection provided by investment treaties, they do show that the vast majority of scholars agree that investment treaties involve competing interests and that, in the abstract, a balance between competing interests is normatively desirable.

Discussion of balance is also an important component of debate about the level of protection provided by investment treaties.[154] Several scholars have argued that the indirect expropriation and FET provisions of investment treaties should be interpreted in a way that balances investors' rights against states' legitimate regulatory prerogatives.[155] More specifically, some scholars have claimed that the concept of sustainable development,

---

[151] Vandevelde, *Bilateral Investment Treaties*, p. 8.
[152] Alvarez, 'Critical Theory and the North American Free Trade Agreements Chapter Eleven' (1997) 28 *University of Miami Inter-American Law Review*, p. 309; Weiler, 'Balancing Human Rights and Investor Protection: A New Approach for a Different Legal Order' (2004) 27 *Boston College International and Comparative Law Review*, p. 430.
[153] Tienhaara, *The Expropriation of Environmental Governance*, p. 206; cf. Paulsson, 'Indirect Expropriation', p. 1.
[154] E.g., Kläger, *'Fair and Equitable Treatment' in International Investment Law* (2011), p. 256.
[155] Kingsbury and Schill, 'Public Law Concepts to Balance Investors' Rights with State Regulatory Actions in the Public Interest – The Concept of Proportionality' in Schill (ed), *International Investment Law and Comparative Public Law* (2010), p. 103; Kläger, *'Fair and Equitable Treatment' in International Investment Law*, p. 151.

in its interstitial sense, should be used as the principle to govern the balancing of competing economic, environmental and social objectives.[156] Sustainable development requires the reconciliation of competing primary norms, with special attention to environmental conservation and the effect that depletion of non-renewable resources would have on future generations.[157]

Other scholars have argued that investment treaty protections should use the principle of proportionality to balance competing primary norms.[158] Proportionality, as a legal principle, has its roots in German jurisprudence on the protection of constitutional rights.[159] It has since been adopted by other legal systems in situations that require a balance to be struck between the protection of private rights and the pursuit of public interests.[160] For a government's interference with a protected right to be justified, the principle of proportionality requires that the interference advance a legitimate public interest objective, that it be the least rights-restrictive means of achieving that objective and that the burden on the rights-holder be proportionate in light of the objective pursued.[161] The cumulative effect of these criteria is to place a significant burden of justification on any interference with a protected right.[162] (Just how significant that burden of justification is turns on a range of more specific questions relating to the application of proportionality in the particular context, including the extent of interference with a protected right required to trigger proportionality review and whether, in examining the proportionality of an interference with a protected right, the court or tribunal

---

[156] Kläger, "Fair and Equitable Treatment' and Sustainable Development' in Cordonier Segger, Gehring and Newcombe (eds), *Sustainable Development in World Investment Law* (2011), p. 249.

[157] Pavoni, 'Environmental Rights, Sustainable Development, and Investor-State Case Law: A Critical Appraisal' in Dupuy, Francioni and Petersmann (eds), *Human Rights in International Investment Law and Arbitration* (2009), p. 556.

[158] Kulick, *Global Public Interest*, p. 168; Diehl, *The Core Standard in International Investment Protection: Fair and Equitable Treatment* (2012), p. 336.

[159] Stone Sweet and Mathews, 'Proportionality Balancing and Global Constitutionalism' (2008) 47 *Columbia Journal of Transnational Law*, p. 104.

[160] Ibid., p. 112.

[161] Kingsbury and Schill, 'Public Law Concepts to Balance Investors' Rights with State Regulatory Actions', pp. 85–7. The requirement that the burden on the rights-holder be proportionate in light of the objective pursued is often called 'proportionality *stricto sensu*'.

[162] Stone Sweet and Mathews, 'Proportionality Balancing and Global Constitutionalism', p. 109, arguing that proportionality requires a court or tribunal 'to put itself in the shoes of policymakers, and then to walk through their decision-making processes, step-by-step'.

defers to findings of fact made by the government decision-maker.[163]) It is not self-evident that proportionality, a secondary norm developed to safeguard primary norms of great weight (i.e., human rights codified in a national constitution) is equally appropriate to balance private economic interests against public interests.[164]

There is clearly room for disagreement about the way in which competing incommensurable interests should be reconciled. For present purposes, there is no need to develop a theory of how tension between competing primary norms should be resolved, nor to determine whether proportionality, or some other principle, should guide the balancing of competing objectives. At this stage of the inquiry, I seek to make a simpler point. My claim is that any meaningful discussion of what balance, sustainable development or proportionality requires is possible only after the primary norms that need to be balanced have been specified and the extent to which they are, in fact, in tension has been determined.

This contention is borne out by the analysis in subsequent chapters. For example, in Section 5.6.1. I argue that, insofar as the principle of proportionality has been used to resolve indirect expropriation claims, tribunals have balanced the impact of a government measure on the value of the foreign investment against the public interest objective pursued by that measure. In Section 6.6.2, I conclude that tribunals should reject this approach in favour of approaches embodied in other arbitral decisions that do not incorporate the principle of proportionality. This is partly because, in the context of indirect expropriation claims, the principle of proportionality has been applied to protect an interest that there is little justification for protecting – namely, the value of an investment as distinct from the rights that inhere in it.

2.6 Synthesis of existing debate as it relates to investment treaty protections

The analysis in previous sections entails a number of important conclusions. The first of these is that much normative debate about investment treaties relies on *methodologies* that are not appropriate for the

---

[163] Henckels, 'Indirect Expropriation and the Right to Regulate', p. 255.
[164] E.g., Vadi and Gruszczynski, 'Standards of Review in International Investment Law and Arbitration: Multilevel Governance and the Commonweal' (2013) 16 *Journal of International Economic Law*, p. 632, arguing for an approach to balancing based on reasonableness and procedural fairness.

prospective evaluation of different levels of protection. Critiques of investment treaties based on historical methodology raise important questions about whether these treaties are desirable, but do not provide much guidance on the level of protection that such treaties should provide. Comparative methodologies describe, with attention to certain features, the similarities and differences between investment treaties and other legal systems. Moving from comparative observations to normative conclusions requires a set of normative criteria by which the compared subjects should be evaluated. Accordingly, comparative methodology is only capable of justifying claims about the level of protection investment treaties should provide insofar as it incorporates or refers to some underlying normative framework.

The second conclusion that can be drawn from the analysis is that some norms invoked in debates about investment treaties are not coherent *criteria* by which to evaluate the merit of adopting a given level of protection. The criteria of sovereignty and consent fall into this class. Criticism that an investment treaty protection constitutes too great an interference with states' sovereignty requires recourse to some further normative framework to determine how much interference with sovereignty can be justified. Justification of existing investment treaty protections on the basis that states have consented to them does not provide grounds for prospective evaluation of different levels of protection. Moreover, reference to a treaty's purpose is not sufficient grounds for normative judgement. Claims that given investment treaty protections advance existing treaties' purpose requires reference to some further normative framework to confirm that the purpose is a desirable one and that pursuit of that purpose does not come at the expense of unjustifiable harm to other interests. Similarly, the desirable degree of deference to decisions taken in the political sphere of host states depends on specification of primary norms implicated by the decision and the decision-making process.

A third conclusion concerns the identification of *primary norms* invoked in existing debate about investment treaties that are capable of justifying a preference between different levels of protection. These norms are the following:

1. The claim that increases in FDI flows and economic efficiency are desirable.
2. The claim that respect for the rule of law in the legal systems of signatory states – in the Razian sense of norms relating to the procedural and formal characteristics of law and legal systems – is desirable.

3. The claim that the conservation of environmental resources is desirable.
4. The claim that the realisation of human rights is desirable.
5. The claim that protection of property rights is intrinsically desirable. The basis for the intrinsic value of property rights is not articulated in the investment treaty literature, but it presumably depends on a theory of distributive justice, most likely libertarian theory.
6. The claim that sustainable development is desirable. In its portmanteau sense, sustainable development functions as an umbrella term for a set of other primary norms, including environmental conservation, realisation of human rights, distributive justice and economic efficiency. Thus, it does not appear to add anything to the five previous norms articulated.
7. The claim that good governance is desirable. Recent justifications for investment treaty protections invoke the concepts of good governance and the rule of law (understood in a broader sense than Razian norms). While focusing attention on the effects of investment treaty protections on the exercise of government power, these umbrella concepts do not appear to expand the criteria by which these effects should be evaluated beyond the first five primary norms articulated here.

These norms form the basis of the framework developed in Chapter 3.

A fourth conclusion that emerges from this chapter's review of normative scholarship is that there is remarkably little dispute that the norms articulated in the previous paragraph are desirable. Few advocates of greater protection for foreign investors disagree that the realisation of human rights or the protection of the environment are normatively desirable. Even critics who doubt whether greater FDI flows and improvements in economic efficiency are worth their perceived environmental and social costs do not dispute that the latter objectives are desirable, all other things being equal. Normative disagreement stems partly from differences between underlying causal assumptions about the likely consequences of investment treaties and partly from disagreement about which norms should be prioritised and how tension between competing norms should be reconciled.

A fifth conclusion is that most normative debate about investment treaty protections is already framed in consequentialist terms. Arguments that investment treaty protections increase FDI flows, improve economic efficiency, discourage governments from taking measures necessary for environmental conservation, reduce the realisation of human rights or encourage good governance in signatory states are all arguments that rest on causal assumptions. Sometimes the causal assumptions underpinning these arguments are made explicit; often they are left unarticulated. Evaluating the strength of these arguments requires examination of the theoretical coherence of the underlying causal assumptions as well as empirical investigation of whether the effects of investment treaty protections are, indeed, those assumed. Moreover, to the extent that deontological arguments are present in the existing literature – for example, the argument that it is *unfair* for a state to interfere with a foreign investor's property without paying compensation – these arguments can usefully be reframed in consequential terms. Rather than starting from a set of abstract libertarian principles and asking what level of protection these principles require, I submit that it is more practical to ask whether adopting a given level of protection would have a set of distributive consequences consistent with those principles.

3 A framework for evaluating different levels of investment treaty protection

3.1 Introduction

This chapter constructs a framework for evaluating different levels of investment treaty protection. Chapter 2 argued that the evaluation of alternative levels of protection should be based on a comparison of the likely consequences of each level of protection, if it were adopted. Therefore, the framework must perform two tasks: it must provide an informed basis for drawing inferences about the likely consequences of adopting given levels of protection; and it must specify the normative criteria by which these consequences should be evaluated.

This chapter draws on the critique and synthesis of scholarship on investment treaties presented in Chapter 2 to propose a categorisation of the consequences of investment treaty protections that is as comprehensive as possible. It argues that a prospective assessment of the consequences of adopting a given level of protection can be divided into five categories: its effect on efficiency, the distribution of economic costs and benefits, flows of foreign direct investment (FDI) into host states, the realisation of human rights and environmental conservation in host states and respect for the rule of law in host states. Within this framework, this chapter provides a synthesis of evidence and theory, on the basis of which conclusions about the likely consequences of differing levels of protection can be drawn.

As for the criteria by which these consequences should be evaluated, this chapter argues that most of the identified consequences are normatively desirable in themselves, Specifically, economic efficiency, the realisation of human rights, environmental conservation and respect for the rule of law are all inherently desirable. Consistently with the existing literature, the attraction of FDI is accepted as a proxy for other desirable consequences. In contrast to the other consequences considered, there is significant disagreement about the normative criteria by which distributive impacts should be evaluated. I propose four normative criteria for the evaluation of the distributive impacts of different levels of protection.

This chapter comprises nine substantive sections. Section 3.2 explains and justifies the approach to theory and evidence adopted in this chapter. Section 3.3 explains and justifies the premise that investment treaty protections should be understood as liability rules. Sections 3.4 to 3.8 constitute the framework, dealing respectively with the likely consequences of alternative levels of investment treaty protection for efficiency, the distribution of economic costs and benefits, flows of FDI, the realisation of human rights and environmental conservation and respect for the rule of law. Each section explains why the identified consequence should form part of the framework and examines how the consequence relates to the other identified consequences. Section 3.9 argues that other categories of consequences are unnecessary. In doing so, it justifies the claim that the framework provides an account of the consequences of different levels of protection that is as comprehensive as possible. Section 3.10 highlights some preliminary conclusions that emerge from the framework.

3.2 Methodology: the relationship between theory and evidence

The framework developed in this chapter provides a basis for determining the consequences of adopting alternative levels of investment treaty protection. To construct this framework, I use a combination of theory and evidence of the consequences of investment treaties as they currently operate. The process of integrating theory and evidence is iterative. The starting point is the set of causal theories that emerge from the review of the existing literature in Chapter 2. In this chapter, I articulate the behavioural assumptions underpinning these theories, examine whether the theories are internally coherent and draw out the predictions that they suggest. These assumptions and predictions then frame the engagement with available evidence. The role of evidence is both to test the validity of underlying assumptions (which may turn out to be valid simplifying assumptions in some circumstances but not others) and to examine whether evidence supports the predictions that a theory implies. Through this process of critique, the original theories are refined (or discarded), new theories are developed and new hypotheses are proposed. These predictions are then subject to further testing.

3.2.1 The influence of the New Haven school of law and economics

The iterative process of building and testing causal theory is common to many forms of inquiry in the social sciences. However, my approach to theory in this chapter has been particularly influenced the New Haven school of law and economics (not to be confused with the New Haven school of international law).[1] There are many different theoretical perspectives within the discipline of law and economics. This chapter has been specifically influenced by the New Haven approach to law and economics in two important respects.

The first concerns basic assumptions about actors' behaviour. The common foundation of law and economics, as a discipline, is the assumption that actors are influenced by incentives, tending to act in a way that minimises the costs and maximises the benefits of their actions.[2] Because law changes the expected costs and benefits of different actions, this behavioural assumption provides a basis for predicting how actors will respond to legal rules.[3] As it turns out, this assumption (or variations of it) also underpins much of the debate about investment treaties – for example, arguments that investment treaties increase FDI flows, that they encourage 'good governance' in host states or that they lead to 'regulatory chill' of human rights or environmental measures.

The hallmark of the new the New Haven school of law and economics scholarship is that the assumption that actors' behaviour responds to incentives is treated as a first approximation – a working hypothesis that may have to be modified or discarded in light of evidence about how actors behave in the context in question. Thus, many of the important contributions of New Haven scholars have focused on the implications of departures from the simplifying assumptions of other forms of law and economics – for example, the implications of the fact that individuals may not have perfect information about the risks associated with their actions[4] and the implications of the fact that there may be significant transaction costs associated with bargaining among individuals.[5] Consistently with

---

[1] On the New Haven school of international law, see Reisman, 'The View from the New Haven School of International Law' (1992) 86 *American Society of International Law Proceedings*, p. 120.

[2] Polinsky and Shavell, 'Economic Analysis of Law' in Durlauf and Blume (eds), *The New Palgrave Dictionary of Economics* (2nd edn, 2008).

[3] Cooter and Ulen, *Law & Economics Law & Economics* (5th edn, 2008), p. 4.

[4] Calabresi and Klevorick 'Four Tests for Liability in Torts' (1985) 14 *Journal of Legal Studies*.

[5] Calabresi and Melamed, 'Property Rules, Liability Rules, and Inalienability: One View of the Cathedral' (1972) 85 *Harvard Law Review*, p. 1119.

the New Haven school of law and economics, I accept the assumption that actors' behaviour responds to incentives as starting point. However, this assumption is only ever a first approximation, subject to testing and revision in light of available evidence through the iterative process described earlier. On this basis, I argue that this simplifying assumption is appropriate in certain contexts and not in others.

A second respect in which this book is influence by the New Haven school of law and economics is that no attempt is made to value the various consequences of a given level of protection within a single metric.[6] In other words, different types of consequence are treated as incommensurable. Most lawyers and legal scholars will find the view that different types of consequences are incommensurable intuitive, requiring little justification. Legal problems regularly raise questions that require the balancing of incommensurable ends.[7] Legal scholars who have applied similar consequentialist methodologies to the study of investment treaties – notably Been and Beauvais – have also proceeded on the assumption of incommensurability.[8] In contrast, economists and policy analysts may be more comfortable with using a single metric to aggregate all the costs and benefits associated with a policy choice. Because these professions form part of the audience for this book, in the following paragraphs I provide a fuller justification for the assumption of incommensurability.

The claim that different types of goods are incommensurable is, above all, an empirical claim. An individual's ability to access an impartial court system, her job – which she finds rewarding – and the fresh apples in her pantry are all qualitatively distinct, even if they are all things she values.[9] Seeking to value all these different goods within a single metric would be inconsistent with individuals' own understanding of how different goods are, and should, be valued.

A second general argument stems from fundamental epistemological problems with plausible bases for commensurability. Even if one wished

---

[6] Similarly, Ibid., p. 1102.
[7] Kronman, *The Lost Lawyer: Failing Ideals of the Legal Profession* (1993), p. 57; Sunstein 'Incommensurability and Valuation in Law' (1994) 92 *Michigan Law Journal*, p. 824.
[8] Been and Beauvais, 'The Global Fifth Amendment?' NAFTA's Investment Protections and the Misguided Quest for an International "Regulatory Takings" Doctrine' (2003) 78 *New York University Law Review*, p. 87. This analysis develops Beauvais' earlier argument: Beauvais, 'Regulatory Expropriations under NAFTA: Emerging Principles & Lingering Doubts' (2002) 10 *New York University Environmental Law Journal*, p. 256.
[9] Sunstein 'Incommensurability and Valuation in Law', p. 782; similarly, Sen, 'Incompleteness and Reasoned Choice' (2004) 140 *Synthese*, p. 44.

to evaluate different consequences within a single metric, there is no non-arbitrary means by which different consequences could be quantified and weighed against each other. Using utility as a common unit of account is problematic because there is no way of quantifying the subjective experience of different individuals within a common metric.[10] An alternative is to use dollar values as a common unit of account and examine individuals' willingness to pay for incommensurable benefits as a mechanism to derive dollar values for them. This approach is particularly associated with the Chicago school of law and economics and is used in formal cost-benefit analyses by some government agencies.[11] Although this approach can be useful, particularly in evaluating regulation that affects a small number of actors in clearly defined ways, it also has its difficulties. Two such difficulties are that individuals' reported willingness to pay for public good provision is not necessarily independent of what other individuals would consent to pay and that willingness to pay is generally not independent of the process by which payment would be collected and allocated.[12] Yet these assumptions underpin the ability of willingness to pay to generate determinate, transitive valuations of policy alternatives.

In the context of this book, there are three more specific arguments in favour of proceeding on the basis that different types of consequences are not commensurable. First, as Chapter 2 has shown, existing debate on investment treaties is premised on the assumption of incommensurability. It would require a considerable reorientation of existing scholarship to bring the range of concerns raised by different scholars into a single metric. Second, the consequences of investment treaties are felt by different classes of individuals across a wide range of countries. As such, it is not clear whose willingness to pay should define the valuation function that would be required if consequences were to be weighed within a

---

[10] Robbins, 'Robertson on Utility and Scope' (1953) 20 *Economica*, p. 109; on the possibility of qualitative, partial interpersonal utility comparisons, see Harsanyi, 'Cardinal Welfare, Individualistic Ethics, and Interpersonal Comparisons of Utility' (1955) 63 *The Journal of Political Economy*, p. 309; Sen, 'Interpersonal Aggregation and Partial Comparability' (1970) 38 *Econometrica*, p. 407.

[11] Posner, 'Cost-Benefit Analysis: Definition, Justification and Comment on Conference Papers' (2000) 29 *Journal of Legal Studies*, p. 1154; Sunstein, *The Cost-Benefit State: The Future of Regulatory Protection* (American Bar Association 2002), p. 15; Australian Government, 'OBPR Guidance Note – Best-Practice Regulation', p. 4.

[12] Sen, 'The Discipline of Cost-Benefit Analysis' (2000) 29 *Journal of Legal Studies*, p. 946; Sen, *Rationality and Freedom* (2004), p. 536

single metric.[13] Third, even if it were possible to identify all those potentially affected by investment treaty protections, there would be enormous practical difficulties in collecting data necessary to determine willingness-to-pay weightings.

The basic principle underpinning the evaluation of incommensurable consequences is maximisation: that desirable consequences should be maximised (and undesirable ones minimised) so far as is possible.[14] More difficult issues arise when evaluation of alternatives requires a trade-off between different types of desirable consequences. That consequences are incommensurable does not mean they are incomparable.[15] Rather, it means that the evaluation of various alternatives must rely on qualitative reasoning. Qualitative reasoning permits a plurality of views about what is reasonable and, accordingly, a range of disagreement on the merits of a given choice.[16]

3.2.2 To what extent do the decisions of arbitral tribunals constitute evidence?

The framework developed in this chapter provides a basis for evaluating various levels of protection that could be adopted and applied consistently. Although the levels of protection evaluated in this book are derived from the awards of arbitral tribunals in past cases, the facts surrounding such cases do not constitute direct evidence of the consequences of adopting a given level of protection generally. This is because arbitral tribunals disagree about the level of protection investment treaties currently provide and because individual awards only specify the level of protection for the purposes of resolving a single case, after a dispute has already arisen. For both reasons, existing decisions are relevant only as an indirect evidentiary source. As an indirect evidentiary source, existing decisions are useful in that they provide highly detailed factual records, which serve as case studies of the issues to which investment treaties apply.[17] Existing

---

[13] Dunoff and Trachtman, 'Economic Analysis of International Law' (1999) 24 *Yale Journal of International Law*, p. 47.

[14] Maximisation should be contrasted with optimisation, which is the search for an ideal or 'optimal' approach given a defined set of constraints. See Sen, 'Maximization and the Act of Choice' (1997) 65 *Econometrica*, p. 772.

[15] Sunstein, 'Incommensurability and Valuation in Law', p. 798.

[16] Sen, *The Idea of Justice* (2009), p. 242.

[17] Franck, 'Empiricism and International Law: Insights for Investment Treaty Dispute Resolution' (2008) 48 *Virginia Journal of International Law*, p. 807.

cases may provide evidence for relatively general hypotheses – for example, that foreign investors sometimes challenge measures motivated by environmental concerns[18] – or for more specific propositions – for example, that states sometimes cite environmental concerns as a justification for measures that are not truly motivated by those concerns.[19]

A significant weakness of existing decisions as an evidentiary source is selection bias. Situations in which foreign investments operate profitably and with cordial relations with the host government do not tend to result in investor-state disputes; those in which a host state treats a foreign investor poorly are more likely to end up before a tribunal. Inferences drawn from the set of cases that result in disputes will be highly unreliable, unless this evidentiary bias is taken into account. Selection bias may explain why certain commentators perceive foreign investors to be treated poorly in comparison to domestic investors,[20] notwithstanding evidence from systematic studies suggesting that, on average, foreign investors are not treated more poorly than domestic investors.[21]

3.3 Investment treaty protections as liability rules

An important premise on which this framework is based is that investment treaty protections function as liability rules – rules that require states to compensate foreign investors for losses caused by conduct that breaches those protections. Other commentators have also argued that

---

[18] Peterson, 'Parties in *Vattenfall v. Germany* Case Suspend Proceedings' (2010), *IA Reporter* [online].

[19] *Metalclad v. Mexico*, Award, para. 69.

[20] Ratner, 'Regulatory Takings in Institutional Context: Beyond the Fear of Fragmented International Law' (2008) 102 *American Journal of International Law*, p. 483; Paulsson, 'Indirect Expropriation' (2005) [online], p. 4; Wälde and Weiler, 'Investment Arbitration under the Energy Charter Treaty: Towards a Global Code of Conduct for Economic Regulation' (2004) 1 *Transnational Dispute Management*, fn. 119; Choi, 'The Present and Future of the Investor-State Dispute Settlement Paradigm' (2007) 10 *Journal of International Economic Law*, p. 735; *Tecmed v. Mexico*, Award, para. 122; *Gallo v. Canada*, Award, para. 335.

[21] Desbordes and Vauday, 'The Political Influence of Foreign Firms in Developing Countries' (2007) 19 *Economics & Politics*, p. 447; Aisbett and McAusland, 'Firm Characteristics and Influence on Government Rule-Making: Theory and Evidence' (2013) 29 *European Journal of Political Economy*, p. 226; Huang, 'Are Foreign Firms Privileged by Their Host Governments?' Evidence From The 2000 World Business Environment Survey' (2005) [online], p. 28.

investment treaty protections should be understood as liability rules.[22] In this section, I explain and justify the claim that investment treaty protections should be understood as liability rules.

The concept of liability rules, as contrasted with property rules and inalienability, derives from an article by Calabresi and Melamed. Liability rules, property rules and inalienability describe three different ways in which a given legal entitlement might be protected. These three forms of protection are distinguished by their associated remedies. An entitlement is protected by a liability rule if the individual that holds the entitlement is unable, *ex ante*, to prevent another actor from interfering with the entitlement but is capable of recovering compensatory damages for interference *ex post*.[23] To be clear, an entitlement protected by a liability rule still entails a corresponding legal obligation on the duty-bearer not to interfere with the entitlement.[24]

Investment treaty provisions that require compensation for expropriation (including indirect expropriation) are clearly liability rules.[25] The wording of expropriation provisions is permissive – it allows a state to expropriate foreign investors' property on payment of compensation, provided that basic legality requirements are satisfied.[26] In contrast, other substantive protections such as fair and equitable treatment (FET) provisions are not phrased in permissive language. They purport to oblige states to provide foreign investors with a certain standard of treatment. Nevertheless, the identifying characteristic of a liability rule is its associated remedy, not the way in which the obligation is phrased. In investor-state disputes, the normal remedy for breach of the FET standard is compensation.[27] For this reason, FET provisions should also be understood as liability rules.

The prevailing view is that tribunals adjudicating investor-state disputes under investment treaties do have the inherent authority to award non-pecuniary remedies, such as injunctions and orders of specific

---

[22] van Aaken, 'Primary and Secondary Remedies in International Investment Law and National State Liability: A Functional and Comparative View' in Schill (ed), *International Investment Law and Comparative Public Law* (2010), p. 746; Montt, *State Liability in Investment Treaty Arbitration* (2009), p. 6.

[23] Calabresi and Melamed, 'Property Rules, Liability Rules, and Inalienability', p. 1092.

[24] Ibid., p. 1116.   [25] Ibid., p. 1106.

[26] Generally, that the expropriation is for a public purpose, non-discriminatory and complies with due process.

[27] Dolzer and Schreuer, *Principles of International Investment Law* (2nd edn, 2012), p. 294; Schill, *The Multilateralization of International Investment Law* (2009), p. 250.

performance, unless this authority is expressly excluded by the investment treaty in question.[28] Both injunctions and orders of specific performance are remedies that purport to constrain the manner in which a government may exercise is powers. That tribunals have authority, in theory, to award these remedies might raise doubts about the characterisation of FET provisions as liability rules. However, non-pecuniary remedies cannot be enforced under the ICSID Convention and, although their enforceability is not specifically excluded by the New York Convention, there is no obvious mechanism by which a successful investor could enforce an injunction in a non-ICSID award.[29]

The difficulty of enforcing non-pecuniary remedies, coupled with tribunals' respect for the sovereign prerogatives of states, explains why the overwhelming majority of arbitral decisions award only damages for breach of investment treaties.[30] Indeed, the literature cites only two cases in which an investment treaty tribunal has awarded a non-pecuniary remedy against a state.[31] (This count does not include the use of non-pecuniary interim orders during proceedings, which raise very different

---

[28] Schreuer, 'Non-Pecuniary Remedies in ICSID Arbitration' (2004) 20 *Arbitration International*, p. 329; Endicott, 'Remedies in Investor-State Arbitration: Restitution, Specific Performance and Declaratory Awards' in Kahn and Wälde (eds), *New Aspects of International Investment Law* (2007), p. 550. The authority to award a non-pecuniary remedy is excluded by NAFTA and partially excluded by the ECT: NAFTA, art. 1135; ECT art. 26(8).

[29] ICSID Convention, art. 54(1); New York Convention, art. III.

[30] Jarvin, 'Non-Pecuniary Remedies: The Practice of Declaratory Relief and Specific Performance in International Commercial Arbitration' in Rovine (ed), *Contemporary Issues in International Arbitration and Mediation: The Fordham Papers 2007* (2008), p. 183; Hobér, 'Remedies in Investment Disputes' in Bjorklund, Laird and Ripinsky (eds), *Investment Treaty Law: Current Issues III* (2009), p. 13; cf. Douglas, 'The ICSID Regime of State Responsibility' in Crawford, Pellet and Olleson (eds) *The Law of International Responsibility* (Oxford University Press 2010), p. 829.

[31] Schreuer, 'Non-Pecuniary Remedies in ICSID Arbitration', p. 329; Jarvin, 'Non-Pecuniary Remedies', p. 172; Hobér, 'Remedies in Investment Disputes', p. 13; *Enron Corporation v. Argentine Republic* ICSID Case No ARB/01/3, Decision on Jurisdiction, 14 January 2007, para. 80. The tribunal in *Occidental I* did hold that the Ecuadorian tax authority's rulings demanding payment from the claimant were 'without legal effect': *Occidental v. Ecuador (I)*, Final Award, para. 202. However, this declaration was made in a section of the award headed 'compensation due' and was part of the tribunal's attempt to make a net pecuniary award settling the financial claims and counter-claims between the claimant and the respondent. Reviewing the decision, the English High Court interpreted the tribunal's statement as a declaration that the tax rulings had breached the applicable treaty, rather than as an attempt to grant a remedy invalidating the tax rulings, *Republic of Ecuador v. Occidental Exploration and Production Co* [2006] EWHC (Comm) 345 124.

issues.)[32] In the first, *Goetz* v. *Burundi*, the tribunal offered the host state a choice between paying compensation to the investor and revoking the measure that breached the treaty. Because the decision allowed the host state the option to maintain its chosen measure and pay compensation, it is consistent with understanding the FET standard as a liability rule.[33] A second, more recent decision, *ATA* v. *Jordan*, also resulted in the award of a non-pecuniary remedy. The tribunal ordered that the respondent restore the claimant's right to arbitration of disputes under a contract, which had been extinguished by legislation.[34] However, in this case it was the respondent state itself that had proposed non-pecuniary remedy.[35] This award is also consistent with the understanding of the FET standard as a liability rule; it appears that the host state could have refused to restore the right to arbitration of contractual disputes and chosen, instead, to pay compensation. The implications of the tribunal's orders have since been the subject of a further dispute, highlighting the practical obstacles to the order and enforcement of non-pecuniary remedies in investment treaty arbitration.[36]

Further questions about characterising the substantive protections of investment treaties as liability rules might be raised by the fact that many investment treaties allow claims of breach to be brought to state-state arbitration.[37] Tribunals resolving state-state disputes may be more inclined to award non-pecuniary remedies than those hearing investor-disputes. At present, however, state-state arbitration does not play a significant role in practice. More than five hundred cases have been brought under investor-state dispute settlement procedures. There are only three publicly known occasions in which the state-to-state dispute settlement procedures have been invoked. The first is a case brought by Peru against Chile in response to an investor-state proceeding that a Chilean investor had brought against Peru. The state-to-state dispute was subsequently discontinued,[38] while the associated investor-state dispute proceeded to a final decision.[39] The second is a recent claim initiated by Ecuador against

---

[32] E.g., *Chevron* v. *Ecuador (II)*, Second Interim Award on Interim Measure, para. 3.
[33] *Goetz* v. *Burundi*, Award (Embodying the Parties Settlement Agreement), para. 133.
[34] *ATA Construction* v. *Jordan*, Award, paras. 127–32.
[35] *ATA Construction* v. *Jordan*, Award, para. 131.
[36] *ATA Construction* v. *Jordan*, Decision on Interpretation and on the Request for Provisional Measures.
[37] Roberts, 'State-to-State Investment Treaty Arbitration' (2014) 55 *Harvard International Law Journal*, p. 3.
[38] UNCTAD, 'Latest Developments in Investor-State Dispute Settlement' (2005), p. 2.
[39] *Lucchetti* v. *Peru*, Award.

the United States. This claim was dismissed on jurisdictional grounds.[40] The third is a claim brought by Italy against Cuba under the bilateral investment treaty (BIT) between those states. In this case the tribunal found that Cuba had not breached the BIT, so the issue of remedies did not arise.[41] In summary, there are no known cases involving the award of non-pecuniary remedies in state-to-state dispute settlement. This observation, coupled with the marginal role of state-state arbitration in the investment treaty system, means that the substantive protections of investment treaties can be safely characterised as liability rules.

Subsequent sections of this chapter show how this characterisation of investment protections as liability rules can clarify a number of issues in existing debate. For example, good governance justifications for investment treaties concern the impact of investment treaty protections on the exercise of public powers. As the remedy for breach of an investment treaty does not directly constrain a state's ability to exercise public power, these concerns are best elaborated through examination of the way that the risk of liability under investment treaties affects governments' exercise of public powers.

3.4 Efficiency - net economic benefits (or costs)

3.4.1 The concept of efficiency

The concept of efficiency is central to economic analysis of public policy, including economic analysis of legal rules. Although the term is used in a number of specific ways, all its uses refer to maximising relationships between ends and means. Neo-classical economics is founded on the notion of Pareto efficiency. A state of affairs is Pareto efficient if commodities are allocated so that no person can be made better off without making someone else worse off. Pareto efficiency is normatively desirable on utilitarian grounds because it implies greater satisfaction of individuals' preferences.

In practice, there are few policy choices for which an option under consideration would be more Pareto efficient than the alternative. The notion of Hicks-Kaldor efficiency, which is derived from Pareto efficiency,

---

[40] Hepburn and Peterson, 'US-Ecuador Inter-State Investment Treaty Award Released to Parties' 2012) *IA Reporter* [online].

[41] Hepburn and Peterson, 'Cuba Prevails in Rare State-to-State Investment Treaty Arbitration Initiated by Italy on behalf of Italian Nationals' (2011) *IA Reporter* [online]. Accessed 11 January 2012.

is more useful. A policy change improves Hicks-Kaldor efficiency if the gains of those who are better off as a result of the change would be sufficient to compensate those made worse off, demonstrating the potential for Pareto improvement.[42] The difference between the two notions is that Hicks-Kaldor efficiency does not require that winners actually compensate the losers, only that they would be capable of doing so. Accordingly, Hicks-Kaldor efficiency denotes the same maximising relationship as Pareto efficiency, discarding the constraint that no person may be left worse off. In more colloquial terms, a policy improves Hicks-Kaldor efficiency if the economic benefits of adopting that policy exceed the economic costs. When economists describe a set of legal arrangements as more efficient than the alternative, they are almost always invoking Hicks-Kaldor efficiency.[43] Throughout the remainder of this book, 'efficiency' refers to Hicks-Kaldor efficiency unless otherwise specified.

There is an ongoing academic debate over whether efficiency – the maximisation of net economic benefits – is an appropriate objective of public policy. Critics have observed that a focus on *net* economic benefits and costs leads to a disregard for the distributive impact of policies under consideration.[44] Moreover, Sen has shown that the exclusive pursuit of efficiency is incompatible with even a mild commitment to individual autonomy.[45] These criticisms are important and well-made, yet they do not undermine the view that efficiency should be one of the criteria by which legal rules are evaluated. A rigorous examination of efficiency is especially important in the context of investment treaties because economic objectives provide the most plausible justification for the protection of foreign investments.[46]

3.4.2 The relationship between efficiency and other consequences

Defining the boundaries of efficiency analysis raises a number of conceptual questions. The first of these is the appropriate geographical scope for efficiency analysis. Throughout this inquiry, examination of questions of efficiency is conducted from a global perspective. Adopting a given level

---

[42] Cooter and Ulen, *Law & Economics*, p. 47.   [43] Posner, *Economic Analysis of Law* (2007), p. 13.
[44] Calabresi, 'The Pointlessness of Pareto' (1991) 100 *Yale Law Journal*.
[45] Sen, 'The Impossibility of a Paretian Liberal' (1970) 78 *Journal of Political Economy*, p. 157.
[46] Ortino, 'The Social Dimension of International Investment Agreements: Drafting a New BIT/MIT Model?' (2005) 7 *International Law FORUM du droit international*, p. 244. References to the objectives of 'economic development', 'prosperity' or similar are also specifically identified in the preambles of US, Canadian, French, German, Dutch, Chinese, Australian and UK investment treaties, among others.

of protection in investment treaties is more efficient than an alternative level of protection if the economic benefits of adopting the former would exceed the costs, regardless of to whom those costs and benefits accrue. In other words, all economic costs and benefits are aggregated. The global approach to efficiency is also justified by the international spread of investment treaties. Most countries are affected by investment treaties in both the capacity of host state and of home state. For this reason, global efficiency improvements are likely to correlate with national efficiency improvements in most states. An examination of whether particular actors – such as, host states, home states or investors – are likely to benefit from a given level of protection raises distributive questions, which are addressed in Section 3.5 of this chapter.

A second issue is the relationship between efficiency assessment and assessment of flows of foreign direct investment. Greater flows of foreign investment do not necessarily entail *net* economic benefits. In the absence of externalities, the most efficient situation is for each investment project to be undertaken by the firm that can produce at the lowest cost, regardless of nationality.[47] However, there is some evidence to suggest that FDI brings benefits – that is, positive externalities – over and above domestic investment, particularly to developing countries.[48] This evidence partially justifies the assumption made in much of the existing social scientific literature that increased FDI is a benefit to host countries. These issues are discussed in greater detail in Section 3.6.1. At this point, I simply note that there is a tension, at a theoretical level, in regarding both efficiency and greater FDI flows as normatively desirable.

A third issue is whether a given consequence should be subsumed into the efficiency analysis or characterised as an incommensurable consequence to be valued on its own terms. In this book, the concept of efficiency is used to assess the consequences of a decision on the production and allocation of resources that are capable of being sold as commodities under existing institutional conditions. The likely consequences of alternative levels of protection for the realisation of human rights, environmental conservation and the rule of law are assessed separately to the efficiency calculus. The boundary between efficiency analysis and other

---

[47] Vandevelde, 'The Political Economy of a Bilateral Investment Treaty' (1998) 92 *American Journal of International Law*, p. 624.

[48] Moran, Graham and Blomström, 'Introduction and Overview' in Moran, Graham and Blomström (eds), *Does Foreign Direct Investment Promote Development?* (Institute for International Economics 2005), p. 4.

consequences is justifiable on both theoretical and practical grounds. The theoretical basis for treating gains and losses of tradable commodities as commensurable with one another is that these gains and losses could be converted into other commodities at prevailing market prices, independently of the subjective value that particular individuals would attribute to the particular commodities involved. This is why gains of apples can be valued in terms of losses of oranges, but improvements in freedom of speech cannot be valued in terms of losses of oranges. The practical justification for limiting efficiency analysis to tradable commodities is that it reflects the structure of existing debate about investment treaties. This permits inferences to be drawn about the net economic benefits of different levels of investment treaty protection while preserving the central insight of incommensurability – that there are likely to be further non-economic consequences that should not be valued within a single metric.

3.4.3 Theory and evidence in the efficiency analysis

This section considers the likely consequences of adopting particular levels of protection primarily from a theoretical perspective. In doing so, it draws on a well-established literature in law and economics concerning the likely economic costs and benefits of legal rules. This theoretical analysis ultimately rests on a set of empirical hypotheses concerning the likely behaviour of various actors in various situations. This section articulates and critically evaluates these underlying assumptions against evidence. For example, I argue that the assumption that investors maximise profits is likely to be a more accurate behavioural hypothesis than assumptions about the way governments respond to monetary incentives created by legal rules. Empirical evidence is integrated into the theoretical analysis in other ways. For example, theoretical arguments suggest that investment treaty protections may create net economic benefits to the extent that they redress discrimination against foreign investors. Whether states do discriminate against foreign investors is an empirical question, and evidence relating to this question is considered.

3.4.4 Free markets and competitive equality: a basic efficiency analysis

There are surprisingly few articles examining the economics of foreign investment protection. Most of the existing academic literature on international investment and efficiency addresses the question of investment liberalisation.[49] Those articles that do examine the impact of investment protection on economic efficiency have taken sophisticated approaches to narrow questions.[50] In the interests of clarity, it is preferable to outline a more basic understanding of the impact of investment protection on economic efficiency before engaging with more complex issues of externalities and regulatory efficiency. This simple analysis shows why the principle of competitive equality – or non-discrimination – should be the point of departure for any efficiency analysis of investment protection.

The foundation for examining the effect of investment treaty protections is the neo-classical theory of markets. This theory is based on a number of simplifying assumptions, including perfect information about investment opportunities, zero transaction costs and no externalities to production that are not reflected in prices. In a simplified world of this sort, competitive equality among producers – within and between industries – will lead to the most efficient organisation of production. This is because more efficient firms will be able to produce more profitably than less efficient firms under conditions of competitive equality. Greater potential profitability – all other things being equal – means that efficient firms will win investment contracts and expand their production at the expense of less efficient firms. The outcome is a more efficient organisation of production (from a global perspective). This association between competitive equality and efficiency is a foundational and uncontroversial economic result.

The application of this model to investment treaties is relatively straightforward. Legal rights that entitle firms to compensation for certain classes of loss are valuable. If all firms are granted the same legal rights a situation of competitive equality prevails. If some firms are granted legal rights beyond those of their competitors, the privileged firms will be able to expand their market share at the expense of their more efficient competitors.[51] On this basis, investment treaty protections that confer equal legal status to domestic and foreign investors are likely

---

[49] E.g., MacDougall, 'The Benefits and Costs of Private Investment from Abroad' (1960) 36 *Economic Record*, p. 13; Salvatore, *International Economics* (9th edn, 2007), p. 427.

[50] E.g., Aisbett, Karp and McAusland, 'Compensation for Indirect Expropriation in International Investment Agreements: Implications of National Treatment and Rights to Invest' (2010) 1 *Journal of Globalization and Development*.

[51] Vandevelde, 'The Economics of Bilateral Investment Treaties' (2000) 41 *Harvard International Law Journal*, p. 478; Stiglitz, 'Regulating Multinational Corporations: Towards Principles of Cross-Border Legal Frameworks in a Globalized World Balancing Rights with Responsibilities ' (2008) 23 *American University International Law Review*, p. 468.

to increase efficiency. Investment treaty protections that confer legal rights on foreign investors that go beyond the legal rights of domestic investors will tend to reduce efficiency.

One objection to this simplified treatment of efficiency might be that foreign firms may face practical obstacles in their regulatory relationships with government that similarly situated domestic firms do not face, despite being entitled to equal treatment as a matter of law. If this were the case, the ideal solution would be to improve government conduct – for governments to treat all firms equally. However, given the difficulties of reforming national bureaucracies, it might be argued that conferring additional legal rights on foreign firms is a simpler and more effective way to redress foreigners' initial disadvantage. This argument is implicit in many of the justifications for investment treaties asserted by lawyers – for example, the suggestion that the international legal rights of foreign investors are a counter-balance to the political influence of domestic firms[52] or systemic bias in domestic courts.[53] The underlying structure of argument has been formalised in the economic theorem of the second best. The theorem implies that if there is a departure from conditions of perfect competition then a further, compensating, distortion may increase efficiency (while still resulting in a less efficient outcome than the removal of the original obstacle to perfect competition).[54]

On closer examination, there are important limitations to the argument that investment treaty protections are an efficiency-improving counter-balance for domestic firms' political influence. Administrative discrimination against foreigners might provide an efficiency justification for strong national treatment protections, even if domestic firms are not protected by reciprocal legal rights to be treated no worse than foreign investors. Similarly, discrimination against foreigners in domestic courts could, plausibly, justify foreign investors' entitlement to initiate investor-state arbitration, which domestic investors are unable to utilise. However, it is difficult to see how the objective of redressing either form of discrimination is advanced by substantive standards of protection that are

---

[52] Ratner, 'Regulatory Takings in Institutional Context: Beyond the Fear of Fragmented International Law' (2008) 102 *American Journal of International Law*, p. 483; Paulsson, 'Indirect Expropriation', p. 4.

[53] Wälde and Weiler, 'Investment Arbitration under the Energy Charter Treaty', fn. 119; Choi, 'The Present and Future of the Investor-State Dispute Settlement Paradigm' (2007) 10 *Journal of International Economic Law*, p. 735.

[54] Lipsey and Lancaster, 'The General Theory of the Second Best' (1956) 24 *The Review of Economic Studies*, p. 16.

defined without reference to the way in which similarly situated domestic investors are treated.

There are further empirical limitations to the applicability of 'second best' arguments to investment treaties. To the extent that quantitative evidence exists, it suggests that foreign investors are not at a disadvantage in their dealings with host governments compared to domestic firms.[55] These findings are also supported by qualitative research into the channels available to foreign investors to influence policy in the countries in which they operate.[56] This does not exclude the possibility that there are particular states in which particular foreign investors suffer discrimination. However, even in such states, investment treaty protections over and above the right to equivalent treatment to domestic investors go beyond what is needed to redress such discrimination. In conclusion, in the absence of externalities, levels of protection that put foreign investors in a better position than domestic investors are likely to be less efficient than alternatives that put foreign and domestic investors in an equivalent legal position.

3.4.5 Efficient government and investor conduct

One of the most common justifications for laws requiring governments to compensate property owners for expropriation of their property is that such laws encourage *governments* to make more efficient decisions.[57] A closely related issue is whether such laws encourage *investors* to make more efficient investment decisions. Although these arguments normally

---

[55] Desbordes and Vauday, 'The Political Influence of Foreign Firms in Developing Countries', p. 447; Aisbett and McAusland, 'Firm Characteristics and Influence on Government Rule-Making', p. 226; Huang, 'Are Foreign Firms Privileged by Their Host Governments?', p. 28. There is also some discussion of the 'liability of foreignness' in management studies journals. This literature is unhelpful for present purposes because it does not include any broad-based empirical testing of the liability of foreignness hypothesis. It also fails to distinguish between the characteristics of foreign firms that make them less efficient than domestic firms – for example, that foreign firms often face higher transport costs – and discriminatory treatment at the hands of government that puts foreign firms at a disadvantage when compared to equally efficient domestic firms. A summary of these issues is contained in Sethi and Judge, 'Reappraising Liabilities of Foreignness within an Integrated Perspective of the Costs and Benefits of Doing Business Abroad' (2009) 18 *International Business Review* p. 405.

[56] Some of this evidence is summarised in Schneiderman, 'Investing in Democracy? Political Process and International Investment Law' (2010) 60 *University of Toronto Law Journal*, pp. 935–7.

[57] Blume, Rubinfeld and Shapiro, 'The Taking of Land: When Should Compensation Be Paid?' (1984) 99 *The Quarterly Journal of Economics*, p. 88.

focus on the question of compensation for expropriation, the underlying economic analysis is not specific to the seizure of assets. The analysis is applicable to any legal rule that requires a government – in some set of legally relevant circumstances – to compensate an investor for losses caused by a government measure.[58] This analysis can provide insights into the likely consequences of different levels of investment treaty protection.

Before examining the economic arguments, it is helpful to clarify the concepts of efficient investment decisions and efficient government decisions. Efficiency, as used in this book, concerns the maximising of net economic benefits. A more efficient investment decision is a decision that creates greater net economic benefits, regardless of to whom those benefits accrue. The profitability of an investment project is a first approximation of the efficiency gain of undertaking the project because profit represents the excess of economic benefits of production over economic costs.[59] However, externalities – external costs and benefits of production that do not accrue to the investor – mean that the (un)profitability of a project does not necessarily imply its (in)efficiency.

The efficiency of a government decision can be understood in the same way. Government measures pursue a range of objectives. Regardless of the end pursued by a government measure, it will have a range of consequences including a set of economic impacts – gains and losses that accrue to those affected directly or indirectly by the measure. A more efficient government measure is a measure that leads to greater net economic benefits. Efficiency is not the only criterion by which government decisions should be assessed; yet efficiency is a desirable characteristic of all government measures, regardless of the end a particular measure pursues. If two measures are equally effective in achieving a common objective and indistinguishable in their other consequences, the more efficient measure should be preferred.

3.4.5.1 The efficiency of government conduct: the problem of fiscal illusion

The most influential economic argument that liability rules can create economic benefits is that such rules can improve the efficiency of

---

[58] See Aisbett, Karp and McAusland, 'Police Powers, Regulatory Taking and the Efficient Compensation of Domestic and Foreign Investors' (2010) 86 *The Economic Record*, p. 370.

[59] Blume and Rubinfeld, 'Compensation for Takings: An Economic Analysis' (1984) 72 *California Law Review*, p. 588.

government decisions.[60] The argument that compensation requirements induce more efficient government decisions is premised on the assumption that public decision-makers tend to undervalue the economic costs of a decision that fall on private actors.[61] This presumed bias is commonly termed 'fiscal illusion'. A compensation requirement might assist in redressing fiscal illusion by forcing government decision makers to reflect on the costs that the measure under consideration would impose on affected individuals and factor these costs into the overall evaluation of that measure.[62] The extent to which government decisions are likely to be influenced by investment treaty protections owed to foreign investors – and whether this influence is likely to lead to more efficient decisions – is an empirical question.

'States' are highly complex institutions,[63] and a set of internal dynamics mediate between legal obligations assumed at the national level and their impact on government decision-making. A whole range of legislative and executive decisions, made by different tiers of government, could potentially become the subject of a claim made by a foreign investor. The associated processes of decision-making, and their sensitivity to a national government's obligations to compensate foreign investors, is likely to vary both within and between countries.

There is little publicly available evidence on the impact of investment treaties on government decision-making before the initiation of arbitral proceedings and still less on the impact of the substantive protections conferred by investment treaties on the way in which governments weigh the various costs and benefits associated with measures under consideration. Although some developed states are now beginning to commission impact studies on investment treaties, such studies have, so far, been limited to the assessment of consequences of increased FDI flows caused by the treaty in question. They have not considered whether investment treaties affect government decision-making.[64] Perhaps more promising is evidence that a handful of states have instituted internal processes to share information between various arms and agencies of government about the state's obligations under investment treaties. UNCTAD cites the examples of the NAFTA parties – that is, Canada, the United States and Mexico – as well as Malaysia, the Philippines and Peru.[65] Other states

---

[60] Blume, Rubinfeld and Shapiro, 'The Taking of Land', p. 90.   [61] Ibid., p. 88.
[62] Blume and Rubinfeld, 'Compensation for Takings', p. 621.
[63] Slaughter, *A New World Order* (2004), p. 5.
[64] See Gehring, 'Impact Assessments of Investment Treaties' in Cordonier Segger, Gehring and Newcombe (eds), *Sustainable Development in World Investment Law* (2011), p. 164.
[65] UNCTAD, *Investor State Disputes: Prevention and Alternatives to Arbitration* (2010), pp. 66–74.

may have similar mechanisms in place. Institutionalisation of investment treaty protections in such countries can be expected to encourage government decision-makers to pay greater attention to the risk of their actions breaching an investment treaty protection. However, little empirical work has been done to examine the effects of such mechanisms.

This shortage of empirical evidence is not unique to investment treaties. Academics writing on the liability of public authorities within national legal systems have noted the lack of evidence of the consequences of such legal rules.[66] To the extent that scholars of domestic law have investigated these issues empirically, they have tended to focus on the volume of litigation and quantum of damages awarded in cases brought against government authorities rather than on the effect of these cases on government authorities' decision-making processes.[67]

In the absence of detailed empirical evidence, it is useful to consider the theoretical argument that providing legal protection to foreign investment is likely to lead to more efficient government decisions. The argument is based on the assumption that decision-makers tend to underestimate (or ignore) economic costs of a decision unless they are directly borne by the government. This indifference to costs borne by private actors leads decision-maker to adopt measures that entail net economic costs.[68] More specifically, it may lead them to act opportunistically – that is, to take measures that are not efficiency improving (on an *ex post* assessment) for the purpose of extracting a benefit for the state at the expense of the foreign investor.[69]

Investment treaties protections could discourage decision-makers from taking inefficient measures of the second type – measures that benefit the government directly at the expense of a greater cost to a foreign investor. Direct expropriation of foreign investment is the archetypal example of

---

[66] Marsh, 'The Impact of Liability on Public Bodies: Lessons from the Literature' (2008) [online], p. 3; Booth and Squires, *The Negligence Liability of Public Authorities* (2006), p. 227; Levinson, 'Making Government Pay: Markets, Politics, and the Allocation of Constitutional Costs' (2000) 67 *University of Chicago Law Review*, p. 416.

[67] E.g., Markesinis and Fedtke, 'Damages for the Negligence of Statutory Bodies: The Empirical and Comparative Dimension to an Unending Debate' (2007); Eisenberg and Schwab, 'The Reality of Constitutional Tort Litigation' (1987) 72 *Cornell Law Review*.

[68] Miceli and Segerson, 'Regulatory Takings: When Should Compensation Be Paid?' (1994) 23 *Journal of Legal Studies*, p. 754; Blume, Rubinfeld and Shapiro, 'The Taking of Land', p. 90.

[69] Similarly, van Aaken, 'International Investment Law between Commitment and Flexibility: A Contract Theory Analysis' (2009) 12 *Journal of International Economic Law*, pp. 515–9.

such a measure.[70] On the other hand, broader liability rules that require decision makers to bear the costs of a policy when they cannot capture its benefits – for example, when some of the benefits of a policy change accrue to actors other than the state itself – would lead to inefficient reluctance to alter the status quo.[71] Furthermore, the assumption that decision-makers suffer from 'fiscal illusion' implies that they are more sensitive to the private costs that the government is forced to bear. Requiring states to compensate foreign investors for their losses, but not extending equivalent protection to other private actors, is likely to lead decision-makers to overvalue the interests of foreign investors. This distortion could only be justified if it corrected a systematic bias in government decision-making, which caused government to value foreign investors' losses less than other private losses.[72] There is little evidence that a bias of this sort exists.[73]

In summary, investment treaty protections may be able to improve the efficiency of government conduct insofar as they discourage a relatively narrow class of measures – those in which the state inefficiently extracts a direct benefit for itself at the expense of the investor. Investment treaty protections are unlikely to improve the efficiency of government conduct more generally.[74] They are particularly unlikely to improve the efficiency of government decisions that entail a range of costs and benefits for actors other than the host state and the investor in question.[75]

3.4.5.2 The efficiency of investor conduct: hold-ups and the problem of moral hazard

The likely effect of liability rules on investors' decisions also raises empirical questions. However, the assumption that investors' behaviour is driven by profitability – a standard assumption in the economic literature that

[70] Aisbett, Karp and McAusland, 'Compensation for Indirect Expropriation in International Investment Agreements', p. 11.

[71] Been and Beauvais, 'The Global Fifth Amendment?', p. 96; Levinson, 'Making Government Pay', pp. 351–3.

[72] This argument is developed in the domestic context in: Fischel, *Regulatory Takings: Law, Economics and Politics* (1995).

[73] Desbordes and Vauday, 'The Political Influence of Foreign Firms in Developing Countries', p. 447; Aisbett and McAusland, 'Firm Characteristics and Influence on Government Rule-Making', p. 226; Huang, 'Are Foreign Firms Privileged by Their Host Governments?', p. 28.

[74] Similarly, Rose-Ackerman S and Rossi J, 'Disentangling Deregulatory Takings' (2000) 86 Virginia Law Review, p. 1482.

[75] Bonnitcha and Aisbett, 'An Economic Analysis of Substantive Protections' in Sauvant, *Yearbook on International Investment Law & Policy 2011–2012* (2013), p. 686.

has been repeatedly empirically verified[76] – means that investors' likely response to legal rules can be inferred with greater confidence. This discussion proceeds on the assumption of investor risk neutrality. Given that the investments in questions are commercial ventures owned by international actors (as opposed to, say, family homes owned by private individuals), it is reasonable to assume risk neutrality. Section 3.4.5.4 considers whether the conclusions of this section would be altered if investors were risk averse.

Taking government conduct as given – that is, assuming that government conduct is independent of investors' investment decisions – investors will only make efficient decisions if they factor the risk that future government action poses to their investments into their investment decisions.[77] Thus, if a host state randomly takes inefficient and unjustified regulatory measures from time to time, requiring the state to compensate foreign investors for losses caused by such measures will generally lead to less efficient investment decisions.[78] There is, however, an important exception to this general argument. Even if investment treaty protections do not influence government decision-making, they could plausibly encourage foreign investors to proceed with efficient investments by solving 'hold-up' problems. (The terms 'obsolescing bargain' and 'dynamic inconsistency' are sometimes used interchangeably with 'hold-up'.)[79] As with the general problem of fiscal illusion, hold-ups only arise when a host state undervalues or ignores the costs its actions entail for a foreign investor. However, hold-ups are a more specific problem that arise only when further empirical conditions exist – namely, that an investment involves sunk costs that are capable of being appropriated by the host state.

Hold-up problems arise from the risk that a host state may take measures that are not efficiency improving on an *ex post* assessment but are, instead, adopted opportunistically for the purpose of extracting a benefit from a foreign investor. The nature of the problem is that, although a foreign investor may wish to invest in a given state, investors will only be able to recover the cost of their investments over a number of years. In contrast, once a foreign investor sinks its capital into a project, the state can acquire an immediate benefit by appropriating (part of) that

---

[76] Trachtman, 'International Economic Law Research' in Picker, Bunn and Arner (eds), *International Economic Law: The State and Future of the Discipline* (2008), p. 50.

[77] Blume, Rubinfeld and Shapiro, 'The Taking of Land', pp. 73–81.

[78] Miceli, *The Economic Theory of Eminent Domain: Private Property, Public Use* (2011), p. 98; I am grateful to Emma Aisbett for discussions clarifying this point.

[79] See Section 3.6.4.

capital.[80] This situation means that the state has an incentive to appropriate the investor's assets or renege on an investment contract after the investor has sunk their capital into a project to gain a greater share of the proceeds of the investment. If foreign investors know that the state has an incentive to renege, they are unlikely to invest in the first place, leaving both investor and state worse off.[81] However, if foreign investors know that they would be entitled to compensation in the event that the state attempted to appropriate the investor's assets, then this risk would not dissuade them from proceeding with otherwise viable projects. This model explains the intuitive economic case for investment protection.

The extent to which investors are faced with hold-up problem in any particular country is an empirical question, the answer to which may vary with circumstances relating to both the investment in question and the host state. For example, if the profitability of a project relies on the investor's expertise and these profits are shared between the host and the investor, it may well be that it is not in the state's interest to renege, so no hold-up arises. Moreover, hold-up problems can be overcome by reputation effects over repeated interaction.[82] Hold-up problems are also less likely to arise in states where the government is effectively constrained by its own courts.

Investment treaty protections may also encourage less efficient investment decisions. This is because such rules encourage moral hazard – a situation in which investors fail to allow for the risk posed to contemplated investments by efficiency-improving measures.[83] Protections that compensate investors for losses cause by efficiency-improving government measures are likely to result in misallocation of capital and inefficiently high levels of investment.[84] This scenario is easier to illustrate with an example. It would be inefficient for an investor to sink capital into building a factory that would operate at a profit of one thousand

---

[80] Guzman, 'Explaining the Popularity of Bilateral Investment Treaties' in Sauvant and Sachs (eds), *The Effect of Treaties on Foreign Direct Investment: Bilateral Investment Treaties, Double Taxation Treaties and Investment Flows* (2009), p. 81.

[81] Markusen, 'Commitment to Rules on Investment: The Developing Countries' Stake' (2001) 9 *Review of International Economics* p. 289.

[82] Doyle and van Wijnbergen, 'Taxation of Foreign Multinationals: A Sequential Bargaining Approach to Tax Holidays' (1994) 1 *International Tax and Public Finance*, p. 212.

[83] Aisbett, Karp and McAusland, 'Police Powers, Regulatory Taking and the Efficient Compensation of Domestic and Foreign Investors', p. 381; Stiglitz, 'Regulating Multinational Corporations', p. 529.

[84] Kaplow, 'An Economic Analysis of Legal Transactions' (1986) 99 *Harvard Law Review*, p. 529; Blume, Rubinfeld and Shapiro, 'The Taking of Land', p. 81.

dollars a year by dumping pollutants in a river that cause two thousand dollars a year worth of damage to a downstream oyster industry. The most efficient investment decision would be for the investor not to undertake the investment in the first place and allocate its capital to some other project. Nevertheless, an investor would be more likely to build such a factory if it knew that the government would be required to compensate it for introducing a future regulation that prohibited such dumping.

There are additional ways in which moral hazard arising from overly expansive legal protection is likely to affect investors' behaviour. The risk to an investment posed by future, efficiency-improving government measures is, perhaps, more important in the discipline it places on investors to internalize external costs associated with their conduct by preferring globally efficient production techniques and project structures to inefficient ones. In this way, substantive protections that leave investors exposed to the risk of efficient regulatory change are likely to affect the pattern, as well as the quantity, of investment undertaken. To return to the previous example, a rational investor that was aware of the risk of efficient regulatory change would be more inclined to incur an additional five hundred dollars of sunk cost by installing treatment facilities to prevent the discharge of pollutants. An investor that knew it would be entitled to compensation for the introduction of any new regulatory requirements would be unlikely to incur such a cost voluntarily.[85]

3.4.5.3 Contract protection as an imperfect substitute for investment treaty protection

The previous sections suggest that investment treaties may be able to improve the efficiency of both government and investment decisions to the extent that they require a state to compensate a foreign investor for losses caused by measures that are not efficiency improving and adopted for the purpose of extracting a benefit from the investor. There are a number of indicators that could assist an arbitral tribunal in determining whether a measure is taken for the purpose of extracting a benefit from a foreign investor. These include whether the state has reneged on a bargain struck with the investor, whether the investor has incurred significant sunk costs in making the investment, whether the state acquires a direct benefit for itself from the conduct that causes loss to the investor, whether

---

[85] Bonnitcha and Aisbett, 'An Economic Analysis of Substantive Protections', pp. 688–9.

the measure applies specifically to the foreign investor and whether there are any plausible public policy justification for it.[86]

On the other hand, determining whether a government measure is inefficient and, therefore, whether compensation might plausibly solve hold-up problems, is likely to pose considerable evidentiary problems. To make such a judgement one would need to be able to identify and value all the economic costs and benefits of a measure, not only those that accrue to the government and the investor in question. Arbitral tribunals are particularly poorly situated to conduct such evidentiary inquiries because they involve the valuation of costs and benefits that accrue to actors that will not be among the parties in investor-state arbitrations. These practical difficulties invite a consideration of alternative institutional arrangements that might be able to provide a compensation structure that encourages efficient investment.

If an investment treaty does not adequately solve hold-up problems, many investors can protect themselves by negotiating additional contractual protection with the host state.[87] Contractual protections can also refer disputes to compulsory international arbitration.[88] Indeed, contractual protections, agreed in project-specific negotiations that can address issues specific to the investment in question, may be more effective than general treaty protections in solving hold-up problems that would otherwise discourage efficient investment.[89]

The possibility of negotiating additional contract protection is not equally accessible to all investors. Investors in sectors that do not involve dealings with the host state, particularly smaller investors in such sectors, may face much higher transaction costs in attempting to secure contract-based protections.[90] However, the majority of investment treaty cases that have been brought up to 2013 have arisen in situations in which

---

[86]   I am indebted to Emma Aisbett for discussions on this point; see Aisbett, 'ISDS through the Lens of Welfare Economics' conference paper presented at 21st Investment Treaty Forum Public Meeting: The Economic and Financial Aspects of Investor-State Arbitration, British Institute of International and Comparative Law, 24 October 2013 (copy on file with the author).

[87]   Yackee, 'Do We Really Need BITs? Toward a Return to Contract in International Investment Law' (2008) 3 *Asian Journal of WTO and Health Law*, p. 129; Halabi, 'Efficient Contracting between Foreign Investors and Host States: Evidence from Stabilization Clauses' (2011) 31 *Northwestern Journal of International Law and Business*, p. 310.

[88]   Yackee, 'Do We Really Need BITs?', p. 129.

[89]   Yackee, 'Conceptual Difficulties in the Empirical Study of Bilateral Investment Treaties' (2008) 33 *Brooklyn Journal of International Law*, p. 452.

[90]   Brower CN and Schill, 'Is Arbitration a Threat or a Boon to the Legitimacy of International Investment Law?' (2009) 50 *Chicago Journal of International Law*, p. 481;

the investor was in a contractual relationship with the state of some sort – whether through a concession contract, contract for the supply of goods or services to the state or its citizens or a permit or licence issued in a regulated industry.[91] For investors that would, in any case, be negotiating a contractual relationship with the host state, incorporating additional protections into the contract is unlikely to entail significant transaction costs. For such investors, additional contract protection does constitute a feasible substitute for substantive protection under investment treaties.

The counter-argument is sometimes made that states would be reluctant to offer the same level of internationalised protections to individual investors in contracts as are commonly found in investment treaties.[92] However, if states were reluctant to offer contractual protections (an empirical question), it would suggest doubts on the part of the state about whether the benefits of offering additional contractual protections exceed the costs in the specific cases in question. It would suggest either that the state was willing to forgo the investment rather than offer the additional contractual protections necessary for it to proceed, or that the state was of the view that the investment would proceed even if additional protections are not offered. Thus, the counter-argument is not an argument in favour of providing substantive protection to foreign investors under investment treaties. It is an argument which, if it were true, would imply that existing investment treaty protections are unjustifiably protective of foreign investment.[93]

Although many investors could use additional contractual protection with the host state as a substitute for investment treaty protection from inefficient government conduct, there is no countervailing penalty that can be levied on investors if investment treaties provide compensation for efficient government conduct.[94] This analysis of substitutes suggests that, from the perspective of encouraging efficient investment decisions,

---

Nottage, 'What Future for Investor-State Arbitration Provisions in Asia Pacific Treaties?' (2011) *East Asia Forum.*

[91] Author's count of all publicly available investor-state arbitrations that have proceeded to the merits phase.

[92] Nottage, 'What Future for Investor-State Arbitration Provisions in Asia Pacific Treaties?'; Brower CN and Schill, 'Is Arbitration a Threat or a Boon to the Legitimacy of International Investment Law?', p. 482.

[93] Bonnitcha and Aisbett, 'An Economic Analysis of Substantive Protections', p. 691.

[94] Aisbett, Karp and McAusland, 'Police Powers, Regulatory Taking and the Efficient Compensation of Domestic and Foreign Investors', p. 370.

it is preferable that investment treaty protections err by under-protecting rather than over-protecting foreign investment.

3.4.5.4 Investor risk aversion and the significance of political risk insurance

Several important contributions to the existing literature consider additional complications to the analysis raised by risk aversion among investors.[95] Risk aversion refers to a preference for more certain outcomes to less certain outcomes. A risk-averse investor would prefer to incur a certain loss of one-quarter of the value of its investment than to take a one in four chance that it might lose the entire value of its investment. A risk-neutral investor would be indifferent between the two scenarios because both entail a loss of 25 per cent of the expected value of the investment in risk adjusted terms *ex ante*. From the outset, it is important to note that the extent to which foreign investors are risk averse is an empirical question. There is little direct evidence on this question. While it may be reasonable to assume that private individuals considering the low probability of a catastrophic event – for example, the destruction of their family home by fire – are risk averse,[96] companies that make international investments are less likely to be risk averse. Nevertheless, this section considers whether the conclusions of the previous sections would be altered if investors were risk averse.

If investors are risk averse, then the possibility that an *efficient* government measure may destroy the value of its investment may discourage an investor from making investments that are socially efficient. This is because the risk of the loss of value of the investment exerts a disproportionately dissuasive effect in the investor's project assessment. The optimal solution to this problem of risk aversion is for the investor to purchase private insurance against the risk of government interference with its investment.[97] Private insurance (for which an investor must pay) allows investors to redress risk aversion without disturbing the balance of incentives influencing the investment decision. Risk aversion of investors only alters the analysis presented in the previous section to the extent

---

[95] Blume, Rubinfeld and Shapiro, 'The Taking of Land', p. 86; Kaplow, 'An Economic Analysis of Legal Transactions', p. 533.

[96] Blume and Rubinfeld, 'Compensation for Takings', p. 585.

[97] Kaplow, 'An Economic Analysis of Legal Transactions', pp. 534, 577; Blume and Rubinfeld, 'Compensation for Takings', p. 592.

that investors are unable to insure against the risk of losses caused by efficient government conduct.

In circumstances in which investors have no access to a private insurance market, the situation is complex.[98] Broader compensation requirements on the state can encourage risk averse investors to proceed with efficient investment by protecting the investor from a wider category of losses caused by the host state, but they also encourage investors to proceed with inefficient projects by allowing investors to ignore the social costs associated with such projects.[99] The balance between these two competing effects depends, among other things, on the extent of risk aversion.[100]

There are, in fact, well-developed private insurance markets that sell political risk insurance to foreign investors.[101] In addition, many investors also have the option of purchasing insurance from government agencies sponsored by their home state, or the Multilateral Investment Guarantee Agency (MIGA).[102] Although investors are not able to insure 100% of the value of their investments, investors are able to reduce their exposure to political risk substantially. The existence of these markets undermines the basic rationale for using investment treaty protections to solve problems of inefficiently low levels of investment that are attributable to risk aversion.

The foregoing analysis raises the question of whether investment treaty protections are ever capable of improving the efficiency of investment decisions in situations in which private insurance is available to investors as an alternative. It is important to emphasise that the availability of private insurance would not redress hold-up problems that discourage efficient investment, regardless of whether investors are risk neutral or risk averse.[103] This qualification is easiest to illustrate with an example. Consider an investor contemplating an investment in a 'risky' state. The investor is able to estimate, with reasonable accuracy, that there is a 25 per cent chance that the state will expropriate its investment. Private

---

[98] The efficiency of various liability rules, given investor risk aversion, is the primary focus of Kaplow, 'An Economic Analysis of Legal Transactions' and Blume and Rubinfeld, 'Compensation for Takings'.

[99] Kaplow, 'An Economic Analysis of Legal Transactions', p. 527.

[100] Blume and Rubinfeld, 'Compensation for Takings', p. 606.

[101] Poulsen, 'The Importance of BITs for Foreign Direct Investment and Political Risk Insurance: Revisiting the Evidence' in Sauvant (ed), *Yearbook on International Investment Law & Policy 2009/2010* (2010), p. 563.

[102] Ibid., pp. 555, 559.   [103] Kaplow, 'An Economic Analysis of Legal Transactions', p. 521.

insurance is available to protect against this risk. If insurance is actuarially fair, the cost of insurance will be 25 per cent of the value of the investment. Even if the investor purchases the insurance, the risk of uncompensated taking would still influence the expected payoffs of the investment in that the investor must bear the cost of purchasing insurance. The investor's investment decision is affected by the risk of expropriation, regardless of whether the investor assumes the risk directly or whether that risk is reflected in the additional cost of insuring the investment. In contrast, if the host state guarantees to pay compensation for expropriation, the risk of expropriation does not influence the expected payoffs of the investment. For this reason, the availability of private insurance does not alter the conclusions regarding the likely impact of given levels of investment treaty protection outlined in the previous sections.[104]

3.4.6 Property rights and efficiency: the Coase theorem

The Coase theorem adds another dimension to the examination of the efficiency of governments' and investors' decisions. Although no scholar has argued that investment treaties are justified by the Coase theorem, a discussion of its implications is warranted by its central position in normative argument in favour of the protection of property rights.[105] The Coase theorem suggests that private bargaining is capable of dealing efficiently with externalities – the provision of public goods, the control of pollution, and so forth – without government regulation.[106] According to the theory, if a person is performing an action that imposes costs on others, and if these costs are greater than the benefit the person derives from the activity, then those affected will pay the person to cease the activity.[107] To return to the example of the polluting factory, if dumping waste in a river causes losses to a downstream oyster industry that are greater than the profits of the factory, the Coase theorem suggests that the affected oyster farmers will band together and pay the polluter to cease dumping. In this way, Hicks-Kaldor efficiency can be maximised through private bargaining so long as property rights are clearly defined.

---

[104] Bonnitcha and Aisbett, 'An Economic Analysis of Substantive Protections', p. 693.
[105] Stiglitz, 'Regulating Multinational Corporations: Towards Principles of Cross-Border Legal Frameworks in a Globalized World Balancing Rights with Responsibilities' (2008) 23 *American University International Law Review*, p. 485.
[106] Stigler, 'Two Notes on the Coase Theorem' (1989) 99 *The Yale Law Journal*, p. 631.
[107] Coase, 'The Problem of Social Cost' (1960) 3 *Journal of Law and Economics*, p. 4.

There is an extensive literature on the Coase theorem and its applicability, which goes far beyond the scope of this inquiry.[108] For present purposes, it is sufficient to observe that there are two plausible arguments that investment protection promotes efficiency based on the Coase theorem: one concerning the efficiency of government measures, and a second concerning the efficiency of investors' actions. The discussion that follows examines the extent to which these arguments add to the analysis contained in the previous section.

The Coase theorem might be cited to support the view that government action is inherently less efficient than private bargaining in addressing externalities. If one accepted this view, then it would follow that investment treaty protections increase efficiency to the extent that they discourage governments from intervening in markets, thereby allowing more scope for private actors to make efficiency-improving bargains. (Such an argument should be clearly distinguished from the proposition, examined in Section 3.4.5.1, that investment treaties can improve the efficiency of government interventions in markets.) This argument can be comprehensively dismissed. The ability of private actors to make Hicks-Kaldor optimal bargains depends on two assumptions: that they both have access to perfect information and that there are neither transaction nor enforcement costs associated with what may be exceedingly complex multi-actor contracts.[109] Real economies are characterised by imperfect information and transaction costs and, under these conditions, there are serious impediments to efficiently dealing with externalities through private bargains.[110] Coase himself thought the assumption of zero transaction costs was 'fanciful' and saw the Coase theorem as an analytical step to better understanding how real economies operate given the existence of transaction costs.[111] These qualifications have been borne out by empirical investigation, with Ellickson famously finding that cattle ranchers whose cows encroached on farmland did not behave in the way predicted by Coase theorem.[112] Even in a world of perfect information and zero transaction costs, there would be further problems of moral

---

[108] See Freidman, *Law's Order: What Economics Has to Do with Law and Why It Matters* (2000), p. 42; Calabresi and Melamed, 'Property Rules, Liability Rules, and Inalienability', p. 1094; Kennedy, 'Cost Benefit Analysis of Entitlement Problems: A Critique' (1984) 33 *Stanford Law Review*, p. 398.

[109] Coase, 'The Problem of Social Cost', p. 7.

[110] Stiglitz, 'Regulating Multinational Corporations', p. 486.

[111] Coase, 'Nobel Prize Lecture' (1991).

[112] Ellickson, *Order without Law* (1991).

hazard. It may be efficient for oyster producers to pay to prevent upstream pollution by a factory, but then any other firm could threaten to set up an identical operation and demand compensation to desist.[113] For these reasons, it cannot be said, *a priori*, that government measures are less efficient than private bargains in addressing problems caused by externalities.

Second, the Coase theorem might be cited to support the view that, in protecting investors' proprietary and contractual rights, investment treaties facilitate private bargaining by foreign investors, thereby increasing efficiency.[114] The problem with this argument is that investment treaties govern foreign investors' legal relationship with host states. They do not create new proprietary rights that foreign investors can exchange with third parties,[115] nor do they confer rights on foreign investors to bring proceedings to enforce contractual agreements with third parties. As such, Coasian arguments do not provide efficiency rationale for protecting foreign investors from losses caused by actions of the host state.

3.4.7 Summary of efficiency

This examination of the impact of investment protection on efficiency can be summarised in the following three propositions:

1. One way in which investment treaty protections might create net economic benefits is by redressing discrimination against foreign investors. In states in which foreign investors suffer discrimination, investment treaty protections that place investors in a position of competitive equality are likely to improve efficiency. In all states, investment treaty protections that give foreign investors greater legal rights than domestic investors are likely to decrease efficiency.

2. Determining whether investment treaty protections that go beyond non-discrimination requirements improve the efficiency of government decisions raises difficult empirical questions about the influences on public sector decision-making. There may be considerable variation in the impact of investment treaty protections on government

---

[113] Stiglitz, 'Regulating Multinational Corporations', p. 518.

[114] '. . . if market transaction were costless, all that matters (questions of equity apart) is that the rights of the various parties should be well-defined and the result of legal actions easy to forecast.' Coase, 'The Problem of Social Cost', p. 10.

[115] Douglas, 'The Hybrid Foundations of Investment Treaty Arbitration' (2003) 74 *British Yearbook of International Law*, p. 197; Diehl, *The Core Standard in International Investment Protection: Fair and Equitable Treatment* (2012), p. 225; Sasson, *Substantive Law in Investment Treaty Arbitration: The Unsettled Relationship between International and Municipal Law* (2010), p. 81.

decision-making, both within and between states. From a theoretical perspective, investment treaty protections are only likely to improve the efficiency of government conduct by discouraging a relatively narrow class of conduct – situations in which a government conduct is in efficient and is designed to extract a benefit for the state itself at the expense of the investor.

3. Insofar as investors are faced with hold-up problems and lack other means to solve them, requiring a host state to compensate investors for measures that are not efficient and are designed to extract a benefit from the investor could also improve the efficiency of investment decisions. However, broader investment treaty protections are likely to have the opposite effect by inducing moral hazard on the part of foreign investors.

4. The net economic cost of adopting a legal rule that provides an overly broad protection to foreign investment is likely to be greater than the net economic cost of adopting a legal rule that provides unduly limited protection to foreign investment.

3.5 Distributive consequences – the fair allocation of economic costs and benefits

If one were only interested in determining the net economic benefits of alternative levels of investment treaty protection, there would be no need to consider their distributive consequences. The only relevant question would be the likely consequences of alternative levels of protection in terms of economic efficiency. However, there are several normative arguments in the existing literature that relate to the allocation of costs and benefits under investment treaty protections. The most significant of these is the argument that it is *unfair* for a state to extinguish property rights that are legitimately owned by an investor without paying compensation. This is not an argument relating to the net economic costs of interference with property rights; it is an argument about the undesirability of a certain class of actor – property owners – having to bear the cost of certain government actions.

There are other good reasons for seeking to understand and evaluate the likely distributive consequences of alternative levels of investment treaty protection. A state that is both a source and a destination of foreign investment in roughly equal proportion may well be content to focus on the net economic benefits of investment treaty protections. In contrast, a state that is disproportionately a source or destination of foreign investment is likely to be interested in the question of which particular class of actor benefits most under various levels of protection.

This section begins by attempting to determine the likely distributive consequences of alternative levels of investment treaty protections. This is an empirical question, considered prospectively. It requires consideration of both the allocation of benefits and costs resulting from the way that disputes would be resolved under a given level of protection (*ex post* effects) and the benefits and costs that accrue to various actors as a result of changes in investor and state behaviour associated with a given level of protection (*ex ante* effects). Overall, the analysis seeks to shed light on the pattern of winners and losers associated with different levels of protection. This section then examines the implications of a range of theories of distributive justice for the evaluation of these consequences.

3.5.1 Evidence and theory in the analysis of distributive consequences

The examination of the likely allocation of economic costs and benefits under various levels of investment treaty protection is an extension of the efficiency analysis developed in the previous section, which concerned the assessment of net economic costs and benefits. Because of the close relationship of this section to the assessment of efficiency, it relies on the same combination of theoretical analysis – based on hypotheses concerning investor and state behaviour – and empirical evidence as the previous efficiency analysis.

3.5.2 The nature and extent of the distributive consequences of investment treaty protections

3.5.2.1 The division of costs and benefits from a purely *ex post* perspective

Ignoring any impact that investment treaty protections have on investment or government decisions, the likely division of costs and benefits between host states and foreign investors under a given level of substantive protection is clear.[116] If a state causes loss to a foreign investor in a manner that breaches an investment treaty protection, the state must compensate the investor; if a state causes loss to a foreign investor in a manner that does not breach an investment treaty, the loss will lie with the investor (subject to domestic law and any relevant contractual arrangements). Thus, broader levels of protection are likely to benefit

---

[116] Similarly, Blume and Rubinfeld, 'Compensation for Takings', p. 580.

foreign investors at the expense of host states and narrower substantive protections benefit host states at the expense of foreign investors. To be sure, it is the honouring of a treaty obligation to compensate, rather than the obligation itself, which has an effect on the allocation of costs and benefits. However, because this book is limited in scope to investment treaties containing compulsory investor-state arbitration, it is reasonable to assume that investors have some capacity to enforce their rights and will, on occasion, choose to do so.

Of course, investment treaty protections are also likely to have some impact on the decisions of investors and states. These behavioural effects may be considerably more significant than their *ex post* effects. Nevertheless, there are still insights to be gained from a pure *ex post* analysis. These insights are particularly important in understanding the distributive consequences of a decision to adopt (or alter) a given level of investment treaty protection *at the moment of adoption*. Consider a case such a *Chevron v. Ecuador (I)*.[117] In that case, Chevron (then Texaco) had invested in Ecuador at a time when the investment was not covered by an investment treaty. All the relevant investment decisions and regulatory decisions were made without the protection of an investment treaty. After Chevron had ceased operations, a BIT entered into force.[118] Chevron was then able to claim compensation for the Ecuadorian courts' delay in deciding tax cases relating to the investment project.[119] In these circumstances, the entry into force of the BIT resulted in an economic benefit to Chevron and an economic cost to Ecuador compared with the situation that would have prevailed if the BIT protections had not entered into force. Similarly, a decision to alter the level of protection provided by an existing investment treaty would entail a set of distributive consequences.

3.5.2.2 The allocation of costs and benefits from an *ex ante* perspective

When the impact of investment treaty protections on the behaviour of investors and states is also considered, determining the likely distribution of costs and benefits between becomes considerably more complicated. The archetypal situation envisaged by proponents of investment treaties is a situation in which, in the absence of investment treaty protection, investors choose not to make investments that would create net

---

[117] *Chevron v. Ecuador (I)*, Interim Award.
[118] *Chevron v. Ecuador (I)*, Interim Award, para. 180.
[119] *Chevron v. Ecuador (I)*, Final Award, para. 87.

economic benefits.[120] In this case, broader substantive protections aim to redress the risk of hold-up problems, thereby making efficient prospective projects viable from the perspective of investors. This situation is likely to entail economic benefits for foreign investors, who would be able to proceed with efficient projects that would not have been profitable in risk-adjusted terms in the absence of investment treaty protection. If investment treaty protections do have this effect, an empirical question for which the evidence is considered later in the chapter,[121] it is likely that the host state will also benefit from such projects proceeding through tax revenue generated. The way in which economic benefits resulting from such investments going ahead are shared between the investor and the host state will depend largely on the taxation policies of the host state and other fiscal terms governing the investment.

Two other scenarios merit discussion. The first is a situation in which an investor contemplates a highly profitable prospective investment in the host state, which the investor would have undertaken even in the absence of investment treaty protections. In a situation of this sort, the availability of investment treaty protections would not affect the investment decision. Broader protections in an investment treaty would, however, benefit a foreign investor at the expense of the host state if a dispute arises. (This situation is an example of the *ex post* effect described earlier.) The second is a situation in which investment treaty protections encourage investors to proceed with projects that do not create net economic benefits or to choose production techniques and project structures for potentially efficient investment that are not globally efficient. This second scenario is likely to occur when investment treaty provisions induce moral hazard on the part of investors.[122] In this situation, foreign investors benefit because investment treaty protection makes inefficiency profitable from the investor's perspective. This scenario may also involve a direct benefit to the host through tax revenues flowing from the project. However, these benefits will be more than offset by the economic costs of the project in the territory the host state – economic damage to the oyster farm, in the example presented in the previous section.[123] (That the economic costs exceed the benefits follows *ex hypothesi* in this situation.)

---

[120] van Aaken, 'Perils of Success? The Case of International Investment Protection' (2008) 9 *European Business Organization Law Review*, p. 2; Guzman, 'Explaining the Popularity of Bilateral Investment Treaties', p. 81.
[121] See Section 3.6.3.   [122] See Section 3.4.5.2.   [123] See Section 3.4.5.2.

In summary, from an *ex ante* perspective, broader investment treaty protections are likely to benefit foreign investors; the broader the protection, the greater the economic benefit to the investor. From the perspective of the state, the situation is more complex. The host state is also likely to benefit from broader investment treaty protections, to the extent that these protections are efficiency improving. However, investment treaty protections that are not efficiency improving necessarily entail net economic costs in the territory of the host state.

The balance between the *ex ante* and *ex post* distributive effects of a given level of protection depends primarily on the extent to which the protection in question affects the behaviour of states and investors. If investment treaty protections have little impact on the behaviour of states and investors, *ex post* effects are likely to predominate; if they have a significant impact on the behaviour of states and investors, *ex ante* effects are likely to predominate.[124] The extent of behavioural impact is an empirical question and is examined in other sections of this chapter. It is likely to vary between and within states. However, independent of questions about the extent of behaviour impacts, two important conclusions can be drawn about the situations when the *ex ante* and *ex post* effects coincide. Adopting broader protections in investment treaties is likely to benefit foreign investors, both from an *ex ante* and an *ex post* perspective. Adopting levels of protection that go beyond what is needed to maximise efficiency is likely to entail a net cost within the host state, both from an *ex ante* and an *ex post* perspective.

3.5.3 Evaluating the distributive consequences of investment treaties

There is no single accepted normative theory by which to judge the desirability of different patterns in the allocation of costs and benefits. Rather, different theories of distributive justice suggest different normative criteria by which distributive outcomes should be evaluated. This section does not attempt to resolve debates about distributive justice that have filled many libraries worth of books. Instead, I begin by showing why a theory of 'compensatory' justice is not a coherent basis for evaluating the distributive consequences of alternative levels of investment treaty protection. I then examine three of the most influential schools of thought on distributive justice – libertarian, egalitarian and utilitarian – and a further, narrower set of arguments that justify compensatory transfers on

---

[124] Miceli and Segerson, 'Regulatory Takings: When Should Compensation Be Paid?' (1994) 23 *Journal of Legal Studies*, pp. 775–6.

the grounds that they protect identifiable minorities from discrimination. Each section explores the implications of each school for a normative evaluation on the allocation of costs and benefits between foreign investors and host states.

3.5.3.1 Disaggregating the state – which individuals benefit from gains and losses?

One potential complication concerns the ultimate distributive impacts on individuals of investment treaties protections. This question is *sometimes* relevant because neither states nor corporate investors are the subject of utilitarian and egalitarian theories of justice, both of which speak exclusively to distribution among individuals. Behind a corporate investor stand shareholders. Losses to foreign investors are likely to be felt, to some extent, by shareholders as reduced dividend payments or reduced stock value.

In contrast, determining the impact of costs and benefits to the host state on the citizens of that state raises deeply complex questions that are likely to vary between states depending on their systems of government. To the extent these issues have been examined, the existing literature proceeds on the assumption that states are democratic.[125] This is not an appropriate generalisation. At the same, developing an account of the way in which losses and gains to national budgets ultimately affect taxation and spending decisions of states would require a monograph of its own. For present purposes, I use a hypothetical democratic state and a hypothetical kleptocratic state as heuristic devices to explore the likely distributive implications of varying levels of protection. In the hypothetical democratic state, it is assumed that costs and benefits to the state are ultimately borne by the citizenry through the tax system; in the hypothetical kleptocratic state, it is assumed that costs and benefits to the state are ultimately borne by a wealthy and corrupt elite.

It is important to note that empirical challenges in disaggregating likely distributive impacts within states are of little relevance to the libertarian and political process theories of distributive justice considered subsequently. Regardless of the internal structure of the state, libertarianism requires a state that interferes with validly acquired property rights to pay compensation. Similarly, the norms of non-discrimination articulated by political process theory set standards of fairness that are independent

---

[125] Been and Beauvais, 'The Global Fifth Amendment?', p. 105.

of government structure. As such, the internal complexity of states does not preclude a detailed assessment of the implications of these theories of justice for the evaluation of the likely distributive consequences of investment treaty protections.

3.5.3.2 Questions of scale in the evaluation of distributive consequences

Questions of scale have been highly controversial in existing academic debate concerning the distributive impact of investment treaties. Critics have noted that the $US 353 million award against the Czech government in *CME* v. *Czech Republic* was roughly equivalent to the country's annual health budget.[126] In doing so, they are implicitly asserting that the appropriate scale for evaluating the scale of the distributive impact of investment treaty protections is national social expenditure foregone. In contrast, proponents of investment treaties have observed that the size of arbitral awards is much smaller than the amount claimed by foreign investors,[127] and even the amounts claimed by investors are relatively small compared with the value of FDI flows. Neither of these is an appropriate scale by which to evaluate the (in)significance of the likely distributive impacts of alternative levels of investment treaty protection. For a state seeking to determine how much protection it should provide to foreign investment through investment treaties, the relevant question is whether the distributive impacts of adopting a given level of protection are significant in light of the scale of other costs and benefits of adopting that level of protection.

3.5.4 A theory of 'compensatory' justice cannot explain why compensation should be paid for some losses caused by the state but not others

Many lawyers invoke an intuitive conception of 'compensatory' justice in debates about investment treaty protections.[128] However, on critical reflection, it is clear that a theory of justice based on causation – the proposition that fairness requires compensation for losses caused by the state – provides little guidance in this context. This principle cannot assist in determining which losses caused by the state should be compensated and which losses may fairly be left uncompensated, without collapsing

---

[126] Van Harten, *Investment Treaty Arbitration and Public Law* (2007), p. 7.
[127] Franck, 'Empirically Evaluating Claims about Investment Treaty Arbitration' (2007) 86 *North Carolina Law Review*, p. 59.
[128] Been and Beauvais, 'The Global Fifth Amendment?', pp. 100–1.

back into an analysis that turns on the likely net economic benefits of the various alternatives.[129] (That is, unless one argues that distributive justice requires a default rule that compensation be paid for *any* loss caused by the conduct of the host state. This is not a position that has been advanced by any commentator in the existing literature. Such a view would face serious conceptual difficulties that have been examined at length elsewhere.[130]) In other contexts, notably analysis of domestic tort law, legal scholars invoke more sophisticated notions of 'corrective justice' that rely on embedded notions of 'harm' or 'fault'.[131] However, this literature concerns legal rules allocating loss between private parties. Scholars who invoke the norm of 'corrective justice' in the context of domestic tort law have been careful to acknowledge that their analysis is not equally applicable to debates about when the state should be required to compensate private parties.[132]

One argument endorsed in the early Fifth Amendment 'takings' jurisprudence of the US Supreme Court is that fairness requires compensation when the state acts to extract a benefit from a property owner but not when it seeks to prevent a harm.[133] This harm/benefit distinction has been heavily criticised as indeterminate in the absence of some prior theory of distributive justice:

> In the absence of some accepted standard of proper conduct, a court or legislature can describe any particular government-imposed rights change equally well as either harm prevention or benefit extraction.[134]

The Supreme Court has abandoned this distinction for this very reason:

> In Justice Blackmun's view . . . the test for required compensation is whether the legislature has recited a harm-preventing justification for its action. . . . Since such a justification can be formulated in practically every case, this amounts to a test of whether the legislature has a stupid staff.[135]

---

[129] Calabresi, *The Costs of Accidents: A Legal and Economic Analysis* (1970), p. 43.
[130] Coase, 'The Problem of Social Cost', p. 2.
[131] Coleman, *Risks and Wrongs* (1992), pp. 332–4; Weinrib, *The Goals of Private Law* (1995), pp. 220–1.
[132] Smith, 'The Rights of Private Law' in Robertson and Hang (eds), *The Goals of Private Law* (2009), p. 116; similarly Coleman, *Risks and Wrongs*, p. 358, arguing that notions of wrongdoing can only be defined within a political community by reference to conventions about acceptable allocation risks among private actors.
[133] Been and Beauvais, 'The Global Fifth Amendment?', p. 101.
[134] Lunney 'Responsibility, Causation, and the Harm-Benefit Line in Takings Jurisprudence': A Response to Professor Dagan' (1990) 99 *Michigan Law Review*, p. 435.
[135] *Lucas* v. *South Carolina Coastal Council* 505 US 1003 (1992) per Scalia J.

These criticisms are perhaps overstated. It is true that when assessed *at the moment a measure is taken*, there is no obvious way to distinguish a benefit conferred from a harm avoided. For example, a regulation prohibiting the dumping of pollutants could be described either as a measure to prevent the harm of pollution or to ensure the benefit of clean water. On the other hand, in situations in which a state seizes an investor's factory, it is clear that the state is better off than if the investment had not been made. This is the essence of the hold-up problem. In contrast, if a new regulation prohibiting the dumping of pollutants results in the closure of an investor's factory the state is no better off than if the investment had not been made. The question of whether government interference with an investment leaves the state better off than the situation that would have existed if the investment had not been made is determinate and central to the foregoing discussion of economic efficiency.

Nevertheless, the basic point remains that the harm/benefit distinction as understood by the US Supreme Court does not provide a general theory to explain why fairness requires the payment of compensation in some circumstances and not others. Arguments about why fairness requires the payment of compensation in certain circumstances must be founded on some other theory of distributive justice. Libertarian theories of distributive justice provide the most compelling justification for the view that fairness requires compensation for the interference with foreign investments.

3.5.5 Libertarian theories of distributive justice

The libertarian conception of distributive justice is based on entitlement to existing, validly acquired property rights.[136] This school of thought is most associated with the theoretical work of Robert Nozick. However, Richard Epstein has done more than any other scholar to apply Nozickian libertarian principles to the law of property protection. Epstein observes that a full commitment to the protection of property would imply a *minimal state* unable to supply even the most basic public goods.[137] For example, an inviolable commitment to property would prevent a state from acquiring the land necessary to build roads, unless every landowner along the planned route was willing to sell their land to the state voluntarily. In such a state, every individual could be worse off than in a state with a

---

[136] Nozick, *Anarchy, State and Utopia* (1974), p. 151.
[137] Epstein, 'One Step beyond Nozick's Minimal State: The Role of Forced Exchanges in Political Theory' (2005) 21 *Social Philosophy and Policy*, p. 290.

well-designed system of limited public good provision.[138] Epstein argues that the appropriate theoretical response for a libertarian is to allow the state to interfere with property rights, provided that no affected individual is left worse off.[139]

Libertarian theory, based on Nozick and developed by Epstein, provides a clear normative criterion by which to evaluate the distributive effects of investment treaty protection: justice requires a host state to compensate a foreign investor for loss caused by interference with the investor's property rights. However, this principle applies only to compensation for interferences with an investor's rights of ownership – its legal entitlements relating to the possession, use and disposition of the property in question.[140] The libertarian claim is for the protection of legal entitlements rather than insurance of the value of those entitlements.[141] Economic loss only comes into the analysis as the measure of compensation once a deprivation of entitlements has been established.[142] The distinction between legal entitlements and value is crucial when it comes to evaluating the distributive consequences of an investment treaty provision in libertarian terms. When an investor validly acquires an investment in a foreign country, it acquires a bundle of legal interests that are defined by domestic law at the time of purchase.[143] A libertarian theory of justice implies that a state should compensate an investor if it alters the scope of those legal entitlements; it does not imply that a state should compensate an investor for losses flowing from changes in policy that do not alter those legal entitlements.

3.5.6 Egalitarian theories of distributive justice

Virtually all theories of justice argue for equality of something, whether it is equal protection of rights, equal weighting of each individual's utility or equality of income and wealth.[144] Egalitarianism, in the sense used in this book, refers to the third form of equality: equality in the distribution of income, wealth and resources. It is important to recognise that egalitarian principles of distributive justice are normally embedded in wider theories of justice. So, for example, in John Rawls' work, every person's entitlement to equal basic liberties is a higher-order principle than the difference

---

[138] Ibid., p. 290.   [139] Ibid., p. 293.
[140] Epstein, *Takings: Private Property and the Power of Eminent Domain* (1985), p. 100.
[141] Eagle, *Regulatory Takings* (1996), p. 62.   [142] Epstein, *Takings*, p. 103.
[143] Douglas, 'The Hybrid Foundations of Investment Treaty Arbitration', p. 197.
[144] Sen, *Inequality Reexamined* (1992), p. ix.

principle, which relates to the distribution of wealth.[145] Understanding the position of egalitarian principles within wider theories of justice is crucial to fully appreciating authors' overarching normative frameworks. However, for the purposes of this book, it is not necessary to provide an overview of complete theoretical works. It is sufficient to identify basic principles that allow evaluation of alternative distributions of economic costs and benefits in normative terms.

The work of Rawls occupies a central position in egalitarian thought. Although different theorists incorporate egalitarian norms into their theories in different ways, the conclusions of many thinkers – among them Pogge, Cohen and Sen – are developed through criticism and extension of Rawls' ideas.[146] My characterisation of the norms of egalitarianism is based on the difference principle in Rawls' *A Theory of Justice*.[147] Rawls' difference principle can be expressed in two simple normative propositions: that primary goods, which include wealth and income, should be distributed equally and that any inequality in the distribution can be justified only to the extent it improves the position of the worst off.[148]

Some critics of investment treaties contend that they benefit wealthy investors at the expense of developing states, implicitly invoking an egalitarian theory of distributive justice.[149] However, in situations in which adopting a given level of protection creates economic benefits both for the foreign investor and within the host state, egalitarian concerns are unlikely to arise. Although it is not possible to be certain as to how such benefits will be shared, the coincidence of mutual economic benefit means that there are no grounds for assuming that the poorest will be disadvantaged.

The potential for egalitarian concerns is limited to a situation in which a given level of protection creates economic benefits for foreign investors but results in economic costs within the territory of the host state. Section 3.5.2.2 has argued that this situation is likely to arise if investment treaties confer broader protection on foreign investors than is necessary to maximise net economic benefits. This situation is likely to be undesirable for a hypothetical democratic host state, in which gains and losses to the state are ultimately borne by the citizenry through taxation, judged from an egalitarian perspective. This is because the shareholders of

---

[145] Rawls, *A Theory of Justice* (rev edn, 1999), p. 53.
[146] Pogge, *Realizing Rawls* (1989), p. 1; Cohen, *Rescuing Justice and Equality* (2008), p. 1; Sen, *The Idea of Justice*, p. 1.
[147] Rawls, *A Theory of Justice*, p. 53.   [148] Ibid., p. 67.
[149] Anderson and Grusky, 'Challenging Corporate Investor Rule' (2007) [online].

foreign investors that benefit are likely to be better off than the citizens of host states, who suffer the loss. This hypothesis is justified by three empirical observations. First, the investors whose claims have come to international investment arbitration are predominantly medium-large corporations from the developed world.[150] Second, in developed countries shares are more commonly owned, and owned in greater proportion, by the wealthy than the poor.[151] Third, the respondent states in investment claims are predominantly developing countries.[152]

In contrast, in a hypothetical kleptocratic state it is not self-evident that benefits to foreign investors that come at the expense of actors within the host state are undesirable from an egalitarian perspective. Indeed, if all costs to the host state are assumed by a corrupt and wealthy elite, there may even be situations in which preferring the economic interests of foreign investors to those of the host state is desirable – the question turns on a comparison of the relative wealth of shareholders and kleptocrats. Accordingly, egalitarian concerns about the distributive consequence of investment treaty protections are most acute in situations in which the level of protection under consideration is broader than is necessary to maximise net economic benefits and in which the host state is broadly democratic.

3.5.7 Utilitarian theories of distributive justice

Classical utilitarianism is based on the norm of seeking 'the greatest happiness for the greatest number'.[153] Happiness, in this sense, is conventionally described as 'utility', but it is also sometimes equated with welfare, pleasure or satisfaction. Whichever word is used, the concept posits a single metric that is capable of fully describing individuals' subjective well-being. If one assumes the population size to be fixed, utilitarianism calls for the maximisation of the aggregate utility of existing individuals.[154]

---

[150] Franck, 'Empirically Evaluating Claims about Investment Treaty Arbitration', p. 29.
[151] E.g., in the United Kingdom, 'wealth is considerably less evenly distributed than income' with the wealthiest half of the population owning 99% of non-dwelling, marketable wealth: Office for National Statistics, 'Share of the Wealth' (2006) [online].
[152] Franck, 'Empirically Evaluating Claims about Investment Treaty Arbitration', p. 32.
[153] This quote is customarily attributed to Bentham: Burns, 'Happiness and Utility: Jeremy Bentham's Equation' (2005) 17 *Utilitas*, p. 46.
[154] Roemer, *Theories of Distributive Justice* (1996), p. 127.

Evaluating distributive impacts in utilitarian terms requires aggregation of the loss of utility of those who suffer economic loss and the gain in utility of those who receive economic benefits from a given level of protection. Such a utilitarian analysis would diverge from an efficiency analysis to the extent that people derive different levels of subjective well-being from the same amount of money in different contexts. However, there is no way of quantifying the subjective experience of different individuals within a common metric.[155] These fundamental epistemological difficulties with cardinal comparison of utilities make it impossible to ascertain empirically whether those who ultimately benefit from the greater wealth of foreign investors derive more subjective well-being from the same amount of money than those who would benefit from greater wealth in host states.

Practical difficulties of this sort have led some to argue that subjective utility is an unworkable and indeterminate normative criterion by which to assess public policy.[156] Those who have invoked utilitarian norms to evaluate distributive consequences rely on the assumption that the utility of additional wealth is higher for the poor than the rich because the poor lack for more of the things that might dramatically improve the quality of their lives.[157] Under this assumption, a utilitarian analysis roughly follows an egalitarian analysis,[158] although without the same insistence that attention focus specifically on the interests of the worst off.

3.5.7.1 Why 'demoralization costs' should not be considered as an additional factor in a utilitarian analysis

Michelman's 1967 article proposes a further, purportedly utilitarian, rationale that would justify compensating property owners who suffer economic loss caused by government action: these are termed 'demoralization costs'. It is important to address Michelman's arguments directly because they have proved influential.[159] Michelman's contention that law should protect the 'investment-backed expectations' of property owners,

---

[155] Robbins, 'Robertson on Utility and Scope' (1953) 20 *Economica*, p. 109. On the possibility of qualitative, partial interpersonal utility comparisons, see Harsanyi, 'Cardinal Welfare, Individualistic Ethics, and Interpersonal Comparisons of Utility', p. 309; Sen, 'Interpersonal Aggregation and Partial Comparability', p. 407.

[156] Posner, *The Economics of Justice* (1981), p. 33.

[157] Pigou, *The Economics of Welfare* (1932), sec. I.VIII.3.

[158] This argument is developed in Lerner, *The Economics of Control* (1944), p. 35.

[159] Other scholars have rejected demoralization costs relying exclusively on *ex ante* efficiency arguments; see Blume, Rubinfeld and Shapiro, 'The Taking of Land', p. 81; and Kaplow, 'An Economic Analysis of Legal Transactions', p. 561.

an argument which relies on his conception of demoralization costs,[160] was subsequently accepted by the Supreme Court in *Penn Central Transportation Co v. New York City*.[161] The appendices of investment treaties based on the 2004 and 2012 versions of the US model BIT and the 2004 Canadian model BIT now identify investment-backed expectations as one of the criteria that distinguishes indirect expropriation from legitimate non-compensable regulation.[162]

Michelman defines demoralization costs as

1. the dollar value necessary to offset disutilities which occur to losers and their sympathizers specifically from the realization that no compensation is offered, and
2. the present capitalized dollar value of lost future production (reflecting either impaired incentives or social unrest) caused by demoralization of uncompensated losers, their sympathizers, and other observers disturbed by the thought that they themselves may be subjected to similar treatment on some other occasion.[163]

The first element of Michelman's formulation is an *additional* (additional, that is, to the economic loss suffered) 'psychological shock...emotional protest' when individual loss due to governmental action goes uncompensated.[164] Although it is plausible to suggest that liability rules may trigger psychological effects of utilitarian significance, Michelman does not provide an empirical basis for his contention. Later scholars have attempted to put this demoralization effect on a firmer conceptual footing by suggesting that it results from concern that uncompensated individuals have been victimized by the majority.[165] However, this reasoning disguises a normative premise – that impartiality and non-discrimination are desirable – as a utilitarian argument. If demoralization costs rely on a truly utilitarian basis, one would also need to consider the possibility that some members of a majority derive psychological utility when they perceive that they are able to advance their interests through the political system at the expense of minorities. Alternatively, the first element of demoralization costs could be a manifestation of risk aversion among

---

[160] Michelman, 'Property, Utility, and Fairness: Comments on the Ethical Foundation of "Just Compensation" Law' (1967) 80 *Harvard Law Review*, p. 1213.

[161] *Penn Central Transportation Co v. New York City* 438 US 104 (1978) 124.

[162] US 2012 Model BIT, annex B, art. 4(a); Canada Model FIPA, annex B.13(1).

[163] Michelman, 'Property, Utility, and Fairness', p. 1214.   [164] Ibid., p. 1228.

[165] Fischel and Shapiro, 'Takings, Insurance, and Michelman: Comments on Economic Interpretations of "Just Compensation" Law' [1988] 17 *Journal of Legal Studies*, p. 281.

property owners.[166] However, risk aversion does not provide a utilitarian justification for compensation for losses when private insurance against such risks is available,[167] as is commonly the case with foreign investment projects.

The second element of Michelman's demoralization costs relates to the consequences that flow from the effect of the relevant legal rules on investors' conduct. This simply reframes the question of whether given legal rules create net economic benefits, considered in Section 3.3, as a utilitarian argument. Although it is true that the risk of uncompensated losses will dissuade investors from pursuing some investment projects, this reallocation of capital to other uses does not necessarily entail net economic costs. Indeed, contrary to Michelman, broad entitlements to compensation for loss caused by government conduct are likely to create net economic costs by inducing moral hazard on the part of investors.[168]

3.5.8 Political process theories and distributive justice

A further school of thought argues that evaluation of the fairness of distributive transfers should be grounded in an analysis of political processes.[169] This literature is particularly concerned, first, with the risk that a majority in a given polity may use its influence over government decision-making to exploit minorities and, second, with the implications of this risk for the design of liability rules.[170] The problem of majoritarian decision-making is cited in the course of at least three distinct arguments. The first is the argument that decisions that enrich a majority at the expense of a minority cause psychological unease, an effect which should be included in utilitarian evaluation of compensatory transfers.[171] This argument is essentially the same as the first limb of Michelman's demoralization costs. It was discussed and dismissed earlier in the chapter.[172] The second is the argument that, in the absence of rules requiring government to compensate individuals (including minorities) for losses caused by

---

[166] Kaplow, 'An Economic Analysis of Legal Transactions', p. 561.
[167] Ibid., pp. 534, 577; discussed above in Section 3.4.5.4.
[168] Cooter, 'Unity in Tort, Contract and Property: The Model of Precaution' (1985) 73 *California Law Review*, p. 21; Blume, Rubinfeld and Shapiro, 'The Taking of Land', p. 81; Kaplow, 'An Economic Analysis of Legal Transactions', p. 561. These arguments are taken up in detail in Section 3.4.5.2.
[169] Been and Beauvais, 'The Global Fifth Amendment?', p. 102.
[170] Levmore, 'Just Compensation and Just Politics' (1990) 22 *Connecticut Law Review*, p. 310; Fischel, *Regulatory Takings*, p. 204.
[171] Fischel and Shapiro, 'Takings, Insurance, and Michelman', p. 281.
[172] See Section 3.5.7.1.

governmental measures, governments will make inefficient decisions.[173] This 'fiscal illusion' argument relates to the effect of investment treaty protections on states' behaviour; it has been addressed in detail.[174] The third is the argument that it is *unfair* for majorities to use political processes to gain advantages at the expense of minorities, where the supposed unfairness is independent of both utilitarian and efficiency-based evaluation.[175] This third argument is sometimes offered as justification for investment treaty protections, without reflection on its normative underpinnings.[176] This section addresses the third argument – that fairness may require compensatory transfers to minorities that are victims of losses inflicted on them by majorities.

Almost every government decision will confer benefits on some individuals and cause losses to others. If the only criterion for unfairness were that the outcome disadvantage a minority, political process theory would approximate Epstein's libertarianism.[177] Indeed, such a theory of fairness would be more expansive than libertarianism, in that it would require compensation for government acts that cause losses to a minority even if the losses did not flow from an interference with property rights. However, political process theorists have been anxious to distinguish their views from libertarians[178] and acknowledge that democratic decision-making can legitimately impose costs on a minority without compensation being required.[179]

The initial challenge for political process theories, then, is to provide a normative basis to distinguish decisions resulting from 'fair' decisions from 'unfair' decisions. Levmore argues that this distinction rests on the procedural question of whether the disadvantaged minority has 'difficulty influencing political bargains' and is therefore 'unprotected'.[180] Influence, in this sense, refers to a minority's *relative* lack of capacity to access and participate in decision-making processes compared with other 'interest groups' that are affected by government decision-making.[181] The

---

[173] Fischel, *Regulatory Takings*, p. 206.   [174] See Section 3.4.5.1.
[175] See Fischel, *Regulatory Takings*, p. 217; Fischel, 'Exploring the Kozinski Paradox: Why Is More Efficient Regulation a Taking of Property?' (1991) 67 *Chicago-Kent Law Review*, p. 911.
[176] Wälde and Kolo, 'Environmental Regulation, Investment Protection and 'Regulatory Taking' in International Law' (2001) 50 *International and Comparative Law Quarterly*, p. 845.
[177] See Ely, *Democracy and Distrust: A Theory of Judicial Review* (1980), p. 136.
[178] Fischel, *Regulatory Takings*, p. 178.
[179] Fischel, 'Exploring the Kozinski Paradox', p. 889.
[180] Levmore, 'Just Compensation and Just Politics', p. 308.   [181] Ibid., p. 306.

normative basis of Levmore's distinction is a procedural conception of non-discrimination: that decision-making processes should provide equal opportunity to all to articulate and defend their interests.[182]

The phenomenon of majoritarianism, however, is not unique to situations in which the minority lacks opportunities for political influence. A minority may be organised, able to access decision-makers, make representations and lobby but then be outvoted by a relatively homogenous majority. Indeed, in Fischel's account of local government, such cases are presented as the archetype of unfair majoritarian exploitation of minorities.[183] This suggests that the unfairness of which political process theorists complain resides as much in the outcome of a decision-making process, as in the process itself.

The objection to majoritarian outcomes appears to be based on a substantive conception of non-discrimination:

[M]ajoritarian, or gang, law is thought unfair because of the equal treatment principle, which is especially compelling when the community's needs would be met just as well by using any piece of land.[184]

According to this account, unfair discrimination occurs when a minority is singled out to bear a cost that might equally have been placed on others. Farber gives this understanding of non-discrimination a more coherent conceptual basis. He argues that politically powerful minorities will invariably be able to obtain compensation for losses caused by government through their influence over political processes.[185] Non-discrimination requires that less politically powerful individuals be legally entitled to equivalent compensatory transfers.[186] A substantive norm of non-discrimination, in this sense, is not grounds for objecting to all decisions that impose costs on minorities; the objection is to the *arbitrary* singling out of particular minorities to bear uncompensated losses.[187] Although the case for horizontal equity rests primarily on a normative premise of fair distribution, some have argued that equal treatment of similarly

---

[182] Ibid., p. 310.   [183] Fischel, 'Exploring the Kozinski Paradox', p. 886.
[184] Levmore, 'Just Compensation and Just Politics', p. 309.
[185] Farber, 'Economic Analysis and Just Compensation' (1992) 12 *International Review of Law and Economics*, p. 137.
[186] Ibid., p. 137.
[187] Treanor, 'The Original Understanding of the Takings Clause and the Political Process' (1995) 95 *Columbia Law Review*, p. 872;. Lunney, 'Takings, Efficiency, and Distributive Justice', p. 159.

situated individuals is also desirable on the grounds of economic efficiency.[188]

A further political process argument that might be raised in defence of investment treaty protections is that, unlike domestic actors, foreign investors are unable to vote. For example, the *Tecmed* Tribunal justified its conclusion, in part, by the observation that

> the foreign investor has a reduced or nil participation in the taking of the decisions that affect it, partly because the investors are not entitle to exercise political rights reserved to the nationals of the State, such as voting for the authorities that will issue the decisions that affect such investors.[189]

This argument can be comprehensively dismissed. Foreign investors are predominantly corporations, and neither domestic nor foreign-domiciled corporations are able to vote in any country.[190] This observation alone is sufficient to reject the argument that foreign investors require invest-ment treaty protections to redress the fact that they are unable to vote. Moreover, in democratic countries, nationals of the host state who benefit from an investment – employees and suppliers, for example – are entitled to vote. This is true regardless of whether the investment is made by a local or a foreign investor.

The foregoing analysis shows that political process theories of fairness rely on two normative premises, both of which are based on the prin-ciple of non-discrimination: that it is unfair for government to impose uncompensated losses on minorities who are at a practical disadvan-tage in decision-making processes and that it is unfair for government decision to *arbitrarily* single out particular minorities to bear uncompen-sated losses.[191] The latter norm implies that investment treaty protec-tions can be justified to the extent they redress situations in which for-eign investors are arbitrarily singled out to bear particular losses. With respect to the former norm, empirical evidence indicates that foreign investors are not a general class of actor that lacks influence in host state

---

[188] Innes, 'Takings, Compensation, and Equal Treatment for Owners of Developed and Undeveloped Property' (1997) 40 *Journal of Law and Economics*, p. 407; cf. Kaplow, 'Horizontal Equity' (2000) [online].

[189] *Tecmed* v. *Mexico*, Award, para. 122. For more detailed discussion of the *Tecmed* Tribunal's recourse to political process theory, see Schneiderman, 'Investing in Democracy? Political Process and International Investment Law' (2010) 60 *University of Toronto Law Journal*.

[190] Schneiderman, 'Investing in Democracy?', p. 926.

[191] Been and Beauvais, 'The Global Fifth Amendment?', p. 104.

decision-making.[192] Therefore, investment treaty protections can only be justified by the former norm to the extent they redress specific and demonstrable instances of discriminatory exclusion from decision-making processes.

3.5.9 Summary of distributive consequences of investment treaties

The foregoing identification and evaluation of likely distributive consequences of investment treaty protections can be summarised in the following seven propositions:

1. The likely scope and extent of distributive effects of investment treaty protections is an empirical question, which requires consideration of both *ex post* and *ex ante* effects.

2. From an *ex post* perspective, broader levels of protection are likely to benefit foreign investors at the expense of host states. From an *ex ante* perspective, levels of protection that improve economic efficiency benefit both the foreign investor and the host state. In contrast, levels of protection that go beyond what is necessary to maximise net economic benefits are likely to entail economic benefits to the foreign investor, which accrue at the expense of greater costs to the host state or actors within the host state.

3. Whether *ex post* or *ex ante* effects predominate is an empirical question that depends on the extent to which investment treaty protections influence the behaviour of investors and states. Regardless of whether *ex post* or *ex ante* effects predominate, broader levels of protection are likely to benefit foreign investors while levels of protection that go beyond what is necessary to maximise net economic benefits are to the detriment of host states (considered territorially).

4. Libertarian theories of justice suggest that validly acquired property rights should be protected. This provides a justification for the payment of compensation to foreign investors when the host state interferes with their property rights. However, libertarian theories do not justify compensation for losses that do not result from an interference with property rights.

5. Egalitarian theories of distributive justice suggest that legal rules are desirable to the extent they improve the position of the worst off. Egalitarian concerns about the distributive consequence of investment treaty protections are most acute in situations in which the level of protection under consideration is broader than is necessary to

---

[192] Desbordes and Vauday, 'The Political Influence of Foreign Firms in Developing Countries', p. 447; Aisbett and McAusland, 'Firm Characteristics and Influence on Government Rule-Making', p. 226; Huang, 'Are Foreign Firms Privileged by Their Host Governments?', p. 28.

maximise net economic benefits and in which the host state is broadly democratic.

6. Utilitarian theories of distributive justice suggest that different patterns in the distribution of costs and benefits should be evaluated according to their impact on aggregate subjective utility. Utilitarian concerns are limited to the same situations as egalitarian concerns.

7. Political process theories suggest that it is unfair for states to impose losses on minorities who were at a practical disadvantage in decision-making processes and that it is unfair for government decisions arbitrarily to single out particular minorities to bear losses. These two norms of non-discrimination provide a justification for investment treaty protections that serve either to compensate investors for decisions made through processes from which they were discriminatorily excluded or to compensate investors for being arbitrarily singled out to bear the costs of a governmental measure.

3.6 Attraction of foreign direct investment

3.6.1 Is additional FDI normatively desirable?

The desire to attract FDI is widely cited as an explanation for states' decisions to sign investment treaties.[193] Presumably this is because FDI is seen as a proxy for other desirable objectives, rather than because increased FDI has any intrinsic value. Consider, for example, a situation in which two companies, one from the United States and one from Canada, are considering where to locate their manufacturing facilities. Both locations would allow the facilities to operate equally efficiently. Ultimately, the US company chooses to locate in Canada, and the Canadian company chooses to locate in the US. In this situation, FDI in both states is higher than it would have been if the US and Canadian companies had located in their respective home states. But it is difficult to see how this increase in FDI could plausibly amount to a benefit to either state. This example illustrates why it is important to be precise about the benefits that supposedly flow from increases in FDI.

There are two possible situations in which additional might FDI have instrumental value. The first is when investment in a country is inefficiently low, perhaps due to hold-up problems. This is the situation described in Section 3.4.5.2. In this situation, greater investment would bring net economic benefits and foreign investors are one (but not the only) source of capital for such investment. Second, FDI may entail

---

[193] See, UNCTAD, *South-South Cooperation in International Investment Agreements* (2006), p. 47.

positive economic externalities – 'spillover' benefits that accrue to a host state beyond those associated with other forms of investment. This raises a threshold question of whether there is any evidence to support a correlation between FDI and identifiable externalities.

There is some evidence that FDI is associated with higher wages, faster productivity growth and greater diffusion of knowledge than domestic investment, particularly in developing countries.[194] However, evidence also suggests that the range of externalities associated with FDI varies. FDI in some sectors is associated with strongly positive externalities and, in other sectors, with no or negative externalities.[195] In particular, empirical studies of extractive industries suggest that FDI in this sector is associated with significant *negative* externalities.[196] Investment in the extractive sector also tends to involve high sunk costs. Thus, investment treaties may, perversely, be more effective in attracting investments that are not associated with positive externalities than those that are.[197] The only published study to examine the impact of investment treaties on FDI flows disaggregated by sector supports this hypothesis.[198]

For the purposes of the analysis that follows, I adopt the simplifying assumption that increases in the volume of FDI correlate with positive economic externalities. There are pragmatic justification for this assumption – specifically, that it seems to be accepted by states[199] and that it is accepted in most of the existing literature.[200] Because I conclude that

---

[194] Moran, Graham and Blomström, 'Introduction and Overview', p. 4; Colen, Maertens and Swinnen, 'Foreign Direct Investment as an Engine of Economic Growth and Human Development' in de Schutter, Swinnen and Wouters (eds), *Foreign Direct Investment and Human Development: The Law and Economics of International Investment Agreements* (2013); cf. Lall and Narula, 'Foreign Direct Investment and Its Role in Economic Development' (2004) 16 *The European Journal of Development Research*, p. 461.

[195] Colen, Maertens and Swinnen, 'Foreign Direct Investment as an Engine of Economic Growth and Human Development', pp. 80–100.

[196] Sachs and Warner, 'Natural Resources and Economic Development The Curse of Natural Resources' (2001) 45 *European Economic Review*, p. 837.

[197] I am grateful to Emma Aisbett for this insight. Bonnitcha and Aisbett, 'An Economic Analysis of Substantive Protections', p. 700.

[198] Colen and Guariso, 'What Type of FDI Is Attracted by BITs', in de Schutter, Swinnen and Wouters (eds), *Foreign Direct Investment and Human Development: The Law and Economics of International Investment Agreements* (2013), p. 168, finding that BITs are more effective at attracting FDI to resource-rich countries.

[199] Sachs and Sauvant, 'BITs, DTTs and FDI Flows: An Overview' in Sauvant and Sachs (eds), *The Effect of Treaties on Foreign Direct Investment: Bilateral Investment Treaties, Double Taxation Treaties and Investment Flows* (2009), p. lx.

[200] de Schutter, Swinnen and Wouters, 'Foreign Direct Investment and Human Development' in de Schutter, Swinnen and Wouters (eds), *Foreign Direct Investment and*

the level of protection provided by investment treaties is unlikely to have a major impact on FDI flows, this simplifying assumption has little influence on the overall analysis. Nevertheless, if further studies were to confirm Colen and Guariso's findings that investment treaties are most effective at attracting FDI in sectors associated with negative externalities, it would be necessary to reconsider the assumption that aggregate FDI is an appropriate proxy for economic benefits.

3.6.2 Evidence and theory on the relationship between investment treaty protections and FDI

Whether adopting a given level of investment treaty protection is likely to lead to greater FDI flows than an alternative level of protection is an empirical question.[201] Currently, there is no direct evidence on the association between particular levels of protection and FDI flows. There are also significant limitations to drawing inferences about the likely impact of different levels of protection from isolated case studies.[202] This is especially so given that anecdotal evidence is mixed. On one hand, it is clear that the timing and structure of certain investment decisions has been influenced by investment treaties.[203] On the other hand, there is the evidence from states such as Brazil, which has seen remarkable growth in FDI since the late 1990s despite never having ratified an investment treaty.[204]

For these reasons, the appropriate starting point for an empirical inquiry is studies that have attempted to examine the link between

---

Human Development: The Law and Economics of International Investment Agreements (2013), p. 12; Yackee, 'Are BITs Such a Bright Idea? Exploring the Ideational Basis of Investment Treaty Enthusiasm' (2005) 12 *University of California Davis Journal of International Law and Policy*, p. 219.

[201] Cf. Sanders, 'Of All Things Made in America Why Are We Exporting the *Penn Central* Test?' (2010) 30 *Northwestern Journal of International Law and Business*, p. 367.

[202] Poulsen, 'The Importance of BITs for Foreign Direct Investment and Political Risk Insurance', p. 541.

[203] *Mobil* v. *Venezuela*, Decision on Jurisdiction, para. 204:

> As stated by the Claimants, the aim of the restructuring of their investments in Venezuela through a Dutch holding was to protect those investments against breaches of their rights by the Venezuelan authorities by gaining access to ICSID arbitration through the BIT. The Tribunal considers that this was a perfectly legitimate goal as far as it concerned future disputes.

[204] UNCTAD, 'Brazil: Total Number of Bilateral Investment Treaties Concluded, 1 June 2013' (2013) [online]; UNCTAD, 'Investment Policy Review of Brazil' (2005) [online], p. 5.

investment treaties and FDI systematically. These studies are sufficient to test some basic hypotheses about the relationship between alternative levels of protection and FDI. For example, if the existence of investment treaties does not increase FDI flows, it is highly unlikely that FDI flows will be influenced by variations in the level of protection within such treaties. As this section argues that empirical evidence on the relationship between investment treaties and FDI is inconclusive, it goes on to consider the implications of the two main theories linking investment treaties to FDI. This analysis would be especially relevant if future empirical evidence revealed that investment treaties did influence FDI.

3.6.3 Empirical evidence on the relationship between BITs and FDI

An ever-growing number of econometric studies have examined the connection between investment treaties and FDI. At the time of going to press, eighteen studies claim statistically significant findings to support the hypothesis that signing investment treaties increases FDI.[205] This count

---

[205] Salacuse and Sullivan, 'Do BITs Really Work? An Evaluation of Bilateral Investment Treaties and Their Grand Bargain' in Sauvant and Sachs (eds), *The Effect of Treaties on Foreign Direct Investment: Bilateral Investment Treaties, Double Taxation Treaties and Investment Flows* (2009), p. 149; Buthe and Milner, 'Bilateral Investment Treaties and Foreign Direct Investment: A Political Analysis' in Sauvant and Sachs (eds), *The Effect of Treaties on Foreign Direct Investment: Bilateral Investment Treaties, Double Taxation Treaties and Investment Flows* (2009), p. 213; Neumayer and Spess, 'Do Bilateral Investment Treaties Increase Foreign Direct Investment to Developing Countries' in Sauvant and Sachs (eds), *The Effect of Treaties on Foreign Direct Investment: Bilateral Investment Treaties, Double Taxation Treaties and Investment Flows* (2009), p. 247; Swenson, 'Why Do Developing Countries Sign BITs?' in Sauvant and Sachs (eds), *The Effect of Treaties on Foreign Direct Investment: Bilateral Investment Treaties, Double Taxation Treaties and Investment Flows* (2009), p. 455; Egger and Pfaffermayr, 'The Impact of Bilateral Investment Treaties on Foreign Direct Investment' in Sauvant and Sachs (eds), *The Effect of Treaties on Foreign Direct Investment: Bilateral Investment Treaties, Double Taxation Treaties and Investment Flows* (2009), p. 262; Grosse and Trevino, 'New Institutional Economics and FDI Location in Central and Eastern Europe' in Sauvant and Sachs (eds), *The Effect of Treaties on Foreign Direct Investment: Bilateral Investment Treaties, Double Taxation Treaties and Investment Flows* (2009), p. 288; Gallagher and Birch, 'Do Investment Agreements Attract Investment?' Evidence from Latin America' in Sauvant and Sachs (eds), *The Effect of Treaties on Foreign Direct Investment: Bilateral Investment Treaties, Double Taxation Treaties and Investment Flows* (2009), p. 305; UNCTAD, 'The Impact on Foreign Direct Investment of BITs' in Sauvant and Sachs (eds), *The Effect of Treaties on Foreign Direct Investment: Bilateral Investment Treaties, Double Taxation Treaties and Investment Flows* (2009), p. 347; Coupé, Orlova and Skiba, 'The Effect of Tax and Investment Treaties on Bilateral FDI Flows to Transition Economies' in Sauvant and Sachs (eds), *The Effect of Treaties on Foreign Direct Investment: Bilateral Investment Treaties, Double Taxation Treaties and Investment Flows* (2009), p. 709; Banga, 'Impact of Government Policies and Investment Agreements on FDI Inflows' (2003) [online], p. 34; Kim, 'Bilateral Investment Treaties, Political Risk and Foreign Direct

includes studies that find that only some investment treaties increase FDI,[206] studies that find that investment treaties increase only some types of FDI,[207] two studies reporting apparently contradictory findings – one that only US BITs increase co-signatories' FDI and another that most BITs increase FDI but US BITs do not increase co-signatories' FDI from the United States,[208] and two studies that find, respectively, only a 'minor and secondary' and a 'slight' relationship between investment and FDI.[209] A further six studies reject the hypothesis that investment treaties increase FDI.[210]

There are several obstacles to reliably testing the causal relationship between FDI and investment treaties. They include measurement problems – finding data on financial flows and determining which financial flows should count as FDI;[211] coding issues – for example, determining whether all investment treaties or only those with certain characteristics

---

Investment' (2007) 11 *Asia Pacific Journal of Economics & Business*, p. 22; Egger and Merlo, 'The Impact of Bilateral Investment Treaties on FDI Dynamics' (2007) 30 *The World Economy*, p. 1546; Oh and Fratianni, 'Do Additional Bilateral Investment Treaties Boost Foreign Direct Investment?' (2010) [online]; Busse, Königer and Nunnenkamp, 'FDI Promotion through Bilateral Investment Treaties' (2010) 146 *Review of World Economics*, p. 170; Kerner, 'Why Should I Believe You? The Costs and Consequences of Bilateral Investment Treaties' (2009) 53 *International Studies Quarterly*, p. 97; Tobin and Rose-Ackerman, 'When BITs Have Some Bite: The Political-Economic Environment for Bilateral Investment Treaties' (2011) 6 *Review of International Organizations*, p. 28; Colen and Guariso, 'What Type of FDI Is Attracted by BITs'; Peinhardt and Allee, 'Devil in the Details? The Investment Effects of Dispute Settlement Variation in BITs' in Sauvant K, *Yearbook on International Investment Law & Policy 2010–2011* (2012), p. 857.

[206] Banga, 'Impact of Government Policies and Investment Agreements on FDI Inflows', p. 34; Kim, 'Bilateral Investment Treaties, Political Risk and Foreign Direct Investment', p. 22; Tobin and Rose-Ackerman, 'When BITs Have Some Bite', p. 28; Peinhardt and Allee, 'Devil in the Details' p. 858.

[207] Colen and Guariso, 'What Type of FDI Is Attracted by BITs', p. 167.

[208] Salacuse and Sullivan, 'Do BITs Really Work?', p. 148; Gallagher and Birch, 'Do Investment Agreements Attract Investment?', p. 305.

[209] UNCTAD, 'The Impact on Foreign Direct Investment of BITs', p. 347; Tobin and Rose-Ackerman, 'When BITs Have Some Bite', p. 22.

[210] Tobin and Rose-Ackerman, 'Foreign Direct Investment and the Business Environment in Developing Countries': The Impact of Bilateral Investment Treaties' (2005) Yale Law and Economics Research Paper No 293, p. 31; Hallward-Driemeier, 'Do Bilateral Investment Treaties Attract FDI? Only a Bit . . . and They Could Bite' in Sauvant and Sachs (eds), *The Effect of Treaties on Foreign Direct Investment: Bilateral Investment Treaties, Double Taxation Treaties and Investment Flows* (2009)', p. 374; Yackee, 'Do BITs Really Work?', p. 390; Aisbett, 'Bilateral Investment Treaties and Foreign Direct Investment', p. 414; Mina, 'External Commitment Mechanisms, Institutions, and FDI in GCC Countries' (2009) 19 *International Financial Markets, Institutions and Money*, p. 383; Berger, Busse, Nunnenkamp and Roy, 'More Stringent BITs, Less Ambiguous Effects on FDI? Not a Bit!' (2011) 112 *Economics Letters*, p. 272.

[211] Lowe, 'Changing Dimensions of International Investment Law', p. 38.

(such as compulsory investor-state arbitration) constitute the indepen-dent variable;[212] and endogeneity problems – disentangling reverse-causality effects and controlling for policy shifts made concurrently with the ratification of investment treaties.[213] The first two problems are easier to address than the third. Although there is no objective way to determine what should count as FDI, so long as the way flows are measured is consistent over time, one can identify trends. Similarly, although a significant weakness of some studies is that they treat investment treaties with com-pulsory investor-state arbitration as equivalent to investment treaties that cannot be enforced in this way, there is no obstacle to addressing this problem through more thoughtful coding. In contrast, controlling for other variables that may influence FDI raises exceedingly difficult pro-blems.

Among earlier studies, those that better control for endogeneity are less likely to find a causal relationship between investment treaties and FDI.[214] Indeed, in an important article, Aisbett shows that the results of two of the studies supporting a causal link between investment treaties and FDI – those of Neumayer and Spess and Salacuse and Sullivan – are not robust once endogeneity effects are controlled for.[215] More recent studies tend to address endogeneity concerns in a more sophisticated manner. However, aside from one study that finds a large effect,[216] these studies tend to find only minor effects of investment treaties on FDI.[217] That many of these studies find that only some investment treaties are effective in attracting FDI and that they are inconsistent with one another as to which subset of treaties are effective,[218] raises further concerns about their reliability. Together, the issues of endogeneity and consistency cast doubt on the hypothesis that investment treaties significantly increase FDI.

---

[212] Yackee, 'Changing Dimensions of International Investment Law' (2007) [online], p. 441.

[213] Aisbett, 'Bilateral Investment Treaties and Foreign Direct Investment', p. 396.

[214] Hallward-Driemeier, 'Do Bilateral Investment Treaties Attract FDI?', p. 358; Yackee, 'Do BITs Really Work?', p. 389; Aisbett, 'Bilateral Investment Treaties and Foreign Direct Investment', p. 414.

[215] Aisbett, 'Bilateral Investment Treaties and Foreign Direct Investment', pp. 395, 410.

[216] Kerner, 'Why Should I Believe You?', p. 90.

[217] Tobin and Rose-Ackerman, 'When BITs Have Some Bite', p. 22; Berger, Busse, Nunnenkamp and Roy, 'More Stringent BITs, Less Ambiguous Effects on FDI? Not a Bit!', p. 272; Peinhardt and Allee, 'Devil in the Details', p. 858.

[218] Tobin and Rose-Ackerman, 'When BITs Have Some Bite', p. 22, finding that BITs are most effective in developing countries with good institutional quality; cf. Busse, Königer and Nunnenkamp, 'FDI Promotion through Bilateral Investment Treaties' p. 164, finding that that BITs are most effective in developing countries with poor institutional quality.

This assessment of the econometric evidence is supported by recent empirical work conducted by Poulsen. In a detailed series of interviews with private and government-sponsored political risk insurers, Poulsen found that the existence of an investment treaty covering a proposed investment had little impact on the pricing of political risk insurance.[219] Similarly, Yackee's econometric analysis of the relationship between political risk ratings and the number of BITs a country has ratified concludes 'either that BITs have no statistically significant impact on political risk ratings, or, if they do have an impact, it is quite small.'[220] Both studies are important because they suggest that investment treaties do not significantly reduce the political risks facing foreign investment. Moreover, Poulsen's findings imply that investors who pay to insure against political risks have little financial incentive to prefer to invest in states covered by a BIT.

Yackee has also surveyed in house general counsel of seventy-five Fortune 500 companies. He asked a series of questions about the level of awareness of BITs and about their impact on company investment decisions. Yackee concludes:

Overall, the responses indicate a low level of familiarity with BITs, a pessimistic view of their ability to protect against adverse host state actions, and a low level of influence over FDI decisions.[221]

On the other hand, in an *Economist* survey of 602 corporate executives, 19% responded that the existence of an international investment agreement influenced their investment decisions 'to a very great extent'.[222] Although doubts have been raised about the reliability of this study's results,[223] it does suggest that investment treaties play at least some role in influencing the destination and volume of FDI in some countries.

In summary, studies of the impact of investment treaties on FDI have been unable to identify consistent causal effects across a range of data sets and methodologies. This is an important conclusion in itself; it

---

[219] Poulsen, 'The Importance of BITs for Foreign Direct Investment and Political Risk Insurance'.

[220] Yackee, 'Do Bilateral Investment Treaties Promote Foreign Direct Investment? Some Hints from Alternative Evidence' (2011) 51 *Virginia Journal of International Law'*, p. 421.

[221] Ibid., p. 429.

[222] Shinkman, 'The Investors' View: Economic Opportunities versus Political Risks in 2007–11' in Kekiz and Sauvant (eds), *World Investment Prospects to 2011* (2007) [online], p. 96.

[223] Sachs, 'Bilateral Investment Treaties and FDI Flows', fn. 5.

suggests that investment treaties are unlikely to have a major impact on FDI flows. However, there is not sufficient evidence to reject the hypothesis that investment treaties have some lesser but still meaningful effect on FDI flows. In other words, it is unclear whether investment treaties have, on average, a minor impact (as opposed to no impact) on FDI and whether that impact varies among different types of states, treaties and investments. This is a more cautious conclusion than that reached by a recent UNCTAD review of the evidence. That review, which was less comprehensive than the one conducted here,[224] concluded that, on balance, the evidence supports the conclusion that BITs have an indirect impact on FDI.[225]

3.6.4 Theoretical insights on investment protection and FDI

Although the previous section argued that existing evidence suggests that investment treaties do not have a major impact on FDI flows, there remains a possibility that future studies might reveal an empirical relationship that is not being consistently picked up in the statistical analysis of current data sets. It is also possible that as investors become more aware of the protections offered by investment treaties, investment treaties will become more effective in attracting FDI.[226] Current evidence is neither sufficiently robust nor sufficiently consistent to rule out either of these two possibilities. Therefore, it is worth proceeding on the assumption that ratifying investment treaties does increase FDI to some extent and considering what this assumption, if it were true, would imply for the relationship between the level of protection provided by such treaties and FDI. Guidance on this relationship can be found in existing theories of the connection between investment treaties and FDI.

There are two, potentially complementary theories of how investment treaties might induce FDI in the existing literature: commitment theory and signalling theory. The more popular theory is that investment treaties act as a commitment device to solve 'hold-up' problems.[227] This theory was introduced in Section 3.4.5.2. In short, according to commitment theory, investment treaties could encourage FDI by allowing states credibly to

---

[224] It considered only fourteen of the twenty-four econometric studies identified here and did not have access to Poulsen's findings.

[225] UNCTAD, *The Role of International Investment Agreements in Attracting Foreign Direct Investment to Developing Countries* (2009), p. 55.

[226] Hallward-Driemeier, 'Do Bilateral Investment Treaties Attract FDI?', p. 354.

[227] van Aaken, 'Perils of Success?', p. 2.

commit to not appropriating an investor's property or otherwise reneg-ing on investment contracts.[228] The implications of hold-up problems (to the extent that they exist) for the design of investment protections are relatively clear. Commitment theory suggests that investment treaty pro-tections that prevent states from reneging on negotiated bargains made with foreign investors will be more effective in attracting FDI.

The extent to which investors actually suffer from hold-up problems is an empirical question. Even when making investments involving large sunk costs, the discipline placed on host states by reputation effects[229] and the availability of other forms of legal protection[230] may be suffi-cient to prevent hold-up problems from arising. If investors are not faced with hold-up problems in practice, commitment theory suggests that investment treaty protections are unlikely to be effective in attracting additional FDI. Two recent studies have examined whether investment treaties that contain advance consent to investor-state arbitration are more effective in attracting FDI than investment treaties that do not pro-vide for investor-state arbitration. Both find that investment treaties that provide for investor-state arbitration are no more effective than invest-ment treaties that lack this enforcement mechanism.[231] These findings are the exact opposite of what commitment theory implies. These findings suggest either that investors have other tools to solve hold-up problems effectively or, if hold-up problems do persist, that investment treaties are ineffective in solving them.

A less widely advocated theory is that investment treaties function as signalling devices. According to this theory, investors lack information about the quality of a host state's domestic policies and institutions.[232] In this situation of asymmetric information, an investment treaty sends a signal to foreign investors from all countries (not just the other parties to the treaty) that the host state does have an adequate regime of domestic governance, encouraging investors to invest. Signalling theory relies on the assumption that it is less costly for states with 'good' regimes of domes-tic governance to become (and remain) parties to investment treaties than it is for states with 'bad' regimes of domestic governance.[233] If this were

---

[228] Neumayer and Spess, 'Do Bilateral Investment Treaties Increase Foreign Direct Investment to Developing Countries', p. 230.

[229] Doyle and van Wijnbergen, 'Taxation of Foreign Multinationals', p. 212.

[230] Yackee, 'Do We Really Need BITs?', p. 130.

[231] Peinhardt and Allee, 'Devil in the Details' p. 856; Berger, Busse, Nunnenkamp and Roy, 'More Stringent BITs, Less Ambiguous Effects on FDI? Not a Bit!', p. 272.

[232] Buthe and Milner, 'Bilateral Investment Treaties and Foreign Direct Investment', p. 176.

[233] Spence, 'Job Market Signaling' (1973) 87 *Quarterly Journal of Economics*, p. 358.

not the case, all states, including those with bad governance, would be equally likely to ratify investment treaties. The result would be that the existence of a treaty would not convey any meaningful information about the quality of domestic governance to prospective investors.

In a 2009 article, Kerner contends that a government that wishes to sign an investment treaty will face opposition from civil society actors and, therefore, that the act of signing the treaty entails a political cost. On this basis, he argues that investment treaties function as credible signals of good governance. Even if the general proposition that the signing of investment treaties entails significant political costs were true (there are good reasons to doubt that it is),[234] Kerner does not explain why this political cost would be greater for states with bad governance. Indeed, when it comes to signing investment treaties, one might reasonably assume that authoritarian states with poor governance face lesser domestic political constraints than Western democracies. Thus, Kerner does not provide a satisfactory account of how investment treaties operate as signals.

A more plausible basis for signalling theory is that the risk of liability under the investment treaty is greater for states with bad governance. As Tobin and Rose-Ackerman argue, the costs of remaining party to an investment treaty may be higher for states with bad governance than those with good governance. On this view, the level of substantive protection provided by an investment treaty could affect FDI flows indirectly, to the extent it increases the cost to a state with 'bad governance' of remaining party to the treaty. This, in turn, would allow an investment treaty to operate more effectively as a signal. The indirect and complex nature of this causal mechanism suggests that the impact of the level of variation in the level of substantive protection in an investment treaty on FDI flows is likely to be weak. Although signalling theory does not explore the characteristics of a 'well-governed' state in detail, they presumably include the norms of intrinsic value identified elsewhere in this chapter. A state that respects the rule of law, acts efficiently and realises human rights could be said to be well-governed. To the extent that investors are attracted by any (or all) of these, signalling theory suggests that

---

[234] Cf. Poulsen and Aisbett, 'When the Claim Hits: Bilateral Investment Treaties and Bounded Rational Learning' (2013) 65 *World Politics*, p. 301; Poulsen, 'Bounded Rationality and the Diffusion of Modern Investment Treaties' (2013) 57 *International Studies Quarterly*, p. 12; Vis-Dunbar and Poulsen, 'Reflections on Pakistan's Investment-Treaty Program after 50 Years: An Interview with the Former Attorney General of Pakistan, Makhdoom Ali Khan' (2009), all suggesting that in many cases investment treaties were not the subject of public controversy or attention at the time they were signed.

protections that penalise states that lack these characteristics tend to increase FDI.

3.6.5 The interaction between investment treaty protections, FDI and other measures affecting the investment climate

Historically, states have often signed investment treaties at the same time as introducing other measures to liberalise the investment climate.[235] This raises questions about the interaction between investment treaties and domestic reforms and the interaction between investment treaties and other treaties – for example, double taxation treaties (DTTs) or the World Trade Organization (WTO) agreements. It is important to state this question precisely. This issue is not whether domestic reforms or the entry into other economic treaties influences FDI flows; it is highly likely that they do. The question is whether investment treaties have an additional (or lesser) impact on FDI when adopted in conjunction with other measures.

So far as I am aware, no study has sought to examine whether investment treaties are more (or less) effective in attracting FDI in the presence of other international agreements. Academics have, however, recently begun to examine the impact of variation in domestic governance on the relationship between investment treaties and FDI. In a 2011 study, Tobin and Rose-Ackerman conclude that, for developing countries, investment treaties are more effective at attracting FDI as domestic governance improves.[236] However, this effect is marginal in comparison to the substantial direct impact of improved domestic governance on FDI, independently of whether an investment treaty is in force. In contrast, Busse, Königer and Nunnenkamp find that investment treaties are more effective in countries with weaker governance.[237] Each of these conflicting results would have to be verified by further studies before any reliable conclusion can be drawn.

The two theories that purport to explain the relationship between investment treaties and FDI provide competing hypotheses about the relationship between investment treaties and the quality of domestic governance. Commitment theory suggests that investment treaties will have the most impact on FDI in conditions where hold-up problems are

---

[235] UNCTAD, *The Role of International Investment Agreements in Attracting Foreign Direct Investment to Developing Countries*, p. 57.

[236] Tobin and Rose-Ackerman, 'When BITs Have Some Bite', p. 22.

[237] Busse, Königer and Nunnenkamp, 'FDI Promotion through Bilateral Investment Treaties' p. 164.

endemic. In other words, commitment theory suggests that investment treaties are most effective in situations of poor governance. In contrast, signalling theory suggests that investment treaties are likely to be most effective when a state has new information to communicate to investors about improvements in governance. In other words, signalling theory suggests that investment treaties will be most effective at attracting FDI in states that have recently improved their internal governance.

3.6.6 Summary of FDI

The examination of the impact of investment protection on FDI can be summarised in the following propositions:

1. FDI has no intrinsic value. However, in some circumstances, additional FDI may be a useful proxy for other desirable objectives – for example, positive externalities such as technological diffusion and skills transfer. Although the assumption that increased FDI is beneficial to host states is a useful first approximation, it is also important to consider whether investment treaties are effective in attracting the types of FDI that are associated with positive externalities.
2. Current evidence suggests that investment treaties do not have a major impact on the destination and volume of FDI and raises doubts about whether they have any significant impact on the destination and volume of FDI.
3. If the presence or absence of an investment treaty does not affect FDI flows, then variation in the level of substantive protection provided by an investment treaty is highly unlikely to affect FDI flows.
4. On the other hand, if entering investment treaties does increase FDI, then one would need to understand why investment treaties increase FDI to draw inferences about whether different levels of investment treaty protection are likely to have different impacts on FDI flows.
5. Commitment theory suggests that investment treaty protections that prevent host states from reneging on bargains with the investor are likely to increase FDI; signalling theory suggests that levels of protection that place greater costs on states with 'bad governance' than states with 'good governance' may increase FDI (a conclusion that refers the inquiry back to the relationship between investment treaty protections and the realisation of the other norms identified in this chapter).

3.7 Regulatory chill: consequences for the realisation of human rights and for environmental conservation

This section examines the consequences of investment treaty protections for the realisation of human rights and the protection of the environment in host states. Because investment treaty protections operate as liability rules they do not have any direct impact on the realisation of human rights or the protection of the environment. Any impact stems from their effect on the way in which host states exercise their regulatory powers – an effect sometimes described as 'regulatory chill'.[238] This section examines the extent to which adopting different levels of investment treaty protection is likely to affect the extent of regulatory chill and the consequences of such chilling effects for the realisation of human rights and the protection of the environment. The analysis proceeds on the premises that the realisation of human rights and environmental conservation are both intrinsically desirable. These normative premises are shared across the existing academic literature and are unlikely to prove controversial.

3.7.1 The relationship of regulatory chill to other consequences

The fact that government measures concerning environmental conservation or human rights may become the subject of investment treaty arbitration does not, in itself, entail consequences for the realisation of these objectives. If host states were indifferent to the possibility of liability under investment treaties and maintained their preferred environmental and human rights policies despite investor opposition and unfavourable arbitral awards, the only consequence of adopting different levels of protection would be to vary *ex post* distributive impacts. However, investment treaty protections will have consequences for the realisation of human rights and environmental conservation to the extent they dissuade host states from enacting or maintaining measures that are effective in realising these objectives. As such, there is likely to be an inverse relationship between the distributive consequences of investment treaties and regulatory chill. The more states modify their behaviour to reduce the distributive impact of investment treaties, the greater potential for regulatory chill. The manner and extent to which states modify their behaviour to avoid liability under investment treaties is an empirical question.

The relationship between economic efficiency and the consequences of investment treaty protections for the realisation of human rights and environmental conservation is more subtle. Investment treaty protections' impact on the efficiency of government decisions (discussed in

---

[238] High Commissioner for Human Rights, *Economic, Social and Cultural Rights: Human Rights, Trade and Investment* (2003), p. 21; Been and Beauvais, 'The Global Fifth Amendment?', p. 132; Schill, 'Do Investment Treaties Chill Unilateral State Regulation to Mitigate Climate Change?' (2007) 24 *Journal of International Arbitration*, p. 470; Tienhaara, *The Expropriation of Environmental Governance: Protecting Foreign Investors at the Expense of Public Policy* (2009), p. 262.

Section 3.4.5.1) and their impact on the realisation of human rights and environmental objectives are components of a single effect: the effect of investment treaty protections on government decision-making. As these two analyses examine components of the same effect, they should be consistent with one another. So, if evidence showed that most government decision-makers are unaware of investment treaties at the time of making regulatory decisions and indifferent to the risk of liability under investment treaties when alerted to that risk, it would suggest that investment treaty protections have little impact on government decision-making. This would imply that they have little effect on the efficiency of government decisions and little effect on the realisation of human rights and environmental conservation.

Despite the need for coherence between the 'efficiency' and 'regulatory chill' analyses of governmental decision-making, there are several reasons to keep the two distinct. The first is that impacts on the realisation of human rights and environmental conservation are incommensurable with economic gains and losses. Incorporating both sets of consequences into a single analysis would require one set of consequences to be valued in terms of the other. The second is that investment treaties might have opposite effects on the two sets of consequences. Investment treaty protections might plausibly encourage decisions that engender net economic benefits – by forcing government decision-makers to consider private costs – but less effective at realising human rights – by discouraging rights-realising measures that entail private costs. The third is that existing literature deals with these sets of consequences separately, so synthesising them into a single analysis of government decision-making would require a substantial re-orientation of existing contributions.

3.7.2 Evidence and theory in the regulatory chill inquiry

Even with highly detailed case studies, past chilling effects are difficult to identify because they require counterfactual evidence about the regulations that would have existed in the absence of the purported chilling.[239] In addition to identifying an apparent chilling effect, one must be able to exclude the possibility that it was attributable to some other cause – for example, the fear of discouraging future investment – and the possibility that reference to the investment treaty was merely a public excuse.[240] This

---

[239] Neumayer, *Greening Trade and Investment* (2001), p. 78.
[240] Tienhaara, *The Expropriation of Environmental Governance*, p. 263.

task is especially difficult because relevant documents relating to govern-ment decision-making are almost never made public. These evidentiary difficulties may explain why, with the occasional notable exception,[241] so little empirical work has been done to examine the extent to which investment treaties cause regulatory chill.

Given these difficulties with existing evidence, this section begins with an overview of theoretical arguments and implicit causal assumptions about regulatory chill in the existing literature. This analysis, in Section 3.7.3, attempts to draw out the assumptions on which existing debate rests, so that these assumptions can be tested against evidence. The review of the existing literature shows that there is remarkable agreement that government measures that breach investment treaty protections are more likely to be chilled than those that do not.[242] Disagreement in exist-ing debate primarily stems from different *doctrinal* views about whether socially desirable measures are likely to breach the substantive provisions of existing treaties. Having mapped out the conceptual structure of exist-ing debate, Section 3.7.4 tests hypotheses implicit in existing debate about regulatory chill against available evidence.

3.7.3 Theoretical debate about regulatory chill in the existing literature

One starting point of existing discussions of 'chilling' effects is doctrinal inquiry – inquiry that examines whether certain types of governmental measures would give rise to liability under investment treaties. Schill, for example, argues that investment treaties will not chill unilateral state reg-ulation to mitigate climate change because proportionate and reasonable mitigation measures would not breach common protections contained in existing treaties.[243] Similarly, Vandevelde argues that the fact that most regulatory expropriation claims are unsuccessful shows that investment treaties do not impede efforts to raise regulatory standards.[244] The twin assumptions implicit in this argument are that states may be dissuaded from adopting or maintaining measures that entail liability but will not be dissuaded from adopting or maintaining measures that do not entail liability. These two assumptions are foundational in existing debate. They are shared by those who argue that investment treaties are likely to have

---

[241] Ibid., p. 263.
[242] Schill, 'Do Investment Treaties Chill Unilateral State Regulation to Mitigate Climate Change?', p. 477; Vandevelde, *Bilateral Investment Treaties*, p. 107; Tienhaara, 'Regulatory Chill and the Threat of Arbitration', p. 626.
[243] Schill, 'Do Investment Treaties Chill Unilateral State Regulation to Mitigate Climate Change?', p. 477.
[244] Vandevelde, *Bilateral Investment Treaties*, p. 107.

significant chilling effects[245] and those, such as Schill and Vandevelde, who argue that they are not.

A further argument made by some critics of investment treaties is that uncertainty about the implications of investment treaty protections for specific regulatory proposals will discourage decision-makers from adopting measures that would likely be permissible.[246] This is the uncertainty argument. Similarly, critics have argued that states' concern about the costs of defending claims under investment treaties in arbitration may chill permissible regulation.[247] This is a species of the uncertainty argument, which is only conceptually coherent if one accepts the basic uncertainty argument. Tribunals have awarded costs against unsuccessful investor-claimants, and such costs awards are more likely if it is clear from the outset that the claim has no arguable basis.[248] Accordingly, a state that was certain that a challenged measure was permissible would know that there was no risk of liability associated with maintaining the measure and could also assume that it had a strong chance of recovering costs from the investor for pursuing a spurious claim.

The division among existing contributions illustrates a useful conceptual distinction between two types of regulatory chill that might be caused by investment treaties protections: the chilling of measures that would clearly give rise to liability and the chilling of measures that may not give rise to liability. The former type of regulatory chill is uncontroversial in the existing literature. For it to occur, at least two empirical conditions would need to be present: decision-makers would need to be aware of the existence of investment treaties[249] and concerned (as opposed to

---

[245] Tienhaara, 'Regulatory Chill and the Threat of Arbitration: A View from Political Science' in Brown and Miles (eds), *Evolution in Investment Treaty Law and Arbitration* (2011), p. 626.

[246] Louthan, 'A Brave New Lochner Era? The Constitutionality of NAFTA Chapter 11' (2001) 34 *Vanderbilt Journal of Transnational Law*, p. 1446; Been and Beauvais, 'The Global Fifth Amendment?', p. 134; Bachand and Rousseau, 'International Investment and Human Rights', p. 21; Mann H, 'Investment Agreements and the Regulatory State: Can Exceptions Clauses Create a Safe Haven for Governments?' (2007) [online], p. 5; Suda, 'The Effect of Bilateral Investment Treaties on Human Rights Enforcement and Realization' (2005) [online], fn. 103; Waincymer, 'Balancing Property Rights and Human Rights in Expropriation' in Dupuy, Francioni and Petersmann (eds), *Human Rights in International Investment Law and Arbitration* (2009), p. 306.

[247] Been and Beauvais, 'The Global Fifth Amendment?', p. 132.

[248] *Methanex v. United States* Final Award, pt V, paras. 5, 10. Current arbitral practice on costs is discussed in *EDF v. Romania*, Award, para. 326 and Dissent Regarding Costs, para. 4.

[249] Franck, 'The Legitimacy Crisis in Investment Treaty Arbitration: Privatizing Public International Law through Inconsistent Decisions' (2005) 73 *Fordham Law Review*, p. 1592.

indifferent) about the possibility of the state being required to compensate foreign investors.[250] For the latter type of regulatory chill to occur a third, additional, empirical condition must be present: there must be uncertainty regarding the application of investment treaty protections to specific proposals under consideration.

There is a further empirical distinction, within both types of regulatory chill, between the effect of investors' invocation of investment treaty protections in disputes with government and the extent to which decision-makers internalise investment treaty protections independently of any action by investors. If an affected investor threatens legal action or lobbies against an existing measure on the basis of an investment treaty, the relevant decision-maker will be alerted to the existence of the treaty.[251] The empirical question that follows is whether such threats of litigation have any influence on decisions to maintain or enforce existing regulations. The threat of litigation could also dissuade a decision-maker from adopting a new measure. However, for the investor to be able to threaten litigation, it would need to be aware that the adoption of a new measure was being contemplated, perhaps because the measure had been proposed in a public consultation. Collectively, I describe these circumstances as 'threat' chill. The situation is entirely different when investors have not opposed a measure on the basis of an investment treaty. In these circumstances, decision-makers would need independent knowledge of the existence of investment treaties for the provisions contained in such treaties to have any influence on their decision-making.[252] I describe the impact of decision-makers general awareness of investment treaty protections on decisions to adopt, maintain and enforce measures as 'internalisation' chill.

3.7.4 Assessing empirical evidence of regulatory chill

3.7.4.1 What sort of evidence would be needed to test hypotheses about regulatory chill?

To empirically test the extent of 'internalisation' and 'threat' regulatory chill effects, different types of case studies would be needed. Investigation of cases in which foreign investors have publicly cited investment

---

[250] Coe and Rubins, "Regulatory Expropriation and the *Tecmed* Case: Context and Contributions' in Weiler (ed), *International Investment Law and Arbitration: Leading Cases from the ICSID, NAFTA, Bilateral Treaties and Customary International Law* (2005) Most scholars accept as self-evident that states will be concerned about the risk of liability, e.g., Mann H, 'Investment Agreements and the Regulatory State', p. 5.

[251] Tienhaara, *The Expropriation of Environmental Governance*, p. 262.

[252] Coe and Rubins, 'Regulatory Expropriation and the *Tecmed* case', p. 599.

treaty protections in opposing regulations, including cases in which the investor commences international arbitration, would be useful in identifying 'threat' chill. Some such research exists, and the factual record of arbitration proceedings provides further relevant source material. Evidence of this sort may also provide limited insight into the effect of investors' opposition to the adoption of new measures. However, a systematic examination of 'internalisation' chill would need to focus on cases of governmental decision-making when there was no public opposition to a measure by foreign investors. To my knowledge, no such research has been published.[253]

3.7.4.2 Disaggregating the state – institutional complexity and regulatory chill

An additional complexity in the study of regulatory chill is that variation in the characteristics of decision-making bodies, both within and between countries, is likely to lead to variation in the extent of regulatory chill. Within countries, it is reasonable to hypothesise that national governments, who sign investment treaties, are more likely to be aware of the protections contained therein than subnational governments.[254] And, as national governments will bear initial responsibility for paying any adverse award in international arbitration, they may be more sensitive to the risk of liability under investment treaties than decision-makers with a high degree of autonomy from national government.[255] This hypothesis is supported by a recent dispute between the owner of the US company Abitibi-Bowater (a paper and pulp mill), and Canada. The Canadian province of Newfoundland expropriated the assets of the Abitibi-Bowater in late 2008, ignoring the objections of the Canadian federal government and seemingly indifferent to risk of liability this action entailed at the national level.[256] The federal government ultimately settled the case $130 million Canadian, apparently having reached the view that it would be unable to defend the case on the merits.[257]

---

[253] Similarly, Tienhaara, 'Regulatory Chill and the Threat of Arbitration', p. 607.

[254] Vicuña, 'Regulatory Authority and Legitimate Expectations: Balancing the Rights of the State and the Individual under International Law in a Global Society' (2003) 5 *International Law FORUM du droit international*, p. 191.

[255] Been and Beauvais, 'The Global Fifth Amendment?', p. 90.

[256] Peterson, 'Canada Settles NAFTA Claim by Pulp & Paper Company for $130 Million; Spotlight Turns to Federal Government's Being on Hook for Actions of Province' (2010) *IA Reporter* [online].

[257] Ibid.

One might also expect that decision-makers in developing countries, which are less able to finance adverse arbitral awards, would be more concerned about avoiding liability under investment treaties than decision-makers in developed countries.[258] The fact that developing countries are less likely to have access to high-quality legal expertise may also contribute to greater chilling of decision-making in those states.[259] This hypothesis receives some evidential support from situations in which, following threats of arbitration under investment treaties by foreign investors, the Indonesian and Costa Rican governments reversed earlier decisions to refuse to grant mining permits.[260] In similar circumstances, the governments of developed countries have maintained refusals to grant mining permits, notwithstanding investor opposition.[261]

Nevertheless, each case of purported regulatory chill involves a complex interplay of factors. There is not yet sufficient evidence to reach firm conclusions about differences in behaviour between national and subnational arms of government or about differences in behaviour between developing and developed states. This highlights the need for caution in making generalisations about regulatory chill.

3.7.4.3 Empirical testing hypotheses of regulatory chill I: liability and chilling

This section examines the hypothesis that states are dissuaded from adopting or maintaining measures that would give rise to liability under investment treaties. It concludes that this hypothesis should be qualified. A brief survey of decided cases reveals a number in which states maintained measures that purported to pursue environmental objectives, notwithstanding the ultimate expense of compensating foreign investors, among them: *Metalclad* v. *Mexico*; *Tecmed* v. *Mexico*; and *Santa Elena* v. *Costa Rica*.[262] One might object that in these cases the decision-makers in question only maintained the measures that became the subject of arbitration because they mistakenly believed them to be investment treaty compliant. However, the fact that states in these cases chose to pay out foreign investors, when they could have bifurcated the merits and quantum stages of arbitral proceedings and, after losing on the merits, negotiated settlements that involved the abandonment of the measure in question, serves to

---

[258] Mann H, 'Investment Agreements and the Regulatory State', p. 5.
[259] Tienhaara 'Regulatory Chill and the Threat of Arbitration', p. 612.
[260] See Section 3.7.4.4   [261] *Glamis Gold* v. *United States*, Award.
[262] *Metalclad* v. *Mexico*, Award; *Tecmed* v. *Mexico*, Award; *Santa Elena* v. *Costa Rica*, Final Award.

illustrate a simple point: states sometimes maintain measures that entail liability under investment treaty protections.

Similarly, in two cases involving water privatisation – *Aguas del Tunari* v. *Bolivia* and *Biwater* v. *Tanzania* – the states in question cancelled water concession contracts, purporting to protect the right to water.[263] The arbitration in *Aguas del Tunari* ultimately settled.[264] In *Biwater*, the Tanzanian government was found liable for breaching the BIT in question, although no economic loss to the foreign investor flowed from the breach.

This survey is unlikely to be representative of the effect of liability under investment treaty protections on regulatory decisions. Arbitration normally involves cases in which states have not been dissuaded from maintaining measures and brings such cases to public attention. In contrast, situations in which a state has been dissuaded from maintaining measures do not have an equivalent mechanism by which they are publicised. Care should be taken not to overestimate the extent to which states maintain measures that will clearly give rise to liability.

The assumption that states will be dissuaded from maintaining measures that would give rise to liability under investment treaties should be qualified rather than rejected. It remains reasonable to assume that states are less likely to maintain measures that give rise to liability than to maintain measures that do not. This is consistent with existing evidence. There are several examples of states being dissuaded from maintaining measures that would have entailed liability under an investment treaty. For example, in *SD Myers* v. *Canada*, the government revoked a ban on PCB exports after the investor initiated arbitration,[265] a measure that the tribunal subsequently found had been in breach of the relevant investment treaty during the time it was in force. Indeed, the cases reviewed in the following section show that, on occasion, the mere risk of liability under an investment treaty has been sufficient to dissuade states from maintaining measures that may well have been investment treaty compliant.

Requiring the state to compensate foreign investors for losses resulting from a regulatory decision adds a cost to maintaining that decision.[266] All other things being equal, the expense of liability is likely to make

---

[263] *Compañia de Aguas del Aconquija and Vivendi* v. *Argentina (II)*, Award; *Biwater* v. *Tanzania*, Award.

[264] Vis-Dunbar and Peterson, 'Bolivian Water Dispute Settled, Bechtel Forgoes Compensation' (2006) *Investment Treaty News*, p. 1.

[265] *SD Myers* v. *Canada*, Partial Award.

[266] Wagner, 'International Investment, Expropriation and Environmental Protection' (1999) 29 *Golden Gate University Law Review*, p. 467.

decision-makers less inclined to maintain a decision. As argued earlier, this hypothesis is accepted by both proponents and critics of investment treaties as the foundation for debate about regulatory chill. These chilling effects are likely to be stronger in states in which internal procedures have been established to encourage compliance with investment treaties.[267] This conclusion is sufficient to allow inferences to be drawn about the likely consequences of different levels of investment treaty protection.

Chilling effects are likely to be stronger in cases in which investor has opposed a measure or threatened arbitration, than situations in which decision-makers consider the adoption of new measures in the absence of controversy. There is a dearth of evidence relating to 'internalisation' effects of this sort[268] and little evidence of the impact of liability rules on government decision-making in domestic legal systems, which might provide guidance by way of analogy.[269] Coe and Rubins argue that administrative decision-makers who do not have direct or regular dealings with foreign investors are unlikely to be aware of investment treaties,[270] which would suggest that such decision-makers do not internalise the constraints of investment treaty protections when evaluating the adoption of new governmental measures.[271] Government lawyers from several developed states speak privately of instances where policies have been modified or abandoned due to internal concerns within government about the risk of liability under investment treaties. It is difficult to assess the reliability or significance of these anecdotes in the absence of publicly available information. Understanding the extent to which governments internalise investment treaties remains an important area for further study. Hypotheses about the extent of 'internalisation' effects must be open to testing and revision if and when future evidence comes to light.

3.7.4.4 Empirical testing hypotheses of regulatory chill II: uncertainty and chilling

This section examines the hypothesis that states are not dissuaded from adopting or maintaining measures that may not have given rise to liability under investment treaties. It is difficult to find evidence to test this assumption. Among Tienhaara's fourteen detailed case studies of foreign

---

[267] See Section 3.4.5.1.
[268] Tienhaara, 'Regulatory Chill and the Threat of Arbitration', p. 607.
[269] See Section 3.4.5.1.
[270] Coe and Rubins, 'Regulatory Expropriation and the *Tecmed* case', p. 599.
[271] Cf. Schneiderman, *Constitutionalizing Economic Globalization: Investment Rules and Democracy's Promise* (2008), p. 114.

investment and environmental regulation, there are three cases in which investment treaty protections arguably affected a state's regulatory conduct. One of these is *SD Myers*, which has been considered in the previous section.

The other two cases Tienhaara examines are the notorious *Ethyl Corp* v. *Canada* and the less well-known events surrounding Vannessa Ventures dealings with the Costa Rican environmental authorities. The facts in *Ethyl* concerned a Canadian government measure that banned the import of gasoline additive MMT on environmental grounds. The Canadian government reversed the ban after an arbitral tribunal ruled it had jurisdiction to hear a claim brought by Ethyl challenging the measure under NAFTA's Chapter 11.[272] It seems the Canadian government's decision to abandon the measure was partly motivated by a Canadian court ruling that the measure breached Canada's Agreement on Internal Trade.[273] Nevertheless, the fact that Canada choose to make settlement payments to Ethyl,[274] rather than scrap the measure and contest the arbitral claim on the merits, suggests that investment treaty protections did play some role in the government's decision.

The case of Vannessa Ventures related to a mining concession owned by the company. In 2003, the Costa Rican environmental agency declined to approve Vannessa Venture's environmental impact assessment, a step necessary for it to commence open-pit mining.[275] This denial of approval reflected a change in policy on open pit-mining, although it was disputed whether Vannessa Ventures had held the necessary environmental permits to commence mining before the change in policy.[276] The environmental agency maintained its position throughout two years of domestic court proceedings. Then, only two months after the investor initiated arbitration proceedings, and with issues still before the Constitutional Court, it approved Vannessa Venture's proposal.[277] Although Tienhaara uncovers no direct evidence that the threat of arbitration caused the agency to issue the approval, the timing of events suggests that it played some role. (In 2010, five years after these events, a Costa Rican court ruled that the concession awarded to Vannessa was inconsistent with Costa Rican law.[278] This decision is now the subject of a dispute. These events do not detract from the conclusion that the earlier actions of the environmental agency constituted a case of regulatory chill.)

---

[272] Tienhaara, *The Expropriation of Environmental Governance*, p. 157.
[273] Ibid., p. 157.   [274] Ibid., p. 157.   [275] Ibid., p. 239.
[276] Ibid., p. 238.   [277] Ibid., p. 239.   [278] Ibid., p. 624.

Gross describes a similar set of circumstances in Indonesia. Although information on the case is limited, it appears that the Indonesia government had legislated to ban open-pit mining.[279] A number of mining companies with undeveloped exploration contracts threatened international arbitration, relying – on Gross's reading of the facts – on the protections of applicable investment treaties.[280] Six months later, the government revoked the measure. The Environment Minister linked the change of policy to the threat of arbitration.[281]

In all three of these cases there seems to have been some chilling effect. The more difficult question is whether the abandoned measures were likely to have been permissible. In each it seems that the state had an arguable case on the merits, suggesting that either uncertainty about the implications of investment treaty protections or concern about the costs of arbitration played a role. The facts of *Ethyl* bear some similarity to a later case, *Methanex v. US*, in which the United States successfully defended a ban on a gasoline additive on environmental grounds.[282] This suggests that the abandoned measure may have been permissible. The Costa Rican and Indonesian cases raise more difficult issues. Arbitral decisions concerning denial of permits to use land in a certain way do not lay down any bright line tests. However, several arbitral awards appear to accept that states are entitled to refuse permission for land to be used in a certain way, so long as fair administrative processes are followed and the state has not made any assurances to the contrary to the investor.[283] This suggests that the strength of both Costa Rica's and Indonesia's defences would have depended on the scope of permission held by and the assurances made to mining companies before the changes in policy. In Gross's view, the Indonesian measure would not have given rise to liability had the case proceeded to arbitration.[284]

Schneiderman presents two additional case studies (his third case study is *Ethyl*) which concern the effect of investment treaties and governmental decision-making.[285] The first is the Canadian attempt to introduce

---

[279] Gross, 'Inordinate Chill: BITs Non-NAFTA MITs and Host State Regulatory Freedom – An Indonesian Case Study' (2003) 24 *Michigan Journal of International Law*, p. 894.
[280] Ibid., p. 897.   [281] Ibid., p. 895.
[282] Gantz, 'Potential Conflict between Investor Rights and Environmental Regulation under NAFTA's Chapter 11' (2001) 33 *George Washington International Law Review* 651, p. 665.
[283] *Tecmed v. Mexico*, Award, para. 173; *Metalclad v. Mexico*, Award, para. 97.
[284] Gross, 'Inordinate Chill', p. 960.
[285] Schneiderman, *Constitutionalizing Economic Globalization*, p. 129.

legislation requiring plain packaging for cigarettes in 1994. This measure was abandoned after the Canadian Supreme Court found similar legislation to be unconstitutional.[286] Opposition of foreign investors based on investment treaties does not appear to have been significant in that decision. Prior to the ruling of unconstitutionality, the relevant legislative committee had recommended the adoption of the measure despite tobacco companies' claims the measure violated investment treaty protections.[287] The second is the case of South African affirmative action policies in the mining sector, which were the subject of arbitration in *Foresti* v. *South Africa*.[288] Schneiderman claims that the case shows that 'South Africa's internal policy options will have been shaped by the external environment for the promotion and protection of foreign investment.'[289] His own evidence does not support this claim. It does not suggest that concern about liability under investment treaties influenced the development and drafting of South Africa's Black Economic Empowerment policies. Although there is some suggestion that the pressure of arbitral proceedings expedited the claimants dealings with the South African authorities,[290] South Africa both maintained and applied its affirmative action policies despite the claim, which was ultimately abandoned by the claimants.[291]

There are other examples in which decision-makers have maintained permissible environmental and human rights measures, despite opposition from foreign investors. In *Methanex* v. *US*, *Glamis Gold* v. *US*, *Chemtura* v. *Canada* and *Lucchetti* v. *Peru*, the respective respondent states maintained the impugned measures throughout arbitration proceedings and ultimately avoided liability.[292] The Uruguayan government has maintained its restrictions on tobacco marketing,[293] which are now the subject of a claim in *Philip Morris Products* v. *Uruguay*.[294]

The circumstances surrounding Australia's introduction of tobacco plain packaging in 2011 also provide a useful case study on regulatory chill. In this case, Philip Morris initiated investor-state arbitration *before*

---

[286] Ibid., p. 128.   [287] Ibid., p. 128.   [288] *Piero Foresti* v. *South Africa, Award.*
[289] Ibid., p. 157.   [290] Ibid., Award, para. 118.   [291] Ibid., Award, para. 117.
[292] *Methanex* v. *United States* Final Award; *Glamis Gold* v. *United States*, Award; *Chemtura* v. *Canada*, Award; *Lucchetti* v. *Peru*, Award.
[293] Peterson, 'ICSID Panels Convened in Disputes over Uruguay's Tobacco Policies, Venezuelan Airport Concession, Polish Health-Care Venture, and Hungarian Energy Investment' (2011) *IA Reporter* [online].
[294] *Philip Morris* v. *Uruguay*, Decision on Jurisdiction.

tobacco plain packaging had been adopted in Australia.[295] Thus, there can be no question that Australia was aware of the risk of liability and elected to proceed with the measure regardless. In contrast, the New Zealand government has made a formal policy announcement that it intends to introduce tobacco plain packaging but that the introduction of this policy will be delayed until the WTO and investment treaty claims arising from tobacco plain packaging in Australia have been resolved.[296] Subsequent comments reportedly made by the prime minister of New Zealand suggest that New Zealand government is particularly concerned about the risk of liability resulting from investment treaty claims.[297] This is a clear case of regulatory chill.

The experience of the United Kingdom differs again. In 2013, it also considered adopting tobacco plain packaging but, after a concerted public campaign by tobacco manufacturers, decided to defer any decision to wait for 'more evidence' of the impact of the measure in Australia. Although the United Kingdom must have been aware of the risk of legal challenge,[298] concerns about the risk of liability under investment treaties were not among the reasons given for postponing consideration of the measure.[299] Late in 2013, the government of the United Kingdom reversed course again, commissioning a review that has put tobacco plain packaging back on the policy agenda. The different experiences of these three states with tobacco plain packaging neatly encapsulates the complex effects of investment treaty protections on domestic decision-making.

Overall, it is clear that foreign investors' invocation of investment treaties does not always lead to the chilling of the governmental measure subject to challenge. There are several cases in which states have maintained measures in the face of arbitral proceedings initiated by investors. That said, there is also evidence that investment treaty protections do, on occasion, dissuade states from adopting or

---

[295] *Philip Morris* v. *Australia*, Notice of Claim.
[296] Turia, 'Government Moves Forward with Plain Packaging of Tobacco Products' (2013) [online].
[297] Wilson P, 'Plain Packaging Bill Passes First Reading' (2014) [online].
[298] The United Kingdom does not have investment treaties with any of the states in which the parent companies of the world's major tobacco manufacturers are domiciled. However, as was the case with Australia, the United Kingdom does have investment treaties with states in which subsidiaries of the major tobacco manufacturers are domiciled. As was the case with Australia, it is possible, at least in theory, that a Hong Kong domiciled subsidiary could bring a claim.
[299] BBC, 'Government Rejects Labour's "Cigarette U-Turn" Claim' (2013) [online].

maintaining measures that may not have given rise to liability. It is also important to recall that there is likely to be significant bias in available evidence, with cases in which regulation is not chilled being more likely to come to public attention. For both reasons, chilling effects are unlikely to be limited exclusively to measure that would ultimately be found to breach investment treaty protections.

This conclusion is consistent with anecdotal evidence about how the legal services of governments in developed states work in practice. When called on to advise on whether a measure under consideration is consistent with a state's international legal obligations, the advice will often take the form of an opinion on the risk or probability that a measure would be found to be non-compliant. This advice will then be one factor that is weighed along with other factors in the decision-making processes.

Although the evidence is complex, the implications of the theory that uncertainty increases regulatory chill are relatively clear: investment treaty protections that provide decision-makers with greater certainty about how the protection would apply to government measures will reduce the chilling of permissible measures. Investment treaty protections that give arbitrators unstructured discretions or that turn on *ex post* judgments that decision-makers cannot easily predict when considering the adoption of measures prospectively are likely to be associated with greater uncertainty and greater chilling of measures that would have been permissible.[300]

3.7.5 The possibility of more complex effects on government decision-making

The previous sections have considered two relatively simple causal hypotheses relating to the likely effect of different levels of investment treaty protection on government decision-making. They highlighted some of the challenges in drawing inferences from current evidence, even with respect to these relatively simple hypotheses. Conscious, perhaps, of these limitations, the academic literature on regulatory chill has not given a great deal of attention to the possibility that investment treaty protections may have more complex effects on government behaviour. In this section, I consider two more complex hypotheses: that international scrutiny of government decision-making improves the effectiveness of

---

[300] Tienhaara, 'Regulatory Chill and the Threat of Arbitration', p. 615.

environmental or human rights-inspired measures and that the extent to which states are held liable for environmental or human rights-inspired measures affects the degree to which they cooperate in addressing such concerns in other international forums.

In other contexts, the argument has been made that international scrutiny of government decision-making improves the effectiveness of measures ultimately adopted. For example, Zahrnt argues that the international process of policy review through the institutions of the WTO can improve domestic decision-making.[301] However, the WTO policy review process differs substantially because it involves technical review of government decisions through a procedure that is not backed by sanctioning mechanisms, rather than legal challenge to policies in contentious proceedings. The judicial review of government decision-making in contentious proceedings in a domestic context is perhaps more closely analogous to the situation that arises under investment treaties. In one of the few studies of the impact of such proceedings, Marsh argues that they tend to encourage 'defensive practice' that makes government measures less effective.[302]

Whether the possibility of review by an international arbitral tribunal improves, reduces or has no impact on the effectiveness of human rights and environmental measures adopted is an empirical question, for which there is little available evidence. Although the argument that international review improves government decision-making offers a justification for the availability of investor-state arbitration, its implications for questions relating to the desirable level of substantive protection to be provided in investment treaties are less clear. To the extent that the argument speaks to the level of protection that should be available, it implies that arbitral review of government conduct should focus on whether the procedures by which a measure was adopted were rational and fair,[303] rather than the question of whether the measure affected the interests of the foreign investor.

The second hypothesis concerns the likely impact of different levels of protection on the behaviour of the state as an international legal actor. On the one hand, one might argue that if a state is held liable for measures perceived to constitute legitimate environmental or human

---

[301] Zahrnt, 'Transparency of Complex Regulation: How Should WTO Trade Policy Reviews Deal with Sanitary and Phytosanitary Policies?' (2011) 10 *World Trade Review*, p. 237.

[302] Marsh, 'The Impact of Liability on Public Bodies', p. 19.

[303] Zahrnt 'Transparency of Complex Regulation', p. 237.

rights regulation, it would strengthen the hand of domestic constituencies that oppose international cooperation, discouraging international cooperation in other fields. Although there is some evidence of countries reacting to controversial cases brought under investment treaties by withdrawing from the ICSID Convention,[304] there is little evidence that this reaction against international cooperation in other fields more generally.

On the other hand, one might argue that if a state were required to compensate a foreign investor following the introduction of an environment or human right-inspired measure that is perceived as legitimate, the state may be encouraged to seek clearer international agreement on the legitimacy of such measures. This argument is consistent with some economic theories of why states cooperate, in that changes in the perceived payoffs of cooperation are thought to drive state behaviour.[305] One difficulty with this argument is that many environmental and human rights measures that have been the subject of investment treaties claims do not appear to be matters that are amenable to international standard setting – for example, the question of when it is legitimate for a state to unilaterally alter the terms of a water concession contract to promote universal access to water[306] or the question of when it is legitimate to require back-filling as an environmental condition for the award of a mining permit.[307] (Tobacco plain packaging is a notable exception.)[308] There is little evidence for the proposition that the risk of liability under investment treaties encourages international cooperation in the field of human rights and environmental standard setting.

3.7.6 The consequence of regulatory chill for human rights and environmental conservation

The previous sections tested hypotheses about the extent of regulatory chill likely to follow from the adoption of different levels of investment treaty protection. The final issue is the likely impact of the chilling of environmental and human rights–inspired measures on the realisation

---

[304] Including Bolivia and Ecuador: Mourra, 'The Conflicts and Controversies in Latin American Treaty-Based Disputes' in Mourra MH (ed), *Latin American Investment Treaty Arbitration* (2007), p. 63; ICSID, 'Ecuador Submits a Notice under Article 71 of the ICSID Convention'.

[305] Dunoff and Trachtman, 'Economic Analysis of International Law' (1999) 24 *Yale Journal of International Law*, p. 14.

[306] *Suez and Vivendi; AWG Group* v. *Argentina*, Decision on Liability.

[307] *Glamis Gold* v. *United States*, Award.

[308] *Guidelines for Implementation of Article 11 of the WHO Framework Convention on Tobacco Control* (Packaging and labelling of tobacco products), FCTC/COP3(10) (22 November 2008).

of human rights and the protection of the environment. Assessing this impact requires a further set of inferences about the likely effect on the realisation of human rights and environmental conservation of regulations that are not adopted (or not maintained) as a result of regulatory chill. This section begins with a survey of the environment and human rights–inspired measures that have been the subject of past investment treaty claims. It then traces the effect that the chilling of such measures would have on the realisation of human rights and environmental protection.

A range of measures purporting to pursue environmental and human rights objectives have been the subject of investment treaty claims. In the field of human rights, investors have challenged measures: banning the use or sale of products purportedly harmful to human health (right to health);[309] regulating the marketing of tobacco (right to health);[310] altering water supply contracts, purportedly to ensure access to drinking water (right to water);[311] promoting affirmative action to redress past institutionalised racial discrimination (right to equality);[312] and failing to control or prevent public demonstrations, which the investor contended had become violent (right to freedom of assembly).[313] Of the claims that have led to an award on the merits, the respondent state was successful in each case, save those relating to the unilateral alteration of water supply contracts.

In the field of environmental protection, investors have challenged measures imposing environmental conditions on the award of mining permits;[314] measures imposing environmental conditions on the award of permits to operate hazardous waste facilities;[315] measures imposing environmental conditions on the award of permits to operate coal power stations;[316] judgments of domestic courts holding the investor liable for pollution allegedly caused by the investor (the investor argues that the

---

[309] *Chemtura* v. *Canada*, Award; *Methanex* v. *United States* Final Award.
[310] *Philip Morris* v. *Uruguay*, Decision on Jurisdiction; Peterson, 'Analysis: Australian Defense Strategy Puts Emphasis on Timing of Philip Morris's Corporate Structuring Moves, Claims "Abuse" of Investment Treaty' (2011) *IA Reporter* [online].
[311] *Suez and Vivendi; AWG Group* v. *Argentina*, Decision on Liability; *Compañia de Aguas del Aconquija and Vivendi* v. *Argentina (II)*, Award; *Biwater* v. *Tanzania*, Award.
[312] *Piero Foresti* v. *South Africa*, Award.
[313] *Tecmed* v. *Mexico*, Award, para. 177; *Plama* v. *Bulgaria*, Award, para. 236.
[314] *Glamis Gold* v. *United States*, Award; *PacRim* v. *El Salvador*, Notice of Arbitration, para. 77.
[315] *Tecmed* v. *Mexico*, Award.
[316] Peterson, 'Parties in *Vattenfall* v. *Germany* Case Suspend Proceedings'.

state had released the investor from liability);[317] the phase out of nuclear power;[318] and measures expropriating the investor's land for the purpose of establishing an environmental reserve.[319]

Environmental measures have also been cited by host state in cases in which it appears that the purported environmental objective was merely a pretext. For example, in *Metalclad* an executive decree establishing a conservation reserve for the preservation of a rare cactus, which prevented the operation of the investor's hazardous waste facility, was made only after other attempts to halt the construction of the facility had failed;[320] and in *SD Myers*, a ban on the transboundary movement of PCB waste, purportedly justified by environmental concerns about the safe transport of the waste, greatly *increased* the distance the waste had to be transported. However, these cases are in the minority. In most cases, disagreement between the investor and the state related to the question of whether the impugned measure constituted an unjustified interference with the investor's interests,[321] rather than the question of whether the human rights or environmental objective was a pretext.

This survey of publicly known cases supports two important conclusions. The first is that a wide variety of environment and human rights–inspired measures have been the subject of investment treaty claims in the past. This is important because it suggests that when negotiating investment treaties, states may not be able to foresee the particular measures that may be the subject of investment treaty claims in the future. Rather, states will need to make prospective judgements based on a more general assessment of the way in which given levels of protection are likely to influence the exercise of regulatory power.

The second conclusion is that, in most cases, the measures to which the investor objected seem to have been taken in good faith to advance the environmental or human rights objective purportedly pursued.[322] If measures of this sort were chilled, it would have a negative effect on realisation of human rights and on environmental conservation. This inference does not rest on the assumption that the measures abandoned

---

[317] *Chevron v. Ecuador (II)*, Notice of Arbitration.
[318] Bernasconi-Osterwalder and Hoffmann, 'The German Nuclear Phase-Out Put to the Test in International Investment Arbitration? Background to the New Dispute Vattenfall v. Germany (II)' (2012) [online].
[319] *Santa Elena v. Costa Rica*, Final Award.
[320] *Metalclad v. Mexico*, Award.   [321] *Tecmed v. Mexico*, Award.
[322] E.g., *Philip Morris v. Australia*, Notice of Claim; *Santa Elena v. Costa Rica*, Final Award; *Chemtura v. Canada*, Award; *Tecmed v. Mexico*, Award; *Piero Foresti v. South Africa*, Award.

would have been the most effective way to achieve a particular human rights or environmental objective. Rather, it is based on the assumption that the abandoned measures would have been somewhat effective in achieving their purported objectives, an assumption that is consistent with the measures reviewed in this section.

3.7.6.1 Can regulatory chill improve the realisation of human right and environmental conservation?

Finally, for the sake of completeness, I consider the possibility that chilling effects could improve the realisation of human rights and environmental conservation. Although it is possible to imagine fact scenarios in which regulatory chill might, counter-intuitively, increase the realisation of these objectives,[323] it is highly unlikely that cumulative impact of chilling effects across the range of cases covered by investment treaty protections would be to achieve these objectives. This is because the effectiveness of measures in realising human rights is a function of their consequences for a wide range of individuals; the effectiveness of measures to protect the environment is a function of their achievement of non-economic conservation objectives. The economic interests of foreign investors may occasionally coincide with these objectives,[324] but they are not representative of them. As such, reluctance on the part of decision-makers to interfere with the economic interests of foreign investors is highly unlikely to lead to the greater realisation of human rights and environmental objectives.

3.7.7 Summary of regulatory chill

The examination of regulatory chill can be summarised in the following propositions:

1. The extent of regulatory chill is likely to vary between decision-makers within and between states.
2. There is little publicly available evidence that sheds light on how, if at all, concerns about liability under investment treaty protections are internalised in decision-making processes. Evidence of chilling consists

---

[323] E.g., in late 2009, Graeme Hall Sanctuary filed a notice of dispute under the Canada-Barbados BIT against Barbados. The prospective claimant alleged that Barbados had violated the BIT by failing to enforce its own environmental laws. Whitsitt, 'Claimant Seeks Enforcement of Environmental Laws in Notice of Dispute Alleging Expropriation of Barbadian Nature Sanctuary', *Investment Treaty News*, p. 4; similarly, *Desert Line* v. *Yemen*, Award, para. 290.

[324] E.g., *Desert Line* v. *Yemen*, Award, para. 290.

primarily of cases in which states have not maintained measures in the face of opposition from foreign investors based on the threat of investment treaty arbitration.

3. Both critics and supporters of investment treaties assume that states are less likely to maintain measures that give rise to liability under investment treat protections than to maintain measures that do not. Existing evidence is consistent with this proposition. On this basis, investment treaty protections which hold a state liable for loss cause by environmental or human rights–inspired measures are likely to lead to greater chilling than investment treaty protections in which the environmental or human right objectives of a measure weighs against a finding of liability.

4. Investment treaty protections that provide greater certainty to decision-makers are likely to reduce the chilling of measures that would not have given rise to liability.

5. Chilling effects are highly unlikely to have positive consequences for the realisation of human rights and environmental conservation. The extent of any negative consequences associated with a given level of protection is likely to depend on the structure of liability under the protection in question.

3.8 Respect for the rule of law

The protections contained in investment treaties may also affect host states' legal institutions, the formal characteristics of the laws promulgated by them and the procedures by which law are applied. Raz's seminal work on the rule of law proposes three desirable characteristics of laws and a further five desirable characteristics of the legal institutions that enforce them.[325] The formal characteristics that law should possess are that it be prospective, open and clear, relatively stable, and that the making of particular (subsidiary) laws should be guided by open, clear and stable general rules.[326] The principles governing legal institutions include that the judiciary should be independent; the courts should be accessible; and natural justice should be observed.[327] I adopt the Razian conception of the rule of law and take as given that the qualities he identifies are intrinsically normatively desirable.[328] There is also a body of social scientific scholarship that links the strength of the rule of law within a

---

[325] Raz, 'The Rule of Law and Its Virtue', p. 202.

[326] Ibid., p. 198.   [327] Ibid., p. 200.

[328] In Raz's work, the normative desirability of the rule of law is grounded in individual autonomy. Respect for the rule of law allows an individual to know the law and organise her or his life according to it: Ibid., p. 198.

state to the state's economic prosperity.[329] While noting this research, this book proceeds on the basis that greater compliance with the rule of law would be desirable even if it were not associated with the attainment of other, instrumental objectives.

Other scholars have argued for broader conceptions of the rule of law that address the substantive content of law.[330] For example, some have argued that, to comply with the rule of law, law must protect human rights,[331] or that it must be reasonable and proportionate.[332] For the purpose of this book, it is unnecessary to resolve debates about whether the Razian conception is unduly narrow. The consequences of investment treaty protections for the substantive content of host government measures were examined earlier in the chapter, in terms of efficiency and the realisation of human rights and environmental conservation. The purpose of this section is to identify the consequences of investment treaty protections on the formal, institutional and procedural qualities of host states' legal systems – their Razian characteristics – that are not assessed in previous sections.

3.8.1 Theory and evidence on investment treaty protections and the rule of law

Although the concept of the rule of law has been invoked in debates about investment treaties with increasing frequency over the past decade, there have been relatively few attempts to link the level of protection provided in investment treaties to the rule of law. One notable exception is in the work of Schill, who has argued that the FET provisions of investment treaties can be understood as 'an embodiment of the rule of law'.[333] In his article, the argument that certain arbitral awards have articulated principles that are consistent with the rule of law is developed in great

---

[329] See Morita and Zaelke, 'Rule of Law, Good Governance and Sustainable Development' (2005) [online], whose definition of the rule of law approximates the Razian conception. However, other empirical studies that purport to establish a connection between the rule of law and economic development use statistics that do not reflect the Razian conception, e.g., Kaufmann, Kraay and Mastruzzi, 'Governance Matters VIII' [online].

[330] Craig, 'Formal and Substantive Conceptions of the Rule of Law', p. 467.

[331] Bingham, The Rule of Law, p. 66.

[332] Schill, 'Fair and Equitable Treatment, the Rule of Law, and Comparative Public Law', p. 169.

[333] Ibid., p. 155; similarly, Vandevelde, 'A Unified Theory of Fair and Equitable Treatment', p. 48.

detail.[334] However, the central causal proposition – that requiring host states to compensate investors for breaching such principles will encourage states to act consistently with the rule of law – is assumed, rather than proved.[335]

This section begins by reviewing existing empirical evidence on the impact of investment treaties on the extent to which states respect the rule of law; it then reviews theories relating to the likely impact of investment treaties on respect for the rule of law; finally, it examines the causal hypothesis implicit in Schill's argument. Before considering the likely effect of adopting different levels of protection in investment treaties for the rule of law, it is important to distinguish academic debate about investor-state arbitration and the rule of law.

3.8.1.1 Distinguishing debate about investor-state arbitration and the rule of law

Most discussion of the relationship between investment treaties and the rule of law centres on the institutions and procedures of investor-state arbitration. Many of the references to the rule of law are somewhat opaque, but they seem to reflect a belief that that the resolution of investment disputes by legal adjudication, rather than by negotiation or political pressure, is more consistent with the rule of law.[336] In this vein, Vandevelde states that 'the rule of law triumphs when sovereign governments commit themselves to legal processes and honor those processes'.[337] Van Harten rejects this view, arguing that arbitration is inconsistent with the rule of law because '[t]here can be no rule of law without an independent judiciary.'[338] Another context in which the rule of law has been invoked is to justify tribunals' decisions to follow earlier awards that are not binding on them.[339]

---

[334] Cf. Section 4.4.2, arguing that arbitral jurisprudence on the FET standard cannot be explained and justified by a coherent set of doctrinal principles, as contended by Schill.
[335] Schill, 'Fair and Equitable Treatment, the Rule of Law, and Comparative Public Law', p. 181.
[336] Sampliner, 'Arbitration of Expropriation Cases under U.S. Investment Treaties' Treaties – A Threat to Democracy of the Dog That Didn't Bark' (2003) 18 *ICSID Review – FILJ*, p. 41; UNCTAD, *Development Implications of International Investment Agreements*, p. 5; Paulsson, 'Indirect Expropriation', p. 2.
[337] Vandevelde, *Bilateral Investment Treaties*, p. 119; similarly, Brower CN and Steven, 'Who Then Should Judge? ?: Developing the International Rule of Law under NAFTA Chapter 11' (2001) 2 *Chicago Journal of International Law*, p. 202.
[338] van Harten, *Investment Treaty Arbitration and Public Law*, p. 174.
[339] *Saipem v. Bangladesh*, Decision on Jurisdiction, para. 67.

For present purposes, it is not necessary to determine the extent to which the resolution of international investment disputes through compulsory investor-state arbitration is consistent with the rule of law, or to determine whether the rule of law requires a *de facto* doctrine of precedent. This book focuses on the level of substantive protection provided by investment treaties. Discussion of the rule of law is of interest to the extent that it draws attention to the consequences that are likely to flow from adopting differing levels of protection, taking the institution of investor-state arbitration as given. Such consequences would depend on the capacity of investment treaty protections to induce changes in host states' domestic legal systems.

3.8.2 Empirical evidence of the impact of investment treaties on the rule of law in host states

Whether investment treaties have an impact on the extent to which states respect the rule of law is an empirical question of some complexity. Thus far, two attempts have been made to investigate some of these issues empirically. Ginsburg's regression analysis suggests that signing a BIT has a minor negative impact on the rule of law in signatory states.[340] Aranguri's regression analysis suggests that signing a BIT has little impact on the rule of law in signatory states and that a foreign investor's successful claim under a BIT has a negative, but statistically insignificant, impact on the rule of law.[341] There are several challenges associated with empirical work of this sort, including the reduction of 'rule of law' to a single metric and controlling for endogeneity.[342] A great deal more evidence is needed before any reliable conclusion can be drawn. Nevertheless, these two studies are important in that they call into question some of the more optimistic claims about investment treaties' impact on the rule of law.

3.8.3 Theories on the relationship between investment treaties and respect for the rule of law

Only a handful of scholars have reflected on the relationship between investment treaties and improvements in the rule of law in host states.

---

[340] Ibid., para. 121.

[341] Aranguri, 'The Effect of BITs on Regulatory Quality and the Rule of Law in Developing Countries' (2010) [online], p. 29.

[342] There are particularly acute endogeneity concerns with respect to the Aranguri study, which does not attempt to control for changes in governance that may make the signing of a BIT more likely.

Their arguments fall into two opposing camps. One view is that investment treaties, and international arbitration under them, complement
domestic legal systems. According to this theory, arbitration under investment treaties demonstrates the benefits of impartial legal institutions,
thereby engendering domestic support in host states for reforms that promote the rule of law.[343] The alternate view is that investment treaties
are, if anything, likely to make the domestic legal systems weaker than
they would otherwise be.[344] The argument is that, by allowing foreign
investors to exit the domestic legal regime, international investment
arbitration removes an important constituency that might advocate for
greater respect for the law and stronger legal institutions at the domestic
level.

Both theories are based on the argument that the ability of foreign
investors to access compulsory investor-state arbitration will have consequences for the respect for the rule of law in host states. As such, both
theories suggest that the extent of any impact on the rule of law in particular states would vary with the presence (or absence) of provisions in
investment treaties that govern the ability of investors to exit the domestic
legal system and access arbitration: exhaustion of local remedies requirements, fork-in-the-road clauses, umbrella clauses and the like.[345] Neither
theory implies an obvious relationship between the level of substantive
protection adopted in investment treaties and consequences for the rule
of law.

3.8.4 Formulating hypotheses about the relationship between levels of investment treaty protection and the rule of law

The causal assumption implicit in Schill's argument is that investment
treaty protections under which a state is more likely to be found liable
when its conduct does not respect the rule of law are more likely to
encourage respect for the rule of law.[346] This hypothesis rests on three
further assumptions: that lawmakers and decision-makers are aware of

---

[343] Franck, 'Foreign Direct Investment, Investment Treaty Arbitration, and the Rule of
Law' (2007) 19 *Global Business and Development Law Journal*, p. 367; similarly, Wälde and
Weiler, 'Investment Arbitration under the Energy Charter Treaty', fn. 22.

[344] Ginsburg, 'International Substitutes for Domestic Institutions: Bilateral Investment
Treaties and Governance' (2005) 25 *International Review of Law and Economics*, p. 119.

[345] E.g., Franck, 'Foreign Direct Investment, Investment Treaty Arbitration, and the Rule of
Law', p. 368.

[346] Schill, 'Fair and Equitable Treatment, the Rule of Law, and Comparative Public Law',
p. 181.

investment treaties; that they are concerned to avoid liability under investment treaties; and know that greater compliance with Razian principles will reduce their likelihood of breaching investment treaties. The hypothesis is consistent with economic theories of the state, in which the monetary incentives are thought to influence decision-making, and is also consistent with the assumptions about the likely extent of regulatory chill that are implicit in the arguments of both critics and supporters of investment treaties.[347] Because this hypothesis is theoretically coherent, intuitively plausible and generally accepted, it constitutes a useful starting point for inferences about the likely consequences of different levels of protection for the rule of law. However, in the absence of evidence to test this proposition, it remains open to revision in light of future evidence.

Two further qualifications should also be added to this hypothesis. The first relies on the distinction between 'threat' and 'internalisation' effects of investment treaty protections, developed in the analysis of regulatory chill.[348] When an investor threatens litigation under an investment treaty, any procedural unfairness or unfairness resulting from application of laws that are unpublicised, unclear and unstable of which the investor complains is likely to have occurred. Although a host state may reverse a substantive decision to avoid the risk of liability to an investor, it cannot undo procedural unfairness which the investor has already suffered. As such, 'threat' effects are probably less significant in tracing the consequences of investment treaty protections for the rule of law than they are in the analysis of regulatory chill. Any impact of investment treaty protections on the degree of respect for the rule of law would then depend on the existence of 'internalisation' effects. (That the benefits of investment treaty protections for the rule of law depend on the internalisation of investment treaty protections has been implicitly recognised in the existing literature.)[349] Section 3.7.4 argued that 'internalisation' effects on government behaviour are likely to be less significant than 'threat' effects on government behaviour.[350] This suggests that the level of substantive protection provided by investment treaties is unlikely to have

---

[347] Schill, 'Do Investment Treaties Chill Unilateral State Regulation to Mitigate Climate Change?', p. 477; Vandevelde, *Bilateral Investment Treaties*, p. 107; Tienhaara, 'Regulatory Chill and the Threat of Arbitration', p. 626.

[348] This distinction is introduced in Section 3.7.3.

[349] Echandi, 'What Do Developing Countries Expect from the International Investment Regime' Alvarez, Sauvant, Ahmed and Vizcaino (eds), *The Evolving International Investment Regime* (Oxford University Press 2011), p. 15.

[350] See Section 3.7.4.3.

a major impact on the degree of respect for the rule of law in host states.

The second qualification concerns the institutional complexity of the host state – specifically, the impact of investment treaties protections on the conduct of the judiciary in host states. Questions about the impact of international legal rules on the conduct of domestic courts raise highly specific and profoundly complex empirical questions. Domestic courts are subject to unique institutional constraints in that they are bound to apply law. For this reason, although it may be reasonable to assume that the behaviour of the executive and legislative arms of states is influenced by the risk of liability under investment treaties, the same assumption cannot be made about the behaviour of states' judiciaries.

3.8.5 Summary of the rule of law

The examination of the rule of law can be summarised in the following three propositions:

1. Little is known about the impact of the substantive protections of investment treaties on the degree of respect for the rule of law in host states. The evidence that does exist casts doubt on some of the more optimistic claims about the impact of investment treaties on the rule of law.
2. One reasonable hypothesis is that investment treaty protections in which a state's liability depends on whether a measure taken by the executive or legislative arms of the state is consistent with Razian norms are more likely to encourage respect for the rule of law.
3. Inferring the likely effect of investment treaties protections on the judicial systems of host states raises highly complex empirical issues. It is unclear what impact, if any, investment treaty protections have on the extent to which host states' judiciaries act consistently with the rule of law.

3.9 The boundaries of the framework

The previous sections of this chapter constitute a framework for conceptualising, identifying and evaluating the consequences of different levels of investment treaty protection. These consequences can be divided into five categories – namely the effect of investment treaty protections on efficiency; the distribution of economic costs and benefits; flows of FDI into host states; the realisation of human rights and environmental conservation in host states; and respect for the rule of law in host states. In the interests of clarity, this section briefly explains why further categories of consequences are unnecessary. This argument is divided into two parts. First, this section shows why the consequences of investment treaty protections, as seen from the perspective of a host state or home state, are adequately addressed within the five-category framework. Second, this section shows that some supposed consequences of investment treaties are unconnected to the consequences of investment treaty protections.

3.9.1 The impact of investment treaty protections on host and on home states

An alternative way to begin an examination of the consequences of investment treaty protections would be to adopt the perspectives of host states and of home states. A state-centric framework for understanding consequences is implicit in some examinations of why states sign investment treaties.[351] The consequences of investment treaty protections for host states are normally understood as loss of sovereignty and increased inflows of FDI. The consequences for home states are normally understood in terms of the protection of the interests of foreign investors, relying on the, often unstated, assumption that home states' interests are aligned with those of their investors abroad.[352]

These consequences of investment treaty protections, as framed by a state-centric perspective, are fully accounted for within the framework developed in this chapter. Concerns about host states' loss of sovereignty can be understood as concerns that investment treaties may leave states unable to enact measures that are normatively desirable.[353] These concerns are addressed within the framework in terms of efficiency and regulatory chill. Moreover, the benefit of FDI flows to host states is addressed directly through inclusion as an element of the framework. The economic costs and benefits of alternative levels of protection for foreign investor were examined in the analysis of distributive consequences. Any benefits of investment treaty protections to home states – for example, increases in revenue from corporate taxation or greater dividends to home state shareholders – follow from these consequences.

---

[351] Guzman, 'Why LDCs Sign Treaties That Hurt Them: Explaining the Popularity of Bilateral Investment Treaties' (1998) 38 *Virginia Journal of International Law*, p. 643.
[352] See, Vandevelde, 'The BIT Program', p. 534.
[353] Yannaca-Small, '"Indirect Expropriation" and the "Right to Regulate" in International Investment Law' (2004) [online], p. 2; see Section 2.3.4.

3.9.2 Rationales for investment treaties that are unrelated to the consequences of investment treaty protections

There are two further arguments in the literature that seek to justify investment treaties on the basis of their consequences for the relationship between signatory states. It is useful to explain why these rationales for signing investment treaties, even if they were empirically verified, are not relevant to debate about the desirable level of investment treaties protection. The first such rationale is that investment treaties remove international investment disputes from the ambit of inter-governmental politics, thereby contributing to friendly relations between states.[354] For the purposes of this book, it is sufficient to note that it is the institution of investor-state arbitration that provides purported independence from inter-governmental politics.[355] Differences in the level of substantive protection to be applied in arbitral proceedings do not jeopardise the achievement of this objective.

A second, related, rationale for international economic agreements, potentially including investment treaties, is that they strengthen diplomatic ties and promote cooperation between states.[356] In the context of investment treaties, the argument would be that the process of negotiating and signing these treaties improves diplomatic relations, with positive consequences for other aspects of the relationship between signatory states. This rationale may go some way towards explaining why states continue to sign investment treaties, despite ambivalent evidence about their economic benefits. However, states can achieve the benefits of cooperation engendered by the negotiation and agreement process regardless of the level of protection they choose to confer within such treaties.

3.10 Conclusion

This chapter has constructed a framework for conceptualising, identifying and evaluating the consequences of different levels of investment treaty protection. These consequences can be divided into five categories: the

---

[354] Caruso, 'Private Law and State-Making in the Age of Globalization' 2006) 39 New York University Journal of International Law and Politics, p. 53.

[355] Shihata, 'Towards a Greater Depoliticization of Investment Disputes: The Roles Of ICSID and MIGA' (1986) 1 ICSID Review – FILJ, p. 24.

[356] Wai, 'Transnational Liftoff and Juridical Touchdown: The Regulatory Function of Private International Law in an Era of Globalization' (2002) 40 Columbia Journal of Transnational Law, p. 224.

effect of investment treaty protections on efficiency, the distribution of economic costs and benefits, flows of FDI into host states, the realisation of human rights and environmental conservation in host states, and respect for the rule of law in host states. More detailed inferences regarding the likely effect of different levels of protections on each category of consequences are summarised in point form at the end of each section. It is unnecessary to restate these conclusions here. These conclusions form the basis for the evaluation of different levels of protection that might be adopted in Chapter 6.

Without wishing to pre-empt the application of this framework in Chapter 6, it is worth drawing attention to two general insights that emerge from the evaluative framework. First, the 'economic' justifications for investment treaty protections are much weaker than is commonly assumed. Protections that are more favourable to the interests of foreign investors are not, self-evidently, associated with net economic benefits. In many cases, lower levels of protection will be more desirable from an economic perspective. Second, levels of protection in which liability turns on an examination of whether the government's conduct in question is consistent with the realisation of human rights, environmental conservation and the rule of law are more likely to lead to the realisation of these objectives than protections in which liability turns on the degree of interference with the interests of the investor.

Chapter 6 explores the implications of these general insights, and the other specific insights of this chapter, in greater detail. Having constructed a framework for evaluating different levels of protection in this chapter, the next task is to identify alternative levels of protection that might be adopted in investment treaties. Chapter 4 and Chapter 5 show that the FET and indirect expropriation provisions of investment treaties have been interpreted as entailing different levels of protection. The levels of protection implied by different arbitral decisions are outlined as options that might be explicitly adopted in future investment treaties or through the amendment of existing investment treaties.

4   Fair and equitable treatment

4.1 Introduction

The use of the phrase 'fair and equitable' in the field of foreign investment protection seems to originate from the 1948 Havana Charter of the International Trade Organisation (ITO), an institution that never came into existence.[1] Article 11(2) conferred power on the ITO to promote international agreements 'to ensure just and equitable treatment for the enterprise, skills, capital, arts and technology from one member country to another.'[2] Soon afterwards, the obligation to provide 'fair and equitable treatment' to both foreigners and their property began to appear in US treaties on Friendship Commerce and Navigation (FCN), the precursors to modern investment treaties.[3] Specific obligations to provide fair and equitable treatment (FET) to foreign property were then included in the 1959 Abs-Shawcross Draft Convention on Investments Abroad and the 1967 Organization for Economic Cooperation and Development (OECD) Draft Convention on the Protection of Foreign Property.[4] From these draft multilateral instruments, the obligation passed into the model bilateral investment treaties (BITs) of developed states.[5] The obligation to accord

---

[1] Cf. Paparinskis, *The International Minimum Standard and Fair and Equitable Treatment* (2013), p. 90, identifying use of the phrase 'fair and equitable' in economic treaties of the mid-1930s, albeit not in the context of investment protection.

[2] Havana Charter (24 March 1948) 62 UNTS 30, para. 143.

[3] Yannaca-Small, 'Fair and Equitable Treatment Standard in International Investment Law' (2004) [online], p. 4.

[4] Abs and Shawcross, 'Draft Convention on Investments Abroad' (1960) 9 *Journal of Public Law*, art. 1; OECD Draft Convention on the Protection of Foreign Property (1967), art. 1(a).

[5] Vasciannie, 'The Fair and Equitable Treatment Standard in International Investment Law and Practice' (1999) 70 *British Yearbook of International Law*, p. 112; Paparinskis, *The International Minimum Standard and Fair and Equitable Treatment*, p. 92.

foreign investment FET is now contained in the majority of investment treaties. Under many of the remaining investment treaties – those that do not contain a FET provision – a foreign investor could rely on an MFN clause to import the standard from another treaty.[6]

The FET standard has risen to prominence remarkably swiftly. Prior to 2000, no publicly available arbitral award applied the FET standard.[7] Since that time, investors have alleged breach of FET in almost every claim brought under an investment treaty.[8] Two of the standard's characteristics are particularly important in explaining its popularity among claimants. The first is that a government may breach the standard even if a foreign investment is treated as well (or better) than local investment.[9] The second is that an exceedingly broad range of government conduct can be challenged for failure to meet the standard.[10] During the past decade, breach of FET is also the claim with which foreign investors have the best record of success in arbitral proceedings.[11] For all these reasons, commentators now suggest that the standard is the most significant substantive protection contained in investment treaties.[12]

The obligation to provide 'fair and equitable treatment' could be read as requiring both fair treatment and equitable treatment. However, arbitral awards are unanimous in reading the two words as a single standard.[13] The legal content of this standard is not immediately obvious. Decisions are replete with observations that the wording of the standard is 'somewhat vague' and 'none too clear and precise.'[14] Indeed, some commentators have gone so far as to argue that FET is

[6] Newcombe and Paradell, *Law and Practice of Investment Treaties: Standards of Treatment* (2009, p. 255; *MTD* v. *Chile*, Award, para. 104; *Bayindir* v. *Pakistan*, Award, para. 157.

[7] Dolzer, 'Fair and Equitable Treatment: A Key Standard in Investment Treaties' (2005) 39 *The International Lawyer*, p. 88.

[8] Salacuse, *The Law of Investment Treaties* (2010), p. 218.

[9] Vasciannie, 'The Fair and Equitable Treatment Standard in International Investment Law and Practice', p. 105.

[10] Dolzer, 'Fair and Equitable Treatment', p. 90.

[11] Dolzer and Schreuer, *Principles of International Investment Law* (2nd edn, 2012), p. 130; Reed and Bray, 'Fair and Equitable Treatment: Fairly and Equitably Applied in Lieu of Unlawful Indirect Expropriation?' in Rovine (ed), *Contemporary Issues in International Arbitration and Mediation: The Fordham Papers 2007* (2008).

[12] Dolzer and Schreuer, *Principles of International Investment Law* (2nd edn), p. 130; Newcombe and Paradell, *Law and Practice of Investment Treaties*, p. 255.

[13] Dolzer and Schreuer, *Principles of International Investment Law* (2nd edn), p. 133.

[14] *CMS Gas* v. *Argentina*, Final Award, para. 273; *Enron* v. *Argentina*, Award, para. 256.

an intentionally vague term, designed to give adjudicators a quasi-legislative authority to articulate a variety of rules necessary to achieve the treaty's object and purpose in particular disputes.[15]

Regardless of whether treaty-makers intended to confer such broad authority on tribunals, it is clear that the text of investment treaties does not provide a great deal of guidance about what distinguishes fair and equitable treatment from unfair and inequitable treatment. This chapter seeks to understand and elucidate the different ways in which tribunals have interpreted the FET standard of investment treaties. I propose a basic taxonomy of the 'elements' of the FET standard and then employ an inductive methodology to locate arbitral reasoning within that taxonomy. The taxonomy divides decisions between those dealing with the protection of the legitimate expectations of the investor; decisions reviewing governmental conduct on procedural grounds; and decisions reviewing governmental conduct on substantive grounds. Although this taxonomy is original, it should not prove controversial. Almost every commentator has argued that FET comprises a number of elements, which include the protection of the investor's legitimate expectations and other doctrines providing for the procedural and substantive review of governmental conduct.[16] These elements function as quasi-independent components of the FET standard, in that a state can be found liable for breach of one element of the standard without any suggestion that it has breached any of the other elements.

Notwithstanding the use of common terminology – for example, reference to an investor's 'legitimate expectations' – I show that tribunals give markedly different legal content to the various elements of FET. I argue that arbitral decisions can be further divided into distinct interpretations of each element. In this chapter, I do not seek to determine which interpretation of each element of the FET standard is 'correct' (although I do return to this question in Section 7.3). Rather, each interpretation is sketched as a level of protection that might be explicitly incorporated

---

[15] Brower CH, 'Structure, Legitimacy, and NAFTA's Investment Chapter' (2003) 36 *Vanderbilt Journal of Transnational Law*, p. 63.

[16] E.g., Newcombe and Paradell, *Law and Practice of Investment Treaties*, p. 275; Dolzer and Schreuer, *Principles of International Investment Law* (2nd edn), p. 145; Choudhury, 'Defining Fair and Equitable Treatment in International Investment Law' (2005) 6 *The Journal of World Investment and Trade*, p. 316; Kläger, *'Fair and Equitable Treatment' in International Investment Law* (2011), pp. 117–8.

in future investment treaties. This analysis and classification is, in itself, a contribution to existing scholarship on the interpretation of the FET standard. The classification also provides the basis for Chapter 6, which applies the framework developed in Chapter 3 to evaluate these different levels of protection.

This chapter comprises seven substantive sections. Section 4.2 examines the differences in the wording of FET provisions between investment treaties and justifies the decision to treat arbitral decisions that interpret differently worded FET provisions as parts of a single body of jurisprudence. Section 4.3 explains and justifies the parameters of this chapter – I do not address decisions in which liability under the FET standard stems from the fact that treatment is discriminatory, or in bad faith, or a denial of justice. Section 4.4 argues that the remaining FET decisions can be divided into those concerned with three distinct elements of the FET standard: protection of an investor's legitimate expectations; procedural review of government conduct; and substantive review of government conduct. Section 4.5 examines tribunals' interpretation of the protection of legitimate expectations under the FET standard; Section 4.6 considers interpretation of the procedural review element; and Section 4.7 considers interpretation of the substantive review element. Each of these three sections argues that arbitral reasoning coalesces around a number of distinct interpretations of the element of FET in question.

4.2 Foundational doctrinal issues in the interpretation of the FET standard

4.2.1 The drafting of FET clauses

Although the obligation of states to treat foreign investment fairly and equitably is common to most investment treaties, there is significant variation in the way in which treaty clauses containing this provision are drafted. Following the classification proposed in the 2008 edition of Dolzer and Schreuer, three basic patterns of drafting can be identified.[17] First, the FET standard can be a freestanding obligation. For example, Article 3(1) of the China-Myanmar BIT provides simply that 'investments of investors of each Contracting Party shall all the time be accorded fair and equitable treatment in the territory of the other Contracting Party.'[18]

---

[17] Dolzer and Schreuer, *Principles of International Investment Law* (1st edn, 2008), p. 121.
[18] China-Myanmar BIT (12 December 2001).

Second, the FET standard can be included in a clause that contains a number of standards of treatment. For example, Article 10(1) of the ECT reads:

Each Contracting Party shall, in accordance with the provision of this Treaty, encourage and create stable, equitable favourable and transparent conditions for Investors of other Contracting Parties to make Investments in its Area. Such conditions shall include a commitment to accord at all times to Investments of Investors of other Contracting Parties fair and equitable treatment. Such Investments shall also enjoy the most constant protection and security and no Contracting Party shall in any way impair by unreasonable or discriminatory measures their management, maintenance, use, enjoyment or disposal.[19]

Third, the FET standard can be identified as a standard that is required by 'international law', where the basic obligation is to comply with an international law standard. For example, Article 1105(1) of the North American Free Trade Agreement (NAFTA) provides that '[e]ach Party shall accord investments of investors of another Party treatment in accordance with international law, including fair and equitable treatment and full protection and security.'[20]

These three basic drafting patterns could be further disaggregated to highlight nuances in treaty language. In a 2007 study, UNCTAD proposed dividing FET provisions into seven model types.[21] The UNCTAD taxonomy draws attention to the different standards that are sometimes included alongside FET within a single treaty clause and to different ways in which clauses refer to international law. A particularly important distinction is between provisions that require treatment according to international law including FET, and those that require FET including treatment 'in no case . . . less favourable than that required by international law'.[22] The latter terminology leaves open the possibility that the FET standard may require treatment beyond that required by international law, whereas the former does not.[23] Of course, questions remain as to what standard of treatment is required by international law and whether 'international law' refers only to customary international law.

---

[19] ECT, art. 10(1).   [20] NAFTA, art. 1105(1).
[21] UNCTAD, *Bilateral Investment Treaties 1995–2006, Trends in Investment Rule-Making* (2007), p. 28.
[22] ECT, art. 10(1).
[23] Vandevelde, *Bilateral Investment Treaties: History, Policy and Interpretation* (2010), p. 191; *Lemire* v. *Ukraine (II)*, Decision on Jurisdiction and Liability, para. 253.

4.2.2 FET: customary international law minimum standard or autonomous treaty standard?

Most academic analysis of textual nuance in FET provisions focuses on the significance of treaty text in determining whether a particular provision embodies the customary international law minimum standard for the treatment of aliens (IMS – international minimum standard) or whether it imposes an autonomous, presumably more exacting, treaty standard.[24] This debate is also central to arbitral analysis of textual variation. Often, an investor alleging breach of FET will argue that the FET provision in the applicable investment treaty imposes an autonomous standard, whereas the respondent state will argue that it imposes the IMS.[25] Thus, the issue put to the tribunal is the implication of a specific textual formulation for the determination of whether a given FET provision simply refers back to the IMS.[26] This determination is analytically prior to subsequent questions about the standard of conduct required by the IMS or by FET, to the extent it is construed as an autonomous standard.

The practical significance of the debate is that, historically, the IMS has been understood as a relatively lenient standard. The point of departure for discussion of the IMS is often the *Neer Claim*,[27] which found that

the treatment of an alien, in order to constitute an international delinquency should amount to an outrage, to bad faith, to wilful neglect of duty, or to an insufficiency of governmental action so far short of international standards that every reasonable and impartial man would readily recognise its insufficiency.[28]

(However, it is important to note that in *Neer*, the tribunal was reviewing Mexico's investigation of the murder of a foreign national, not the way in which a foreign investment had been treated.)[29]

The debate about the relationship between FET and the IMS has been going on for some time,[30] and a great deal of intellectual energy has been expended on it. The ascendant view is that, unless the text of the

---

[24] Kinnear, 'The Continuing Development of the Fair and Equitable Treatment Standard' in Bjorklund, Laird and Ripinsky (eds), *Investment Treaty Law: Current Issues III* (2009), p. 215.

[25] Tudor, *The Fair and Equitable Treatment Standard in the International Law of Foreign Investment* (2008), pp. 140, 142.

[26] E.g., *Siemens* v. *Argentina*, Award, para. 289.

[27] Yannaca-Small, 'Fair and Equitable Treatment Standard in International Investment Law', fn. 37.

[28] *Neer Claim*, Mexico-US General Claims Commission, RIAA, IV 60.

[29] *Mondev International* v. *United States*, Award, para. 115.

[30] See, Mann FA, 'British Treaties for the Promotion and Protection of Investments' 1981) 52 *British Yearbook of International Law*, p. 244.

investment treaty in question specifically provides otherwise, FET is an autonomous standard.[31] However, a minority view – buttressed by some supporting state practice and the recent scholarly work of Paparinskis – is that FET provisions should always be understood as references to the IMS.[32] This book does not attempt to resolve this doctrinal debate. Instead, this section provides a brief overview of tribunals' discussion of the relationship between treaty text, the FET standard and the IMS. The purpose of this review is to ascertain the extent to which tribunals' interpretation of the legal content of FET provisions is predetermined by their view of whether the FET provision in question embodies the IMS.

4.2.2.1 The IMS versus autonomous standard debate in arbitral awards

When confronted with investment treaties in which the FET provision is not explicitly limited to international law, few tribunals have found that FET refers to the IMS. In *Genin v. Estonia*, a case sometimes cited as authority for the proposition that FET does refer to the IMS,[33] the tribunal was confronted with a BIT that provided for FET including treatment not 'less favourable than that required by international law.'[34] The tribunal described the FET standard as 'an "international minimum standard" that is separate from domestic law' but did not make a specific finding that the FET standard referred to *the* customary international law minimum standard.[35] The tribunal in *MCI Power v. Ecuador* went further. Interpreting a similarly worded FET provision, it held that FET obliges states to provide the standard of treatment required by international law, and that 'international law' meant 'customary international law'.[36]

Most tribunals have come to the opposite conclusion – that, absent express textual linkage, the FET standard is not limited to the IMS. The

[31] Vasciannie, 'The Fair and Equitable Treatment Standard in International Investment Law and Practice', p. 144; Dolzer and Schreuer, *Principles of International Investment Law* (2nd edn), p. 137; Salacuse, *The Law of Investment Treaties*, p. 228; Muchlinski, *Multinational Enterprises and the Law* (2nd edn, 2007), p. 635.

[32] Paparinskis, *The International Minimum Standard and Fair and Equitable Treatment*, p. 162; Montt, *State Liability in Investment Treaty Arbitration* (2009), p. 306; Newcombe and Paradell, *Law and Practice of Investment Treaties*, p. 268.

[33] Salacuse, *The Law of Investment Treaties*, p. 223.   [34] *Alex Genin v. Estonia*, Award, para. 13.

[35] *Alex Genin v. Estonia*, Award, para. 367; *Saluka v. Czech Republic*, Partial Award, para. 295.

[36] *MCI Power v. Ecuador*, Award, para. 369; similarly, *Lauder v. Czech Republic*, Final Award, para. 292; *Suez and InterAgua v. Argentina*, Separate Opinion of Arbitrator Pedro Nikken, paras. 6–18.

relevant paragraph of the decision in *Bayindir* v. *Pakistan* is representative of these decisions and is worth quoting in full:

> As an initial matter, the Tribunal notes that Article 4 of the Pakistan-Switzerland BIT makes no reference to general international law. However, as already mentioned, customary international law and decisions of other tribunals may assist in the interpretation of this provision. This is particularly apposite here given that Article 4(2) of the Pakistan-Switzerland BIT simply states a general obligation of fair and equitable treatment. The Tribunal must therefore set forth the meaning of such a general obligation.[37]

Other decisions could be cited to similar effect.[38] Moreover, at least one tribunal has interpreted treaty language that might have been read as limiting FET to the IMS as imposing an autonomous standard. The tribunal in *Vivendi* v. *Argentina (II)* found that an obligation to provide 'fair and equitable treatment according to the principles of international law' set a standard that was more demanding than international law.[39]

Of the decisions that find that the applicable FET provision is autonomous, many go on to observe that the autonomous standard's content is 'not materially different from the content of the minimum standard of treatment in customary international law.'[40] The purported equivalence results from the fact that customary international law has evolved over time to a point where the IMS approximates FET,[41] rather than the 'watering down' of the treaty standard to the level of the IMS. According to these decisions, the evolution of the IMS has been driven, in part, by the proliferation of investment treaties. Investment treaty provisions, along with arbitral awards interpreting them, are the primary evidence cited for evolution.[42] Proceeding on the assumption that the two standards are similar, at least three more tribunals have found it

---

[37] *Bayindir* v. *Pakistan*, Award, para. 176.

[38] Including *Enron* v. *Argentina*, Award, para. 258; *National Grid* v. *Argentina*, Award, para. 167; *MTD* v. *Chile*, Award, paras. 110–12; *Plama* v. *Bulgaria*, Award, para. 163; *PSEG* v. *Turkey*, Award, para. 239; *Sempra Energy* v. *Argentina*, Award, para. 302; *Suez and Vivendi; AWG Group* v. *Argentina*, Decision on Liability, paras. 177–9; *Tecmed* v. *Mexico*, Award, para. 155; *Rompetrol* v. *Romania*, Award, para. 197.

[39] *Compañia de Aguas del Aconquija and Vivendi* v. *Argentina (II)*, Award, paras. 7.4.1, 7.4.6.

[40] *Biwater* v. *Tanzania*, Award, para. 592; similarly, *Azurix* v. *Argentina*, Award, para. 361; *CMS Gas* v. *Argentina*, Final Award, paras. 282–4; *Occidental* v. *Ecuador (I)*, Final Award, para. 190; *Rumeli* v. *Kazakhstan*, Award, para. 610; *Saluka* v. *Czech Republic*, Partial Award, para. 291; *Siemens* v. *Argentina*, Award, para. 299.

[41] *Azurix* v. *Argentina*, Award, paras. 361–2.   [42] *Ibid.*, paras. 361–2.

unnecessary to determine whether the FET provisions in question were autonomous or whether they were references to the IMS.[43]

The situation in cases when tribunals have confronted treaty language in which FET is explicitly limited to international law is more complex. Most claims of this sort have arisen under Article 1105(1) of NAFTA, which demands 'treatment in accordance with international law, including fair and equitable treatment'. Early decisions under Article 1105(1) took the view that this provision did not equate FET with *customary* international law.[44] However, in the context of NAFTA, the FET-IMS debate has now been resolved. In June 2001, the tribunal in *Pope & Talbot* v. *Canada* issued a partial award in which it interpreted Article 1105(1) as including obligations of fair treatment – 'fairness elements' – that were 'additive to the requirements of international law.'[45] The tribunal justified its 'additive' interpretation by reference to the NAFTA parties' BITs with other states.[46] In response the three NAFTA parties used the powers conferred on the NAFTA Free Trade Commission (FTC) to issue a binding interpretation of Article 1105(1), which affirms that Article 1105(1) does not go beyond the IMS.[47] The statement reads as follows:

B. Minimum Standard of Treatment in Accordance with International Law

1. Article 1105(1) prescribes the customary international law minimum standard of treatment of aliens as the minimum standard of treatment to be afforded to investments of investors of another Party.

2. The concepts of 'fair and equitable treatment' and 'full protection and security' do not require treatment in addition to or beyond that which is required by the customary international law minimum standard of treatment of aliens.

3. A determination that there has been a breach of another provision of the NAFTA, or of a separate international agreement, does not establish that there has been a breach of Article 1105(1).[48]

Subsequent tribunals have accepted that they are bound by the FTC interpretation of Article 1105(1).[49] BITs and free trade agreements (FTAs) signed

---

[43] *Duke Energy* v. *Ecuador*, Award, paras. 333–7; *BG Group* v. *Argentina*, Final Award, para. 291; *Impregilo* v. *Argentina*, Award, para. 289.

[44] *SD Myers* v. *Canada*, Partial Award, para. 264; similarly, *Metalclad* v. *Mexico*, Award, para. 76; although this portion of the *Metalclad* decision was overturned on review, *The United Mexican States* v. *Metalclad Corporation* 2001 BCSC 664, paras. 68–72.

[45] *Pope & Talbot* v. *Canada*, Award on the Merits of Phase 2, para. 110.

[46] Ibid., paras. 110–8.   [47] NAFTA, art. 1131(2).

[48] Notes of Interpretation of Certain Chapter 11 Provisions (31 July 2001).

[49] *Mondev International* v. *United States*, Award, para. 120; *ADF Group* v. *United States*, Award, para. 177.

by the United States and Canada since 2002 also contain, within the treaty text, statements based on the FTC interpretation.[50] Questions remain as to the standard of conduct required under the IMS and how this standard relates to autonomous FET obligations in other investment treaties. In answering the former question, the majority of NAFTA tribunals have begun by observing that the IMS is an evolving standard, concurring with the view of tribunals under other investment treaties. The tribunal in *Mondev v. US* noted a development in 'both the substantive and procedural rights of the individual in international law' and the broad spread of investment treaties containing FET provisions.[51] It concluded that 'the content of the minimum standard today cannot be limited to the content of customary international law as recognised in arbitral decisions in the 1920s.'[52] Similar statements have been made by many other NAFTA tribunals.[53] Only the tribunal in *Glamis Gold v. US* found that the IMS had not evolved since the 1920s – or, more precisely, that, although conduct that may once have seemed acceptable might now be deemed outrageous, the legal standard itself could still only be breached by conduct that was 'outrageous', egregious' or 'shocking'.[54]

Most NAFTA tribunals have found it unnecessary to determine whether the IMS has evolved to such an extent that it has converged with the standard set by autonomous FET provisions.[55] It seems that only two tribunals have made findings squarely on the point. In *Merrill & Ring v. Canada*, the tribunal held that the two standards were equivalent, arguing that to allow any difference in the scope of the IMS and autonomous FET provisions 'would be to countenance an unacceptable double standard.'[56] In contrast, the tribunal in *Glamis Gold*, having adopted a restrictive interpretation of the IMS, found that it was bound to ignore the decisions of tribunals interpreting autonomous FET provisions.[57]

---

[50] E.g., Dominican Republic-Central America-United States of America Free Trade Agreement (5 August 2004) (CAFTA), art. 10.5; interpreted and applied in *Railroad Development Corporation v. Guatemala*, Award, para. 212.

[51] *Mondev International v. United States*, Award, paras. 116–17.

[52] *ADF Group v. United States*, Award, para. 123.

[53] *ADF Group v. United States*, Award, para. 179; *Waste Management v. Mexico (II)*, Final Award, para. 92; *GAMI Investments v. Mexico*, Final Award, para. 95; *Merrill & Ring Forestry v. Canada*, Award, paras. 205–13; *Chemtura v. Canada*, Award, para. 121. Similarly, *Railroad Development Corporation v. Guatemala*, Award, para. 218.

[54] *Glamis Gold v. United States*, Award, para. 616.

[55] E.g., *ADF Group v. United States*, Award, para. 183.

[56] *Merrill & Ring Forestry v. Canada*, Award, para. 213.

[57] *Glamis Gold v. United States*, Award, para. 611.

A further dimension to the FET-IMS debate is the claim that FET is a general principle of law.[58] The argument is that general principles of law are a legitimate source of guidance in interpreting treaty provisions because they are among the 'relevant rules of international law applicable in the relations between the parties' referred to by Article 31 of the Vienna Convention of the Law of Treaties (VCLT).[59] As such, tribunals might be justified in interpreting differently worded treaty provisions according to the common, underlying general principles which they embody.[60]

For the purpose of this book, it is not necessary to resolve the doctrinal question of whether FET is a general principle of law and, if so, what the implications for treaty interpretation would be. It is sufficient to observe that the view that FET is a general principle of law has not yet taken hold among tribunals.[61] Only Professor Wälde's dissent in *Thunderbird v. Mexico* endorses this view and, even then, only with respect to protection of the investor's legitimate expectations.[62] Thus, the foundational question for this chapter remains the relationship among treaty text, the IMS and the interpretation of FET provisions.[63]

4.2.3 Is it legitimate to abstract from textual variation in FET provisions in an analysis of FET decisions?

The question of whether it is permissible to analyse decisions interpreting different FET provisions as a group, or as uniquely tied to a particular treaty text, is particularly pressing when it comes to NAFTA and other recent treaties that follow NAFTA in limiting FET to the IMS.[64] Although some academic commentary does treat NAFTA and non-NAFTA investment

---

[58] Tudor, *The Fair and Equitable Treatment Standard in the International Law of Foreign Investment*, p. 103; similarly, Schill, 'Fair and Equitable Treatment, the Rule of Law, and Comparative Public Law' in Schill (ed), *International Investment Law and Comparative Public Law* (2010), p. 175.

[59] Montt, *State Liability in Investment Treaty Arbitration*, p. 304; *Golder v. the United Kingdom*, Judgment 21 February 1975, para. 35.

[60] Schill, 'Book Reviews' (2009) 20 *European Journal of International Law*, p. 237.

[61] The relationship between customary international law and general principles of law is briefly discussed in *ADF Group v. United States*, Award, para. 185; *Enron v. Argentina*, Award, para. 257; *Merrill & Ring Forestry v. Canada*, Award, para. 187.

[62] *International Thunderbird Gaming v. Mexico*, Separate Opinion, paras. 28–30; similarly, Snodgrass, 'Protecting Investors' Legitimate Expectations: Recognizing and Delimiting a General Principle' (2006) 21 *ICSID Review – Foreign Investment Law Journal*, p. 11. There are, however, doubts about whether this view is correct: see Potesta, 'Legitimate Expectations in Investment Treaty Law' (2013) 28 *ICSID Review*, p. 98.

[63] Newcombe and Paradell, *Law and Practice of Investment Treaties*, p. 271.

[64] E.g., CAFTA, art. 10.5.

treaty decisions as separate lines of jurisprudence,[65] most text writers treat all investment treaty decisions on FET as a single body of cases.[66] In this chapter, I follow the dominant practice in academic writing – treating all FET decisions as a single body of cases, while explicitly noting the cases that were decided under a treaty, such as NAFTA, that limits FET to the IMS. This section explains why such an abstraction from textual variation is justified.

The primary justification for treating FET decisions as a group is the high degree of consensus among tribunals that FET embodies a common set of legal elements – protection of the investor's legitimate expectations and protection from procedural unfairness, substantive unreasonableness and denial of justice in the courts of a host state.[67] This consensus in the elements of the standard exists, notwithstanding differences in treaty text. Relative agreement as to the common legal elements of FET makes it sensible to talk of *an* FET standard and provides a basis for the comparison of the reasoning of different tribunals interpreting this standard.[68]

In this vein, Vandevelde goes so far as to assert:

International arbitral awards have been uniform in their interpretation of the standard, regardless of the context in which it appears, whether alone, combined with other general absolute standards of treatment, linked with non-discrimination standards, or linked with customary international law.[69]

His statement is too sweeping. In subsequent sections, this chapter shows that there is considerable variation in the way in which tribunals have understood the meaning of various elements of the FET standard.

---

[65] Dolzer and von Walter, 'Fair and Equitable Treatment – Lines of Jurisprudence on Customary Law' in Ortino, Sheppard and Warner (eds), *Investment Treaty Law: Current Issues Volume 1* (2006), p. 103; Kinnear, 'The Continuing Development of the Fair and Equitable Treatment Standard', p. 223.

[66] Tudor, *The Fair and Equitable Treatment Standard in the International Law of Foreign Investment*, p. 154; Newcombe and Paradell, *Law and Practice of Investment Treaties*, p. 275; Grierson-Weiler and Laird, 'Standards of Treatment' in Muchlinski, Ortino and Schreuer (eds), *The Oxford Handbook of International Investment Law* (2008), p. 272; Dolzer and Schreuer, *Principles of International Investment Law* (2nd edn), p. 145; Salacuse, *The Law of Investment Treaties*, p. 228; McLachlan, Shore and Weiniger, *International Investment Arbitration* (2007), p. 226; Vandevelde, *Bilateral Investment Treaties*, p. 194.

[67] E.g., Dolzer and Schreuer, *Principles of International Investment Law* (2nd edn), p. 145; Kläger, '*Fair and Equitable Treatment*' in International Investment Law, pp. 117–18.

[68] Note the similarity between the analysis of legitimate expectations in the NAFTA case, *International Thunderbird Gaming v. Mexico*, Arbitral Award, para. 147, and the US-Argentina BIT case, *Enron v. Argentina*, Award, para. 262.

[69] Vandevelde, *Bilateral Investment Treaties*, p. 194.

However, for the purposes of this inquiry, the crucial point is that the pattern of variation in interpretation of FET provisions is not predetermined by nuances in treaty text, nor by tribunals' views about the relationship between FET and the IMS.

A second justification for treating FET decisions as a group is that NAFTA contains a MFN clause. Other tribunals have interpreted similarly worded MFN clauses in a way that permits a claimant to rely on an FET clause contained in a BIT between the respondent state and a third state.[70] Both Mexico and the United States have signed BITs that post-date the entry into force of NAFTA[71] and contain FET provisions that are not explicitly tied to the IMS.[72] It is certainly arguable that a NAFTA claimant could have recourse to one of these autonomous FET clauses via NAFTA's MFN clause, rendering any difference in the FET standard between NAFTA and other investment treaties meaningless. Surprisingly, it seems that the NAFTA MFN clause has only been invoked once in this manner. In that case, the tribunal was able to avoid the issue on the grounds that it would make no difference to the outcome of the case.[73]

A third justification for treating FET decisions as a group is the convergence of the IMS with autonomous understandings of FET. Recall that, among NAFTA decisions, the predominant view is that the IMS is evolving and that this evolution is, to some extent, influenced by the proliferation of investment treaties and arbitral decisions under them.[74] Tribunals outside NAFTA agree with this position, and a significant number of them suggest that the IMS has evolved to the point where it is equivalent with autonomous FET treaty provisions.[75] These observations are not sufficient to definitively resolve debate about the relationship between FET and the IMS, but they do highlight the close relationship between decisions interpreting different FET provisions.

A final justification for treating all FET decisions as a single group is the cross-citation of decisions of tribunals constituted under different treaties. Tudor, for example, suggests that NAFTA and BIT tribunals freely

---

[70] *MTD* v. *Chile*, Award, para. 104; *Bayindir* v. *Pakistan*, Award, para. 157.
[71] Art. 1108(6) of NAFTA recognises an exception to the MFN provision for more favourable treatment accorded by treaties listed in the Schedule to Annex IV. Each NAFTA party has an exception for more favourable treatment accorded by treaties signed or in force prior to the NAFTA agreement.
[72] US-Estonia BIT (19 April 1994), art. 2(3); Netherlands-Mexico BIT (13 May 1998), art. 3(1). On the other hand, Canada's BITs from the mid-1990s up to the redrafting of the Canadian model BIT in 2004 require 'fair and equitable treatment in accordance with the principles of international law': e.g., Canada-Lebanon BIT (11 April 1997), art. 2(2)a.
[73] *Chemtura* v. *Canada*, Award, para. 235.   [74] See Section 4.2.2.1.   [75] See Section 4.2.2.1.

cite each other's decisions.[76] This is not strictly true. Many tribunals under other investment treaties do cite NAFTA decisions. However, only three of the seventeen NAFTA decisions that interpret and apply article 1105(1) cite the decisions of investor-state tribunals from beyond NAFTA.[77] Nevertheless, the regular citation of NAFTA decisions in non-NAFTA awards is both a cause and evidence of the co-evolution of FET jurisprudence. This observation buttresses the decision to treat FET decisions as single group.

4.2.4 Other standards equivalent to the FET standard

Although use of the term 'fair and equitable treatment' is remarkably widespread, occasionally investment treaties employ some other synonym for the word 'fair'. Tribunals have not given these variations legal significance. In *Parkerings v. Lithuania*, the tribunal confronted a treaty provision that required 'equitable and reasonable treatment'. It found that this provision was identical to the FET standard.[78] In the consolidated claims of *Suez and InterAgua v. Argentina* and *Suez and Vivendi; AWG Group v. Argentina*, the tribunal was required to apply the French-Argentine BIT. The treaty provided – in its French and Spanish language version respectively – for 'un traitement juste et équitable' and 'un tratamiento justo y equitativo'.[79] The decision (rendered in English) translated the treaty provision as an obligation of 'just and equitable treatment'. It went on to hold that there was no difference in meaning between this provision and the FET standard.[80] The analysis in this chapter includes arbitral decisions interpreting treaty terms that tribunals understand to be *identical* to FET.

4.3 Parameters: the scope of the FET standard and the limitations of this chapter

The FET standard allows investors to challenge the treatment of their investments by any arm of the host state's government in a wide range of circumstances. Arbitral tribunals have developed different doctrines to

---

[76] Tudor, *The Fair and Equitable Treatment Standard in the International Law of Foreign Investment*, p. 154.

[77] Author's citation count, noting *Chemtura* v. *Canada*, Award, para. 137; *GAMI Investments* v. *Mexico*, Final Award, para. 88; *International Thunderbird Gaming* v. *Mexico*, Arbitral Award, para. 194.

[78] *Parkerings* v. *Lithuania*, Award, para. 278.

[79] *Suez and InterAgua* v. *Argentina*, Decision on Liability, para. 176; *Suez and Vivendi; AWG Group* v. *Argentina*, Decision on Liability, para. 183.

[80] *Suez and InterAgua* v. *Argentina*, Decision on Liability, para. 176.

deal with different categories of cases under the standard. In this chapter, I do not address the full range of circumstances in which the FET standard has been applied. Three sets of decisions are excluded: those dealing with treatment of foreign investment by a host state's judicial system, those dealing with liability under the FET standard for discriminatory conduct and those dealing with situations in which a state has embarked on a deliberate and coordinated campaign to ruin an investment. These excluded circumstances correspond roughly with those that would be covered by the doctrines of denial of justice, national treatment and bad faith respectively. Each of these limitations excludes only a small minority of FET cases. Setting these parameters allows this chapter to go into greater depth in analysing the remaining cases – those in which claimants have argued that a state's legislative or administrative actions have breached FET, understood as an objective, non-contingent standard. This section provides a brief description of each of these parameters and explains why, in the context of this book, these limitations are justified.

4.3.1 Conduct of a state's judicial institutions that breaches the FET standard

There is no doubt that the treatment of foreign investment by a host state's judicial system can breach the FET standard. In determining whether the improper conduct of judicial proceedings constitutes a breach of FET, tribunals have looked to the customary international law principles governing the treatment of aliens by foreign courts – the principles of denial of justice.[81] Investment treaty tribunals agree that, with respect to the conduct of judicial proceedings, the FET standard does not go beyond what is required by the doctrine of denial of justice.[82] This position is also endorsed in academic commentary.[83]

The principles of denial of justice are highly specific to the treatment of a foreigner by the judicial institutions of a host state. A full exposition of these principles would require a review of customary international law on the subject, going well beyond the decisions of investment treaty

---

[81] On the principles of denial of justice, see Paulsson, *Denial of Justice in International Law* (2005).

[82] *Mondev International* v. *United States*, Award, para. 126; *Jan de Nul* v. *Egypt*, Award, para. 188; *Víctor Pey Casado* v. *Chile*, Laudo, para. 657.

[83] Paparinskis, *The International Minimum Standard and Fair and Equitable Treatment*, p. 211; Tudor, *The Fair and Equitable Treatment Standard in the International Law of Foreign Investment*, p. 160; Salacuse, *The Law of Investment Treaties*, p. 241.

tribunals.[84] Moreover, consideration of the level of protection that investment treaties should provide from losses caused by the judiciary of a host
state (such as losses caused by unfavourable court judgments or delays
in judicial proceedings) would raise different issues to the examination
of the level of protection that investment treaties should provide from
losses caused by legislative and administrative action. For both reasons,
I exclude analysis and evaluation of the interpretation of the principles
of denial of justice, so as to focus in greater detail on state liability for
legislative and administrative action.

4.3.2 Conduct that breaches the FET standard because it is discriminatory

A government may breach the FET standard even if a foreign investment
is treated as well (or better) than local investment.[85] However, many tribunals have observed that discrimination against a foreign investment
may also constitute a breach of the FET standard.[86] Some tribunals even
go far as to suggest that nationality-based discrimination against a foreign
investment will always breach the FET standard.[87]

The assessment of whether impugned treatment is discriminatory is
seldom decisive in the application of the FET standard. Two decisions
serve to illustrate this point. In *Eureko* v. *Poland*, the investor challenged
the failure of the Polish government to sell it a second tranche of shares
in a Polish bank, as had been agreed in a privatisation contract between
the investor and the government. In *Eastern Sugar* v. *Czech Republic*, the
investor challenged the reallocation of the national sugar production
quota that followed the European Union's (EU) reduction of the Czech
national quota; the reallocation reduced Eastern Sugar's quota by more
than the entire reduction in the national quota.[88] In both cases, the tribunals accepted that it was likely that the governments' actions had been
motivated by nationalist or protectionist sentiment.[89] However, the reasoning of these decisions confirms that these inferences of discriminatory

---

[84] For a full treatment of these issues, see Paparinskis, *The International Minimum Standard and Fair and Equitable Treatment*, pp. 182–217; Paulsson, *Denial of Justice in International Law*.
[85] Vasciannie, 'The Fair and Equitable Treatment Standard in International Investment Law and Practice', p. 105.
[86] *Saluka* v. *Czech Republic*, Partial Award, para. 292; *Waste Management* v. *Mexico (II)*, Final Award, para. 98; cf. *Grand River* v. *United States*, Award, para. 208.
[87] *Noble Ventures* v. *Romania*, Award, paras. 180–2; *Parkerings* v. *Lithuania*, Award, para. 287; *CMS Gas* v. *Argentina*, Final Award, para. 290.
[88] *Eastern Sugar* v. *Czech Republic*, Partial Award, para. 291.
[89] *Eureko* v. *Poland*, Partial Award, para. 233; *Eastern Sugar* v. *Czech Republic*, Partial Award, paras. 314, 338.

motive were not decisive. In *Eureko*, liability rested on the fact that the state had repudiated the fundamental terms of the privatisation contract with the investor;[90] in *Eastern Sugar*, liability was based on the fact that the state could not provide *any* rational justification for the way in which it had reallocated the sugar quota.[91]

There are only two cases in which treatment that arguably would have satisfied the FET standard (in the absence of discrimination) was found to breach the standard on account of being discriminatory. One of these cases is *SD Myers*, in which the tribunal simply stated that breach of the NAFTA national treatment provision entailed breach of the FET standard on the facts in question.[92] The subsequent FTC Interpretation of Article 1105(1) makes it unlikely that the case would now be decided in the same way.[93] The other case is *Saluka v. Czech Republic*, a case distinguished by the fact that the tribunal subsumed its discussion of breach of the national treatment provision of the BIT into its analysis of FET.[94]

It is easy to understand why discrimination is seldom determinative of FET cases. Most investment treaties contain a specific provision dealing with discriminatory treatment – either a national treatment clause or a provision prohibiting 'arbitrary or discriminatory measures', or sometimes both.[95] An investor that was able to show that it had suffered discrimination would be able to succeed in a claim under one of these provisions. An additional basis of liability under the FET standard would then be of little consequence. This was the situation in *SD Myers*. On the other hand, an investor that was unable to show that it had suffered discrimination, often due to difficulties in identifying a similarly situated comparator, would be left to advance its claim under the non-contingent elements of the FET standard. This was the situation in the *Parkerings v. Lithuania, Loewen v. US, BG v. Argentina* and *CMS Gas v. Argentina* awards, among others.[96]

Because allegations of discrimination are seldom decisive in FET cases, this chapter is justified in omitting analysis of discriminatory treatment, so as to focus on the non-contingent elements of the FET standard.

[90] *Eureko v. Poland*, Partial Award, paras. 232–5.
[91] *Eastern Sugar v. Czech Republic*, Partial Award, paras. 333–7.
[92] *SD Myers v. Canada*, Partial Award, paras. 264, 268.
[93] Notes of Interpretation of Certain Chapter 11 Provisions (31 July 2001).
[94] *Saluka v. Czech Republic*, Partial Award, para. 283.
[95] Newcombe and Paradell, *Law and Practice of Investment Treaties*, p. 290.
[96] *Parkerings v. Lithuania*, Award, para. 290; *Loewen v. United States*, Award, para. 140; *BG Group v. Argentina*, Final Award, para. 357; *CMS Gas v. Argentina*, Final Award, para. 295.

However, state liability for discriminatory treatment under investment treaties remains an important issue, and there is not yet consensus among tribunals about the interpretation of non-discrimination obligations.[97] The framework developed in Chapter 3 could be used to evaluate the varying levels of protection implied by different interpretations of non-discrimination provisions of investment treaties. For example, it could be used to evaluate different understandings of the requirement that the foreign investor and the domestic investor to which it is compared be 'in like circumstances'. The framework could also be used to evaluate whether various justifications for differences in treatment should prevent a finding of liability against the host state.

4.3.3 Conduct that breaches the standard because it is in bad faith

Tribunals and academic commentary agree that bad faith – governmental conduct motivated by the conscious intent to harm an investment – will breach the FET standard.[98] An allegation of bad faith requires a tribunal to examine the subjective intentions that motivate state conduct. For example, in *Tokios Tokelés* v. *Ukraine*, the claimant alleged that the Ukrainian state mounted a coordinated campaign to punish it 'for its impertinence in printing [political] materials opposed to the regime'.[99] The tribunal accepted that such a campaign would breach the FET standard, although, on the facts, it found that the claimant was unable to establish that the state's conduct was motivated by the objective of retaliation.[100]

Tokios Tokelés is broadly representative of cases in which bad faith is alleged. Although tribunals occasionally suggest that the impugned conduct of a state approaches bad faith,[101] outright findings of bad faith are rare.[102] This is due to the difficulty of proving the subjective intention of the host state.[103] To succeed in a claim based on allegations of bad faith, an investor must be able to establish that the ruin of an investment was the specific *intention* of coordinated governmental conduct, rather than

---

[97] Ortino, 'Non-Discriminatory Treatment in Investment Disputes' in Dupuy, Francioni and Petersmann (eds), *Human Rights in International Investment Law and Arbitration* (2009), p. 351.

[98] *Frontier Petroleum* v. *Czech Republic*, Final Award, para. 300; *Waste Management* v. *Mexico (II)*, Final Award, para. 138.

[99] *Tokios Tokelés* v. *Ukraine*, Award, para. 123.   [100] Ibid., para. 136.

[101] *Azurix* v. *Argentina*, Award, para. 376; *Petrobart* v. *Kyrgyzstan*, Arbitral Award, p. 76; *Compañia de Aguas del Aconquija and Vivendi* v. *Argentina (II)*, Award, paras. 7.4.19, 7.4.45–46.

[102] *Waste Management* v. *Mexico (II)*, Final Award, para. 139; *Bayindir* v. *Pakistan*, Award, para. 258; *Chemtura* v. *Canada*, Award, para. 138.

[103] *Bayindir* v. *Pakistan*, Award, para. 223; *Chemtura* v. *Canada*, Award, para. 137.

simply a result of government conduct.[104] Of the decisions rendered since 2005, only *Anatolie Stati and others* v. *Kazakhstan*, *Cargill* v. *Mexico* and *Vivendi II* could, arguably, be read as relying on a finding of bad faith.[105] Investors invariably find it easier to succeed by framing their claim under some other element of the FET standard. On this basis, this chapter is justified in focusing on the elements of the FET standard that are usually legally determinative.

4.4 The elements of FET

This section presents and justifies a taxonomy of the elements of the FET standard, which provides a useful heuristic device for understanding arbitral decisions applying the FET standard. This section argues that arbitral reasoning is best understood by distinguishing decisions (or, more commonly, parts of decisions) dealing with the protection of the legitimate expectations of the investor, those reviewing governmental conduct on procedural grounds, and those reviewing governmental conduct on substantive grounds. This is a functional taxonomy in that it looks to the structure of arbitral reasoning, rather than whether arbitral decisions adopt common terminology. In arbitral reasoning, these three elements function as conceptually distinct, although potentially overlapping, bases for liability of the FET standard.

Two objections might be raised to dividing FET decisions into those dealing with different elements of the standard. The first is the argument that all FET decisions can be explained by a single, unified jurisprudential theory – that is, the standard should be understood as having only one element. The second is the argument that any apparent inconsistency in legal reasoning between arbitral decisions can be explained by the different factual situations that tribunals were addressing in each case – that is, the standard should be understood as having *no* elements capable of restatement in the abstract. This section discusses and addresses each objection in turn.

4.4.1 The taxonomy of the elements of FET used in this chapter

Since 2006, protection of the investor's legitimate expectations has emerged as the most significant element of the FET standard. The

[104] *Tokios Tokelés* v. *Ukraine*, Award, para. 136.
[105] *Anatoile Stati and others* v. *Kazakhstan*, Award, para. 1095; *Cargill* v. *Mexico*, Award, para. 298; *Compañia de Aguas del Aconquija and Vivendi* v. *Argentina (II)*, Award, paras. 7.4.19, 7.4.45–46.

doctrine of legitimate expectations has been sufficiently widely accepted that arbitral decisions now spend more time examining the contours of the doctrine than determining whether compliance with the doctrine is an element of FET.[106] This shared recognition of legitimate expectations as an element of FET is reflected in academic commentary.[107] Despite differences of opinion about the scope of the doctrine, the common understanding of arbitral decisions and commentators is that a breach of legitimate expectations is *sufficient* to establish liability.[108] This book, like most contemporary commentary, identifies legitimate expectations as an element of the FET standard.[109] This element of the standard, and arbitral tribunals' differing understandings of it, is examined in Section 4.5.

Classifying the remaining FET decisions is more challenging. Tribunals employ a range of terminology to describe situations in which a state's liability for breach of the FET standard does not rest on violation of an investor's legitimate expectations. Such terms include transparency, stability, reasonableness, consistency, (non-)arbitrariness and due process. The use of common terms is not always consistent between decisions. For example, *Maffezini* v. *Spain* held that a Spanish state entity's withdrawal of funds from an investor's bank account breached the FET standard because of the 'lack of transparency'.[110] However, the basis of liability was that the investor had not consented to the withdrawal, not that the state had failed to disclose the withdrawal.[111] The tribunal's reasoning is difficult to reconcile with the way in which the word 'transparency' is used in other

---

[106] E.g., *International Thunderbird Gaming* v. *Mexico*, Arbitral Award, para. 147; *International Thunderbird Gaming* v. *Mexico*, Separate Opinion, para. 4.

[107] Schreuer and Kriebaum, 'At What Time Must Legitimate Expectations Exist?' in Werner and Ali (eds), *A Liber Amicorum: Thomas Wälde – Law beyond Conventional Thought* (2010); von Walter, 'The Investor's Expectations in International Investment Arbitration' in Reinisch and Knahr (eds), *International Investment Law in Context* (2008), p. 173; Snodgrass, 'Protecting Investors' Legitimate Expectations', p. 1.

[108] Cf. Paparinskis, *The International Minimum Standard and Fair and Equitable Treatment*, p. 227, recognising that most recent FET decisions endorse the view that a breach of legitimate expectations is sufficient to establish liability, but doubting whether this view is correct.

[109] Newcombe and Paradell, *Law and Practice of Investment Treaties*, p. 279; Dolzer and Schreuer, *Principles of International Investment Law* (2nd edn), p. 145; Tudor, *The Fair and Equitable Treatment Standard in the International Law of Foreign Investment*, p. 163; Kläger, 'Fair and Equitable Treatment' in International Investment Law, p. 164; Diehl, *The Core Standard in International Investment Law: Fair and Equitable Treatment* (2012), p. 366.

[110] *Maffezini* v. *Spain*, Award, para. 83.

[111] *Maffezini* v. *Spain*, Award, para. 75; Vandevelde, *Bilateral Investment Treaties*, p. 404; Newcombe and Paradell, *Law and Practice of Investment Treaties*, p. 293.

decisions.[112] Such difficulties in classifying the remaining FET decisions are reflected in academic writing. Although all commentators propose some division of FET decisions, no two text writers propose an identical system of classification.[113]

In light of the range of terminology used in arbitral awards, I propose a *functional* division of the FET decisions that do not relate to an investor's legitimate expectations. I distinguish between decisions which examine whether the state has followed fair procedures and those which examine the substantive justification for government measures that have affected an investor.[114] The former category encompasses concepts such as transparency, lawfulness and procedural fairness. The latter encompasses concepts such as rationality, reasonableness and proportionality when they refer to the substance of an impugned measure. This is a functional distinction, in that it looks to the structure of reasoning that tribunals use to determine liability, rather than to whether decisions employ common terminology. For example, arbitrariness connotes procedural review when it is used to mean 'a wilful disregard of due process of law'[115] and substantive review when it is used to mean conduct 'not related to legitimate policy objectives'.[116]

Although many FET decisions involve both substantive and procedural review, it appears that both are capable of operating as independent elements of the FET standard. Several tribunals have held that an irrational measure may breach the standard without any criticism of the procedures by which it was adopted and applied,[117] and an investor that is subjected to unfair administrative procedures may succeed in a claim even if the

---

[112] *LG&E Energy* v. *Argentina*, Decision on Liability, para. 128, arguing that transparency implies that 'all relevant legal requirements . . . should be capable of being readily known'.

[113] Cf. Newcombe and Paradell, *Law and Practice of Investment Treaties*, p. 275; Dolzer and Schreuer, *Principles of International Investment Law* (2nd edn), p. 145; Tudor, *The Fair and Equitable Treatment Standard in the International Law of Foreign Investment*, p. 154; Salacuse, *The Law of Investment Treaties*, p. 218; Vandevelde, *Bilateral Investment Treaties*, pp. 190, 234; McLachlan, Shore and Weiniger, *International Investment Arbitration*, p. 226; Kläger, 'Fair and Equitable Treatment' in International Investment Law, pp. 117–18.

[114] The recent decision in *Micula* v. *Romania* adopts essentially the same distinction: *Micula* v. *Romania*, Award, para. 520. Vandevelde and Kläger have also drawn similar distinctions: Vandevelde, 'A Unified Theory of Fair and Equitable Treatment' (2010) 43 *International Law and Politics*, p. 49; Kläger, 'Fair and Equitable Treatment' in International Investment Law, p. 154.

[115] *Elettronica Sicula SpA (United States of America* v. *Italy)* Judgment of 20 July 1989, para. 128.

[116] Vandevelde, *Bilateral Investment Treaties*, p. 204.

[117] E.g., *Eastern Sugar* v. *Czech Republic*, Partial Award, paras. 33–7.

decisions ultimately taken by the administrative body are reasonable.[118] These two elements of the FET standard, including the degree to which they function as independent grounds of liability, are examined in Sections 4.6 and 4.7, respectively.

4.4.2 A unified jurisprudential theory of FET?

There have been various attempts to offer a unified jurisprudential theory that would explain and justify the full range of FET decisions. Some commentators suggest that the standard embodies the principle of good faith;[119] others that it embodies the rule of law.[120] Writing in dissent in *Thunderbird*, Professor Wälde argued that the standard embodies norms of good governance.[121] Kläger has recently added to this debate with the argument that the FET standard embodies 'justice'.[122] There are difficulties with all four theories.[123]

The suggestion that FET is grounded in the principle of good faith is difficult to reconcile with the observation that 'FET is an objective standard that does not depend on whether the Respondent has proceeded in good faith or not.'[124] Theories based on the rule of law and good governance must address the fact that these concepts are contestable. Even if a common understanding of the meaning of these concepts could be reached, they sit uneasily with awards holding that a change of government policy may breach the FET standard, even though the change was made and applied through lawful procedures and was the 'result of reasoned judgment rather than simple disregard of the rule of law.'[125]

The theory that the FET standard embodies justice is both the most ambitious and the most problematic attempt to provide an overarching rationalisation of arbitral jurisprudence. Drawing on the work of Thomas Franck, Kläger identifies six competing objectives implicated by

---

[118] *Pope & Talbot v. Canada*, Award on the Merits of Phase 2, para. 181.

[119] Grierson-Weiler and Laird, 'Standards of Treatment', p. 272; see also *Tecmed v. Mexico*, Award, paras. 154–5; *Siemens v. Argentina*, Award, para. 308.

[120] Schill, 'Fair and Equitable Treatment, the Rule of Law, and Comparative Public Law', p. 154; Vandevelde, 'A Unified Theory of Fair and Equitable Treatment', p. 48; Diehl, *The Core Standard in International Investment Protection*, p. 337.

[121] *International Thunderbird Gaming v. Mexico*, Separate Opinion, para. 13.

[122] Kläger, *'Fair and Equitable Treatment' in International Investment Law*, p. 153.

[123] Newcombe and Paradell, *Law and Practice of Investment Treaties*, p. 279.

[124] *Occidental v. Ecuador (I)*, Final Award, para. 186.

[125] *LG&E Energy v. Argentina*, Decision on Liability, para. 162.

cases in which the FET standard has been applied – 'fair procedure, non-discrimination, transparency, the protection of the investor's legitimate expectations ... sovereignty and sustainable development.'[126] While conceding that this set of objectives is not necessarily complete,[127] his basic claim is that justice requires a balance to be struck between these (and other) competing objectives.[128]

There are problems with this argument at both the theoretical and the practical level. As a matter of normative theory, Kläger does not explain why the six objectives that happen to figure prominently in existing arbitral jurisprudence should be central to a theory of justice. For example, he does not explain why the protection of investors' expectations is an important component of a normatively attractive conception of justice[129] or how the argument that justice requires the protection of *expectations* relates to influential theories of justice that suggest that justice requires the protection of validly acquired property *rights*.[130] Nor does he explain why the objective of maximising economic benefits (or, stated at a higher level of abstraction, net social welfare) does not feature in his theory of justice, even though the vast majority of investment treaties identify 'economic' objectives as among their principal objectives.[131] For present purposes, there is also an important practical objection. No arbitral award of which I am aware has sought to articulate or defend an overarching conception of justice, nor to use such a conception of justice to justify a particular interpretation of the FET standard. When tribunals have referred to an unelaborated concept of 'justice', it is just as often to explain that FET standard only allows a tribunal to intervene in cases of 'manifest' or 'serious' injustice[132] as it is to argue that the FET standard embodies justice.[133] Thus, Kläger's theory does not provide a useful *explanatory* account of existing jurisprudence.

While noting these difficulties with unified jurisprudential theories, I do not go so far as to suggest that the search for such a theory is a

---

[126] Kläger, *'Fair and Equitable Treatment' in International Investment Law*, p. 150.
[127] Ibid., p. 150.   [128] Ibid., pp. 149, 151–3.   [129] Ibid., p. 149.
[130] E.g., Nozick, *Anarchy, State and Utopia* (1974); for more detailed discussion, see Section 3.5.5.
[131] References to the objectives of 'economic development', 'prosperity' or similar appear in the preambles of US, Canadian, French, German, Dutch, Chinese, Australian and UK investment treaties, among others; for more detailed discussion, see Section 2.2.
[132] *Glamis Gold v. United States*, Award, paras. 626–627; similarly, *AES Summit Generation v. Hungary*, Award, para. 38; *Chemtura v. Canada*, Award, para. 148.
[133] *El Paso v. Argentina*, Award, para. 373; *PSEG v. Turkey*, Award, para. 239.

fruitless exercise. I make only a more modest claim, from which I draw a modest conclusion. My claim is that a generally accepted jurisprudential theory of the FET standard has yet to emerge in either arbitral decisions or academic commentary. My conclusion is that inductive methodology can help understand and elucidate similarities and differences in the interpretation of the FET standard in decided cases. The application of inductive methodology in subsequent sections strongly supports the conclusion that the FET standard comprises a number of relatively autonomous elements. Even if a consensus were to coalesce around a general jurisprudential theory that could explain and justify all the elements of the standard, inductive methodology would still be a useful way to understand the specific legal content that tribunals give to the unifying jurisprudential principles.

4.4.3 Fact-specific reasoning and the FET standard

Rather than attempt to construct a single jurisprudential theory of the FET standard, one might take a radically different approach and begin from the premise that the reasoning of each arbitral decision is specific to the factual matrix before the tribunal.[134] This understanding of the standard receives some support from arbitral awards. For example, in *Mondev*, the tribunal noted that '[a] judgment of what is fair and equitable treatment cannot be reached in the abstract; it must depend on the facts of the particular case.'[135] A doctrinal theory based on this understanding of FET might simply amount to a list of factors that suggest that the standard has been breached, a list of factors that suggest the standard has not been breached and the claim that each case involves an ad hoc exercise of characterisation.[136]

Notwithstanding that characterisation of contested facts is sometimes determinative, I submit that apparent inconsistencies in the reasoning of FET decisions are not solely attributable to factual nuances. Rather, a close examination of existing arbitral decisions reveals very different understandings of the legal content of the FET standard. These differences entail divergent patterns of legal reasoning and would lead to different decisions on an identical set of facts. These divergent patterns of reasoning

---

[134] Tudor, *The Fair and Equitable Treatment Standard in the International Law of Foreign Investment*, p. 129.

[135] *Mondev International* v. *United States*, Award, para. 118.

[136] E.g., *Renée Rose Levy de Levi* v. *Republic of Peru*, Award, para. 320; Malik, 'Fair and Equitable Treatment' (2009) [online].

are best understood by distinguishing the different elements of FET and then comparing decisions applying each element. The sections of this chapter that follow constitute a detailed and sustained argument for these propositions.

4.5 Legitimate expectations

As an element of the FET standard, the doctrine of legitimate expectations is of relatively recent origin. Its foundations are normally traced to comments made in the early arbitral awards of the twenty-first century.[137] In 2000, the tribunal in *Metalclad* v. *Mexico* observed that the investor 'was led to believe, and did believe, that the federal and state permits allowed for the construction and operation of the landfill.'[138] Subsequent actions of the authorities to halt construction of the landfill on the grounds that an additional, municipal permit was required breached the FET standard.[139] The following year, the *CME* v. *Czech Republic* Tribunal held that the FET standard was breached by the 'evisceration of the arrangements in reliance upon which the foreign investor was induced to invest.'[140] In 2003, the *Tecmed* v. *Mexico* Tribunal referred, for the first time, to the protection of an investor's expectations in general terms. It stated that the FET standard requires treatment 'that does not affect the basic expectations that were taken into account by the foreign investor to make the investment.'[141] In 2004, the *Waste Management* v. *Mexico (II)* Tribunal took a more restrained view. It held that in determining whether treatment breached the FET standard it was 'relevant that the treatment is in breach of representations made by the host State which were reasonably relied on by the claimant.'[142]

By 2005, academic commentators were already arguing that the FET standard protected investors' legitimate expectations.[143] However, it was not until the *Thunderbird* decision of 2006 that an arbitral tribunal first invoked the terms 'legitimate expectations' in resolving an FET claim.[144] Since that time, the majority of FET cases have examined whether the

---

[137] E.g., Dolzer and Schreuer, *Principles of International Investment Law* (2nd edn), pp. 146–7.
[138] *Metalclad* v. *Mexico*, Award, para. 85.   [139] Ibid., para. 89.
[140] *CME* v. *Czech Republic*, Partial Award, para. 611.   [141] *Tecmed* v. *Mexico*, Award, para. 154.
[142] *Waste Management* v. *Mexico (II)*, Final Award, para. 98.
[143] Dolzer, 'Fair and Equitable Treatment', p. 103; Schreuer, 'Fair and Equitable Treatment in Arbitral Practice' (2005) 6 *The Journal of World Investment and Trade*, p. 386.
[144] *International Thunderbird Gaming* v. *Mexico*, Arbitral Award, para. 196; Snodgrass, 'Protecting Investors' Legitimate Expectations', p. 2.

investor's legitimate expectations were violated.[145] For investors, part of the appeal of the doctrine is that it allows a claim to be framed as an interference with a protected interest of the claimant – a legitimate expectation. Under the other elements of the FET standard, liability turns primarily on the characteristics of governmental conduct, not the extent of interference with the investor's interests. For tribunals, the utility of the doctrine seems to be that it provides a basis for resolving claims that involve a wide range of fact-patterns common in FET claims, including claims arising from changes to the general regulatory arrangements governing an investment and breaches of investor-state contracts by the host state.

Identifying the basis for state liability under the doctrine of legitimate expectations requires answers to three consecutive questions:

1. On what basis must an expectation rest to qualify for protection under the FET standard?
2. Of expectations that rest on a recognised basis, by what criteria are *legitimate* expectations identified?
3. To what extent must a claimant rely on a legitimate expectation to recover for its breach?

One might expect that a final question would arise as to whether the frustration of the investor's expectations was justified in the circumstances, with a state only liable to the investor in the event that interference with its legitimate expectations was not justified. In the early *Saluka* v. *Czech Republic* decision, the tribunal hinted that it would, indeed, be necessary to include this final stage of analysis.[146] However, the occasional notable exception aside,[147] other tribunals have not incorporated this final stage of analysis into their inquiry. Instead, the consistent practice of tribunals is to integrate any discussion of the justifications for a state's conduct into the second stage of the inquiry – that is, the determination of whether a given expectation was legitimate in the circumstances.[148]

In the three-stage inquiry utilised by tribunals, the first of these questions is the most significant because it defines the scope of the doctrine.

---

[145] Author's count of publicly available arbitral awards rendered since January 2006.
[146] *Saluka* v. *Czech Republic*, Partial Award, para. 305.
[147] E.g., *Total* v. *Argentina*, Decision on Liability, para. 123.
[148] E.g., *International Thunderbird Gaming* v. *Mexico*, Arbitral Award, para. 147; *Duke Energy* v. *Ecuador*, Award, para. 340; *Continental Casualty* v. *Argentina*, Award, para. 261; *International Thunderbird Gaming* v. *Mexico*, Separate Opinion, para. 64; *Enron* v. *Argentina*, Award, para. 264; *Sempra Energy* v. *Argentina*, Award, para. 303.

The way tribunals answer this question is central to understanding the different ways in which they have interpreted the doctrine. Although tribunals also disagree on the second and third questions, their views on these questions are shaped by the way they answer the first question. This section organises arbitral decisions according to the way in which they answer the first question. I submit that distinct interpretations of the doctrine of legitimate expectations have coalesced around four different answers to this question:[149]

i) Expectations can only rest on specific rights that the investor has acquired under domestic law.

ii) In addition to i), expectations may rest on specific representations made to the investor by government officials.

iii) In addition to ii) expectations may rest on the regulatory framework in force in the host state at the time the investor made the investment.

iv) In addition to iii), expectations may rest on the business plans of the investor.

Two final observations will help clarify the analysis that follows. First, the legitimate expectations of investors have been mentioned in the determination of whether given interests qualify as 'investments' for the purpose of establishing jurisdiction under an investment treaty and in the determination of whether an indirect expropriation has occurred.[150] This section is limited to the protection of legitimate expectations as an element of the FET standard. Second, tribunals have occasionally held that an investor may legitimately expect the full range of treatment required by the FET standard.[151] This is incoherent.[152] To say that an investor legitimately expects the treatment that is required by the FET standard is to make a circular argument – an argument that does not shed any light on the treatment that is required by the FET standard. The doctrine of

---

[149] Potesta proposes a division of fact scenarios that roughly follows the first three elements of this taxonomy: Potesta, 'Legitimate Expectations in Investment Treaty Law', pp. 100–19.

[150] On the definition of investment: *Southern Pacific Properties* v. *Egypt*, Award, paras. 82–3; *EnCana* v. *Ecuador*, Partial Dissenting Opinion, paras. 17–21. On indirect expropriation: *Azurix* v. *Argentina*, Award, para. 316. For discussion of investors' expectations beyond FET claims: von Walter, 'The Investor's Expectations in International Investment Arbitration', p. 177.

[151] *Saluka* v. *Czech Republic*, Partial Award, para. 303; similarly, *Plama* v. *Bulgaria*, Award, para. 176; *Kardassopoulos and Fuchs* v. *Georgia*, Award, paras. 438, 441.

[152] McLachlan, Shore and Weiniger, *International Investment Arbitration*, p. 234.

legitimate expectation is only meaningful to the extent it gives content to the FET standard.[153]

4.5.1 The legal rights approach

The narrowest interpretation of the doctrine of legitimate expectations is that it protects only specific, enforceable legal rights that have vested in the investor under domestic law. Further criteria then determine the circumstances in which an interference with a particular legal right will amount to a breach of legitimate expectations. According to this interpretation, the doctrine functions as an additional, international layer of protection for existing rights, rather than as a source of new rights. As such, this interpretation best conforms to Crawford's opinion that 'the doctrine of legitimate expectations should not be used as a substitute for the actual arrangements agreed between the parties, or as a supervening and overriding source of the applicable law.'[154]

4.5.1.1 LG&E Energy v. Argentina

The first case to articulate this view of legitimate expectations was LG&E v. Argentina. The facts of the case relate to the privatisation of the Argentine gas-distribution sector in the early 1990s. The Argentine government created a regulatory framework to make the privatisation attractive to foreign investors. This framework included guarantees that tariffs would be based on the US Producer Price Index, calculated in US dollars and adjusted twice annually.[155] These guarantees were specifically incorporated in the terms of the gas licenses awarded to the privatised entities.[156] '[T]he government could not rescind or modify the licenses without the consent of the licensees.'[157] LG&E became a shareholder in three licensee companies.

In 2001, Argentina entered a period of deep economic and social crisis. One of the government's responses to the crisis was the January 2002 Emergency Law. The Emergency Law unilaterally modified gas licenses, removing licensees' right to the calculation of tariffs in US dollars and to the indexation of tariffs.[158] LG&E argued that the repudiation of key rights conferred by the gas distribution licenses breached its 'basic expectations'

---

[153] Vandevelde, *Bilateral Investment Treaties*, p. 235.
[154] Crawford, 'Treaty and Contract in Investment Arbitration' (2008) 24 *Arbitration International*, p. 374; similarly, *MTD* v. *Chile*, Decision on Annulment, para. 67.
[155] *LG&E Energy* v. *Argentina*, Decision on Liability, para. 49.
[156] Ibid., para. 42.   [157] Ibid., para. 41.   [158] Ibid., para. 65.

relating to the investment and, therefore, the FET standard.[159] The claims in *CMS Gas* v. *Argentina*, *Sempra Energy* v. *Argentina*, *Enron* v. *Argentina* and *BG* v. *Argentina* were brought by other gas licensees as a result of these same events.

Addressing LG&E's FET claim, the tribunal quoted the passages from *Tecmed* and *Waste Management II* dealing with investors' expectations.[160] It then stated its own view of the protection provided to an investor's expectations by the FET standard, as if it followed naturally from these early decisions:

> It can be said that the investor's fair expectations have the following characteristics: they are based on the conditions offered by the host State at the time of the investment; they may not be established unilaterally by one of the parties; they must exist and be enforceable by law; in the event of infringement by the host State, a duty to compensate the investor for damages arises except for those caused in the event of state of necessity; however, the investor's fair expectations cannot fail to consider parameters such as business risk or industry's regular patterns.[161]

The tribunal held that tariff regime was 'not merely an economic and monetary policy of the Argentine government' but a set of rights granted and specifically guaranteed by the state. LG&E relied on these 'key guarantees' in making its decision to invest. By abandoning the tariff regime, Argentina breached LG&E's legitimate expectations and, therefore, the FET standard.[162]

The key clause in the *LG&E* Tribunal's statement is the requirement that expectations 'must exist and be enforceable by law'. The requirement that expectations must *exist by law* imposes a condition that an expectation be grounded in the legal entitlements of the investor under the domestic law of the state (or in the proper law of a contract or licence on which the expectation is based). An expectation that is based on a unilateral statement made by the host state would not meet this condition, except in the narrow circumstance in which domestic law itself recognises the unilateral statement as creating a right vested in the investor. The requirement that expectations must be *enforceable by law* further circumscribes the set of legal entitlements that are capable of supporting a legitimate expectation. At any given time, a state will have a number of laws and regulations in force. However, it would be rare for an investor to have an *enforceable* right for its entitlements under general regulations to remain

---

[159] Ibid., paras. 102–5.   [160] See Section 4.5.
[161] *LG&E Energy* v. *Argentina*, Decision on Liability, para. 130.   [162] Ibid., paras. 133–4.

unchanged unless the state has specifically agreed to maintain or guarantee the continuation of existing arrangements through a contract or licence agreement with the investor.

Under the criteria laid down by the *LG&E* Tribunal, the requirement that an expectation rest on a specific legal right vested in the investor is necessary, but not sufficient, for the expectation to be protected by the FET standard. The tribunal also held that an expectation must be 'fair', an assessment that required consideration of 'parameters such as business risk or industry's regular patterns.'[163] Moreover, the tribunal held that to recover for breach of a legitimate expectation, an investor must have relied on the expectation in making its initial investment.[164]

4.5.1.2 Other decisions consistent with *LG&E*

The *LG&E* Tribunal's interpretation of the doctrine of legitimate expectations was cited and applied in *BG* v. *Argentina*, a case brought by another gas investor based on the same facts. The *BG* Tribunal emphasised that both the tariff regime itself and provisions relating to the stability of the tariff regime were incorporated in the gas licences and stressed that Argentine law recognised these interests as 'legitimately acquired rights' vested in the investor.[165] The reversal of these commitments breached the claimant's legitimate expectations.

In another case brought against Argentina, the consolidated *Suez* claims, the claimants alleged that a number of measures affecting their investment in a Buenos Aires water concession breached the FET standard. Foremost among these was Argentina's refusal to revise water tariffs according to the legal framework established by the concession contract.[166] The tribunal noted that the claimants' expectations were basic terms of the concession contract. These expectations 'were not established unilaterally but by the agreement between Argentina and the Claimants; and they existed and were enforceable by law.'[167] Accordingly, Argentina was liable under the FET standard.

Other decisions have limited the doctrine of legitimate expectations to the protection of enforceable legal rights without citing the *LG&E* award. The case of *MCI* v. *Ecuador* arose from a dispute under an electricity contract between the investor and INECEL, a governmental entity.

---

[163] Ibid., para. 130.   [164] Ibid., para. 130.
[165] 'derecho legítimamente adquirido', *BG Group* v. *Argentina*, Final Award, para. 308.
[166] *Suez and Vivendi; AWG Group* v. *Argentina*, Decision on Liability, paras. 79–80.
[167] Ibid., para. 231.

Suez + Interaguas   para 212

The tribunal rejected the notion that the doctrine of legitimate expectations protected 'the basic assumptions on which the investor made the investment.'[168] It held that

[t]he legitimacy of the expectations for proper treatment entertained by a foreign investor protected by the BIT does not depend solely on the intent of the parties, but on certainty about the contents of the enforceable obligations.[169]

As the claimant could not prove the violation of an 'enforceable obligation' owed by INECEL or an 'acquired right' vested in the claimant, it could not succeed in its claim for breach of legitimate expectations.[170]

Similar issues were raised in *EDF v. Romania*. The claim arose from a set of contractual disputes between the investor and state entities relating to its investment in airport duty-free shops. The central claims of the investor were that the state had failed to extend its contract to provide duty free sales beyond its initial term and that the state subsequently abolished duty free sales in airports. The claimant argued that it had a legitimate and reasonable expectation of the continued operation of its business.[171] The tribunal disagreed:

The idea that legitimate expectations, and therefore FET, imply the stability of the legal and business framework, may not be correct if stated in an overly-broad and unqualified formulation.[172]

It went on to state that the claim for breach of legitimate expectations 'presupposes that the acts or the conduct in question were in breach of AIBO's and TAROM's [the state entities] contractual obligations.'[173]

The decision is particularly significant for its attempt to clarify the relationship between unilateral governmental statements and the doctrine of legitimate expectations. The tribunal held that

[t]o validly claim a breach of the FET standard under the BIT, Claimant should have proven not only a breach of the SKY Contract, but also that such other assurances had been given by the Government and had been breached.[174]

In the tribunal's view, the relevance of governmental representations was that they weigh in the determination of which expectations based on legal rights rise to the status of *legitimate* expectations that are protected by the FET standard.

In the case of *Metalpar v. Argentina*, the investor alleged that the changes made during the Argentine financial crisis to Argentina's regime of

---

[168] *MCI Power v. Ecuador*, Award, para. 237.   [169] Ibid., para. 278.
[170] Ibid., paras. 322–5.   [171] *EDF v. Romania*, Award, para. 243.
[172] Ibid., para. 217.   [173] Ibid., para. 240.   [174] Ibid., para. 298.

currency convertibility breached its legitimate expectations relating to its investment in a bus manufacturing company.[175] The tribunal gave the claim short shrift. It reviewed a range of decided cases and found that, in every case where a legitimate expectations claim had been successful, 'the government [had] refused to renew or comply with [a] contract, license or permit.'[176] The fact that the claimant had 'no bid, license, permit or contract of any kind' with the state was sufficient to show that it could have no legitimate expectation that the currency regime would not change.[177]

A further set of decisions is consistent with the proposition that the doctrine of legitimate expectations is limited to the protection of vested legal rights, without expressly foreclosing the possibility that expectations could be based on other forms of state conduct in other cases. In the recent decision *Paushok* v. *Mongolia*, the claimant, an investor engaged in the mining of gold, argued that the introduction of windfall profits tax on the sale of gold breached its legitimate expectations. The tax was calculated at the rate of 68 per cent on the portion of the sale price exceeding a base price of USD 500 an ounce.[178] While noting that the tax imposed a significant burden on the operation of the investment, the tribunal held that governments regularly change their tax policies and that, in the absence of a stabilisation agreement with the host state, an investor could not legitimately expect tax arrangements to remain unchanged.[179] In *Eureko* v. *Poland*, the tribunal held that the Polish state 'consciously and overtly' refused to respect the terms of its contract with the investor, thereby breaching 'the basic expectations' of the investor.[180] The NAFTA claim in *GAMI* v. *Mexico* failed because the investor's expectation that the state would enforce sugar quotas was not based on any obligation on the state under Mexican law.[181]

4.5.1.3 Restatement of the legal rights approach

Taken together, these cases constitute a coherent interpretation of the doctrine of legitimate expectations under the FET standard. This interpretation of the doctrine can be restated as follows:

---

[175] *Metalpar* v. *Argentina*, Award on the Merits, para. 116.
[176] Ibid., para. 185.   [177] Ibid., paras. 186–7.
[178] *Sergei Paushok* v. *Mongolia*, Award on Jurisdiction and Liability, para. 104.
[179] Ibid., Award on Jurisdiction and Liability, para. 302.
[180] *Eureko* v. *Poland*, Partial Award, para. 232; similarly, *Alpha Projektholding* v. *Ukraine*, Award, paras. 421–2.
[181] *GAMI Investments* v. *Mexico*, Final Award, para. 76.

1. An expectation can only qualify for protection under the FET standard if it is based on a specific and enforceable legal right vested in the investor.
2. Not all expectations based on specific legal rights qualify for protection under the doctrine. An expectation must also be legitimate and reasonable in the circumstances. This determination must be made in light of normal business risk, the regulatory patterns in the industry and any specific representations made by the state to the investor. The expectation must also be basic to the investment.
3. To recover for the infringement of a legitimate expectation, the investor must have relied on the expectation in making the decision to invest.

The domestic law of the host state plays an important role in this interpretation of the doctrine of legitimate expectations. However, this understanding of legitimate expectations does not reduce to a question of the legality of state conduct under domestic law. For example, what was crucial for the LG&E and BG Tribunals was that the gas licences granted gas companies specific and enforceable legal rights under Argentine law. It may well have been that, under Argentine constitutional law, it was legal for the state to subsequently repudiate these rights in an emergency situation. This issue was not decisive. Having created specific and enforceable legal rights under domestic law, the doctrine of legitimate expectations was activated; the subsequent treatment of these rights was then assessed according to an international standard.

4.5.2 The representations approach

A broader view of the scope of the doctrine of legitimate expectations is that it protects investors from prior unilateral statements made by the state. Further criteria then determine the circumstances in which an interference with expectations arising from representations will amount to a breach of legitimate expectations. The principle that justifies this view is that representations amount to official 'positions' taken by a host government, even when they are not legally binding. The doctrine of legitimate expectations then functions as a liability rule requiring a state to compensate an investor when it changes a position on which the investor has relied.[182] In keeping with this rationalisation of the doctrine, tribunals

---

[182] Grierson-Weiler and Laird, 'Standards of Treatment', p. 275, arguing that the doctrine is based on the 'concept of detrimental reliance'; Newcombe and Paradell, *Law and Practice of Investment Treaties*, p. 279, arguing that the doctrine is 'closely related to the principle of estoppel and state responsibility under public international law for unilateral acts'; Reisman and Arsanjani, 'The Question of Unilateral governmental

have described the protection of investors' expectations as embodying principles of 'certainty', 'consistency' and 'predictability'.[183] The overwhelming majority of academic commentary accepts that the doctrine of legitimate expectations protects expectations based on specific unilateral representations.[184] I call this the 'representations approach'.

4.5.2.1 The representations approach

The majority in the NAFTA tribunal in *Thunderbird* articulated the view that expectations protected by the FET standard could be derived from the host state's conduct without any requirement that such conduct create legal rights vesting in the investor:

[T]he concept of 'legitimate expectations' relates, within the context of the NAFTA framework, to a situation where a Contracting Party's conduct creates reasonable and justifiable expectations on the part of an investor (or investment) to act in reliance on said conduct, such that a failure by the NAFTA Party to honour those expectations could cause the investor (or investment) to suffer damages.[185]

In this paragraph, the majority also indicates that, to be *legitimate*, an expectation based on a state's conduct must be 'reasonable and justifiable'. In applying this standard to the facts, the tribunal gave more precise content to these limitations.

Thunderbird was a gaming company, seeking to install its gaming machines in Mexico. Mexican law banned gambling machines. Thunderbird requested an official opinion concerning the legality of its gaming machines under Mexican law from SEGOB, the relevant regulatory authority.[186] In its request Thunderbird declared that its machines operated according to the users' 'skills and abilities', not 'chance and wagering or betting'.[187] In its official response, SEGOB explained that Mexican law banned machines in which 'the principal factor . . . is luck or gambling'; and stated that if the investor's machines operated in the manner

---

Statements as Applicable Law in Investment Disputes' (2004) 19 *ICSID Review – FILJ*, p. 342; similarly, *International Thunderbird Gaming* v. *Mexico*, Arbitral Award, para. 147.

[183] *Total* v. *Argentina*, Decision on Liability, para. 129; *Saluka* v. *Czech Republic*, Partial Award, para. 307; *CMS Gas* v. *Argentina*, Final Award, para. 276.

[184] E.g., Potesta, 'Legitimate Expectations in Investment Treaty Law', p. 121; Diehl, *The Core Standard in International Investment Protection*, p. 411; Snodgrass, 'Protecting Investors' Legitimate Expectations', p. 34; Fietta, 'Expropriation and the "Fair and Equitable Treatment" Standard' in Ortino et al. (eds), *Investment Treaty Law: Current Issues II* (2007), p. 189;

[185] *International Thunderbird Gaming* v. *Mexico*, Arbitral Award, paras. 147, 196.

[186] Ibid., para. 48.   [187] Ibid., para. 50.

in which the investor had described, they would be permissible under Mexican law.[188] One year later, on its own motion, the Mexican authorities held an administrative hearing to determine whether Thunderbird's machines complied with Mexican law. Thunderbird appeared and gave evidence. SEGOB subsequently determined that Thunderbird's machines did not comply with Mexican law.[189] Thunderbird argued that on the basis of SEGOB's official response, it had a legitimate expectation that its machines were compliant with Mexican law.

The majority held that Thunderbird's legitimate expectations had not been breached. It noted that the information provided in Thunderbird's request for an official opinion was both incomplete and inaccurate.[190] SEGOB's response was explicitly conditional on the accuracy of this information. As such, it had not made a clear and specific statement on which Thunderbird could reasonably have relied.[191] In addition, the tribunal noted that Thunderbird had already begun to install its machines in Mexico prior to SEGOB's official response. On this basis, it doubted whether Thunderbird's investment had been made in reliance on SEGOB's response.[192]

In the recent decision in *Total* v. *Argentina* – another case arising out of events in the Argentine gas sector – the tribunal agreed that unilateral representations were capable of creating legitimate expectations. However, it was careful to limit the scope of the doctrine to situations where the representations were clear and specific to the investor:

Representations made by the host State are enforceable and justify the investor's reliance only when they are specifically addressed to a particular investor.[193]

It argued that the assessment of whether a given expectation was legitimate required consideration of the state's 'right to regulate' and an assessment of whether the state's actions were reasonable and proportionate.[194] On the facts, the tribunal distinguished the findings of the other Argentine gases. It held that Total had invested a decade after other investors and, as such, was not an addressee of the promises made at the time of privatisation.[195]

In *Duke Energy* v. *Ecuador*, the tribunal accepted that expectations could be derived from 'conditions that the State offered the investor' at the time of the investment, without any requirement that the offer be embodied

---

[188] Ibid., para. 55.   [189] Ibid., paras. 70–3.   [190] Ibid., para. 151.   [191] Ibid., paras. 159–61.
[192] Ibid., para. 167.   [193] *Total* v. *Argentina*, Decision on Liability, para. 119.   [194] Ibid., para. 123.   [195] Ibid., para. 144.

in a legally effective form.[196] The tribunal also noted that the assessment of whether an expectation is legitimate:

[M]ust take into account all circumstances, including not only the facts surrounding the investment, but also the political, socioeconomic, cultural and historical conditions prevailing in the host State.[197]

The tribunal held that a state's contractual agreement to guarantee payments owed to the investor by the electricity regulator created a legitimate expectation.[198] The tribunal dismissed a further claim arising from an arbitration agreement on the grounds that the doctrine of legitimate expectations did not protect expectations created by the state after an investor has made its investment.[199]

The tribunal in *Bayindir* v. *Pakistan* affirmed the comments made in *Duke Energy*.[200] It held that the claimant could not derive legitimate expectations from the fact that the former prime minister had been a key supporter of its highway construction project.[201] Specifically, the claimant could not expect that, after a change of government, the state would refrain from exercising its right to terminate a construction contract as a result of the claimant's defective performance.[202]

The *Biwater* v. *Tanzania* Tribunal also stressed the importance of weighing 'countervailing factors' in the assessment of whether an expectation is legitimate. These included the following:

[T]he responsibility of foreign investors, both in terms of prior due diligence as well as subsequent conduct; the limit to legitimate expectations in circumstances where an investor itself takes on risks in entering a particular investment environment; and the relevance of the parties' respective rights and obligations as set out in any relevant investment agreement.[203]

In *National Grid* v. *Argentina*, the investor was a shareholder in a privatised electricity transmission and distribution company. The case raised essentially the same issue as the *LG&E*, *BG* and the other Argentine gas cases – whether the abandonment of a dollar-denominated tariff regime during the Argentine crisis, which had applied to a public utility and to which the utility was contractually entitled, breached the claimant's

---

[196] *Duke Energy* v. *Ecuador*, Award, para. 340; similarly, *GEA Group* v. *Ukraine*, Award, paras. 287, 291.
[197] *Duke Energy* v. *Ecuador*, Award, para. 340.   [198] Ibid., paras. 362–4.   [199] Ibid., para. 365.
[200] *Bayindir* v. *Pakistan*, Award, paras. 190–1.   [201] Ibid., para. 194.   [202] Ibid., para. 197.
[203] *Biwater* v. *Tanzania*, Award, para. 601.

legitimate expectations.[204] The tribunal began by observing that the FET standard 'protects the reasonable expectations of the investor at the time it made the investment and which were based on representations, commitments or specific conditions offered by the State concerned.'[205] The tribunal recognised much the same limitations on the doctrine as *Duke Energy*, including that Argentina's financial crisis must carry some weight in the assessment of legitimate expectations.[206] However, it went on to find that the claimant had a legitimate expectation that the tariff regime would continue in force, because the tariff regime had been specifically advertised to the claimant in the prospectus that the Argentine government used to attract foreign investors to the electricity transmission industry.[207] As such, the tribunal found that the liability of the state stemmed from its departure from a prior unilateral statement (the prospectus), not from the fact that it had repudiated rights created by the concession contract.

4.5.2.2 The significance of general regulatory arrangements in the representations approach

Thunderbird, *Total*, *Duke Energy*, *Bayindir*, *National Grid* and *Biwater* all dealt with factual scenarios in which the purported expectations were based on investor-state contracts or representations made by the host state. Other tribunals have considered the role of representations relating to the maintenance of general regulatory arrangements. Tribunals that adopt the representations approach agree that the general regulatory arrangements in force at the time of the investment are not a sufficient basis for a legitimate expectation that will be protected by the FET standard. This is the main point of contrast between the representations approach and the stability approach, which is introduced in Section 4.5.3. However, tribunals within the representations approach do agree that representations that the general regulatory framework would be maintained may, on occasion, be a sufficient basis for a legitimate expectation.

Tribunals that follow the representations approach have emphasised that general regulatory arrangements in force at the time an investment is made are not a sufficient basis for a legitimate expectation. For example, In *PSEG* v. *Turkey*, the tribunal addressed a claim based on changes of the legal regime governing the award of build, operate and transfer power

---

[204] *National Grid* v. *Argentina*, Award, paras. 117–25.   [205] Ibid., para. 173.
[206] Ibid., para. 175.   [207] Ibid., paras. 176–9.

contracts under Turkish law.[208] In rejecting this element of the claim, it held that 'legitimate expectations by definition require a promise of the administration on which the Claimants rely to assert a right that needs to be observed.'[209]

Similarly, in rejecting a legitimate expectations claim, the NAFTA tribunal in *Glamis Gold* held that no 'quasi-contractual inducement' had been offered by the state to the investor.[210] In the absence of such an inducement, a change in the environmental remediation regulations that would apply to the gold mine that the claimant was seeking to construct could not have breached its legitimate expectations. It was irrelevant that the 'imposition of mandatory backfilling requirements surprised the claimant and upset its [subjective] expectations.'[211]

The claim in *CMS* v. *Argentina* raised the same set of facts involving the Argentine gas industry as *LG&E* and *BG*.[212] Although the *CMS Gas* Tribunal observed elsewhere in the decision that the tariff regime was embodied in the terms of licence held by the investor, it did not refer to these facts in its application of the FET standard.[213] Rather, the tribunal found the liability of the state arose from changes to the general regulatory framework governing the investment in light of representations that this framework would not be changed. The tribunal noted that Argentina's changes to the tariff regime 'did in fact entirely transform and alter the legal and business environment under which the investment was decided and made.'[214] These comments seem to endorse the stability approach, which is outlined in the following section. However, the tribunal ultimately decided the case on the narrower grounds that, in light of 'specific commitments' that the regime would not be changed, the claimant was entitled expect that the tariff regime would not be abandoned.[215]

The tribunal in *Continental Casualty* made a more structured attempt to reconcile the principles governing the protection of expectations based on unilateral representations made by the state with the possibility that those representations might refer back to the stability of general regulatory arrangements. It held that in the assessment of whether a

---

[208] *PSEG* v. *Turkey*, Award, paras. 13–44.

[209] Ibid., para. 241; similarly, *Plama* v. *Bulgaria*, Award, para. 219; *AES Summit Generation* v. *Hungary*, Award, para. 9.3.18.

[210] *Glamis Gold* v. *United States*, Award, para. 767; similarly, *Cargill* v. *Mexico*, Award, para. 293.

[211] *Glamis Gold* v. *United States*, Award, para. 810.   [212] See Section 4.5.1.1.

[213] *CMS Gas* v. *Argentina*, Final Award, para. 133.   [214] Ibid., para. 275.

[215] Ibid., para. 277.

breach of legitimate expectations has occurred, a tribunal should consider:

   i)   [T]he specificity of the undertaking allegedly relied upon which is
mostly absent here, considering moreover that political statements
have the least legal value, regrettably but notoriously so;

  ii)   general legislative statements engender reduced expectations,
especially with competent major international investors in a context
where the political risk is high. Their enactment is by nature subject to
subsequent modification, and possibly to withdrawal and
cancellation ... ;

 iii)   unilateral modification of contractual undertakings by governments,
notably when issued in conformity with a legislative framework and
aimed at obtaining financial resources from investors deserve clearly
more scrutiny, in the light of the context, reasons, effects, since they
generate as a rule legal rights and therefore expectations of
compliance;[216]

In these three paragraphs, the tribunal suggests a hierarchy in the
sources of expectations in which specific legal rights deserve the most
protection, followed by specific undertakings made to the investor. In the
tribunal's hierarchy, general representations that the state would maintain the existing legislative framework deserve the least protection. The
question of whether any expectation was legitimate would then involve a
further balancing exercise in which the centrality of the expectation to the
investment was weighed against the public interest of the state.[217] Continental Casualty had asserted an expectation of the continued operation of
Argentina's regime of currency convertibility based on a combination of
the general legislative position of the state and public pronouncements of
the relevant minister that the regime would be maintained.[218] Applying
its understanding of the doctrine, the tribunal held that the prior legislative framework did not provide the basis for a legitimate expectation.[219]

4.5.2.3 Restatement of the representations approach

There are certain differences in emphasis among these decisions. However, they coalesce around a set of propositions about the doctrine of
legitimate expectations that can be restated with a degree of precision.
With respect to the scope of the doctrine:

---

[216] *Continental Casualty* v. *Argentina*, Award, para. 261.   [217] Ibid., para. 261.
[218] Ibid., para. 252.   [219] Ibid., paras. 259–60.

1. An expectation need not be based on a legal right vested in the investor. A unilateral statement made by the host state may be the basis for an expectation. For a statement to be the basis for an expectation, it must be made by government officials in their official capacity and be clear, with a degree of specificity to the claimant. An expectation cannot be based on general regulations in force at the time the investment was made unless the state has made specific representations to the investor that the regulations would not be changed.

With respect to the criteria by which *legitimate* expectations are identified:

2. The assessment of whether a given expectation is legtimate is a balancing exercise involving consideration of all the circumstances relating to the investment. This includes consideration of whether the expectation goes beyond what the investor is legally entitled to under domestic law, as well as whether the expectation is reasonable given the 'political, socioeconomic, cultural and historical conditions' in the host state.

With respect to the reliance:

3. To recover for the infringement of a legitimate expectation, the investor must have relied on the expectation in making the decision to invest.

4.5.2.4 Postscript: are contractual rights excluded from the doctrine of legitimate expectations?

The tribunal in *Parkerings* v. *Lithuania* observed that an expectation

is legitimate if the investor received an explicit promise or guaranty from the host-State, or if implicitly, the host-State made assurances or representation that the investor took into account in making the investment.[220]

This much is consistent with the representations approach to the protection of legitimate expectations under the FET standard. However, the *Parkerings* Tribunal went on to contend that 'contracts involve intrinsic expectations from each party that do not amount to expectations as understood in international law.'[221] This comment suggests an investor's contract with the host state cannot form the basis of an expectation protected by the FET standard. Arbitral decisions are unanimous in agreeing that not all breaches of contract are breaches of legitimate expectations,[222] but there are serious doctrinal difficulties with the position that a breach of

---

[220] *Parkerings* v. *Lithuania*, Award, para. 331.
[221] Ibid., para. 344.   [222] E.g., *Hamester* v. *Ghana*, Award, para. 335.

contract is never a breach of legitimate expectations. The latter proposition entails the result that when an investor enters into a legally binding agreement with a host state about the arrangements to govern a particular investment, it *reduces* the degree of protection which the FET standard provides from change to these arrangements. This result is not doctrinally coherent.

The situation in *Parkerings* was complicated by an exclusive forum selection clause in the investor's contract with the state.[223] However, even this cannot justify the view that breaches of contract are excluded from review under the FET standard.[224] A claim for breach of the FET standard is a claim for breach of a treaty standard, not a claim for breach of a contract.[225] It may be relevant for a tribunal to come to a view about whether a contract has been breached, but only to the extent it goes to the question of whether the treaty standard has been breached. The jurisdictional basis for an FET claim is the parties' consent to arbitration of disputes under the treaty, not the jurisdiction to resolve contractual disputes; it is the latter that is constrained by a contractual choice of forum clause.[226] In any case, the *Parkerings* Tribunal's comments were not confined to rights created by contracts with forum selection clauses.

The decision in *Impregilo v. Argentina* shows how the *Parkerings* dicta might be reconciled with other decisions applying the FET standard. The *Impregilo* Tribunal cited *Parkerings* for the proposition that 'legitimate expectations and the existence of contractual rights are two separate issues.'[227] But the tribunal immediately retreated from this claim, arguing instead that a breach of contract could amount to a breach of legitimate expectations when a host state exercises 'sovereign power'.[228] In this way, the tribunal distinguished ordinary breaches of contract that might occur in a relationship between commercial counter-parties from interferences with contractual rights that can amount to a breach of

---

[223] *Parkerings v. Lithuania*, Award, para. 436.
[224] *Franck Charles Arif v. Moldova*, Award, para. 536; Spiermann, 'Premature Treaty Claims' in Binder and others (eds), *International Investment Law for the 21st Century* (2009), p. 484; Kriebaum, 'Local Remedies and the Standards for the Protection of Foreign Investment: The Interface between International Investment Protection and Human Rights' (2006) 3 *Transnational Dispute Management*, p. 447.
[225] Crawford, 'Treaty and Contract in Investment Arbitration', p. 358; *Compañía de Aguas del Aconquija and Vivendi v. Argentina (II)*, Decision on Annulment, paras. 101, 105.
[226] The situation is more complex when a claim is brought before an international tribunal under an 'umbrella clause' of an investment treaty. The jurisdictional and substantive issues relating to umbrella clauses are beyond the scope of this book.
[227] *Impregilo v. Argentina*, Award, para. 292.   [228] Ibid., para. 296.

legitimate expectations under the FET standard. On the facts of the case, the tribunal found that Argentina had indeed breached a concession contract with the claimant in a manner that breached the claimant's legitimate expectations.[229]

4.5.3 The stability approach

A third approach to the protection of investors' legitimate expectations holds that the FET standard grants investors a freestanding entitlement to the stability of the legal arrangements under which the investment was made. Decisions within this approach also adopt a more permissive view of the extent to which expectations may be based on unilateral representations made by the host state. This is consistent with the greater emphasis on ensuring stability for the investor. Many academic commentators endorse the view that FET standard does protect expectations based on the general legal framework in force at the time the investment was made.[230] However, there are some dissenting voices that question whether, in the absence of a clear and specific representation made by the host state, a foreign investor can legitimately expect laws of general application to remain unchanged.[231] The justification for protecting expectations based on general regulatory arrangements in force at the time an investment is made seems to be the assumption that stability in the domestic legal system 'facilitate[s] rational planning and decision making' by foreign investors.[232]

Many of the decisions adopting the stability approach are sparsely reasoned. The possibility of liability arising from changes to general regulations in force at the time an investment is made greatly expands the potential scope of the doctrine of legitimate expectations. As such, the second stage of the legitimate expectations inquiry – the issue of how legitimate expectations based on general regulatory arrangements should be distinguished from expectations of stability that are not protected by the FET standard – assumes special importance. However, the criteria by

---

[229] Ibid., paras. 324, 331.

[230] E.g., Kläger, 'Fair and Equitable Treatment' in International Investment Law, p. 169; Dolzer, 'Fair and Equitable Treatment', p. 103; Schreuer, 'Fair and Equitable Treatment in Arbitral Practice', p. 386; Westcott, 'Recent Practice on the Fair and Equitable Treatment' (2007) 8 The Journal of World Investment and Trade, p. 425; Kinnear, 'The Continuing Development of the Fair and Equitable Treatment Standard', p. 227; Salacuse, The Law of Investment Treaties, p. 232.

[231] Paparinskis, The International Minimum Standard and Fair and Equitable Treatment, p. 259; Potesta, 'Legitimate Expectations in Investment Treaty Law', p. 121.

[232] Frontier Petroleum v. Czech Republic, Final Award, para. 285.

which *legitimate* expectations should be identified are not fully articulated in these decisions.

4.5.3.1 Expectations based on general regulatory arrangements: the stability approach

A key decision developing the stability approach is *Occidental* v. *Ecuador (I)*. The dispute concerned the reimbursement of value-added tax (VAT) paid by the investor under a petroleum contract between the investor and the state. For the first two years of the contract, the Ecuadorian tax authorities refunded VAT on application from Occidental. The tax authorities then issued a resolution denying further refunds and demanding the repayment of refunds previously paid. The authorities justified this change in policy on the basis that the contract itself, through a participation formula that entitled the claimant for reimbursement of its expenses, already provided the investor with the refunds to which it was entitled.[233] The investor argued that the change in policy of the tax authorities breached the legitimate expectations on which the investment was based.[234]

The two issues of domestic law put to the tribunal were whether Occidental was entitled to a refund of VAT under Ecuadorian tax law and, if so, whether this reimbursement was accounted for by the participation formula. The tribunal found in Occidental's favour on both issues.[235] These findings would have been sufficient for the tribunal to hold that the FET standard had been breached by the tax authority's refusal to honour Occidental's acquired right under Ecuadorian law to a refund on tax already paid. However, the tribunal did not structure its reasoning in this way. Instead, it held that 'the stability of the legal and business framework is . . . an essential element of fair and equitable treatment.'[236] While noting that the tax authorities had justified their change of policy by asserting a 'manifestly wrong' interpretation of the contract, the primary basis for liability in the tribunal's decision was that 'the framework under which the investment has been made and operates has been changed in an important manner.'[237]

Both *Sempra* v. *Argentina* and *Enron* v. *Argentina* were based on the events in the Argentine gas industry considered in *LG&E*, *BG* and *CMS Gas*.[238] The same arbitrator presided over both tribunals, and the reasoning of the two follows a similar pattern. In addressing the claimant's FET claim,

---

[233] *Occidental* v. *Ecuador (I)*, Final Award, paras. 27–32.   [234] Ibid., para. 181.
[235] Ibid., para. 143.   [236] Ibid., para. 183.   [237] Ibid., para. 184.   [238] See Section 4.5.1.1.

the *Enron* Tribunal held that the doctrine of legitimate expectations protects 'expectations derived from the conditions that were offered by the State to the investor at the time of the investment'.[239] It understood 'conditions offered' as a category that includes the regulatory framework at the time an investment is made, in addition to those derived from unilateral statements made by the host state.[240] The tribunal found that Argentina breached the FET standard when it 'substantially changed the legal and business framework under which the investment was decided and implemented.'[241]

Although the *Enron* Tribunal also referred to 'the guarantees of the tariff regime' – a comment that could be read as an allusion to the fact that the tariff regime was incorporated into the terms of the licence acquired by the investor – its conclusion that Argentina had breached the FET standard did not turn on an analysis of the legal rights vested in the investor.[242] For the tribunal, the crucial finding was that the '"stable legal framework" that induced the investment is no longer in place and that a definitive framework has not been made available for almost five years.'[243]

In *Frontier Petroleum* v. *Czech Republic*, the tribunal attempted to articulate the stability approach in general terms:

Stability means that the investor's legitimate expectations based on this legal framework and on any undertakings and representations made explicitly or implicitly by the host state will be protected. The investor may rely on that legal framework as well as on representations and undertakings made by the host state including those in legislation, treaties, decrees, licenses, and contracts.[244]

However, on the facts of the case before it, the tribunal did not need to apply this understanding of the FET standard to resolve the claim.

Tribunals who allow the protection of expectations derived from the general regulatory arrangements in force at the time an investment is made have not provided a complete account of the criteria by which *legitimate* expectations are to be identified. The *Enron* Tribunal observed that the protection of expectations based on the framework 'does not mean the freezing of the legal system or the disappearance of the regulatory

---

[239] *Enron* v. *Argentina*, Award, para. 262.
[240] Ibid., para. 265; similarly, *Sempra Energy* v. *Argentina*, Award, para. 298.
[241] *Enron* v. *Argentina*, Award, para. 264; similarly, *Sempra Energy* v. *Argentina*, Award, para. 303.
[242] *Enron* v. *Argentina*, Award, paras. 154, 266.   [243] Ibid., para. 267.
[244] *Frontier Petroleum* v. *Czech Republic*, Final Award, para. 285.

power of the State.'[245] However, it did not explain the limits to the doctrine in any greater detail. To the extent that tribunals have engaged with this question, they seem to envisage a balancing process similar to that which occurs within the representations approach but with greater weight given to investors' general expectations of stability.[246] Thus, the tribunal in *Lemire v. Ukraine (II)* agreed that general laws in force when an investment is made could form the basis for legitimate expectations, but that legitimacy of any expectations based on such laws would have to be assessed in light of 'the State's sovereign right to pass legislation and to adopt decisions for the protection of its public interests.'[247] In *Alpha Projektholding v. Ukraine*, the tribunal said that the question was whether the regulatory change was 'arbitrary'.[248] In *El Paso v. Argentina*, the tribunal said the issue was whether the expectation was 'reasonable' in all the circumstances.[249] Both these tribunals seemed to have envisaged a similar balancing process to that prescribed by the *Lemire II* decision.

4.5.3.2 The stability approach to unilateral representations

Within the stability approach, legitimate expectations may also be based on unilateral representations but, in contrast to the representations approach, there is no requirement that such representations be clear and specific to the investor.[250] The roots of this approach can be found in *Tecmed v. Mexico*. The case concerned a hazardous waste facility. The investor held a licence to operate the facility for one year, which was renewable annually. In response to community opposition to the facility, the authorities and the investor agreed that the facility should be moved to a different location. This agreement was not documented in written form. Within months of this agreement, the authorities declined to renew the annual licence that allowed the facility to operate at its original site.[251] The investor argued that it had a legitimate expectation that the facility would be permitted to continue to operate until it could be relocated.

The tribunal's reasoning is difficult to follow. There is no doubt that it took a dim view of the authorities' conduct, which seems to have been

---

[245] *Enron v. Argentina*, Award, para. 261.
[246] E.g., *Electrabel v. Hungary*, Decision on Jurisdiction, Applicable Law and Liability, para. 7.77.
[247] *Lemire v. Ukraine (II)*, Decision on Jurisdiction and Liability, para. 285.
[248] *Alpha Projektholding v. Ukraine*, Award, para. 420.
[249] *El Paso v. Argentina*, Award, para. 364.
[250] *Electrabel v. Hungary*, Decision on Jurisdiction, Applicable Law and Liability, para. 7.78.
[251] *Tecmed v. Mexico*, Award, para. 160.

coloured by earlier changes to the licensing regime that had occurred before the entry into force of the BIT.[252] What is clear is that the tribunal found that the decision not to renew the licence breached the investor's legitimate expectation that the old facility would be permitted to continue to operate until it could be relocated.[253] What distinguishes the decision from those discussed in the context of the representations approach to legitimate expectations is that the tribunal did not identify a specific assurance that the investor's licence would be renewed. The closest the Mexican authorities had come to such a statement was in issuing a declaration that the original facility 'shall be closed as soon as the new facilities are ready to operate.'[254] The tribunal did not find that this declaration constituted an implicit promise *relating to the licence*. Rather, liability under the FET standard stemmed from the fact that, in a context in which there had been active negotiations between the investor and the authorities, the authorities had not given 'an explicit, transparent and clear warning' that the facility would be closed prior to relocation.[255]

In *Tecmed*, any expectations derived from the statements and negotiations concerning relocation could only have arisen *after* the investor had made its original investment in the facility. Moreover, the tribunal did not make a finding that the relocation exercise itself constituted an investment. As such, on the facts found, it is clear that the investor did not make an investment in reliance on the expectation identified by the tribunal. This did not preclude the investor from succeeding in its claim.

Professor Wälde's dissent in *Thunderbird* provides a way to rationalise the *Tecmed* decision, so far as it concerns legitimate expectations. The facts of *Thunderbird* are described in the previous section.[256] Professor Wälde agreed with the majority that Thunderbird's request for an opinion was 'factually – with the hindsight of this tribunal's expertise – incorrect' and that the regulator's response was phrased as conditional on the accuracy of the investor's information.[257] Professor Wälde also stressed that legitimate expectations could only be created by officials acting in their official capacity and that SEGOB had been acting in its official capacity.[258] (This was not a point of contrast with the majority; it is a condition of the creation of a legitimate expectation accepted, either explicitly or implicitly,

---

[252] Ibid., paras. 68, 171–2.   [253] Ibid., para. 173.   [254] Ibid., para. 160.
[255] Ibid., paras. 160, 163.   [256] See Section 4.5.2.1.
[257] *International Thunderbird Gaming v. Mexico*, Separate Opinion, paras. 63–64.
[258] Ibid., para. 31.

by all arbitral decisions that allow expectations to be based on unilateral statements of the host state.)

The key difference between Professor Wälde and the majority concerned a question of law, not a finding of fact. The difference was the degree of specificity required of a unilateral statement for it to justify a legitimate expectation. The majority had held that because SEGOB's response did not contain any clear or specific assurance that Thunderbird's machines were permitted under Mexican law, Thunderbird could not expect that its machines were permitted. In contrast, Wälde held 'that the risk of ambiguity falls square on the shoulders of the assurance-issuing public authority'.[259] The fact that SEGOB's response could reasonably have been understood by the investor as suggesting approval of the machines was, on his interpretation of the doctrine, sufficient to establish a legitimate expectation.[260]

4.5.3.3 Restatement of the stability approach

Again, there are differences in emphasis among these decisions. However, they are distinguished from decisions with the representations approach in that they accept that legitimate expectations may be based on general regulations in force at the time the investment is made or on unilateral representations made by the host state that lack the clarity and specificity that would be required by the representations approach. With respect to the scope of the doctrine:

1. Legitimate expectations may be based on general regulations in force at the time the investment was made. Legitimate expectations may also be based on unilateral statements made by the host state. Insofar as legitimate expectations are based on unilateral representations, they need not be based on a clear and specific statement of the state's position.

With respect to the criteria by which *legitimate* expectations are identified:

2. The assessment of whether a given expectation is legitimate still involves a balancing exercise but, consistently with the focus of providing stability to the investor, the perspective of the investor weighs more heavily in this balance than it would under the representation approach. The key issue is whether the altered

---

[259] Ibid., paras. 57, 77.   [260] Ibid., para. 64.

regulation was a basic element of the legal regime governing the investment at the time it was made.

With respect to the reliance:

> 3. To recover for the infringement of a legitimate expectation based on a general regulation, the investor must have relied on the expectation in making the decision to invest. However, there is some suggestion that an investor may recover from the breach of expectations created by unilateral statements that it did not rely on in making an investment.

4.5.4 The business plan approach

A handful of decisions take a still broader view of the doctrine of legitimate expectations. What distinguishes these cases from those reviewed in previous sections is that, in each of them, the investor succeeded in a claim for breach of legitimate expectations when the protected expectation was neither based on a legal right vested in the investor nor on a unilateral statement of the host state, nor on the regulations in force at the time the investment was made. These decisions are best rationalised as protecting expectations based on the business plans of the investor, when the state knew, or should have known, that the impugned conduct would upset the investor's business plans. There are difficulties in finding a jurisprudential justification for these decisions. Most commentators agree that, as a matter of legal doctrine, an investor's subjective expectations are not protected by the FET standard.[261] However, the three decisions reviewed in this section come close to allowing an investor to recover for interference with its subjective expectations.

4.5.4.1 MTD, Bogdanov and Walter Bau

The case of *MTD* v. *Chile* concerned an investor's proposal to redevelop land near Santiago. The investor acquired land that was not zoned for redevelopment. It then applied for permission to import capital into Chile to fund the project, a transfer which required the approval of the Chilean Foreign Investment Commission (FIC).[262] The application to transfer funds into Chile required the investor to specify the location and nature of the investment project to which the funds related. The FIC, a national agency,

---

[261] Kinnear, 'The Continuing Development of the Fair and Equitable Treatment Standard', p. 230; similarly, *Saluka* v. *Czech Republic*, Partial Award, para. 304.

[262] *MTD* v. *Chile*, Award, para. 162.

approved the transfer of funds into Chile. The relevant local authority subsequently refused MTD's request to rezone the land for redevelopment. MTD claimed that the FIC's decision created an expectation that the proposed redevelopment could proceed in the specified location.[263]

The tribunal accepted Chile's argument that, as a question of Chilean law, approval of the import of capital did not entitle the investor to proceed with the project without complying with local planning regulations.[264] Indeed, the FIC's approval explicitly noted that all investment projects were required to comply with other applicable national laws.[265] Moreover, the tribunal did not identify any unilateral statement made by the host state which suggested that the land would be rezoned; or that the national authorities would override normal local zoning procedures; or that the investment would be exempted from zoning requirements. Nevertheless, the tribunal characterised the approval of capital transfer and rejection of rezoning as an 'inconsistency of action between two arms of the same Government vis-a-vis the same investor'.[266] In its view, the authorisation to import capital gave 'prima facie to an investor the expectation the project is feasible in that location from a regulatory point of view.'[267] The local authority's refusal to rezone the land breached this expectation.[268]

The tribunal's assertion that liability rested on the inconsistency of Chile's conduct is problematic. In many legal systems, an investor must comply with a range of different regulations simultaneously. The fact that a factory owner must comply with both environmental regulations and tax law is not normally regarded as constituting an inconsistency. Rather, the *MTD* decision seems to rest on the findings of fact that the Chilean state was put on notice of MTD's business plans; it acted in a way that allowed MTD to pursue these plans and then subsequently acted in a way that upset these plans. According to the tribunal's interpretation of the doctrine of legitimate expectations, these three facts were *sufficient* to establish Chile's liability.

The case of *Bogdanov* v. *Moldova* also arose from a relatively simple set of facts. The claimant had signed a privatisation contract with the state. The contract provided that the claimant would transfer assets to the state in exchange for shares in other, unspecified state-owned companies. After the contract had been signed, the Moldovan authorities drew up a list of Eligible Compensation Shares in state-owned companies with which

---

[263] Ibid., para. 116.   [264] Ibid., para. 163.   [265] Ibid., para. 188.
[266] Ibid., para. 163.   [267] Ibid., para. 163.   [268] Ibid., para. 189.

the claimant could be compensated. The claimant argued that all the available shares deprived the compensation mechanism of its substance because the market value of the shares was below their face value.[269] The tribunal found that, under the proper law of the contract at the time it was signed (and at all subsequent times), there was no limit on the state's discretion to nominate which shares in state-owned companies would be offered as compensation shares. It also found that the contract entitled the state to offer shares at their face value, rather than their market value.[270]

Notwithstanding these findings of fact and law, the tribunal held that the claimant had a 'legitimate expectation of obtaining compensation (even if not necessarily a fully satisfactory compensation).' It agreed with the claimant that the compensation mechanism had been 'deprived of its value' and, therefore, held that the claimant's legitimate expectation had been breached.[271] To understand the tribunal's reasoning, it is important to note that the principle that a contractual compensation term should not be 'deprived of its value' was not a principle of Moldovan contract law. The expectation of the claimant was a *business* expectation that existed independently of the terms of the agreement the claimant had made with the state.

The business plan approach to legitimate expectations is articulated most clearly in *Walter Bau v. Thailand*. Walter Bau was a minority investor in a Thai tollway project. The investment consortium invested under a concession contract, which required it to build the tollway and then allowed it to collect the toll on the road for 25 years.[272] Ten years into the project, the terms of the concession were renegotiated, with the renegotiated agreement (MoA2) providing for an increase in the toll and the removal of an on-ramp. The Thai authorities subsequently refused to increase the toll, citing the consortium's failure to remove the on-ramp.[273] Then, in further negotiations to which the claimant objected, the consortium agreed to a reduction in the toll in exchange for the settlement of other legal disputes with the authorities.[274] The claimant sold its stake in the consortium and claimed that its legitimate expectations had been breached by the failure of the authorities to increase the toll.

The tribunal held that the state's failure to increase the toll had breached the claimant's legitimate expectation of a reasonable rate of

---

[269] *Bogdanov* v. *Moldova*, Arbitral Award, p. 3.   [270] Ibid., p. 13.   [271] Ibid., p. 17.
[272] *Walter Bau* v. *Thailand*, Award, para. 2.36.
[273] Ibid., para. 12.14.   [274] Ibid., paras. 12.26–30.

return on its investment. It was explicit that these expectations stemmed from the claimant's business plans:

> The Respondent could not reasonably have expected that foreign investors would enter into an arrangement of the nature proposed, over such a long period, without being fairly confident of a reasonable rate of return on investment. . . .

> In spite of the fact that there was no guarantee by the Respondent of an explicit rate of return, the Tribunal considers that a reasonable rate of return – reasonable in all the circumstances, including the signing of MoA2 [which had the effect of reducing the expected rate of return] – was part of the Claimant's legitimate expectations and the failure to fulfil such a reasonable expectation was a breach of the Respondent's obligations.[275]

The tribunal acknowledged that, as a question of Thai corporate law, the minority investor was bound by the decision of the consortium to consent to the toll reduction. However, it held that it would be unfair for this fact to preclude the claimant from recovering for breach of the FET standard.[276]

The tribunal did not consider whether, to recover for breach of a legitimate expectation, a claimant had to rely on that expectation in making its investment. It would be difficult to reconcile Walter Bau's expectation of a reasonable rate of return with such a requirement of reliance. The original concession agreement did not confer any entitlement on the consortium to an increase in the toll. In the quantum section of the award, the tribunal stated that the claimant's legitimate expectations that had been breached were those that existed at the time of the signing of MoA2 in 1996.[277] The claimant's original investment in the consortium had been made ten years earlier and there was no evidence that it made any subsequent investment in reliance on MoA2 or the business plans it engendered.

4.5.4.2 Restatement of the business plan approach

These three decisions constitute a coherent, albeit expansive, interpretation of the doctrine of legitimate expectations. This interpretation can be restated in the following propositions. With respect to the scope of the doctrine:

1. An expectation may be based on the business plans of the investor if the host state knew or should have known of those plans.

---

[275] Ibid., paras. 12.2–3.   [276] Ibid., para. 12.31.   [277] Ibid., para. 13.10.

With respect to the criteria by which *legitimate* expectations are identified:

2. Business plans must be reasonable to justify a legitimate expectation. However, a business plan is not unreasonable simply because it is premised on assumptions about the way the state will act in the future that are based neither on the legal rights of the investor, nor on the regulatory arrangements in force when the investment was made, nor on any unilateral statement made by the state.

With respect to reliance:

3. A claimant may recover for a breach of an expectation even if did not rely on that expectation in making the investment.

4.5.5 Summary: the four interpretations of the legitimate expectations element of FET

This chapter has argued that the protection of investors' legitimate expectations is a recognised element of the FET standard. The preceding sections have categorised decisions dealing with this element according to their understanding of the scope of the doctrine of legitimate expectations. Decisions embody four different views of the basis for expectations protected by the FET standard. Each of these views can be characterised as a distinct, coherent interpretation of the legitimate expectations element of the FET standard. The four views are as follows:

i) Expectations must rest on specific rights that the investor has acquired under domestic law. This is the legal rights approach.
ii) In addition to i), expectations may rest on specific unilateral representations of government officials. This is the representations approach.
iii) In addition to ii), expectations may rest on the regulatory framework in force in the host state at the time the investor made the investment. This is the stability approach.
iv) In addition to iii), expectations may rest on the business plans of the investor. This is the business plan approach.

4.6 Procedural review of government conduct under the FET standard

This section examines decisions in which state liability under the FET standard turns on failure to meet procedural standards of conduct, excluding cases associated with the conduct of judicial proceedings. (Such cases are governed by the doctrine of denial of justice.) It is widely recognised in arbitral decisions that a state's failure to meet a minimum standard of procedural fairness in non-judicial conduct may breach its obligation to provide FET.[278] Academic commentators agree that the FET standard imposes procedural obligations on host states, whether these obligations are classified under the label of 'procedural propriety and due process',[279] 'regulatory fairness and transparency'[280] or simply 'transparency'.[281]

Few decisions have attempted to articulate complete accounts of the principles of procedural review. Nevertheless, there seems to be a degree of consensus around some fundamental propositions. These include the proposition that the obligation of due process in administrative conduct is lower than that required in judicial proceedings under the doctrine of denial of justice,[282] and the proposition that, although a failure to follow the procedural requirements of national law may make a breach of FET more likely, the determination ultimately involves the application of an international standard.[283]

There are also significant differences between decisions in their interpretation of the procedural element of the FET standard. To make sense of these differences, I organise arbitral jurisprudence around key decisions. Three interpretative approaches are identified in this way:

i) A narrow approach, based on *Genin*, in which procedural unfairness must be aggravated either by being intentional or by having led to an outcome that cannot be justified on substantive grounds for it to breach the FET standard;

ii) An intermediate approach, based on *Chemtura*, in which procedural unfairness is sufficient to breach the FET standard, but in which the intensity of review is lenient – requiring 'procedurally improper behaviour . . . both serious itself and material to the outcome' of an administrative process; and

---

[278] E.g., *Waste Management v. Mexico (II)*, Final Award, para. 98; *Methanex v. United States* Final Award, pt. IV, chp. C, para. 12; *Saluka v. Czech Republic*, Partial Award, para. 308.

[279] Dolzer and Schreuer, *Principles of International Investment Law* (2nd edn), p. 154; Tudor, *The Fair and Equitable Treatment Standard in the International Law of Foreign Investment*, p. 162; similarly, Kläger, 'Fair and Equitable Treatment' in International Investment Law', p. 213.

[280] Grierson-Weiler and Laird, 'Standards of Treatment', p. 277.

[281] Newcombe and Paradell, *Law and Practice of Investment Treaties*, p. 292.

[282] *International Thunderbird Gaming v. Mexico*, Arbitral Award, para. 200; Kreindler, 'Fair and Equitable Treatment', p. 14.

[283] *International Thunderbird Gaming v. Mexico*, Arbitral Award, para. 194; *Elettronica Sicula SpA (United States of America v. Italy)*, Judgment of 20 July 1989, para. 127.

iii)   An exacting approach, based on the detailed set of procedural
       requirements outlined in *Tecmed*.

Each set of decisions is characterised as a coherent, if conceptually incomplete, interpretation of the scope of procedural review under the FET standard. Although the majority of cases are broadly consistent with the intermediate approach, decisions that fall within the narrow and exacting approaches deserve to be taken seriously; they are forthright and unambiguous in proposing interpretations strikingly different from the intermediate approach. Moreover, the narrow approach remains relevant to current arbitral practice, having been applied in the *Glamis Gold* decision.

Finally, some mention must be made of the relationship between the procedural element of the FET standard and principles governing compensation for breach of FET. Although investment treaties do not generally specify the formula by which compensation for a breach of FET should be determined, tribunals have calculated damages on the basis of the principle laid down in *Chorzów Factory*:[284]

[R]eparation must, as far as possible, wipe out all the consequences of the illegal act and re-establish the situation which would, in all probability, have existed if that act had not been committed.[285]

The application of this principle in cases of procedural review is not straightforward. Consider for example, a situation in which a domestic regulatory authority must determine whether an investor has satisfied the conditions required for the renewal of its licence to operate the investment. A state may be liable for breach of the FET standard if the procedure by which the authority determines whether to renew the licence fails to meet some minimum standard of fairness. However, it will not necessarily be the case that the investor's licence would have been renewed if fair procedures had been followed. Quantification of the extent of loss *caused* by the procedural unfairness would then require the tribunal to consider what would have occurred if the state had followed a fair procedure.

---

[284] Paradell, 'The BIT Experience of the Fair and Equitable Treatment Standard' in Ortino et al. (eds), *Investment Treaty Law: Current Issues II* (2007), p. 137.
[285] *Case concerning certain German interests in Polish Upper Silesia (Germany v. Poland) (Claim for Indemnity)* (hereafter, *Chorzów Factory*) PCIJ Rep Series A No 17, p. 47.

This counter-factual inquiry may raise issues of some complexity.[286] For present purposes, it is sufficient to note that, on a given set of facts, the compensation to which a claimant is entitled may be affected by whether the tribunal finds that the breach of FET resulted from procedural unfairness or some other element of the FET standard.

4.6.1 Genin: a narrow approach

The facts in *Genin* v. *Estonia* concerned the revocation of the banking licence of an Estonian bank, EIB, in which the claimant was a major shareholder. The decision to revoke the licence was made on 'extremely technical' grounds. Authorisation to acquire shares in EIB had been granted to Eurocapital Group Company but EIB's share register showed that shares were acquired by Eurocapital Group Limited, which the regulator took to be a different and unauthorised entity.[287] The central question for the tribunal was whether Estonia breached the FET standard by revoking the licence in a manner that was procedurally unfair.[288] In answering this question, the tribunal also took into account the fact that EIB had previously failed to disclose information on the ultimate ownership of its shareholders, as it was required to do under domestic law.[289] The tribunal found that

[n]o notice was ever transmitted to EIB to warn that its licence was in danger of revocation unless certain corrective measures were taken, and no opportunity was provided to EIB to make representations in that regard.[290]

The decision to revoke the licence 'was made immediately effective, giving EIB no opportunity to challenge it in court before it was publicly announced.'[291]

The tribunal held that, to breach the FET standard, conduct must fall 'far below international standards':[292]

[A]ny procedural irregularity that may have been present would have to amount to bad faith, a wilful disregard of due process of law or an extreme insufficiency of action.'[293]

---

[286] *Chevron* v. *Ecuador (I)* Partial Award on the Merits, paras. 380–4; *Lemire* v. *Ukraine (II)*, Award, para. 171.

[287] *Alex Genin* v. *Estonia*, Award, para. 359.   [288] Ibid., Award, para. 357.

[289] Ibid., paras. 351–7.   [290] Ibid., para. 358.   [291] Ibid., para. 364.

[292] Ibid., para. 367.   [293] Ibid., para. 371.

In the tribunal's assessment, the conduct did not fall below this standard. It relied heavily on the finding that, regardless of the procedural failings, the decision to revoke the licence was *substantively* justified – 'ample grounds existed for the action'.[294] Moreover, it found no evidence that departures from 'generally accepted banking and regulatory practice' were intentional or in bad faith.[295]

This approach was reinforced by the *Glamis Gold* Tribunal, which took a similarly restrained view of the procedural element of the FET standard. It accepted the United States' argument that the FET standard does not impose a freestanding requirement of transparency.[296] The tribunal went on to hold that Article 1105(1) of NAFTA imposed 'a floor, an absolute bottom, below which conduct is not accepted by the international community.' Procedural impropriety could only breach this standard if it constituted 'blatant unfairness, [or] a complete lack of due process' – something 'far beyond the measure's mere illegality, an act so manifestly arbitrary, so unjust and surprising as to be unacceptable from the international perspective.'[297]

The facts of the case did not provide the tribunal with the opportunity to explore the threshold set by this adjective-enriched formulation. Among a patchwork of related claims, the claimant alleged that an official administrative re-interpretation of US mining law breached the FET standard because it did not comply with the requirements under US federal law to afford interested parties notice and the opportunity for comment.[298] The tribunal held that this claim did not raise a live issue because, 'if there was a procedural error, it was corrected quickly and effectively through domestic channels' by the adoption of a new interpretation two years later.[299]

4.6.1.1 Restatement of the narrow approach

Genin and *Glamis Gold* are united by the view that procedural unfairness will only breach the FET standard if it exceeds some very high threshold of seriousness. These decisions are defined by their examination of procedural conduct that *does not* breach the FET standard, rather than by detailed exploration of the forms of conduct that might be sufficiently extreme to cross the threshold of liability. Nevertheless, they provide enough guidance to outline a coherent interpretation of the procedural element of FET, one that is embodied in the following propositions:

---

[294] Ibid., para. 367, similarly, paras. 361, 363.
[295] Ibid., paras. 364, 371.   [296] *Glamis Gold v. United States*, Award, paras. 578, 605, 627.
[297] Ibid., paras. 627, 626.   [298] Ibid., para. 771.   [299] Ibid., para. 771.

1. To breach the FET standard, administrative action must amount to 'bad faith, a wilful disregard of due process of law or an extreme insufficiency of action.'
2. This requirement places only minimal procedural obligations on host states. It seems that procedural unfairness will only breach the FET standard if it is aggravated either by being intentional or by having led to an outcome that cannot be justified on substantive grounds.
3. There is no freestanding requirement of transparency under the FET standard. A failure to act transparently could only breach the FET standard to the extent it falls within still uncharted concepts such as 'extreme insufficiency of action'.

4.6.2 Chemtura: *an intermediate approach*

The NAFTA case *Chemtura* concerned a Canadian ban on pesticides containing lindane, the claimant was a producer of such pesticides. The events leading to the ban were triggered by the US government's decision to prohibit the import of lindane-treated canola seed.[300] The Canadian Pest Management Regulatory Agency (PMRA) then launched a 'Special Review' of the use of lindane. The review took two years and reached the conclusion that the health risks to workers handling lindane-containing pesticides justified a Canadian ban of these products.[301] At the claimant's request, a government 'Board of Review' was established to review the decision of the PMRA. Its report recommended that the PMRA reconsider alternatives to mitigate the occupational-health issues relating to the use of lindane.[302] The PMRA then launched a re-evaluation process, to which the claimant made submissions. The re-evaluation confirmed the findings of the original Special Review and concluded with a letter to the claimant addressing the submissions it had made on alternative mitigation measures.[303]

The claimant made two principal allegations: that the Special Review was a sham, motivated by the need to avoid trade complications with the United States rather than legitimate health and environmental concerns and that the process of the Special Review was flawed.[304] The tribunal dismissed the first claim on the facts.[305] However, it accepted that, even if the Special Review of lindane had been conducted in good faith, it could still have breached the claimant's right to procedural fairness under the FET standard.[306] It held that the review process should be assessed 'as a whole' taking into account the subsequent procedures that constituted 'an additional opportunity offered to the claimant to put forward its

---

[300] *Chemtura* v. *Canada*, Award, para. 13.   [301] Ibid., paras. 21–9.   [302] Ibid., paras. 35–40.
[303] Ibid., paras. 41–5.   [304] Ibid., para. 133.   [305] Ibid., para. 143.   [306] Ibid., para. 145.

position.'[307] The claimant advanced a range of contentions, including that it had not been given sufficient notice of the Special Review; it had not been given sufficient practical opportunities to make submissions; the Special Review did not incorporate adequate scientific evidence; and that the Special Review was not completed in a timely manner. The tribunal found a degree of factual support for some of the claimant's contentions, particularly the argument that the claimant lacked opportunities to make submissions to the original Special Review. However, it felt that these facts did not reach the threshold of 'procedurally improper behaviour by the PMRA which was both serious in itself and material to the outcome of its inquiry' that would amount to a breach of the FET standard.[308]

Several other decisions are consistent with the threshold that procedural impropriety must be both serious in itself and material to the outcome of the proceedings to breach the FET standard. The tribunal in AES v. Hungary held that

not every process failing or imperfection... will amount to a failure to provide fair and equitable treatment. The standard is not one of perfection. It is only when a state's acts or procedural omissions are, on the facts and in the context before the adjudicator, manifestly unfair or unreasonable (such as would shock, or at least surprise a sense of juridical propriety)... that the standard can be said to be infringed.[309]

The procedural element of the claimant's FET claim turned on an assessment of the procedures by which the government implemented regulated pricing in the electricity industry. Although the tribunal held that there were 'procedural shortcomings', the most serious being the tight deadlines for comment on the draft price decrees, it held that these did not rise to the level of breaches of FET.[310] The tribunal noted that claimants had been given an opportunity to comment on the draft decrees that would be applied to them; that, notwithstanding the tight deadlines, they had been able to make comments; that the Ministry considered the claimant's comments and, at times, had adjusted the decrees accordingly; and that the claimants had the opportunity to seek review of the process in Hungarian courts.[311]

In Lemire v. Ukraine (II) the claimant alleged that a series of administrative decisions relating to the award of radio licenses under tender were

---

[307] Ibid., para. 145.   [308] Ibid., para. 148.
[309] AES Summit Generation v. Hungary, Award, para. 9.3.40.
[310] Ibid., para. 9.3.66.   [311] Ibid., paras. 9.3.50–69.

unfair.[312] In considering the claims, the tribunal held that the FET standard did not place a general obligation on the licensing authority to provide reasons for its decisions.[313] However, the licensing authority repeatedly awarded licenses to politically well-connected individuals, notwithstanding the claimant's uncontested evidence that it better-satisfied the criteria for award of particular licenses.[314] In this context, the licensing body's failure to state reasons for its decisions was central to the tribunal's decision that the licensing authority's decision-making procedures had breached the FET standard.[315] Similarly, in *Teco v. Guatemala*, the tribunal held that, in setting electricity tariffs, the Guatemalan electricity regulator could not ignore the recommendations of the independent Expert Commission that formed part of regulatory framework governing the sector without providing reasons for its decision.[316]

In *Middle East Cement v. Egypt* the procedure by which an administrative seizure and sale of a ship owned by the claimant was executed was deemed to have breached the FET standard. The serious procedural shortcoming in the case was that the authorities did not notify the claimant that the ship would be seized, even though claimant's and its lawyer's addresses were known to the authorities.[317] In *Waste Management II*, the tribunal agreed that the FET standard could be breached by 'a complete lack of transparency and candour in an administrative process.'[318] In *Thunderbird*, the facts of which are described above,[319] the tribunal held that the procedure by which SEGOB had determined that Thunderbird's machines did not comply with gaming legislation satisfied the FET standard because the claimant had been given an opportunity to be heard and present evidence.[320] In *PSEG v. Turkey*, the tribunal held that 'continuous and endless' changes in the legislation governing an investment and in the interpretation and implementation of that legislation by the Turkish authorities breached the FET standard.[321]

4.6.2.1 Procedural fairness in contractual dealings?

Chemtura, *AES v. Hungary*, *Lemire II*, *Middle East Cement* and *Thunderbird* all concerned the degree of procedural fairness to which a claimant was

---

[312] *Lemire v. Ukraine (II)*, Decision on Jurisdiction and Liability, para. 315.
[313] Ibid., para. 394.   [314] Ibid., para. 384.
[315] Ibid., paras. 419–20; Hepburn, 'The Duty to Give Reasons for Administrative Decisions in International Law' (2012) 61 *International and Comparative Law Quarterly*, p. 650.
[316] *Teco v. Guatemala*, Award, paras. 583-8.   [317] *Middle East Cement v. Egypt*, Award, para. 143.
[318] *Waste Management v. Mexico (II)*, Final Award, para. 98.   [319] See Section 4.5.2.1.
[320] *International Thunderbird Gaming v. Mexico*, Arbitral Award, para. 198.
[321] *PSEG v. Turkey*, Award, paras. 250–4.

entitled in administrative proceedings that directly affected the claimant's interests. Other decisions have considered whether these requirements extend to contractual dealings. The leading case on this point is *Bayindir*. The claimant argued that it had been denied a right to be heard in the Pakistani government's decision to terminate a contract with the claimant, a decision that had been made on the basis of the claimant's non-performance.[322] The tribunal accepted that a lack of procedural fairness in administrative proceedings could breach the FET standard but held that these procedural guarantees were not available in every situation.[323] A claimant was not entitled to be heard in a government's internal decision-making processes relating to the exercise of rights created by a contract.[324] Similarly, in *Biwater* the tribunal held that the FET standard did not place a procedural obligation on the Tanzanian water-regulator to consider a proposal to modify an existing contract to the benefit of the claimant (and the detriment of the host state) because the claimant had no contractual right to renegotiation.[325]

On the other hand, a state's failure to follow the *procedures specified by the contract* in cancelling a contract with the investor was central to finding a breach of FET in *Rumeli v. Kazakhstan*.[326] The tribunal held that the conduct of an administrative review of the validity of the contract cancellation procedure constituted a further breach of FET because the claimants were unable to present their position and the review's finding of validity relied on different grounds to those that formed the basis for the original decision.[327]

An exception to the principle that a claimant is not entitled to procedural fairness in contractual dealings was articulated in the decision *Jan de Nul v. Egypt*. The tribunal held that the state's failure to disclose key contractually relevant information in pre-contractual negotiations could amount to a breach of FET.[328] On the facts, the tribunal found that this failure of disclosure did not breach the FET standard as the claimant was on notice that it should rely on its own inquiries and was in a position to ascertain the information.[329] Similarly, in *PSEG v. Turkey*, the tribunal held that 'evident negligence' on the part of the host state in contractual negotiations with the claimant breached the FET standard.[330] These two

---

[322] *Bayindir v. Pakistan*, Award, para. 338.   [323] Ibid., para. 344.   [324] Ibid., para. 345.
[325] *Biwater v. Tanzania*, Award, para. 673.   [326] *Rumeli v. Kazakhstan*, Award, para. 615.
[327] Ibid., para. 617.   [328] *Jan de Nul v. Egypt*, Award, para. 221.
[329] Ibid., para. 229.   [330] *PSEG v. Turkey*, Award, para. 246.

decisions can be read as imposing a requirement of procedural fairness in contractual negotiations broadly equivalent to the standard of procedural fairness required in administrative proceedings, as understood in *Chemtura*. Both decisions can be distinguished from *Bayindir* and *Biwater* on the basis that they did not impose procedural obligations on a state to enter into contractual negotiations nor additional obligations relating to the performance of existing contracts.

4.6.2.2 A requirement of lawfulness?

A state's compliance with domestic law can be understood as one aspect of procedural fairness, as a requirement of lawfulness constitutes a constraint on the manner in which a state may exercise its powers. Several decisions have examined the extent to which the FET standard requires a host state to act lawfully. In the NAFTA case *ADF* v. *US*, the claimant alleged that an administrative authority's failure to comply with the terms of its empowering statute breached the FET standard.[331] The tribunal held that 'something more than simple illegality or lack of authority under domestic law of a State is necessary' to breach the FET standard.[332] In another NAFTA case, *GAMI*, the claimant argued that the failure of the Mexican sugar industry regulator to fully implement the pricing and quota regulations that governed the industry breached the FET standard. The tribunal held that a 'failure to fulfil the objective of administrative regulations without more does not necessarily rise to a breach of international law.'[333] It found that the claimant had not proved that the regulator had a 'simple and unequivocal' duty to achieve the objectives of the regulatory regime, nor that the regulator had made an '"outright and unjustified repudiation" of the relevant regulations.'[334] These two decisions are consistent with the threshold defined in *Chemtura* – that procedural unfairness, here a failure to comply with domestic law, must be both serious and material to breach the FET standard.

The extent of a requirement of lawfulness was further explored in the decision *Noble* v. *Romania*. The tribunal held that the FET standard precluded a state from treating an investment in an arbitrary manner.[335] It quoted the ICJ's decision in *ELSI* to explain that arbitrariness, in this context, referred to

---

[331] *ADF Group* v. *United States*, Award, para. 190.   [332] Ibid., para. 190.
[333] *GAMI Investments* v. *Mexico*, Final Award, para. 97.   [334] Ibid., paras. 110, 103.
[335] *Noble Ventures* v. *Romania*, Award, para. 182.

[n]ot so much something opposed to a rule of law, as something opposed to the rule of law.... It is a wilful disregard of due process of law, an act which shocks, or at least surprises, a sense of juridical propriety.[336]

The tribunal held that commencement of insolvency proceedings against the claimant was not arbitrary because the proceedings were 'initiated and conducted according to the law and not against it.'[337] The suggestion that unlawfulness must be wilful appears to introduce a requirement of intent.[338] However, the following phrase – which affirms that arbitrariness includes action that surprises juridical propriety – appears to leave the possibility open that serious disregard of national law would breach FET, even if an intention to ignore national law were not established.

4.6.2.3 Transparency

Several tribunals have held that the FET standard imposes an obligation of transparency on host states. Discussion of 'transparency' in the reasoning of FET decisions is complicated by differences in the way the term is used.[339] Transparency is best understood as one aspect of the procedural element of the FET standard. Although both commentators and tribunals have linked the requirement of transparency to the protection of legitimate expectations,[340] this association is not doctrinally sound. A state may change domestic law in a way that an investor did not anticipate and still inform the investor openly, promptly and clearly that the law has so changed. Such a situation could not be said to lack transparency (save, perhaps, in the narrow circumstance in which a state had concealed a prior intention to change the law). Conversely, a state may refuse to make new regulations publicly available – yet, if the content of such secret regulations were entirely consistent with an investor's expectations, such a situation could not be said to breach an investor's legitimate expectations.

The better view is that any requirement of transparency under the FET standard refers to an obligation on the host state that

---

[336] Ibid., para. 176, citing: *Elettronica Sicula SpA (United States of America v. Italy)*, Judgment of 20 July 1989, para. 128.

[337] *Noble Ventures v. Romania*, Award, paras. 178.

[338] Similarly, *Teco v. Guatemala*, Award, para. 458.   [339] See Section 4.4.1.

[340] E.g., Dolzer and Schreuer, *Principles of International Investment Law* (2nd edn), p. 149; Wälde, 'Energy Charter Treaty-based Investment Arbitration' (2004) 5 *Journal of World Investment and Trade*, p. 387; *Occidental v. Ecuador (I)*, Final Award, para. 185.

all relevant legal requirements for the purpose of initiating, completing and successfully operating investments made, or intended to be made under an investment treaty should be capable of being readily known to all affected investors.[341]

This is consistent with the threshold articulated in *Chemtura*. A state that did not make it possible for an investor to ascertain the content of the laws that applied to its investment would perpetrate a serious unfairness, material to the investor's ability to operate its investment. The tribunal in *Champion Trading* v. *Egypt* applied this understanding of transparency in a claim brought by a cotton company regarding administrative decrees that determined the sale price of cotton.[342] The tribunal dismissed the claim, finding that the claimants 'were in a position to know beforehand all rules and regulations that would govern their investments for the respective [cotton] season to come.'[343]

4.6.2.4 Restatement of the intermediate approach

Chemtura concerned the degree of procedural fairness to which an investor is entitled in administrative proceedings that directly affected the claimant's interests. The threshold articulated in that decision is capable of explaining and justifying a number of other decisions concerning the procedural element of the FET standard. This set of cases provides the outline of a coherent interpretation of the procedural element of FET, one embodied in the following propositions:

1. Procedural unfairness will breach the FET standard if it is both serious in itself and material to the outcome of proceedings that directly affect the investor.
2. A state may breach this threshold without the procedural unfairness leading to an outcome that is substantively unjustified or irrational.
3. A state may breach this threshold without acting in bad faith.
4. The record as a whole, including the availability of recourse under domestic law, determines whether the threshold has been breached.
5. Whether administrative proceedings breach this threshold will depend on assessment of what is fair in the specific context, which may include review of the following: whether the investor was notified of proceedings and given an opportunity to be heard in them; whether

---

[341] *LG&E Energy* v. *Argentina*, Decision on Liability, para. 128.
[342] The claimant originally framed this claim as a breach of the FET provision of the treaty but later framed it simply as a breach of 'international law'. The tribunal referred to a decision of the WTO Appellate Body and the *Tecmed* tribunal's discussion of the FET standard in addressing the claim. *Champion Trading* v. *Egypt*, Award, paras. 157–64.
[343] *Champion Trading* v. *Egypt*, Award, para. 164.

proceedings were conducted according to the requirements of domestic law; whether decision-making was based on the consideration of evidence; whether reasons were given for the decision; and whether the decision was reached in a timely manner.

6. Investors are not entitled to procedural fairness in contractual dealings, save that if a state does enter contractual negotiations with an investor, it must conduct itself fairly in those negotiations.

7. A state's serious and material failure to comply with its own law will breach the FET standard.

8. The procedural element of FET includes a transparency requirement that laws that apply to an investment should be readily capable of being known.

4.6.3 Tecmed: *an exacting approach*

The facts of *Tecmed* were described earlier in the chapter.[344] In its decision, the tribunal articulated a comprehensive conception of the FET standard, much of which addressed procedural requirements imposed by the standard. Portions of the relevant paragraph read as follows:

> The foreign investor expects the host State to act in a consistent manner, free from ambiguity and totally transparently in its relations with the foreign investor, so that it may know beforehand any and all rules and regulations that will govern its investments, as well as the goals of the relevant policies and administrative practices or directives, to be able to plan its investment and comply with such regulations. Any and all State actions conforming to such criteria should relate not only to the guidelines, directives or requirements issued, or the resolutions approved thereunder, but also to the goals underlying such regulations. . . . The investor also expects the State to use the legal instruments that govern the actions of the investor or the investment in conformity with the function usually assigned to such instruments.[345]

This tribunal's reasoning has been criticised for failing to apply its statement of the law to the facts of the case.[346] While noting this criticism, there can be no doubt that the paragraph purported to lay down the tribunal's understanding of the FET standard. It is introduced with the sentence '[t]he Arbitral Tribunal considers that this provision of the Agreement [the FET provision] . . . requires the Contracting Parties to . . . '.[347] The paragraph has also been cited as a statement of the content of the FET

---

[344] See Section 4.5.3.2.   [345] *Tecmed v. Mexico*, Award, para. 154.

[346] Douglas, 'Nothing If Not Critical for Investment Treaty Arbitration: Occidental, Eureko and Methanex' (2006) 22 *Arbitration International*, p. 28.

[347] *Tecmed v. Mexico*, Award, para. 154.

standard by other tribunals.[348] It may be that the tribunal felt no need to chart the outer boundary of the legal standard it had articulated because Mexico's conduct fell short of less exacting standards of conduct.

It is clear that the tribunal's interpretation of the procedural element of FET is more exacting than that of the *Chemtura* Tribunal. The *Tecmed* Tribunal's language is unqualified: a state must act 'totally transparently'; '[a]ny and all state actions' should be lawful and consistent with the goals underlying the laws in question. In this way, the *Tecmed* Tribunal suggests that *any* finding of procedural unfairness would breach the FET standard. The obvious contrast with the *Chemtura* approach is the absence of a threshold of seriousness or materiality before the identified classes of unfairness rise to the level of breaches of FET.

4.6.3.1 Transparency

The *Tecmed* dicta focused closely on unfairness that results from a state's failure to act in a way that is 'free from ambiguity and totally transparent'.[349] This entails a more exacting obligation on host states than the requirement that laws be capable of being known.[350] An investor may know the law that applies to its investment yet be faced with ambiguity, either because the terms of the law are not sufficiently precise or because the law confers a degree of discretion on the authorities that administer it. On the facts of the case, the *Tecmed* Tribunal held that the 'ambiguity and uncertainty' relating to the legal situation of the landfill breached the FET standard.[351] This ambiguity did not stem from any lack of clarity about the conditions governing the claimant's licence or the fact that the licence was – formally – only of one year's duration. Rather, the lack of transparency in the case stemmed from uncertainty about the way in which an administrative authority would exercise a discretion conferred by clear and certain general laws; specifically, the question of whether the investor's licence would be renewed.[352]

A similar understanding of the obligation of transparency under the FET standard was developed in *Metalclad* v. *Mexico*.[353] One of the reasons for the tribunal's decision that Mexico breached the FET standard was that it had failed to provide this degree of transparency.[354] Under Mexican

---

[348] *MTD* v. *Chile*, Award, para. 114; *Roussalis* v. *Romania*, Award, para. 316.
[349] *Tecmed* v. *Mexico*, Award, para. 154.
[350] Cf. *LG&E Energy* v. *Argentina*, Decision on Liability, para. 128; *Champion Trading* v. *Egypt*, Award, para. 164.
[351] *Tecmed* v. *Mexico*, Award, para. 172.   [352] *Tecmed* v. *Mexico*, Award, para. 172.
[353] *Metalclad* v. *Mexico*, Award, para. 76.   [354] Ibid., para. 88.

law, which was readily capable of being known, it was not clear whether the approval of the claimant's landfill by federal authorities exempted the claimant from the normal requirement of obtaining a municipal construction permit.[355] The fact that the municipal construction permit was denied at a meeting 'of which Metalclad received no notice, to which it received no invitation, and at which it was given no opportunity to appear' constituted further grounds for the finding that Mexico had breached the FET standard.[356]

4.6.3.2 Administrative proceedings

The *Tecmed* Tribunal did not explore the implications of its interpretation for the conduct of administrative proceedings in great detail. The tribunal did find that the environmental agency: failed to give the investor reasonable notice that, in the agency's view, the investor was in breach of its licence conditions; and that it failed to inform the investor that this could constitute grounds for non-renewal of the licence.[357] The tribunal did not consider whether these events would have constituted an independent breach of the FET standard.

Another case that held that procedural unfairness would breach the FET standard, without identifying a minimum threshold of gravity that such unfairness would need to exceed, is the early NAFTA decision *Pope & Talbot*.[358] The relevant facts concerned a Canadian government agency's 'verification review' of the investor's compliance with lumber regulations. The American investor was required to transport truckloads of documents to Canada for the review. Despite a request from the investor, the agency refused to consider holding the review at the claimant's offices in the United States or to provide reasons justifying its refusal. The tribunal characterised this conduct as placing a 'substantial and disruptive burden' on the claimant, a burden caused by agency's 'imperious insistence on having its own way.'[359] The tribunal drew further support for its conclusion from the fact that the agency refused to disclose what legal authority (if any) entitled it to conduct a review.[360] Although the claimant could have sought judicial review of these administrative actions,[361] the tribunal did not consider that this weighed against a finding of liability.[362]

---

[355] Ibid., paras. 81–6.   [356] Ibid., para. 91.   [357] *Tecmed* v. *Mexico*, Award, para. 161.
[358] *Pope & Talbot* v. *Canada*, Award on the Merits of Phase 2, paras. 116–18.
[359] Ibid., paras. 172–3.   [360] Ibid., para. 174.
[361] Ibid., para. 183.   [362] Ibid., paras. 156–81.

4.6.3.3 Procedural fairness in contractual dealings?

Although the *Tecmed* decision did not discuss procedural fairness in contractual dealings, it is consistent with the exacting approach of *Saluka*. The principal finding in *Saluka* was that the claimant's investment (a bank) had not been treated as well as locally owned banks.[363] However, the tribunal made a further finding that the procedural unfairness suffered by the claimant constituted an *independent* breach of FET. The claimant's bank was struggling to meet the capital adequacy requirements necessary to remain solvent and was seeking to negotiate the terms of a bailout with the host state. The claimant had no legal entitlement to be bailed out, nor had it received assurances that it would be bailed out. The host state made it clear from the outset that it would not gift funds to the claimant's bank unless the investor also injected new capital.[364] The bank subsequently failed.

The Tribunal held that the FET standard imposed a procedural obligation:

[T]hat the host State [take] seriously a proposal that has sufficient potential to solve the problem and deal with it in an objective, transparent, unbiased and even-handed way.[365]

The tribunal found that the Czech Republic breached this obligation by declining to consider plans proposed by the investor in which the state would bailout the bank without the investor having to make any co-contribution.[366] The decision implies a duty on the state actively to consider (and to consider fairly) an investor's contractual proposals, even those that the state views as substantively unacceptable. This principle contrasts with the *Biwater* decision, which expressly rejected arguments that the FET standard imposes an obligation on host states to consider contractual proposals made by investors.[367]

4.6.3.4 Restatement of the exacting approach

The *Tecmed* decision articulated a clear and detailed interpretation of the procedural element of the FET standard. Although the trend in recent jurisprudence has been towards less exacting interpretations of the procedural element of the FET standard, the key paragraph from *Tecmed* award

---

[363] *Saluka* v. *Czech Republic*, Partial Award, paras. 314–47.   [364] Ibid., paras. 385, 396.
[365] Ibid., paras. 363, 407.   [366] Ibid., para. 398.
[367] Cf. *Biwater* v. *Tanzania*, Award, para. 673.

remains influential and is still cited by arbitral tribunals with approval.[368] The decisions identified in this section provide a basic outline of an interpretation of the procedural element of FET that differs significantly from *Chemtura*, one embodied in the following propositions:

1. Procedural unfairness will breach the FET standard. A finding of unfairness is sufficient to breach the standard without any additional finding that the unfairness exceeds a threshold of seriousness.
2. The availability of further administrative or judicial recourse does not necessarily weigh against a finding of unfairness.
3. The FET standard imposes an exacting transparency obligation on host states. Not only must laws be capable of being known, but the policies that underpin them and the manner in which they will be applied to particular fact scenarios must also be capable of being known in advance.
4. The FET standard entails a procedural obligation on states to actively and fairly consider contractual proposals made by investors.

4.6.4 Summary: the three interpretations of the procedural element of FET

This chapter has identified three interpretations of the procedural element of the FET standard:

i) A narrow approach, based on the *Genin*, in which procedural unfairness must be aggravated either by being intentional or by having led to an outcome that cannot be justified on substantive grounds for it to breach the FET standard;
ii) An intermediate approach, based on *Chemtura*, in which procedural unfairness is sufficient to breach the FET standard if it is 'both serious itself and material to the outcome' of an administrative process; and
iii) An exacting approach, based on the detailed set of procedural and transparency requirements outlined in *Tecmed*.

4.7 Substantive review of government conduct under the FET standard

Many arbitral awards have held that the FET standard also allows tribunals to review government conduct on substantive grounds. For example, in *Saluka* the tribunal stated that any government conduct affecting an investment must be 'reasonably justifiable by public policies'

---

[368] E.g., *Roussalis* v. *Romania*, Award, para. 316.

in order to comply with the FET standard.[369] Academic commentators generally agree. In commentary, discussion of this substantive element of the FET standard is organised under the labels of 'unreasonableness',[370] proportionality,[371] or 'arbitrariness' (using arbitrariness to mean absence of substantive justification).[372] However, unlike the legitimate expectations and procedural review elements of the FET standard, there is a small but significant set of arbitral decisions that rejects the possibility of review of government conduct on substantive grounds under the FET standard.

The recent popularity, and potential breadth, of the doctrine of legitimate expectations has meant that fewer decisions have considered the substantive element of the FET standard than would otherwise be the case. The review of government conduct on substantive grounds bears a particularly close similarity to the 'stability approach' to legitimate expectations. This similarity is clearest in the reasoning of *El Paso v. Argentina* tribunal, in which the two concepts were largely merged:

> [T]he legitimate expectations of a foreign investor can only be examined by having due regard to the general proposition that the State should not unreasonably modify the legal framework or modify it in contradiction with a specific commitment not to do so.[373]

Nevertheless, there are several good reasons to distinguish substantive review under the FET standard from the protection of legitimate expectations. First, most tribunals agree that a foreign investor must have *relied* on the legal status quo in making its investment in order to claim a legitimate expectation protected by the FET standard.[374] In contrast, substantive review of government conduct under the FET standard would allow a foreign investor to challenge any government conduct that affects its investment without needing to show reliance. Second, and contrary to the extract of the *El Paso* decision quoted earlier, the majority of tribunals have held that the doctrine of legitimate expectations is limited to situations in which a state infringes either a legal right vested in the investor or a specific representation made to the investor. In contrast, substantive review of government conduct under the FET standard would,

---

[369] *Saluka v. Czech Republic*, Partial Award, para. 307.
[370] Vandevelde, *Bilateral Investment Treaties*, p. 202.
[371] Kläger, *'Fair and Equitable Treatment' in International Investment Law*, p. 236.
[372] Salacuse, *The Law of Investment Treaties*, p. 240.   [373] *El Paso v. Argentina*, Award, para. 364.
[374] E.g., *Frontier Petroleum v. Czech Republic*, Final Award, paras. 287–8.

however conceived, allow a tribunal to examine government conduct that is neither inconsistent with a representation made to the investor nor in breach of the investor's legal rights. In both of these respects, the substantive review element of the FET standard would allow foreign investors to challenge a broader range of government conduct than could be challenged under the doctrine of legitimate expectations. (Although a greater range of government conduct could be challenged under principle of substantive review, the legal principles applied in the course of substantive review under the FET standard may be more lenient, from the perspective of the state, than those applied under the doctrine of legitimate expectations.)

In this section, I identify four different interpretations of the substantive review element of the FET standard. Section 4.7.1 examines decisions that have held that the FET standard does not provide for the review of government conduct on substantive grounds. Section 4.7.2 introduces the concept of reasonableness, which operates as an organising principle for several decisions interpreting the substantive review element of the FET standard. Sections 4.7.3 and 4.7.4 consider two different interpretations that are based on the principle of reasonableness. These two interpretations are distinguished by their different understandings of how a tribunal should determine whether government conduct pursues a 'rational' objective. Section 4.7.5 examines decisions endorsing the view that the substantive review element of the FET standard requires a tribunal to consider whether government conduct is proportionate.

Before examining arbitral reasoning, it is important to note that some investment treaties contain provisions that specifically prohibit the impairment of an investment by 'arbitrary and discriminatory' or 'unreasonable and discriminatory' measures. In applying these provisions, tribunals also engage in substantive review of government conduct. This chapter examines decisions interpreting and applying these provisions only insofar as the tribunal in question held that arbitrariness or unreasonableness in breach of these provisions would *necessarily* constitute a breach of FET. Some of the key decisions examining the substantive element of the FET standard – notably, *AES* v. *Hungary* and *Biwater* – are based on reasoning incorporated into the FET standard in this way.

4.7.1 The 'no substantive review' approach

The view that the FET standard does not allow for the substantive review of government conduct is most clearly articulated in Paparinskis' scholarship on the history and development of the IMS. Having reviewed a range of legal material, both within and beyond investment treaty arbitration, he concludes that

> international law defers to the legitimacy of the purpose and means chosen to pursue it as such (unless they are entirely indefensible), but scrutinizes the formal and procedural safeguards against abuse in their implementation (the absence of which permits a more critical engagement with the ends and means).[375]

On this view, the FET standard does not grant arbitral tribunals a general jurisdiction to review government conduct on substantive grounds. Questions of whether government conduct is substantively justified arise only if a state has breached an investor's legal rights or treated the investor in a way that lacks procedural fairness. In these situations, any questions of substantive justification are purely internal to the legitimate expectations and procedural review elements outlined earlier.[376]

In the context of investment treaty arbitration, the view that the FET standard does not provide for generalised substantive review can be traced to the NAFTA decision *SD Myers* v. *Canada*. In the course of its brief discussion of the FET standard, the tribunal held that:

> [w]hen interpreting and applying the "minimum standard", a Chapter 11 tribunal does not have an open-ended mandate to second-guess government decision-making. Governments have to make many potentially controversial choices. In doing so, they may appear to have made mistakes, to have misjudged the facts, proceeded on the basis of a misguided economic or sociological theory, placed too much emphasis on some social values over others and adopted solutions that are ultimately ineffective or counterproductive.[377]

Two more recent decisions have endorsed the same view. In *Paushok* v. *Mongolia*, the investor, a company engaged in gold mining, argued that a significant increase in the tax on gold sales breached the FET standard.[378] In rejecting the claim, the tribunal explained that

> the fact that a democratically elected legislature has passed legislation that may be considered as ill-conceived, counter-productive and excessively burdensome does not automatically allow to conclude that a breach of an investment treaty has occurred. If such were the case, the number of investment treaty claims would

---

[375] Paparinskis, *The International Minimum Standard and Fair and Equitable Treatment*, p. 243.
[376] See, e.g., Section 4.5.1.1; Section 4.6.1.1.
[377] *SD Myers* v. *Canada*, Partial Award, para. 261.
[378] *Sergei Paushok* v. *Mongolia*, Award on Jurisdiction and Liability, para. 104.

increase by a very large number. Legislative assemblies around the world spend a good part of their time amending substantive portions of existing laws in order to adjust them to changing times or to correct serious mistakes that were made at the time of their adoption.[379]

The tribunal's view that 'ill-conceived, counter-productive and excessively burdensome' legislation would not breach the FET standard clearly precludes substantive review under the FET standard. The tribunal did not consider whether different principles would apply to the review of non-legislative measures.

Comments made by the NAFTA tribunal in *Mobil and Murphy Oil v. Canada* can also be read as rejecting the possibility of substantive review under the FET standard. In the course of rejecting the claimant's argument that the FET standard requires a state to provide stable legal framework, the tribunal explained:

> Article 1105 is not, and was never intended to amount to, a guarantee against regulatory change, or to reflect a requirement that an investor is entitled to expect no material changes to the regulatory framework within which an investment is made. Governments change, policies changes and rules change. These are facts of life with which investors and all legal and natural persons have to live with.[380]

That the tribunal rejected the possibility of substantive review under the FET standard is confirmed by the way it formulated its conclusions. It held that, in order to show that the FET standard had been breached, the claimant would have had to show either that the host state had breached a specific representation made to the investor or that the state's conduct amounted to serious procedural impropriety.[381]

4.7.1.1 Restatement of the 'no substantive review' approach

A small but significant number of tribunals, mostly within NAFTA, have held that the FET standard does not grant foreign investors a freestanding right to challenge government conduct on substantive grounds. This approach can be summarised as follows:

1. There is no freestanding substantive element to the FET standard; investors cannot challenge government conduct under the standard solely on the grounds that it lacks substantive justification.

---

[379] Ibid., para. 299.
[380] *Mobil and Murphy Oil v. Canada*, Decision on Liability and Principles of Quantum, para. 153.
[381] Ibid., paras 170–1.

2. Questions of whether government conduct is substantively justified arise only if a state has breached an investor's legal rights or treated the investor in a way that lacks procedural fairness. In these situations, any substantive review is internal to the scope and application of these doctrines.

4.7.2 Reasonableness review in general

Contrary to the view that the FET standard is not concerned with the strength of substantive justifications for conduct affecting foreign invest-ments, several tribunals have held that the standard imposes a require-ment of reasonableness. Among decisions that adopt reasonableness as the organising principle for the substantive review element of the FET standard, there is relative consensus on some issues and disagreement on others. These decisions agree on the following:

1. To comply with the FET standard, state conduct must be justifiable by some *rational objective* and be a *reasonable* attempt to advance that objective.
2. The substantive element of the FET standard is an independent basis for liability. A sufficiently irrational measure will breach the FET standard even if it is introduced and applied through a fair procedure and does not upset an investor's legitimate expectations.
3. The FET standard does not empower a tribunal to review the legal arrangements in place when the investor makes the initial investment (although it may review the subsequent exercise of a power or discretion conferred by a pre-existing law).[382]

Despite consensus on these basic issues, there is disagreement as to the degree of scrutiny to which a tribunal should subject a state's choice of policy objectives. This disagreement is particularly evident in the way in which tribunals deal with the 'politicisation' of government decision-making, which I use as a fault line to identify to distinct strands of rea-soning within the set of decisions that endorses reasonableness as the basic organising principle. In one set of decisions, the politicisation of a measure is irrelevant to the assessment of whether it has a rational objec-tive. In these decisions, tribunals allow states a wide discretion to define the objectives of their public policy. This interpretation is the subject of Section 4.5.3. I label it the margin of appreciation approach.[383] In a second

---

[382] *GAMI Investments* v. *Mexico*, Final Award, para. 91; Dolzer, 'Fair and Equitable Treatment', p. 102.

[383] I adopt the term 'margin of appreciation' from the jurisprudence of the European Court of Human Rights (ECtHR). The ECtHR allows states a margin of appreciation in

set of decisions, 'political reasons' are contrasted to rational objectives.[384] In these decisions tribunals scrutinise the motivations for a government's conduct and, in effect, invoke a presumption that a politically motivated measure does not pursue a rational objective. This interpretation is the subject of Section 4.5.4. I label it the politics-as-irrationality approach.

4.7.3 Reasonableness review: the margin of appreciation approach

AES v. Hungary concerned the reintroduction of regulated pricing in the electricity industry. The tribunal held that this change in the regulatory framework would breach the FET standard if it was substantively unreasonable.[385] The tribunal's expression of this legal standard was clear and concise:

10.3.7   There are two elements that require to be analyzed to determine whether a state's act was unreasonable: the existence of a rational policy; and the reasonableness of the act of the state in relation to the policy.

10.3.8   A rational policy is taken by a state following a logical (good sense) explanation and with the aim of addressing a public interest matter.

10.3.9   Nevertheless, a rational policy is not enough to justify all the measures taken by a state in its name. A challenged measure must also be reasonable. That is, there needs to be an appropriate correlation between the state's public policy objective and the measure adopted to achieve it. This has to do with the nature of the measure and the way it is implemented.[386]

The tribunal then assessed the three reasons Hungary argued had justified the reregulation of pricing. The first was that it was necessary to overcome electricity generators' refusal to reduce the capacity that they produced and sold to the state under existing contracts. The tribunal

its assessment of whether a given interference with property rights pursues a 'legitimate aim "in the public interest"': James v. UK (1986) 8 EHRR 123, para. 50; Winisdoerffer, 'Margin of Appreciation and Article 1 of Protocol No 1', p. 19. However, I do not intend to suggest that the way these arbitral tribunals approach the question of the existence of a 'rational policy' is identical to the way the ECtHR approaches the question of the existence of a 'legitimate aim "in the public interest"'. Nor do I intend to suggest that arbitral tribunals consciously imported this concept from the jurisprudence of the ECtHR.

384   Peterson was the first to note this contrast between the AES and Biwater decisions: Peterson, 'Hungary Prevails in First of Three Energy Charter Treaty (ECT) Arbitrations over Power Pricing Disputes; Arbitrators Affirm That "Politics" Is Not a Dirty Word' (2010) IA Reporter [online].

385   AES Summit Generation v. Hungary, Award, paras. 9.3.37–38.   386   Ibid., paras. 10.3.7–9.

held that the *aim* of forcing a private party to give up contractual rights could not, in itself, qualify as a rational public policy. It contrasted this to a situation in which pursuit of some other rational policy affects an investor's contractual rights, a situation that would be consistent with the rational objective requirement.[387] (At this point, it is important to note that the contracts in question did not fix the price at which the state was required to purchase electricity but only the volume of electricity that generators were entitled to sell to the state).[388] The second was that the measure was necessary for Hungary to comply with European law. The tribunal accepted that this could be a rational policy, although, because concerns under European law had not crystallised until after the measure was introduced, they could not provide a rational justification for it on the facts of the case.[389] The third reason for reregulation was that 'in the absence of either competition or regulation' the generators' profits on the fixed-volume electricity sale contracts 'exceeded reasonable rates of return for public utility sales.'[390] The tribunal held that it was

a perfectly valid and rational policy objective for a government to address luxury profits. And while such price regimes may not be seen as desirable in certain quarters, this does not mean that such a policy is irrational.[391]

Perhaps the most significant finding of the tribunal related to the significance of the politicisation of electricity pricing, stemming from public opposition to the higher prices that resulted from unregulated pricing. The tribunal held that

the level of the generators' returns became a public issue and something of a political lightning rod in the face of upcoming elections.

10.3.23   However, the fact that an issue becomes a political matter, such as the excessive profits of the generators and the reintroduction of the Price Decrees, does not mean that the existence of a rational policy is erased.

10.3.24   In fact, it is normal and common that a public policy matter becomes a political issue; that is the arena where such matters are discussed and made public.[392]

Having accepted that redressing excessive profitability in one sector of the economy was a rational public policy objective, the tribunal held that reregulating pricing was a reasonable way to achieve that objective.[393]

---

[387] Ibid., para. 10.3.13.   [388] Ibid., para. 4.4–11.   [389] Ibid., para. 10.3.16.
[390] Ibid., para. 10.3.20.   [391] Ibid., para. 10.3.34.   [392] Ibid., para. 10.3.22.
[393] Ibid., para. 10.3.35.

The regulated price was set to allow investors an annual profit of 7.1% of the value of the investment.

A line of earlier decisions are consistent with the principles of substantive review under the FET standard articulated in *AES v. Hungary*. In these cases, the analysis of whether conduct is justified by a rational policy and the assessment of whether it is a reasonable attempt to achieve this policy are often closely intertwined. For example, in *Pope & Talbot*, the tribunal held that adjustment of lumber quotas to the claimant's detriment did not breach the FET standard because it was a 'reasonable response to the difficulty with which it [the host state] had to deal'.[394]

In a more recent NAFTA decision, *Glamis Gold*, the tribunal observed that 'it is not for an international tribunal to delve into the details of and justifications for domestic law.'[395] In isolation, this statement could be read as implying that the FET contains no substantive element. However, the tribunal went on to confirm that conduct with a 'manifest lack of reasons' would breach the standard.[396] By lack of reasons, the tribunal meant lack of rational justification, not a failure to state reasons. It found that the host state had met this requirement because a new measure requiring backfilling of goldmines was 'rationally related to its stated [environmental] purpose and reasonably drafted to address its objectives.'[397] The tribunal also addressed the fact that the new backfilling regulation appeared to be partially motivated by public opposition to the mine on environmental grounds. Indeed, one member of Californian legislature had stated as much.[398] The tribunal held that the fact that the mine was politically contentious and the new measure had been designed to apply to it did not foreclose the question of whether the measure had a rational policy objective:

> [E]ven if an individual [legislator] did single out the Imperial Project, it could be in the nature of describing a symbol that has come to represent the harm that the legislature is striving to remedy. Symbols often can serve as a rallying call for expedited action; if, however, this symbolic project is merely a very visible member of a larger class of projects that are viewed as harmful by the legislature, and which also are addressed by the subsequent litigation [sic], it cannot be said that this project alone was 'targeted.'[399]

The decision in *Merrill Ring* was unusual in that the members of the tribunal were unable to agree on the interpretation of Article 1105(1) of

---

[394] *Pope & Talbot v. Canada*, Award on the Merits of Phase 2, para. 125.
[395] *Glamis Gold v. United States*, Award, para. 762.   [396] Ibid., para. 779.
[397] Ibid., para. 803.   [398] Ibid., paras. 703–10.   [399] Ibid., para. 792.

NAFTA.[400] To sidestep this disagreement, the tribunal applied both the interpretation of the FET standard asserted by the claimant and that asserted by the respondent to the facts.[401] It found that the host state had not breached either threshold. Nevertheless, the split reasoning of the tribunal neatly encapsulates the difference between the two interpretations of reasonableness identified in this chapter. The interpretation advanced by the host state echoed the *AES* v. *Hungary* decision. Applying this interpretation, the tribunal held that encouraging local processing of timber was a rational policy objective, notwithstanding that it benefited the Canadian timber processing industry at the expense of the Canadian logging industry.[402] The lumber export quota system, of which the claimant (a US investor in the Canadian logging industry) complained, was a reasonable attempt to encourage local processing.[403]

Two further decisions focus more closely on the second-stage of substantive review – the requirement that a measure be reasonable in relation to its objective. Discussing Argentina's response to its financial crisis, without specific reference to the FET standard, the *Metalpar* Tribunal held that

[e]xcept in very obvious situations, it is extremely difficult to determine at the time such decisions are made, and even some time afterwards, whether said decisions were the best they could have been.... Resolving whether the actions taken by the Argentine Republic...were correct and taken in a timely manner...are discussions that go beyond this Tribunal's sphere of action.[404]

This decision suggests that reasonableness under the FET standard requires only a rational connection between the measure and the achievement of the policy objective pursued by the measure – an interpretation that is consistent with the *AES* v. *Hungary* Tribunal's requirement of an 'appropriate correlation' between means and ends.[405] The same understanding of reasonableness – rational connection between means and ends – was applied in *Eastern Sugar*. The majority of the tribunal held that two reorganisations of the Czech sugar production quota, both of which disadvantaged the claimant relative to other producers, did not breach the FET standard.[406] In making these findings, the tribunal implicitly accepted that reduction of the sugar quota in line

---

[400] *Merrill & Ring Forestry* v. *Canada*, Award, para. 246.   [401] Ibid., para. 219.
[402] Ibid., para. 236.   [403] Ibid., para. 237.
[404] *Metalpar* v. *Argentina*, Award on the Merits, paras. 198–9.
[405] *AES Summit Generation* v. *Hungary*, Award, para. 10.3.9.
[406] *Eastern Sugar* v. *Czech Republic*, Partial Award, paras. 277, 284–5.

with European Community rules was a rational policy objective and that, although poorly designed and implemented, these two measures had a reasoned connection to the realisation of this objective.[407] It was only a third reorganisation of the quota, in which the claimant's quota was cut by more than the entire national quota reduction, that the tribunal found could not be justified by this objective. The state offered no rational justification for the fact the burden was concentrated on the claimant.[408] A measure that *increased* other producers' quotas at the expense of the claimant had no rational connection with the objective of reducing the industry's total sugar production.

4.7.3.1 Restatement of the margin of appreciation approach

This set of decisions is best explained and justified by the doctrinal principles carefully articulated in *AES* v. *Hungary*. To comply with the substantive element of the FET standard:

1. Conduct must be capable of justification by a rational policy and be a reasonable attempt to achieve that policy.
2. A tribunal should show a high degree of deference to a state's choice of policies. The fact that a policy objective is highly politicised does not bear on the question of whether the objective is rational.
3. The assessment of reasonableness requires a rational connection between means and ends; it does not impose a requirement of proportionality or 'least restrictive means'.

4.7.4 Reasonableness review: the politics-as-irrationality approach

In *Biwater* v. *Tanzania*, the tribunal was required to apply an investment treaty provision prohibiting unreasonable or discriminatory measures. It cited the *Saluka* decision as authority for the proposition that 'the standard of "reasonableness" has no different meaning than the "fair and equitable treatment" standard'.[409] The tribunal held that the standard of reasonableness requires that government conduct 'bears a reasonable relationship to some rational policy'.[410] Stated at this level of generality, this interpretation of the substantive element of the FET standard is no different to that articulated in *AES* v. *Hungary*. However, when it came to apply the law to the facts, the tribunal showed less deference to the host state's choice of policy objectives.

---

[407] Ibid., paras. 261, 290–1.   [408] Ibid., para. 336.
[409] *Biwater* v. *Tanzania*, Award, para. 692.   [410] Ibid., para. 693.

The case arose out of events relating to the termination of a Tanzanian water concession held by the claimant. The privatisation of the water supply and the poor performance of the concessionaire had become contentious political issues. Although the host state was entitled to terminate the concession on account of the claimant's defective contractual performance, the tribunal held that the state's conduct up to the termination could not be justified by rational policies. The tribunal identified a number of occasions on which the state's conduct lacked substantive justification, of which two are particularly relevant. On 13 May 2005, the water minister held a press conference at which he criticised the claimant's performance of the contract and announced that the contract had been terminated. On 17 May 2005, the minister addressed the concession's staff and also claimed that concession had been terminated. Although the tribunal agreed that, by early May, the government had initiated the process necessary to terminate and that termination was 'inevitable', it found that the concession was not legally terminated until the end of the contractual cure period on 24 June 2005.[411]

In this context, Tanzania argued that the premature claims of termination could be justified by the 'rational policy of keeping citizens apprised of matters that affect their lives.'[412] The tribunal rejected this argument as an attempt to provide an 'ex post facto' justification for statements that were, in fact, politically motivated:

> The press conference exceeded the bounds of normal information, included severe criticisms of BGT [the claimant] which were at least in part clearly motivated by political considerations.[413]

In other cases, tribunals have reviewed the justifications for government conduct, without explicitly identifying the standard as one of rationality. Nevertheless, these cases are consistent with rationality review in which politically motivated conduct is presumptively unreasonable. In *Merrill Ring*, the tribunal applied the two distinct interpretations of the substantive element of FET to the facts. In the application of the broader interpretation, the tribunal held that the investor was entitled to be free from 'interference from government regulations which are not underpinned by appropriate policy objectives.'[414] The tribunal suggested that the objective of supporting an industry, when such support was to the detriment of another industry, would not be a rational policy objective.[415]

---

[411] Ibid., paras. 625–6.   [412] Ibid., paras. 683, 686.   [413] Ibid., paras. 696, 698.
[414] *Merrill & Ring Forestry v. Canada*, Award, para. 233.   [415] Ibid., para. 233.

Applying this interpretation, the tribunal noted that the lumber regulations of which the claimant complained 'appear to be geared towards some sort of benefit to the local [timber processing] industry.'[416] It also noted that the regulations were designed by an industry co-regulatory institution of which representatives of the timber processing industry were members. This politicised institution was contrasted with a 'truly independent body'.[417] Despite these criticisms, the tribunal concluded that the FET standard had not been breached, a conclusion that is difficult to reconcile with the reasoning that precedes it.[418]

Azurix v. *Argentina*, like *Biwater*, concerned the termination of a water concession operated by the claimant. The dispute arose out of a long-running disagreement between the parties about tariffs and costs under the contract. The claimant sought to terminate the concession on the basis of non-compliance by the provincial government. The government denied that it was in breach and insisted that the claimant had abandoned the concession.[419] In its assessment of the facts, the tribunal accepted some of the claimant's contentions relating to the contract and rejected others; it did not make an ultimate finding of whether, under Argentine law, the claimant was entitled to terminate on the basis of the province's non-compliance.[420] Instead, the tribunal resolved the FET claim by examining whether the province's conduct was justified. It held that Argentina had breached the FET standard because the positions taken by the water regulator in the dispute with the concessionaire were motivated by popular opposition to tariff increases: 'the tariff regime was politicized because of concerns with forthcoming elections'.[421]

The tribunal in *Tecmed*, the facts of which were described earlier in the chapter, displayed a similar understanding of the substantive element of FET.[422] Although the primary basis for the state's liability in the case was breach of the investor's legitimate expectations, the tribunal also held that conduct 'arbitrarily revoking any pre-existing decisions or permits issued by the State' would breach the FET standard.[423] When it came to apply this element, the tribunal noted that the environmental agency's decision not to renew Tecmed's operating permit was motivated by the fact the waste facility had become 'a nuisance due to political reasons relating to the community's opposition'.[424] Because the decision

---

[416] Ibid., para. 226.   [417] Ibid., para. 228.   [418] Ibid., paras. 226–30.
[419] *Azurix* v. *Argentina*, Award, para. 374.   [420] Ibid., paras. 225–61.
[421] Ibid., paras. 375, 92, 378.   [422] See Section 4.5.3.2.
[423] *Tecmed* v. *Mexico*, Award, para. 154.   [424] Ibid., para. 164.

was motivated by political concerns it was not, in the tribunal's view, justified by environmental or public health objectives.[425]

The *Biwater*, *Azurix* and *Tecmed* decisions all concluded with findings that the measure impugned in the case was not related to a rational policy. These awards had no need to continue to the second stage of analysis – whether the measure in question was reasonable in relation to a rational policy.[426] It is impossible to know whether they would have required a rational connection between means and ends or whether they would have adopted some other, perhaps stricter, understanding of reasonableness. As such, the legal content of this interpretation of the substantive element of FET is not yet fully defined.

4.7.4.1 Restatement of the politics-as-irrationality approach

Of these four decisions, only *Biwater* employs the language of reasonableness and rationality. Nevertheless, it is clear that the *Merrill Ring*, *Azurix* and *Tecmed* Tribunals determined states' liability under the FET standard by reviewing the conduct of the host state on substantive grounds. In all these decisions, the tribunals sought to determine whether the host state's conduct was justified by a rational policy objective. These tribunals (including *Biwater*) engaged in a more detailed examination of the objectives that did, in fact, motivate the conduct of the state in question than tribunals adopting the margin of appreciation approach. This distinction is clearly illustrated by the former's approach to politically motivated conduct. None of these decisions explored the legal contours of the second-stage of substantive review: the requirement that a measure must bear a reasonable relationship to the rational policy that provides its justification. However, it is important to note that they did not purport to introduce requirements of proportionality or a 'least restrictive measure' test. According to these decisions, to comply with the substantive element of the FET standard:

1. Conduct must be capable of justification by a rational policy and be a reasonable attempt to achieve that policy.
2. A tribunal should not defer to a state's choice of objectives. The fact that a policy objective is politicised creates a presumption that it is not rational.

---

[425] Ibid., paras. 129–30. This aspect of the *Tecmed* Tribunal's reasoning has been criticised in detail in Schneiderman, 'Investing in Democracy? Political Process and International Investment Law' (2010) 60 *University of Toronto Law Journal* 909.

[426] *Biwater v. Tanzania*, Award, para. 693.

4.7.5 The proportionality approach to substantive review

A final interpretation of the substantive element of the FET standard is based on the principle of proportionality. In recent years, several academic commentators have argued that the principle of proportionality should be applied in the review of government conduct under the FET standard.[427] However, arbitral tribunals have been less enthusiastic.[428] Reasonableness is still more commonly cited and applied as the basis for substantive review under the FET standard. Nevertheless, in light of the *Occidental v. Ecuador (II)* decision, there is now a line of cases endorsing an approach to substantive review under the FET standard based on the principle of proportionality.

In some early arbitral awards, the concept of proportionality is mentioned alongside other principles of substantive review. For example, in *Vivendi II*, the tribunal concluded that the respondent's 'irresponsible, unreasonable and disproportionate' actions breached the FET standard.[429] Similarly, in *El Paso*, the tribunal opined that 'fair and equitable treatment is a standard entailing reasonableness and proportionality.'[430] However, despite these general statements, neither tribunal conducted a proportionality analysis when it came to apply the FET standard to the facts of the case.

The suggestion – implicit in both the *Vivendi II* and *El Paso* awards – that the principles of 'reasonableness' and 'proportionality' are equivalent is at odds with the academic literature and with the way that other tribunals have understood these concepts.[431] Review of whether government conduct is reasonable involves an examination of whether government conduct pursues a rational policy and is a reasonable attempt to achieve that policy, in the sense of their being a rational connection between the means adopted and the end pursued.[432] Proportionality review is significantly more intrusive. In addition to the examination required by

---

[427] Kingsbury and Schill, 'Public Law Concepts to Balance Investors' Rights with State Regulatory Actions in the Public Interest – The Concept of Proportionality' in Schill (ed), *International Investment Law and Comparative Public Law* (2010), p. 97; Diehl, The Core Standard in *International Investment Protection*, p. 337; Montt, *State Liability in Investment Treaty Arbitration*, p. 357.

[428] Kläger, 'Fair and Equitable Treatment' in International Investment Law, p. 245.

[429] *Compañia de Aguas del Aconquija and Vivendi v. Argentina (II)*, Award, para. 7.4.26; similarly, *MTD v. Chile*, Award, para. 109.

[430] *El Paso v. Argentina*, Award, para. 373.

[431] E.g., Henckels, 'Indirect Expropriation and the Right to Regulate', p. 229.

[432] E.g., *AES Summit Generation v. Hungary*, Award, paras. 10.3.7–9.

reasonableness review, proportionality review in most legal systems requires two further stages of scrutiny.[433] For government conduct to be proportionate, it must be the least restrictive means of achieving the objective in question, and the burden on the claimant must be proportionate in light of the objective pursued.[434] Tribunals that suggest 'reasonableness' and 'proportionality' are equivalent misunderstand both concepts and should not be taken as persuasive authority for the application of either principle.

The tribunal in *EDF v. Romania* was the first decision to apply the principle of proportionality in the course of substantive review of government conduct under the FET standard. The facts of the case are described earlier in the chapter. In the course of reviewing Romania's decision to abolish airport duty-free sales on substantive grounds, the tribunal held that

in addition to a legitimate aim in the public interest there must be 'a reasonable relationship of proportionality between the means employed and the aim sought to be realized'; that proportionality would be lacking if the person involved 'bears an individual and excessive burden.'[435]

As Kläger has noted, the *EDF v. Romania* Tribunal proceeded directly from the question of whether a measure pursued a legitimate aim to the question of whether the burden on the claimant was proportionate in light of the objective pursued.[436] In doing so, the tribunal skipped over the question of whether the measure was the least means available to achieve Romania's chosen objective. As Section 2.5 explained, this step would normally be included in proportionality analysis in other legal systems.

The decision in *Occidental II* is the first, and so far the only, arbitral decision to apply a full proportionality analysis in the course of substantive review under the FET standard. The claim arose out of an oil participation contract between the claimant and the host state. The claimant had assigned its interest in the concession to a third party, conduct which the tribunal found was in breach of both the terms of the contract and the Ecuadorian Hydrocarbon Law.[437] Both the contract and Hydrocarbon Law (which had been in force at the time the contract was signed) were

---

[433] See Section 2.5.
[434] Kingsbury and Schill, 'Public Law Concepts to Balance Investors' Rights with State Regulatory Actions', pp. 85–7; Stone Sweet and Mathews, 'Proportionality Balancing and Global Constitutionalism' (2008) 47 *Columbia Journal of Transnational Law*, p. 75.
[435] *EDF v. Romania*, Award, para. 293.
[436] Kläger, *'Fair and Equitable Treatment' in International Investment Law*, pp. 244–5.
[437] *Occidental v. Ecuador (II)*, Award, para. 337.

explicit that any attempt by the claimant to assign its rights to a third party would give the state the right to terminate the contract.[438] Ecuador invoked its powers under the Hydrocarbon Law to terminate the contract, purportedly on the grounds of the claimant's breach of the Hydrocarbon Law. Although the tribunal recognised Ecuador's right to terminate the contract under the applicable law, the tribunal held that both Ecuador's constitution and the FET standard required Ecuador to exercise this right to terminate proportionately.[439] In a crucial passage, the tribunal argued that the requirement of substantive proportionality under the FET was binding, even if its analysis of Ecuadorian constitutional law proved to be incorrect.[440]

The tribunal then conducted a full proportionality review of Ecuador's decision to exercise its right to terminate the contract. It began by considering whether Ecuador's decision to cancel the contract advanced a public interest objective. The tribunal characterised Ecuador's objective as deterring future violations of contracts and accepted that this could be a legitimate objective.[441] The tribunal then conducted a detailed examination of whether this objective could have been achieved by other means. It identified a range of different courses of action the government might have adopted – for example, requiring the claimant to pay a fee – which would have achieved the objective of deterring contractual violations without having such a harsh impact on the claimant.[442] The tribunal did not conclude that the existence of equally effective alternatives involving lesser interference with the claimant's investment *automatically* meant that the government's conduct was in breach of the FET standard. However, the fact that such alternatives were available played an important role in justifying the tribunal's conclusion that termination of the contract was not proportionate on an overall assessment. On this basis, the tribunal found that Ecuador had breached the FET standard.[443]

4.7.5.1 Restatement of the proportionality approach to substantive review under the FET standard

A handful of arbitral tribunals have suggested that government conduct that affects foreign investment must be proportionate to be consistent with the FET standard. Many of these statements are incoherent in that they imply that the principles of 'proportionality' and 'reasonableness' are interchangeable. However, following the decision in *Occidental II*, a

---

[438] Ibid., paras. 119–21.   [439] Ibid., paras. 396–409.   [440] Ibid., para. 427.
[441] Ibid., paras. 416–18.   [442] Ibid., para. 434.   [443] Ibid., para. 452.

new interpretation of the substantive review element of the FET standard has emerged. This proportionality approach can be summarised in the following propositions:

1. To comply with the substantive element of the FET standard government conduct must advance a legitimate public interest objective.
2. In addition to advancing a legitimate objective, the interference with the claimant's investment must be proportionate in light of the objective pursued.
3. In examining whether the conduct is proportionate it is relevant, but not conclusive, that there are other means of achieving the public interest objective that involve lesser interference with the investment.

4.7.6 Summary: the four interpretations of the substantive element of FET

This chapter has identified four interpretations of the substantive element of the FET standard or, more precisely, three different interpretations of the substantive element of the FET standard along with a line of cases holding that the FET standard does not provide for substantive review of government conduct. The four approaches are as follows:

i) The FET standard does not provide for review of government conduct on substantive grounds.
ii) Government conduct must be reasonable to comply with the FET standard. This means that conduct must be capable of justification by a rational policy and be a reasonable attempt to achieve that policy. A state is entitled to a margin of appreciation in its choice of policy objectives.
iii) Government conduct must be reasonable to comply with the FET standard. This means that conduct must be capable of justification by a rational policy and be a reasonable attempt to achieve that policy. However, politically motivated conduct is presumptively irrational.
iv) Government conduct must be proportionate to comply with the FET standard.

4.8 Conclusion

Section 4.2 of this chapter argued that decisions interpreting differently worded FET provisions should be understood as one body of decisions interpreting the FET standard. The FET standard, as understood in these decisions, comprises several distinct elements, each of which is capable of operating as a quasi-independent liability rule. Having explained and justified the parameters of this chapter in Section 4.3, Section 4.4 argued that decisions interpreting the FET standard are best understood by dividing them into decisions concerning the legitimate expectations, procedural and substantive elements of the standard.

Section 4.5 showed that tribunals have interpreted the legitimate expectations element in four different ways: the legal rights approach; the representations approach; the stability approach; and the business plan approach. Section 4.6 showed that tribunals have interpreted the procedural element of FET in three different ways: the narrow approach; the intermediate approach; and the exacting approach. Section 4.7 showed that tribunals have interpreted the substantive element of FET in four different ways: the 'no substantive review' approach; the margin of appreciation approach; the politics-as-irrationality approach; and the proportionality approach. This doctrinal analysis is, in itself, a contribution to scholarship on the FET standard. In the context of this book, the analysis in this chapter also performs a more specific function. Each interpretation identified in this chapter constitutes a different level of protection that might be explicitly adopted in future investment treaties or by the amendment of existing investment treaties. Chapter 6 applies the framework developed in Chapter 3 to evaluate these different levels of protection. This evaluation leads to a set of conclusions about the level of protection that investment treaties should provide to foreign investors.

5   Indirect expropriation

5.1 Introduction

The expropriation of foreign property has long been a subject of international law.[1] Clauses in US treaties requiring states to pay compensation if they expropriate foreign-owned property date from the mid-nineteenth century.[2] European states have espoused the position that customary international law requires a state to pay compensation for the expropriation of foreign property since at least that time.[3] Although capital importing states have, at various points, resisted the notion that customary international law requires compensation for expropriation,[4] provisions guaranteeing foreign investors compensation for expropriation are included in almost every investment treaty.[5]

There is an exceedingly high degree of uniformity in the drafting of expropriation provisions of investment treaties.[6] Common formulations require host states to compensate foreign investors for both direct and indirect forms of expropriation.[7] Direct expropriation refers to a situation in which a state formally transfers or extinguishes an investor's

---

[1] Dolzer and Schreuer, *Principles of International Investment Law* (2nd edn. 2012), p. 98.

[2] Vandevelde, 'The Bilateral Investment Treaty Program of the United States' (1988) 21 *Cornell International Law Journal*, p. 205.

[3] Shea, *The Calvo Clause: A Problem of Inter-American and International Law and Diplomacy* (1955), p. 13.

[4] Freeman, 'Recent Aspects of the Calvo Doctrine and the Challenge to International Law' (1946) 40 *American Journal of International Law*, p. 121; UNGA Res 3171 (XXVIII) (17 December 1973); UNGA Res 3281 (XXIX) (9 December 1974).

[5] UNCTAD, *International Investment Agreements: Key Issues, Volume 1* (2004), p. 19; Dolzer and Schreuer, *Principles of International Investment Law* (2nd edn), p. 98.

[6] Lowenfeld, *International Economic Law* (2nd edn, 2008), p. 559.   [7] E.g., NAFTA, art. 1110(1).

title to property.[8] Direct expropriations are relatively easy to identify and seldom controversial. Indirect expropriation refers to a situation in which an investor's legal title is not extinguished but the actions of a state are, in legally significant respects, analogous to direct expropriation. Most government regulations, decisions and policies that affect foreign invest-ments do not constitute indirect expropriation. However, the text of the vast majority of investment treaties (subject to a small but growing num-ber of exceptions) does not provide arbitral tribunals with any guidance on how to draw the boundary between these non-compensable government measures and indirect expropriation.[9]

This chapter seeks to understand and elucidate the different ways in which tribunals interpret the concept of indirect expropriation under investment treaties. I propose a basic taxonomy of the structures of inquiry that tribunals use to distinguish indirect expropriation from legit-imate, non-compensable government measures. The taxonomy divides decisions between those: that look exclusively to the effects of the mea-sure on the protected investment; those that define expropriation by its effects, subject to exceptions for measures with certain characteristics; and those that balance the effects on the investment and the characteris-tics of the impugned measure in determining whether an expropriation has occurred. This chapter then employs an inductive methodology to locate arbitral reasoning within the taxonomy. In this way, five alterna-tive interpretations of indirect expropriation are identified. Each interpre-tation constitutes a level of protection that might be adopted explicitly in future investment treaties. This analysis and classification is, in itself, a contribution to scholarship on indirect expropriation. This classifica-tion also provides the basis for Chapter 6, which applies the framework developed in Chapter 3 to evaluate the five identified levels of protection.

This chapter comprises six substantive sections. Section 5.2 examines the text of expropriation provisions of investment treaties. Section 5.3 introduces and justifies the taxonomy used to classify arbitral reason-ing in this chapter. Section 5.4 examines arbitral decisions that define indirect expropriation exclusively by the effects of the measure in ques-tion; it identifies two distinct interpretations of indirect expropriation that look exclusively a measure's effects. Section 5.5 examines arbitral

---

[8] *Biwater* v. *Tanzania*, Award, para. 454; *Continental Casualty* v. *Argentina*, Award, para. 276.

[9] UNCTAD, *Investor-State Dispute Settlement and Impact on Investment Rulemaking*, p. 56; Dolzer, 'Indirect Expropriation of Alien Property', p. 56.

decisions that define legitimate, non-compensable regulation (measures that do not constitute indirect expropriation) by looking exclusively to the characteristics of a measure; it identifies one such interpretation. Section 5.6 examines arbitral decisions that identify indirect expropriation by balancing the effects and the characteristics of a measure; it identifies two distinct interpretations that employ this structure of inquiry.

5.2 Expropriation provisions of investment treaties

The expropriation provisions of investment treaties are normally drafted in a way that precludes the expropriation of foreign investments unless the host state satisfies certain conditions. The Australia-Mexico BIT is typical:

Neither Contracting Party shall expropriate or nationalise an investment either directly or indirectly through measures tantamount to expropriation or nationalisation (hereinafter referred to as 'expropriation'), except:

a) for a public purpose;
b) on a non-discriminatory basis;
c) in accordance with due process of law; and
d) accompanied by payment of compensation.[10]

Thus, expropriation provisions incorporate three analytically distinct stages of legal inquiry. The first stage of inquiry determines whether given legal interests constitute 'investments' covered by the expropriation provision; the second stage determines whether a given investment, identified in the first stage of the analysis, is expropriated by given government measures; and the third stage of inquiry determines whether an expropriation that has occurred satisfies the criteria of a legal expropriation specified in the treaty, including the criterion that compensation be paid.[11]

This chapter is concerned with the second stage of analysis: the way in which arbitral tribunals determine whether a measure constitutes indirect expropriation for which compensation is required. Within this second stage of analysis, the definition of the term 'measure' is seldom contentious. Tribunals appear to accept that any legislative, regulatory

---

[10] Australia-Mexico BIT (23 August 2005), art. 7(1).
[11] Dolzer and Schreuer, *Principles of International Investment Law* (2nd edn), p. 99.

or administrative action by the state would amount to a measure.[12] Arbitral and academic attention focuses on whether given measures amount to indirect expropriation. Before entering this debate, a key preliminary issue is whether variations in the drafting of expropriation provisions of investment treaties are legally significant, particularly the use of other terms in place of the term 'indirect expropriation'. I argue that this chapter is justified in abstracting from textual difference on the grounds that tribunals interpret differently drafted provisions as if they all embody a common legal concept of indirect expropriation.

Although this chapter focuses on the second stage of the expropriation inquiry, some brief discussion of the first and third stage of inquiry is also warranted because tribunals' approaches to these questions may influence their determination of whether an expropriation has occurred. This section considers questions relating to the characterisation of the 'investment' in indirect expropriation cases and the significance of legality requirements for an expropriation to comply with an investment treaty.

5.2.1 Indirect expropriation and variation in treaty text

The drafting of expropriation provisions is relatively uniform, but there is a modicum of variation between provisions. The key issue is the words used to specify the type of government conduct that will trigger a state's obligation to pay compensation. A brief survey of expropriation provisions reveals a range of formulations. Article 1110 of NAFTA provides that '[n]o Party may directly or indirectly nationalize or expropriate an investment ... or take a measure tantamount to expropriation';[13] the Energy Charter Treaty (ECT) stipulates that investments 'shall not be nationalized, expropriated or subjected to a measure or measures having effect equivalent to nationalization or expropriation';[14] Dutch bilateral investment treaties (BITs) speak of 'measures depriving, directly or indirectly nationals of the other Contracting Party of their investments';[15] and French BITs are sometimes translated as requiring compensation for 'measure[s] having an effect similar to dispossession'.[16] This survey illustrates that investment treaties employ a variety of synonyms for the term

---

[12] *Suez and Vivendi; AWG Group* v. *Argentina*, Decision on Liability, para. 13; Newcombe and Paradell, *Law and Practice of Investment Treaties*, p. 337.
[13] NAFTA, art. 1110(1).   [14] ECT, art. 13(1).
[15] Netherlands-Mexico BIT (13 May 1998), art. 5(1).
[16] Argentina-France BIT (3 July 1991), art. 5(2), as translated in *Compañía de Aguas del Aconquija and Vivendi* v. *Argentina (II)*, Award, para. 7.5.1.

expropriation – including 'nationalisation', 'deprivation' and 'dispossession'. It also reveals that expropriation provisions use different words to indicate that the provision applies to measures that are analogous to direct expropriation – including the phrases 'indirect expropriation', 'measures tantamount to expropriation' and 'measures having effect equivalent to expropriation'.

In general, arbitral tribunals have not given legal significance to the particular words an expropriation provision uses to refer to conduct analogous to direct expropriation. Rather, tribunals interpret differently worded provisions as if they refer to a common concept of indirect expropriation.[17] For example, tribunals regularly frame their analysis in terms of indirect expropriation,[18] even when the expropriation provision of the applicable investment treaty does not contain the words 'indirect expropriation'.[19] An example is tribunals' interpretation of Article 1110 of NAFTA. Although this provision could be read as requiring compensation for both indirect expropriation and a broader category of 'measures tantamount to expropriation', tribunals have rejected the argument that the phrase tantamount to expropriation goes beyond the concept of indirect expropriation.[20]

One possible exception to this general disregard of textual nuance is tribunals' interpretation of provisions that require compensation for measures 'having an *effect* equivalent to nationalization or expropriation.'[21] The tribunals in *National Grid* v. *Argentina* and *Siemens* v. *Argentina* argued that this treaty text requires measures analogous to direct expropriation to be identified exclusively by their effect on an investment.[22] However, most tribunals interpreting identical provisions have not given the 'effect equivalent' formulation special significance, holding instead that this phrase is synonymous with indirect expropriation.[23] Via this interpretative process, several tribunals have arrived at the conclusion that a measure's characteristics, as well as its effects, are relevant in

---

[17] E.g., *Electrabel* v. *Hungary*, Decision on Jurisdiction, Applicable Law and Liability, paras. 6.60–2.

[18] E.g., *LG&E Energy* v. *Argentina*, Decision on Liability, para. 185.

[19] *BG Group* v. *Argentina*, Final Award, para. 259; *Tecmed* v. *Mexico*, Award, para. 114.

[20] *Pope & Talbot* v. *Canada*, Interim Award, para. 96; *Feldman* v. *Mexico*, Award, para. 100; *SD Myers* v. *Canada*, Partial Award, para. 286; *Glamis Gold* v. *United States*, Award, para. 355; cf. *Waste Management* v. *Mexico (II)*, Final Award, para. 155.

[21] *National Grid* v. *Argentina*, Award, para. 147, emphasis in original.

[22] Ibid., para. 147; *Siemens* v. *Argentina*, Award, para. 270.

[23] *Telenor* v. *Hungary*, Award, para. 63; *BG Group* v. *Argentina*, Final Award, para. 259.

determining whether a measure requires compensation under an 'effect equivalent to expropriation' provision.[24]

On these grounds, this chapter is justified as treating arbitral decisions that interpret differently worded provisions as comprising a single body of indirect expropriation cases. This conclusion is buttressed by the frequency with which tribunals cite other arbitral awards that apply differently worded expropriation provisions.[25] It is also consistent with vast majority of academic writing.[26]

A final comment should be made on the terms 'de facto expropriation', 'constructive expropriation', 'creeping expropriation' and 'regulatory expropriation'. These terms rarely appear in the text of expropriation provisions but are sometimes used in academic writing.[27] To the extent tribunals have discussed these terms, they have found that *de facto* expropriation and constructive expropriation are synonymous with indirect expropriation.[28] The term creeping expropriation is more analytically useful:

Creeping expropriation is a form of indirect expropriation with a distinctive temporal quality in the sense that it encapsulates the situation whereby a series of acts attributable to the State *over a period of time* culminate in the expropriatory taking of such property.[29]

As such, the concept of creeping expropriation clarifies, rather than expands, the concept of indirect expropriation. Likewise, the term

---

[24] *Tecmed* v. *Mexico*, Award, para. 114; *Suez and Vivendi; AWG Group* v. *Argentina*, Decision on Liability, para. 139; *Suez and InterAgua* v. *Argentina*, Decision on Liability, para. 128.

[25] See, among others, *National Grid* v. *Argentina*, Award, paras. 148–55; *Fireman's Fund* v. *Mexico*, Award, para. 172; *Telenor* v. *Hungary*, Award, para. 63.

[26] Hoffmann, 'Indirect Expropriation' in Reinisch (ed), *Standards of Investment Protection* (2008), p. 153; Reinisch, 'Expropriation' in Muchlinski, Ortino and Schreuer (eds), *The Oxford Handbook of International Investment Law* (2008), p. 420; Schreuer, 'The Concept of Expropriation under the ECT and Other Investment Protection Treaties' in Ribeiro (ed), *Investment Arbitration and the Energy Charter Treaty* (2006), p. 114; Salacuse, *The Law of Investment Treaties* (2010), p. 300; Newcombe and Paradell, *Law and Practice of Investment Treaties* (2009), p. 341; Dolzer and Schreuer, *Principles of International Investment Law* (2nd edn), pp. 107–12; McLachlan, Shore and Weiniger, *International Investment Arbitration* (2007), p. 275; Montt, *State Liability in Investment Treaty Arbitration* (2009), p. 231.

[27] Newcombe and Paradell, *Law and Practice of Investment Treaties*, p. 432; Knahr, 'Indirect Expropriation in Recent Investment Arbitration' (2009) 6 *Transnational Dispute Management*, p. 2; Weston, '"Constructive Takings" under International Law' under International Law: A Modest Foray into the Problem of "Creeping Expropriation"' (1975) 16 *Virginia Journal of International Law*, p. 111.

[28] *Petrobart* v. *Kyrgyzstan*, Arbitral Award, p. 77; *CME* v. *Czech Republic*, Partial Award, para. 604; *Tecmed* v. *Mexico*, Award, para.114.

[29] *Generation Ukraine* v. *Ukraine*, Award, para. 20.22.

'regulatory expropriation' clarifies that a regulation can amount to an indirect expropriation, rather than expanding the meaning of indirect expropriation.[30]

5.2.2 Indirect expropriation in customary international law

A number of academic writers have argued that the expropriation provisions of investment treaties codify customary international law, including customary law that defines indirect expropriation.[31] If the expropriation provisions of investment treaties all embodied a common rule of customary international law, tribunals would be justified in overlooking differences in the wording that different provisions use to refer to that common rule.[32] While noting that there are strong arguments for this view,[33] for the purposes of this chapter, it is unnecessary to determine whether the expropriation provisions of investment treaties embody customary international law. The purpose of this chapter is to identify and clarify the different understandings in existing arbitral jurisprudence of the level of protection provided by the indirect expropriation provisions of investment treaties.

5.2.3 What is an investment, and why does it matter?

Investment treaties invariably designate the investments that fall within expropriation provisions.[34] The term 'investment' is usually defined broadly to include both physical assets and intangible assets, such as contracts.[35] In this respect the ECT is typical. It defines 'investment' to mean 'every kind of asset, owned or controlled directly or indirectly by an investor' and goes on to provide an extensive list of tangible and intangible assets that would fall within this definition.[36] One might think that such clear treaty definitions of the term 'investment' conclusively resolve

---

[30] Reinisch, 'Expropriation', p. 432; Salacuse, *The Law of Investment Treaties*, p. 297.
[31] Hoffmann, 'Indirect Expropriation', p. 154; Reinisch, 'Expropriation', p. 420; Newcombe and Paradell, *Law and Practice of Investment Treaties*, p. 332; Montt, *State Liability in Investment Treaty Arbitration*, p. 232; cf. Subedi, 'The Challenge of Reconciling the Competing Principles within the Law of Foreign Investment with Special Reference to the Recent Trend in the Interpretation of the Term "Expropriation"' (2006) 40 *The International Lawyer*', p. 128.
[32] *SD Myers* v. *Canada*, Partial Award, para. 280; *Saluka* v. *Czech Republic*, Partial Award, para. 261.
[33] McLachlan, Shore and Weiniger, *International Investment Arbitration*, p. 286.
[34] UNCTAD, *International Investment Agreements: Key Issues Volume 1*, p. 115.
[35] E.g., NAFTA, art. 1139.   [36] ECT, art. 1(6).

any disagreement at the first stage of an expropriation inquiry. This is not so.

Conceptual problems arise when an investor owns a set of assets that might be characterised with different degrees of generality, all of which would fall within the treaty definition of an investment. For example, many investment treaties expressly provide that a licence falls within the definition of an investment; a factory would also fall within the definition of an investment.[37] If a host state repudiates an investor's licence to operate a factory, should the tribunal ask if the licence was expropriated or whether the repudiation of the licence amounted to an expropriation of the factory? A tribunal's characterisation of a particular collection of assets pertaining to a single project as a number of distinct investments would make a finding of indirect expropriation more likely (admittedly, a finding that a more circumscribed investment had been expropriated). A tribunal's characterisation of the same collection of assets as a single investment would make a finding of expropriation less likely.[38]

One of the few arbitral awards to directly address this issue is the decision in *Electrabel* v. *Hungary*. The claimant owned a power plant in Hungary and claimed that Hungary's termination of a contract for the purchase of electricity from the power plant amounted to an expropriation *of the contract*. The tribunal rejected the claimant's contention that the contract was the appropriate unit of analysis for the expropriation claim:

[T]he test for expropriation is applied to the relevant investment as a whole, even if different parts may separately qualify as investments for jurisdictional purposes.[39]

It justified its conclusion on the grounds the grounds that

[i]f it were possible so easily to parse an investment into several constituent parts each forming a separate investment (as Electrabel here contends), it would render meaningless that tribunal's approach to indirect expropriation based on 'radical deprivation' and 'deprivation of any real substance' as being similar in effect to a direct expropriation or nationalisation. It would also mean, absurdly, that an investor could always meet the test for indirect expropriation by slicing its investment as finely as the particular circumstances required, without that investment as a whole ever meeting that same test.[40]

---

[37] ECT, art. 1(6).
[38] Vandevelde, *Bilateral Investment Treaties: History, Policy and Interpretation* (2010), p. 280.
[39] *Electrabel* v. *Hungary*, Decision on Jurisdiction, Applicable Law and Liability, para. 6.58.
[40] Ibid., para. 6.57.

For the same reason, the US Supreme Court and European Court of Human Rights (ECtHR) have also held that the relevant unit of analysis in an indirect expropriation claim should be a claimant's 'parcel [of property] as a whole'.[41]

Although few other tribunals have engaged in detailed discussion of these conceptual issues,[42] several decisions are consistent with the view that, for the purpose of an indirect expropriation claim, a claimant's 'investment' is its economic undertaking in a host state as a whole.[43] For example, in *MCI Power v. Ecuador*, the claimant argued that its permit to operate as a company in Ecuador constituted an investment.[44] Even though the US-Ecuador BIT included 'any right conferred by law or contract, and any licenses and permits pursuant to law' within the definition of an investment,[45] the tribunal held that the relevant investment was the claimant's business of installing and operating power plants in Ecuador.[46] Similarly, in *Occidental v. Ecuador (I)*, the tribunal rejected the claimant's argument that its right under Ecuadorian law to a refund on taxes already paid was an investment,[47] notwithstanding the fact that the definition of investment in the BIT included 'a claim to money or a claim to performance having economic value, and associated with an investment'.[48]

Less controversially, tribunals have followed investment treaty definitions of the term 'investment' when these definitions provide textual support for the principle that a claimant's overall economic undertaking is the relevant investment. *Chemtura v. Canada* concerned a factual scenario in which a government measure had severely affected one aspect of a claimant's business in a foreign country, while the other components

---

[41] For the US Supreme Court's adoption of the 'parcel as a whole' rule, see *Concrete Pipe v. Construction Laborers Pension Trust* 508 US 602 (1993) 644; *Penn Central Transportation Co v. New York City* 438 US 104 (1978) 130. For examples of the ECtHR's approach, see *Fredin v. Sweden* (App no 12033/86) (1991) 13 EHRR 784, para. 45; *Baner v. Sweden* (App no 11763/85) (1989) 60 DR 128, p. 140; Harris, O'Boyle and Warbrick *Law of the European Convention on Human Rights* (1995), p. 529.

[42] Lowe, 'Changing Dimensions of International Investment Law' (2007), [online], p. 65.

[43] Kriebaum and Schreuer, 'The Concept of Property in Human Rights Law and International Investment Law' in Breitenmoser (ed), *Human Rights, Democracy and the Rule of Law* (2007), p. 760.

[44] *MCI Power v. Ecuador*, Award, para. 289.   [45] US-Ecuador BIT (27 August 1993), art. 1(1).

[46] *MCI Power v. Ecuador*, Award, paras. 300; similarly, *Parkerings v. Lithuania*, Award, para. 455; *Tecmed v. Mexico*, Award, para. 117; *Bogdanov v. Moldova*, Arbitral Award, para. 4.2.5.

[47] *Occidental v. Ecuador (I)*, Final Award, para. 86; similarly, *Nykomb Synergistics v. Latvia*, Award, para. 4.3.1; *Metalpar v. Argentina*, Award on the Merits, para. 174.

[48] US-Ecuador BIT (27 August 1993), art. 1(1).

of the business continued to operate profitably.[49] The tribunal held that the relevant investment was the claimant's overall business, reflecting the NAFTA definition of an investment, which includes 'an enterprise'[50] and the fact that the claimant had not been able to identify any narrower investment that fell within the NAFTA definition.[51] (It is unclear whether the relevant investment would have been characterized differently if the affected component of the claimant's business had been carried out through a separate subsidiary corporation.)

In contrast to the decisions in *Electrabel*, *Occidental I* and *MCI Power*, a minority of tribunals have relied on the definition of 'investment' in the applicable investment treaty to characterise a single specific asset that comprised part of a wider economic undertaking as an investment capable of indirect expropriation. In *Middle East Cement v. Egypt*, the tribunal characterised the investor's licence to import cement as an investment capable of expropriation and subsequently concluded that the licence had been expropriated.[52] Faced with essentially the same facts as *Occidental I*, the tribunal in *Encana v. Ecuador* held that the right to a tax refund under Ecuadorian law was an investment capable of expropriation.[53]

Comments made by the tribunal in *GAMI v. Mexico* might be read as further support for characterising the relevant investment narrowly, so long as such a characterisation falls within the definition relevant investment treaty. The tribunal asked:

> Should *Pope & Talbot* [the principle that expropriation requires a substantial deprivation of property] be understood to mean that property is taken only if it is so affected in its entirety? That question cannot be answered properly before asking: what property? The taking of 50 acres of a farm is equally expropriatory whether that is the whole farm or just a fraction. The notion must be understood as this: the affected property must be impaired to such an extent that it must be seen as 'taken.'[54]

It is doubtful whether the principle that the relevant investment is 'the affected property' provides much guidance in cases of *indirect*

---

[49] *Chemtura* v. *Canada*, Award, para. 258.   [50] NAFTA, arts. 1139, 201(1).

[51] *Chemtura* v. *Canada*, Award, para. 258; similarly, *Feldman* v. *Mexico*, Award, para. 111; *Merrill & Ring Forestry* v. *Canada*, Award, para. 144; *Grand River* v. *United States*, Award, para. 152; *Telenor* v. *Hungary*, Award, para. 67.

[52] *Middle East Cement* v. *Egypt*, Award, paras. 101, 107; similarly, *Eureko* v. *Poland*, Partial Award, paras. 239–41; *Waste Management* v. *Mexico (II)*, Final Award, para. 163; *Bayindir* v. *Pakistan*, Award, para. 442.

[53] *EnCana* v. *Ecuador*, Award, para. 183.

[54] *GAMI Investments* v. *Mexico*, Final Award, para. 150.

expropriation. Conceptual difficulties relating to the characterisation of the investment in indirect expropriation claims are qualitative, rather than the quantitative problems of characterisation discussed in *GAMI*. For example, if a host state repudiates an investor's licence to operate a factory, both the licence and the factory could reasonably be regarded as 'affected property'. In any case, *GAMI* can be distinguished from the decisions reviewed earlier on the grounds that the tribunal was discussing an example of direct expropriation.[55]

This review of arbitral practice reveals that arbitral tribunals are yet to develop a coherent doctrinal approach to the characterisation of the relevant investment in indirect expropriation claims.[56] It also supports a cautious conclusion: tribunals tend to characterise an investor's economic undertaking as a whole as the relevant investment.[57] Thus, when a tribunal that speaks of the 'effect' of a government measure that repudiates an investor's licence or the 'effect' of a restriction on the use of a physical asset it is normally referring to its effect *on the full collection of assets and legal rights that constitute the investor's business*. The examination in Sections 5.4, 5.5 and 5.6 of the second stage of the expropriation inquiry – the stage in which a tribunal determines whether an expropriation has occurred – proceeds on the basis that this is the more common practice. Specific mention is made of decisions that characterises the relevant investment more narrowly.

5.2.3.1 Can part of an investment be the subject of an indirect expropriation claim?

A subsidiary issue in the first stage of the expropriation inquiry is whether part of an investment may be the subject of an expropriation claim. The provisions of investment treaties are clear. Only interests that qualify as investments fall within the scope of treaty expropriation provisions, and, in resolving a claim that falls within the scope of an expropriation provision, a tribunal can only conclude that an investment in question was expropriated or that the investment was not expropriated.[58] The possibility of a state being liable for 'partial expropriation' must be rejected.[59] Academic discussion of partial expropriation is best understood as

---

[55] Vandevelde, *Bilateral Investment Treaties*, p. 281.
[56] Montt, *State Liability in Investment Treaty Arbitration*, p. 268.
[57] Vandevelde, *Bilateral Investment Treaties*, p. 280; Newcombe and Paradell, *Law and Practice of Investment Treaties*, p. 350.
[58] Cf. Kriebaum, 'Partial Expropriation' (2007) 8 *Journal of World Investment and Trade*, p. 69; Dolzer and Schreuer, *Principles of International Investment Law* (2nd edn), p. 119.
[59] *Grand River* v. *United States*, Award, para. 155.

drawing attention to two analytically distinct possibilities that are consistent with these textual foundations. The first is a situation in which a host state's interference with particular aspects of an investment is so significant that a tribunal would find that it amounts to an indirect expropriation of the entire investment, including the unaffected aspects.[60] (Almost every claim of indirect expropriation is partial in this sense.) The second is a situation in which one component of a larger investment constitutes, in itself, an investment within the meaning of the applicable investment treaty.[61] In this situation, if a tribunal rejected the approach of the *Electrabel* decision, it could find that a narrower investment had been expropriated but that the broader investment had not.[62]

5.2.4 The requirements for an expropriation to be legal, including compensation

Investment treaties place conditions on states' right to expropriate foreign investments. Expropriation – of either the direct or indirect variety – will normally be permitted only if compensation is paid and if the expropriation is undertaken for a public purpose, in a non-discriminatory way and complying with a minimum due process requirement.[63] Investment treaties usually specify that compensation should be equal to the market value of the investment.[64] The inquiry into whether a measure constitutes an expropriation is logically prior to the question of whether these four requirements have been met;[65] these requirements are of no immediate relevance to the determination of whether an indirect expropriation has occurred.[66] In cases in which a state has disputed an investor's claim of indirect expropriation, the state will invariably have failed to pay compensation for the purported expropriation. Thus, a textual reading of investment treaties suggests that a tribunal's finding of indirect expropriation will normally entail a further finding that the expropriation was illegal.[67] Such a finding would render the other legality requirements moot.

---

[60] *SD Myers* v. *Canada*, Partial Award, para. 283.
[61] Kriebaum, 'Partial Expropriation', p. 83.
[62] This appears to be what the tribunal meant in *Waste Management* v. *Mexico (II)*, Final Award, para. 141.
[63] UNCTAD, *International Investment Agreements: Key Issues, Volume 1*, p. 239.
[64] Reinisch, 'Legality of Expropriations', p. 195.
[65] *Fireman's Fund* v. *Mexico*, Award, para. 174; *Parkerings* v. *Lithuania*, Award, para. 456.
[66] *Feldman* v. *Mexico*, Award, para. 99.
[67] Dolzer and Schreuer, *Principles of International Investment Law* (2nd edn), p. 100.

This analysis raises the question of whether there is any difference between the remedial obligations attached to legal and illegal expropriations. The prevailing view in academic commentary is that, in contrast to the treaty-defined compensation required for a legal expropriation, an illegal expropriation requires a state to pay damages for breach of the treaty according to the principle laid down in *Chorzow Factory*:[68]

> [R]eparation must, as far as possible, wipe out all the consequences of the illegal act and re-establish the situation which would, in all probability, have existed if that act had not been committed.[69]

However, in practice, there is seldom any difference between the amount of compensation required for a legal expropriation and the damages required for an illegal one.[70] The reference point for both is the market value of the expropriated investment, which necessarily reflects its ability to generate future profits.[71] For the purpose of this chapter, it is unnecessary to delve further into these issues, which have been the subject of detailed discussion elsewhere.[72] It is sufficient to note that the remedial obligations associated with both legal and illegal expropriations are consistent with the characterisation of expropriation provisions as liability rules, with liability triggered by a finding of indirect expropriation.

5.3 The taxonomy

This section introduces and justifies the taxonomy used in this chapter to classify arbitral reasoning on indirect expropriation. The taxonomy divides decisions into the following categories: those that distinguish indirect expropriation from non-compensable government measures by looking exclusively to the effects of the measure; those that define expropriation by its effects, subject to exceptions or 'carve-outs' for measures with certain characteristics; and those that balance the effects on the

---

[68] Reinisch, 'Legality of Expropriations', p. 200; cf. Sheppard, 'The Distinction between Lawful and Unlawful Expropriation' in Ribeiro (ed), *Investment Arbitration and the Energy Charter Treaty* (2006), p. 195.

[69] *Chorzów Factory*, p. 47.

[70] One situation in which the standards diverge is in cases where the value of the investment has increased since the date of expropriation; e.g., *ADC Affiliate v. Hungary*, Award, para. 499.

[71] Newcombe and Paradell, *Law and Practice of Investment Treaties*, p. 381.

[72] See, generally, Marboe, *Calculation of Compensation and Damages in International Investment Law* (2009).

investment and the characteristics of the impugned measure in determining whether an indirect expropriation has occurred. This section then confronts three objections that might be raised to the use of this taxonomy. The first is the objection that arbitral decisions on indirect expropriation can be explained and justified by a single jurisprudential theory. The second is the objection that each decision concerning indirect expropriation is uniquely tied to the facts of the case, with the result that these decisions are not amenable to abstract examination. The third is the objection that decisions concerning the expropriation of contracts raise unique doctrinal issues, which prevents discussion of these decisions being assimilated with other cases of indirect expropriation.

5.3.1 The taxonomy used in this chapter

This chapter follows in a long line of academic scholarship that contends that arbitral decisions have interpreted the concept of indirect expropriation in different ways. Much of this scholarship divides decisions on indirect expropriation between those that focus exclusively on the effects of a measure and those that also consider its purpose.[73] Application of this taxonomy has yielded important insights – notably, insight into deep-seated disagreement about whether an expropriation should be identified exclusively by its effects. Nevertheless, this taxonomy has two serious limitations. The binary nature of the taxonomy elides the analytical distinction between a legal inquiry in which a legitimate purpose conclusively characterises a measure as non-compensable and an inquiry in which a legitimate purpose is weighed against the measure's effect. This distinction is of significant practical importance.[74] The second limitation is the use of the word 'purposes' to stand for everything that is not an effect. This tends to obscure the fact that tribunals have examined a range of measures' characteristics in determining whether the measure in question is an indirect expropriation.[75]

---

[73] E.g., Dolzer, 'Indirect Expropriations' (1986) 1 *ICSID Review – Foreign Investment Law Journal*, p. 79; Dolzer and Bloch, 'Indirect Expropriation: Conceptual Realignments?' (2003) 5 *International Law FORUM du droit international*, para. 158; Fortier and Drymer, 'Indirect Expropriation in the Law of International Investment', p. 308; Paparinskis, 'Regulatory Expropriation and Sustainable Development' in Cordonier Segger, Gehring and Newcombe (eds), *Sustainable Development in World Investment Law* (2011), p. 300; Hoffmann, 'Indirect Expropriation', p. 156; *Azurix* v. *Argentina*, Award, para. 309.

[74] Cf. *Methanex* v. *United States* Final Award, pt. IV, chp. D, para. 7, with *Tecmed* v. *Mexico*, Award, para. 122.

[75] E.g., *Fireman's Fund* v. *Mexico*, Award, para. 176.

This chapter proposes a taxonomy that builds on the sole-effects/ purposes taxonomy by addressing these two limitations. Indirect expropriation decisions fall within one of three possible structures of inquiry:[76]

1. The inquiry could be directed exclusively to the effect of the measure on the protected property. An inquiry of this sort might look at the effect of the measure on the rights of ownership, the effect of the measure on the value of the investment or whether the investment is appropriated by some other party. These approaches share in common the structural characteristic that the legal inquiry is addressed solely to the effect on the investment. This is the 'effects' structure.

2. The inquiry could define expropriation exclusively by its effects, subject to exceptions defined exclusively by the characteristics of the measure in question. Determining whether a measure falls within the exceptions might involve consideration of any number of features of the measure and the manner of its application, including, but not limited to, its purpose. This is the 'exception' structure.

3. The inquiry could consider both the effects on the investment and the characteristics of the impugned measure in determining whether an expropriation has occurred. A balancing rule of some sort would then be needed to mediate between the two sets of interests. This is the 'balancing' structure.

The categories of the taxonomy are mutually exclusive. Thus, decisions applying different structures of reasoning constitute different interpretations of indirect expropriation unless they follow from a higher legal rule that allocates distinct classes of cases to different structures of reasoning. At the same time, the taxonomy does not foreclose important questions of detail within each of the three possible structures of reasoning. This allows this chapter to identify points of disagreement between decisions that rely on the same structure of inquiry.

5.3.2 Can arbitral decisions be explained by a unified jurisprudential theory of indirect expropriation?

One objection that might be made to this taxonomy is that, notwithstanding apparent differences in their reasoning, all arbitral decisions on indirect expropriation can be explained and justified by a single jurisprudential theory. Several academic writers have attempted to construct such

---

[76] Stern and Kriebaum both propose broadly similar taxonomies: Stern, 'In Search of the Frontiers of Indirect Expropriation' in Rovine (ed), *Contemporary Issues in International Arbitration and Mediation: The Fordham Papers 2007* (2008), p. 44; Kriebaum, 'Regulatory Takings', p. 724.

unified theories. The most prominent theories all contend that an indirect expropriation is defined by the effect of a measure, subject to certain, qualified exceptions. Different unified theories explain the nature of the qualified exceptions in different ways: Paparinskis argues that there is an exception for regulatory measures, subject to the condition that they are applied with due process;[77] Newcombe and Paradell argue that there are exceptions for measures for the purposes of public order, health and the environment and taxation, subject to proportionality and reasonableness review;[78] and Montt argues that there are exceptions for the 'termination of investments according to law' and for measures advancing 'pre-eminent public interests', both of which are subject to further counter-exceptions.[79]

There are two initial difficulties with these unified theories. The first is that only a fraction of tribunals have articulated the test for indirect expropriation in the terms proposed by each theory. This observation is not conclusive – it could be that tribunals' reasoning can be reconciled to principles that they do not expressly articulate – but it does indicate the scale of the challenge that confronts attempts to construct a unified theory. The second difficulty is decisions in which a finding of liability for indirect expropriation rests exclusively on an analysis of the effects of the measure in question. It is arguable that some such decisions failed to discuss exceptions to expropriation because no exception was arguable on the facts.[80] However, in other decisions, tribunals have expressly rejected the argument that consideration of a measure's characteristics is ever relevant.[81] It is not possible to reconcile such decisions with any of the theories discussed in the preceding paragraph.

In the light of these difficulties with unified theories, the taxonomy proposed in this chapter provides a useful heuristic to frame inductive inquiry. This inductive inquiry, in turn, can help elucidate differences and similarities in the interpretation of indirect expropriation – a methodology that provides the basis for further reflection on the explanatory power of unified theories. Relying on this methodology, the subsequent sections of this chapter justify the conclusion that tribunals have interpreted the concept of indirect expropriation in a number of identifiably distinct

---

[77] Paparinskis, 'Regulatory Expropriation and Sustainable Development', p. 315.
[78] Newcombe and Paradell, *Law and Practice of Investment Treaties*, p. 358.
[79] Montt, *State Liability in Investment Treaty Arbitration*, p. 273.
[80] Paparinskis, 'Regulatory Expropriation and Sustainable Development', p. 311.
[81] E.g., *Siemens v. Argentina*, Award, para. 270.

ways that cannot satisfactorily be reconciled by a single jurisprudential theory.

5.3.3 Fact-specific reasoning and indirect expropriation

Another objection that might be made to the taxonomy is that each arbitral decision should be understood as being uniquely tied to the facts of the case in question. This argument finds its most coherent expression in claims that there is no 'magical formula, susceptible to mechanical application' that can identify indirect expropriation; that arbitrators must, and do, 'exercise their judgment in each case'.[82] On this basis, one might attribute apparent inconsistencies in arbitral reasoning to factual nuances of the cases in question, rather than see them as evidence of different understandings of the legal content of indirect expropriation.

This objection can be addressed simply. There is no doubt that identifying an indirect expropriation requires an exercise of judgement specific to the factual nuances of the case in question. However, tribunals have taken remarkably different positions about which facts are relevant and which are irrelevant in the exercise of their judgement. These different interpretations of the legal content of indirect expropriation exist prior to an assessment of the facts in a given case. The subsequent sections of this chapter constitute a sustained argument for these propositions.

5.3.4 Are decisions dealing with the expropriation of contracts distinct?

Both arbitral tribunals and academic writing accept that contracts can be the subject of expropriation claims under investment treaties.[83] This reflects the definition of the term 'investment' in investment treaties, which normally includes contracts.[84] The text of investment treaties provides no reason to think that different legal principles govern the question of whether a contract has been expropriated. However, in practice, claims that an investor's contract with the host state has been expropriated raise unique factual issues: the state is both the counter-party to the contract

---

[82] Paulsson, 'Indirect Expropriation: Is the Right to Regulate at Risk?' (2005), [online], p. 1; Paulsson and Douglas, 'Indirect Expropriation in Investment Treaty Arbitrations' in Horn (ed), *Arbitrating Foreign Investment Disputes: Procedural and Substantive Legal Aspects* (2004), p. 146; Lowe, 'Changing Dimensions of International Investment Law', p. 76; *Generation Ukraine* v. *Ukraine*, Award, para. 20.29.

[83] Dolzer and Schreuer, *Principles of International Investment Law* (2nd edn), p. 126; *Southern Pacific Properties* v. *Egypt*, Award, paras. 164–7.

[84] UNCTAD, *International Investment Agreements: Key Issues, Volume 1*, p. 118.

and the governmental authority with the power to alter the law and regulations governing the contract.

Tribunals have been anxious to draw a distinction between a state's breach of a contract with an investor and the expropriation of the contract. To draw this distinction, many tribunals distinguish between a state's behaviour 'as a party to the contract' and a state's exercise of 'superior governmental power'.[85] For the actions of a state to expropriate a contract, it is necessary, but not sufficient, that its actions involve the exercise of governmental power. Although the distinction between the two types of behaviour is not always clear cut,[86] the basic principle underpinning it is that a state does not expropriate an investment by breaching a contract in a way that any private party might have done.[87] This doctrinal principle is specific to the expropriation of contracts.

In the context of this chapter, the issue is whether decisions concerning the expropriation of contracts can be analysed alongside decisions concerning the expropriation of other investments. In my view, they can.[88] The principle that only exercises of governmental authority can expropriate a contract can be explained and justified by general principles governing expropriation. A breach of contract, whether by a private party or a state acting as a private party, does not deprive an investor of its rights under the contract; these rights still exist and can be enforced through a court of the host state.[89] Nor does a breach deprive the investor of the value of the contract; the rights under the contract subsist, including any attendant rights to damages for defective performance. Regardless of the way one interprets the concept of indirect expropriation, it is clear that a breach of contract does not, of itself, amount to an indirect expropriation. On the other hand, when a state enacts a law declaring that its obligations under a contract cease to exist, it extinguishes the investor's rights in the investment, as well as the value of those rights.[90] All interpretations of the concept of indirect expropriation would recognise that this conduct is potentially expropriatory. As such, the fact that an expropriation claim

---

[85] E.g., *Siemens* v. *Argentina*, Award, paras. 248, 253; *Parkerings* v. *Lithuania*, Award, para. 433; *Consortium RFCC* v. *Morocco*, Award, para. 65.

[86] Salacuse, *The Law of Investment Treaties*, p. 304.

[87] *Waste Management* v. *Mexico (II)*, Final Award, para. 174.

[88] Similarly, *Suez and InterAgua* v. *Argentina*, Decision on Liability, para. 140; cf. Paparinskis, 'Regulatory Expropriation and Sustainable Development', p. 311.

[89] *Waste Management* v. *Mexico (II)*, Final Award, para. 175.

[90] Vandevelde, *Bilateral Investment Treaties*, p. 303.

involves a contract does not alter the set of basic legal questions that confront a tribunal.

Moreover, in determining whether a contract has been indirectly expropriated, arbitral tribunals rely on the same range of interpretative approaches as tribunals faced with claims of the indirect expropriation of other types of investment. Some tribunals look to whether the state's action has seriously diminished the value of the contract,[91] some examine whether the rights in the contract were destroyed[92] and others ask whether the interference with the contract was proportionate.[93] The combination of common basic principles and shared approaches to points of interpretative disagreement is sufficient grounds for subsuming the discussion of the indirect expropriation of contracts into wider discussion of indirect expropriation.

5.4 The effects structure of inquiry

This section examines arbitral decisions that hold that an indirect expropriation should be *exclusively* by its effects. Several academic writers have argued that this is the correct view, both under investment treaties and as a matter of customary international law.[94] This section identifies two interpretations of indirect expropriation that turn exclusively on a measure's effects: one following the decision of *Metalclad* v. *Mexico* that looks to the loss of economic value of the investment caused by a measure, the other following *Pope & Talbot* v. *Canada* that looks to the extent to which a measure interferes with the claimant's property interests in the investment. Although both *Metalclad* and *Pope & Talbot* are relatively early decisions, the approaches they outline have been affirmed, applied and developed in more recent arbitral awards. On this basis, the award in the recent *Chemtura* case observed that two lines of indirect expropriation jurisprudence have developed, which have their roots in the *Metalclad* and *Pope & Talbot* decisions, respectively.[95]

---

[91] *Compañia de Aguas del Aconquija and Vivendi* v. *Argentina (II)*, Award, para. 7.5.34.
[92] *Biwater* v. *Tanzania*, Award, para. 464.   [93] *Azurix* v. *Argentina*, Award, paras. 311–15.
[94] With respect to investment treaties: Reisman and Sloane, 'Indirect Expropriation and Its Valuation in the BIT Generation' (2003) 74 *British Yearbook of International Law*, p. 121; Schreuer, 'The Concept of Expropriation', p. 153; Vandevelde, *Bilateral Investment Treaties*, p. 296. With respect to customary international law: Higgins, 'The Taking of Property by the State: Recent Developments in International Law' (1982) 176 *Recueil des Cours de l'Académie de Droit International*, p. 331.
[95] *Chemtura* v. *Canada*, Award, para. 249.

5.4.1 The Metalclad approach: effect on economic value

Metalclad had purchased a site in Mexico on which to build a hazardous waste landfill. It obtained the permits to operate the landfill from both state and federal agencies and had been told by federal officials that it did not need any additional authorisations.[96] When construction was well underway, the municipality issued a stop work order, claiming that a municipal construction permit was also required. The municipality ultimately refused to grant the permit and, despite having been completed in the interim, the landfill could not begin operation.[97] Metalclad alleged that the municipality's refusal to issue the permit expropriated its investment. After Metalclad had initiated proceedings, the state governor issued an 'Ecological Decree' establishing a Natural Area for the protection of rare cacti. The Natural Area encompassed Metalclad's landfill and 'effectively and permanently precluded [its] operation'.[98] The Ecological Decree was the basis for a second, distinct expropriation claim.

In evaluating the denial of permit claim, the tribunal defined expropriation as

covert or incidental interference with the use of property which has the effect of depriving the owner in whole or in significant part of the use or reasonably-to-be-expected economic benefit of property even if not necessarily to the obvious benefit of the state.[99]

The legal equivalence of covert and incidental interference in the *Metalclad* decision implies that the characteristics of a measure are irrelevant. Covert interference suggests measures calculated to expropriate a particular investment by pretence of form. On the other hand, incidental interference includes the inadvertent effect of general regulations pursuing some other objective in good faith. The tribunal was more explicit in evaluating the second claim. It held that it 'need not decide or consider the motivation or intent of the adoption of the Ecological Decree'.[100] The Ecological Decree was an expropriation on the basis that it 'had the effect of barring forever the operation of the landfill'.[101]

The definition of expropriation provided by the *Metalclad* Tribunal refers to incidental interference with the *reasonably-to-be-expected benefits* of an investment. This approach focuses on the loss of economic value attributable to a measure, independent of any examination of the degree of interference with the investor's legal rights or entitlements relating

---

[96] *Metalclad* v. *Mexico*, Award   [97] Ibid., paras. 46–62.   [98] Ibid., paras. 58–9.
[99] Ibid., para. 103.   [100] Ibid., para. 111.   [101] Ibid., para. 109.

to the investment. The decision suggests that an investor may reasonably expect future economic benefits that follow from the assumption that a state will act consistently with any prior unilateral representations it has made to the investor.[102] (Although the tribunal did assert that Metalclad was denied the 'the right to operate the landfill',[103] this assertion was not based on a determination of the powers of Mexican municipalities to issue construction permits under Mexican law.)[104]

The reasoning of the *Metalclad* decision was criticised on review by the Supreme Court of British Columbia.[105] In reviewing the second expropriation finding the judge noted that 'the Tribunal gave an extremely broad definition of expropriation for the purposes of Article 1110 ... [which was] sufficiently broad to include a legitimate rezoning of property'.[106] Despite these doubts, he held that the legal test for regulatory expropriation concerned a question of law that the reviewing court did not have jurisdiction to revisit.[107]

5.4.1.1 Subsequent decisions applying the *Metalclad* approach

In *CME* v. *Czech Republic*, a Dutch media investor challenged changes made to the regulatory regime governing the foreign ownership of television broadcast licences in the Czech Republic. The case was argued on the basis that the changes allowed the claimant's local business partner to alter its contractual relationship with the claimant, undermining the value of the claimant's business. The key finding of fact was that the media regulator eliminated the legal protection of the use of the licence, allowing the investor to lose the exclusive use of the licence at a later point.[108]

The tribunal began its discussion of expropriation by asserting that measures 'that effectively neutralize the benefit of the property, are subject to expropriation claims'.[109] The tribunal found that the facts in question amounted to regulatory expropriation because the government's actions 'destroyed ... the commercial value of the investment'.[110] The focus on the commercial value of the investment, independent of any analysis of the legal rights of which the investor had been deprived, was justified by the authority of *Metalclad*.[111] In a single paragraph, the *CME*

---

[102] Ibid., para. 107.   [103] Ibid., para. 105.
[104] Ibid., para. 86; Lowe, 'Changing Dimensions of International Investment Law', p. 64.
[105] *The United Mexican States* v. *Metalclad Corporation*, paras. 68–83.   [106] Ibid., para. 99.
[107] Ibid., para. 99.   [108] *CME* v. *Czech Republic*, Partial Award, para. 599.
[109] Ibid., paras. 604–8.   [110] Ibid., para. 591.   [111] Ibid., para. 606.

Tribunal acknowledged that 'deprivation of property... must be distinguished from ordinary [regulatory] measures in the proper execution of the law'.[112] However, the tribunal did not articulate any basis for identifying ordinary regulatory measures, other than the absence of economic loss that would constitute indirect expropriation.

Although *Metalclad* is one of the earliest investment treaty decisions, the approach outlined in the award has been endorsed and elaborated in the more recent decisions of *Occidental v. Ecuador (II)*, *Tokios Tokelés v. Ukraine* and *Vivendi v. Argentina (II)*.[113] In *Vivendi II* the tribunal applied the *Metalclad* approach to resolve a case in which the investor alleged the expropriation of a water concession contract. The tribunal sought to determine whether the concession had been rendered valueless by the state's actions, rather than examining whether these actions had breached or extinguished the rights of the claimant in the concession. On this basis, the tribunal found that the provincial government's public announcement, which had the effect of discouraging water consumers from paying their bills, indirectly expropriated the concession.[114]

Other decisions have used the *Metalclad* approach differently. In *Occidental v. Ecuador (I)*, the tribunal held that it need not elect between competing interpretations of indirect expropriation. It accepted that *Metalclad* established a 'rather broad' legal test for indirect expropriation but held that the measure in question would not be expropriatory, even under the *Metalclad* test.[115] The *Metalclad* approach was similarly applied, without being accepted, in *Waste Management v. Mexico (II)*, *Chemtura v. Canada* and *Telenor v. Hungary*.[116] In this way the approach continues to play an important role in shaping current arbitral jurisprudence.

5.4.1.2 Restatement of the Metalclad approach

The *Metalclad* approach looks exclusively to the effects of a measure. A measure that causes an investment to lose significant economic value will amount to an indirect expropriation, independent of an assessment of the measure's interference with legal rights in the investment. Removing the

---

[112] Ibid., para. 603.
[113] *Tokios Tokelés v. Ukraine*, Award, para. 120; *Occidental v. Ecuador (II)*, para. 455; *Compañia de Aguas del Aconquija and Vivendi v. Argentina (II)*, Award, para. 7.5.34.
[114] *Compañia de Aguas del Aconquija and Vivendi v. Argentina (II)*, Award, para. 7.5.28.
[115] *Occidental v. Ecuador (I)*, Final Award, para. 87.
[116] *Waste Management v. Mexico (II)*, Final Award, paras. 154, 159; *Chemtura v. Canada*, Award, paras. 249, 263; *Telenor v. Hungary*, Award, para. 67.

disjunctives, 'incidental interference with the use of property which has the effect of depriving the owner . . . in significant part of . . . reasonably-to-be-expected economic benefit of property' establishes expropriation.[117] This loss of economic value may, but need not, be attributable to interference with an investor's legal rights and entitlements in the investment. *Tokios Tokelés* described the standard as requiring deprivation 'of a "substantial" part of the value of the investment.'[118]

5.4.2 *The* Pope & Talbot *approach: substantial deprivation of property interests*

In *Pope & Talbot*, the investor challenged the introduction of Canada's Export Control Regime, which imposed a quota on the investor's export of softwood lumber to the United States. The tribunal described the ability to export lumber as a 'property interest' pertaining to the claimant's investment, a wood products company.[119] To determine whether this interference with the entitlement to export lumber under Canadian law amounted to an expropriation, the tribunal examined whether it was 'sufficiently restrictive to support a conclusion that the property has been 'taken' from the owner'.[120] The tribunal restated the standard: 'expropriation requires a substantial deprivation', making it clear that the test of 'taking' refers to the effects of the measure. The tribunal rejected the investor's claim because, although it suffered reduced profits, the measure did not destroy the claimant's ability to 'use, enjoy or dispose of the property';[121] Pope & Talbot retained full rights of ownership and control over its business.[122]

The *Pope & Talbot* standard of substantial deprivation of an investor's property interests in the investment has been widely cited since. A number of cases invoking balancing and exception structures require an effect of substantial deprivation before the balancing or exception question arises.[123] The basis for treating *Pope & Talbot* as authority for an effects structure of inquiry is the tribunal's statement that Article 1110 of NAFTA 'does cover non-discriminatory regulation that might be said to fall within the exercise of a state's so-called police powers'.[124] However, the tribunal

---

[117] *Metalclad* v. *Mexico*, Award, para. 103.   [118] *Tokios Tokelés* v. *Ukraine*, Award, para. 120.
[119] *Pope & Talbot* v. *Canada*, Interim Award, paras. 4, 98.   [120] Ibid., para. 102.
[121] Ibid., para. 102; citing American Law Institute, *Restatement of the Law Third – The Foreign Relations Law of the United States, Volume 2* (1987).
[122] *Pope & Talbot* v. *Canada*, Interim Award, para. 100–1.
[123] E.g., *Fireman's Fund* v. *Mexico*, Award, para. 176; *Chemtura* v. *Canada*, Award, para. 249.
[124] *Pope & Talbot* v. *Canada*, Interim Award, para. 96.

did accept that 'special care' should be taken when reviewing the state's exercise of police powers.[125] The *Pope & Talbot* decision did not indicate what special care would involve.

5.4.2.1 Subsequent decisions developing the *Pope & Talbot* approach

Although *Pope & Talbot* is one of the earlier investment treaty decisions, subsequent awards have applied and developed the approach by sharpening the distinction between a deprivation of property interests and an effect on the economic value of an investment. There is a degree of variation in terminology among these decisions; some speak of deprivation of 'property rights', or simply 'rights',[126] rather than deprivation of 'property interests'.[127] This variation in terminology does not appear to be significant. Tribunals use all three terms to focus the expropriation inquiry on the extent to which a measure alters an investor's entitlements under domestic law to use, enjoy or dispose of its investment in certain ways.

In this chapter, I use the term 'property interest' in discussion of the *Pope & Talbot* approach to avoid confusion with the term 'specific and enforceable legal right' as it relates to the doctrine of legitimate expectations under the FET standard. The meaning of 'property interest' in this chapter is broader than the meaning of 'specific and enforceable legal right' in Chapter 4. An investor's entitlement to use property in a certain way under prevailing regulatory arrangements would qualify as a property interest; it would not amount to a specific and enforceable legal right unless the investor held an *enforceable* right for general regulations to remain unchanged (for example, a right under a contract or licence). According to this understanding of property interest, an investor's ability to use an investment in a way that is permitted under prevailing domestic law is a property interest; an investor's ability to use an investment in a way that requires a permit under prevailing domestic law is a limited property interest circumscribed by the duration and terms of the permit; an investor's expectation or hope that it will be able to use an investment in a way that is not currently permitted under domestic law is not a property interest.

The tribunal in *Sempra* v. *Argentina* gave perhaps the most comprehensive articulation of the *Pope & Talbot* approach, equating indirect

---

[125] Ibid., para. 99.   [126] *Sempra Energy* v. *Argentina*, Award, para. 284.
[127] *Grand River* v. *United States*, Award, para. 154.

expropriation with the interference with an investor's ownership or control of an investment:

> Substantial deprivation results . . . from depriving the investor of control over the investment, managing the day-to-day operations of the company, arresting and detaining company officials or employees, supervising the work of officials, interfering in administration, impeding the distribution of dividends, interfering in the appointment of officials or managers, or depriving the company of its property or control in whole or in part.[128]

The tribunal acknowledged that its list was not exhaustive but explained that indirect expropriation 'would still have to meet the standard of having as a result a substantial deprivation of rights.'[129]

More recent decisions have been particularly important in clarifying the implications of a focus on the claimant's legal entitlements in cases concerning the expropriation of contracts. The dispute in *Bayindir* v. *Pakistan* arose from a situation in which Pakistan had terminated a construction contract with Bayindir and expelled it from the country, citing its poor contractual performance. The tribunal held that 'if the expulsion was lawful under the Contract, then there would be no taking of or interference with Bayindir's rights.'[130] The fact that the state's action was consistent with a 'reasonable interpretation of the Contract' was, according to the tribunal's interpretation of indirect expropriation, sufficient to show that Bayindir's contractual rights had not been indirectly expropriated.[131] The majority in the recent *Impregilo* v. *Argentina* decision came to the same view.[132]

In another contract case, *Biwater* v. *Tanzania*, the tribunal applied the *Pope & Talbot* approach, stressing the distinction between rights and value. It said that a 'distinction must be drawn between (a) interference with rights and (b) economic loss. A substantial interference with rights may well occur without actually causing any economic damage'.[133] The tribunal found that Tanzania had effectively extinguished Biwater's rights in a water concession contract. It quantified the compensation owing for this expropriation at zero.[134]

The *Grand River* v. *US* Tribunal discussed the converse factual scenario, the situation in which serious economic loss is not accompanied by a

---

[128] *Sempra Energy* v. *Argentina*, Award, para. 284.   [129] Ibid., para. 284.
[130] *Bayindir* v. *Pakistan*, Award, para. 458.   [131] Ibid., paras. 458–60.
[132] *Impregilo* v. *Argentina*, Award, para. 272.   [133] *Biwater* v. *Tanzania*, Award, para. 464.
[134] Ibid., para. 519.

substantial interference with property interests. The tribunal observed that

ICISD tribunals have rejected expropriation claims involving significant diminu-
tion of the value of a claimant's property where the claimant nevertheless retained
ownership and control.[135]

It held that 'expropriation must involve the deprivation of all, or a very
great measure, of a claimant's property interests.'[136] The tribunal in
Bosh v. Ukraine reached essentially the same conclusion.[137]

The Pope & Talbot formula of 'substantial deprivation' of property interests has been cited and applied by a number of other decisions, including
Enron v. Argentina, Nykomb v. Latvia and CMS Gas v. Argentina.[138] There are
also occasional decisions within the effects structure that mix discussion
of the effect a measure on a claimant's property interests with discussion of its effect on the value of the investment, such as BG v. Argentina
and National Grid v. Argentina.[139] Although these decisions do not fall
neatly within the Pope & Talbot approach, they are consistent with it.
Their examination of loss of economic value caused by a measure goes
to the assessment of whether the deprivation of property interests was
substantial.[140] These decisions do not appear to countenance the possibility that severe loss of economic value would be sufficient for a finding
of indirect expropriation in the absence of interference with property
interests.

5.4.2.2 Restatement of the Pope & Talbot approach

The Pope & Talbot Tribunal requires a substantial deprivation for a finding of expropriation. This approach looks to the deprivation of property
interests; the catalogue of examples of regulatory expropriation provided
by the Pope & Talbot Tribunal are all 'actions ousting the investor from full
ownership or control of the investment.'[141] The approach does not provide precise guidance as to when a given interference with an investor's

---

[135] Grand River v. United States, Award, para. 151.
[136] Ibid., para. 154.   [137] Bosh v. Ukraine, Award, para. 210.
[138] Enron v. Argentina, Award, para. 245; Nykomb Synergistics v. Latvia, Award, p. 33; CMS Gas
v. Argentina, Final Award, para. 263.
[139] BG Group v. Argentina, Final Award, para. 266; National Grid v. Argentina, Award, para. 149.
[140] BG Group v. Argentina, Final Award, paras. 270–1; National Grid v. Argentina, Award, paras.
150–4.
[141] Pope & Talbot v. Canada, Interim Award, para. 100.

entitlements to use, enjoy or dispose of an investment will amount to expropriation. Nevertheless, it is clear that qualitative judgements about the extent of interference in the context of the claimant's investment are more important than quantitative assessments of the economic loss suffered by the claimant.

5.4.3 *The effect of appropriation: an alternative approach?*

Newcombe argues that the competing strands of jurisprudence on indirect expropriation in international investment law can be reconciled by 'rereading' them as instances of the *appropriation* of property by the state or a third party.[142] Only two arbitral decisions arguably support Newcombe's view: *Lauder v. Czech Republic* and *Olguin v. Paraguay*.[143] The statements in both decisions were intimately tied to their contexts and did not purport to establish a general interpretative approach. In *Olguin,* the relevant passage justified the finding of fact that an omission of the government had not *caused* the alleged loss.[144] In *Lauder*, the tribunal accepted that indirect expropriation normally involved appropriation but explicitly formulated its finding in terms of deprivation.[145] Notwithstanding the policy merits of a legal test based on appropriation,[146] no established strand of jurisprudence in international investment law supports this approach.

5.4.4 *Summary: the effects structure of inquiry*

This section has identified two interpretations of indirect expropriation that turn exclusively on a measure's effects. The first is based on the *Metalclad* decision; it looks to whether a measure deprives the investor of the reasonably expected economic benefits of the investment. The second is based on the *Pope & Talbot* decision; it looks to whether a measure substantially deprives the investor of property interests in the investment, particularly rights of ownership and control.

---

[142] Newcombe, 'The Boundaries of Regulatory Expropriation in International Law' (2005) 20 *ICSID Review – Foreign Investment Law Journal*, p. 7.
[143] *Lauder* v. *Czech Republic*, Final Award, para. 203; *Olguin* v. *Paraguay*, Award, para. 84.
[144] *Olguin* v. *Paraguay*, Award, para. 84.
[145] *Lauder* v. *Czech Republic*, Final Award, paras. 200–1.
[146] The economic analysis of Section 3.4.4 suggests that a state should only be held liable when it appropriates property or sunk costs associated with an investment.

5.5 The exception structure of inquiry

Investment treaties rarely contain exception clauses to their expropriation provisions.[147] If an exception or 'carve-out' for certain regulatory
measures exists, it must be found within the meaning of 'indirect expropriation'. This section examines arbitral decisions that have held that measures with certain characteristics do not amount to compensable indirect
expropriation. To be sure, such decisions still require that a measure have
a sufficient effect on an investment for it to be potentially expropriatory.
Decisions that recognise exceptions to indirect expropriation draw on a
particular understanding of the doctrine of 'police powers' in customary
international law, the view that

a state is not responsible for loss of property ... resulting from bona fide general
taxation, regulation, forfeiture for crime, or other action of the kind that is commonly accepted as within the police power of states, if it is not discriminatory.[148]

This section identifies one interpretation of indirect expropriation within
the exception structure of inquiry.

5.5.1 The Methanex approach: a police powers carve-out

The leading arbitral decision within the exception structure of inquiry is
Methanex v. US. Methanex was the world's largest producer of methanol,
the chemical building block of the fuel additive MTBE.[149] Methanex
claimed that a Californian regulation that banned the sale and use of
MTBE amounted to expropriation because it significantly deprived it of
its 'customer base, market share and goodwill'.[150] This regulation was
motivated by the public health and environmental concerns relating to
MTBE contamination of groundwater.[151]

The tribunal might have resolved the claim by considering whether
customer base, market share and goodwill constitute investments, or

---

[147] Two investment treaties that do provide an exception to indirect expropriation are
COMESA Investment Agreement, art. 20(8); and the ASEAN Comprehensive Investment
Agreement. Article 4 of annex 2 to the latter treaty reads:

Non-discriminatory measures of a Member State that are designed and applied to
protect legitimate public welfare objectives, such as public health, safety and the
environment, do not constitute an expropriation of the referred to in sub-paragraph
2(b) [indirect expropriation].

This is variation on annex B of the US 2012 Model BIT; see Section 5.6.2.2.

[148] See American Law Institute, *Restatement of the Law Third – The Foreign Relations Law of the
United States*, sec. 712 g.

[149] *Methanex v. United States* Final Award, pt. I, para. 1.   [150] Ibid., pt. IV, chp. D, para. 5.

[151] Ibid., pt. III, chp. A, paras. 1–12.

whether a regulation that affects these economic interests can amount to an expropriation of a claimant's enterprise (which did, undoubtedly, constitute an investment). Instead, it dealt with the exception first, allowing it to avoid the question of whether the measure would otherwise have amounted to an expropriation. It held that

> a non-discriminatory regulation for a public purpose, which is enacted in accordance with due process, and which affects, inter alios a foreign investor or investment is not deemed expropriatory and compensable unless specific commitments had been given by the regulating government ... to refrain from such regulation.[152]

This statement defines a categorical carve-out from the scope of liability for indirect expropriation, an interpretation that went beyond the more qualified submissions of both the parties to the dispute.[153] In applying this legal test to the facts, the tribunal concentrated on the criteria of non-discrimination, due process and non-violation of commitments. Through a detailed inquiry into the history of the regulation, it found them all easily satisfied.[154]

Another decision that applied an exception structure in the regulatory expropriation inquiry was *Saluka v. Czech Republic*. Saluka was a major foreign shareholder in the Czech bank IPB. The Banking Act required all banks to maintain payment ability through a minimum 'liquidity cushion'. In 2000, the Czech Banking Regulator found that IPB had continuously failed to maintain payment ability and forced it into liquidation, as it was entitled to do under the Banking Act.[155] Unlike *Methanex,* the *Saluka* decision began with a finding that the claimant had been deprived of its investment.[156]

The tribunal cited the *Third Restatement of the Foreign Relations Law of the United States* (*Third Restatement*) and *Methanex* to support the statement of customary international law that

> states are not liable to pay compensation to a foreign investor when, in the normal exercise of their regulatory powers, they adopt in a non-discriminatory manner bona fide regulations that are aimed at the general welfare.[157]

---

[152] Ibid., pt. IV, chp. D, para. 7.
[153] *Methanex v. United States*, Rejoinder of the Respondent, para. 194; *Methanex v. US*, Reply of Claimant to Amended Statement of Defence, para. 207.
[154] *Methanex v. United States* Final Award, pt. IV, chp. D, paras. 8–15.
[155] *Saluka v. Czech Republic*, Partial Award, paras. 271–2.   [156] Ibid., para. 267.
[157] Ibid., para. 255.

The tribunal confirmed that these characteristics of the regulation were not to be balanced against its effects; satisfaction of these criteria was sufficient to find that the measure did not amount to indirect expropriation.[158]

Despite the differences in terminology, the legal tests in both *Methanex* and *Saluka* were remarkably similar. The *Saluka* Tribunal appears to have inferred low-level requirements of procedural and substantive justification of the measure from the concept of 'normal exercise'.[159] On the facts, the measures were justified because both the final decision of the banking regulator and the process by which the decision was reached were reasonable.[160] These two observations are consistent with the public purpose and due process requirements of *Methanex*.

In the 2010 decision in the consolidated claims of *Suez and InterAgua v. Argentina* and *Suez and Vivendi; AWG Group v. Argentina* the claimants alleged that a series of measures culminating in the termination of their water concession with the Santa Fe provincial government amounted to indirect expropriation.[161] The tribunal held that 'an indirect expropriation requires a substantial deprivation of an investment.'[162] To determine whether the state's termination of the contract fell afoul of this standard, it examined whether the state acted consistently with the framework of legal rights established by the contract.[163] This much is consistent with the *Pope & Talbot* approach.

In addition to the threshold requirement that a measure constitute a substantial deprivation, the tribunal recognised an exception to indirect expropriation for measures within a state's police powers, citing the *Third Restatement*, *Methanex* and *Saluka* as authority.[164] The tribunal then applied this exception in the review of Argentina's unilateral cancellation of the tariff indexation mechanism in public service contracts, including the claimant's concession contract. It concluded that deindexation was a general measure taken in the context of a severe crisis

---

[158] Ibid., para. 275.   [159] Ibid., paras. 265, 271.   [160] Ibid., para. 272.
[161] *Suez and Vivendi; AWG Group v. Argentina*, Decision on Liability, para. 135; *Suez and InterAgua v. Argentina*, Decision on Liability, para. 124.
[162] *Suez and Vivendi; AWG Group v. Argentina*, Decision on Liability, para. 145; *Suez and InterAgua v. Argentina*, Decision on Liability, para. 134.
[163] *Suez and Vivendi; AWG Group v. Argentina*, Decision on Liability, paras. 151–5; *Suez and InterAgua v. Argentina*, Decision on Liability, para. 141.
[164] *Suez and Vivendi; AWG Group v. Argentina*, Decision on Liability, para. 139; *Suez and InterAgua v. Argentina*, Decision on Liability, para. 128.

and therefore fell within the state's police powers; it also held that the measure did not, in any case, meet the threshold of substantial deprivation.[165] Perhaps for this reason, the decision did not consider the significance of the *Methanex* Tribunal's condition that, to fall within the police power exception to indirect expropriation, a measure must not be contrary to 'specific commitments by the regulating government to refrain from such regulation.'[166] Arguably, Argentina had made contractual commitments not to deindex tariffs.

In *Chemtura* v. *Canada*, the claimant alleged that the cancellation of its registration to sell lindane-containing pesticide, a product it produced and sold, constituted indirect expropriation.[167] The Canadian Pest Management Regulatory Agency (PMRA) had imposed the ban due to concerns about the health risks of lindane-containing pesticides.[168] The tribunal began by noting differences between the *Metalclad* and *Pope & Talbot* decisions, so far as they relate to the effects required for a measure to constitute expropriation. It found no need to resolve the controversy, holding that the standard was, broadly, one of 'substantial deprivation' and that this standard required 'fact-sensitive' application.[169] Because the claimant remained in control of the company and it remained profitable, the tribunal found that there had been no substantial deprivation. The tribunal added that, in any case, the measure would have fallen within the police powers exception to indirect expropriation:

The PMRA took measures within its mandate, in a non-discriminatory manner, motivated by the increasing awareness of the dangers presented by lindane for human health and the environment. A measure adopted under such circumstances is a valid exercise of the State's police power and, as a result, does not constitute an expropriation.[170]

5.5.1.1 Restatement of the *Methanex* approach

The *Methanex* decision is the archetype of the exception structure of the indirect expropriation inquiry. The legal test stated in that decision is schematic and clear, and has been endorsed and applied in the more

---

[165] *Suez and Vivendi; AWG Group v. Argentina*, Decision on Liability, para. 140; *Suez and InterAgua v. Argentina*, Decision on Liability, para. 129.
[166] *Methanex v. United States* Final Award, pt. IV, chp. D, para. 7.
[167] *Chemtura v. Canada*, Award, para. 251.   [168] Ibid., paras. 21–9.
[169] Ibid., para. 249.   [170] Ibid., para. 266.

recent decisions such as the consolidated *Suez* claims. A measure will not be classed as expropriatory if it meets the requirements of being

1. a regulation,
2. that is non-discriminatory,
3. for a public purpose,
4. enacted in accordance with due process, and
5. made without specific commitments by the regulating government to refrain from such regulation.

The cases that adopt the exception structure of inquiry have not fully specified the extent of effect on an investment required for a measure to be classed as potentially expropriatory, although there appears to be a preference for the *Pope & Talbot* approach. Nor have these cases fully fleshed out the *Methanex* criteria for a noncompensable exercise of police powers. In particular, none of these decisions provides a comprehensive account of the range of public purposes capable of justifying a measure that would otherwise amount to indirect expropriation.[171] Taken together, they suggest that public health, environmental protection, banking regulation and economic restructuring in a time of crisis are among the legitimate public purposes that could justify an otherwise expropriatory measure.

5.6 The balancing structure of inquiry

This section examines arbitral decisions that consider both the effects and the characteristics of a measure in determining whether it constitutes indirect expropriation. Decisions that employ this structure of inquiry can be distinguished from those within the exception structure in that, within the balancing structure, a measure may have the indicia of legitimate noncompensable regulation, yet still constitute indirect expropriation on account of its severe effect on an investment. A number of academic writers support the view that determination of whether an indirect expropriation has occurred involves a 'case-by-case' approach in which both the effects and the characteristics of the measure are relevant.[172] This section

---

[171] Weiner, 'Indirect Expropriations: The Need for a Taxonomy of "Legitimate" Regulatory Purpose' (2003) 5 *International Law FORUM du droit international*, p. 171; *Saluka* v. *Czech Republic*, Partial Award, paras. 262–3.

[172] Yannaca-Small, 'Indirect Expropriation and the Right to Regulate: How to Draw the Line' in Yannaca-Small (ed), *Arbitration Under International Investment Agreements* (2010), p. 476; McLachlan, Shore and Weiniger, *International Investment Arbitration*, p. 298; Salacuse, *The Law of Investment Treaties*, p. 317.

identifies two interpretative approaches within the balancing structure: the proportionality approach and an approach based on characterisation of the impugned measure that has its roots in arbitral jurisprudence and now finds expression in the interpretative annexes of new US and Canadian BITs. I label the latter the 'US annex approach'.

5.6.1 The Tecmed approach: proportionality balancing

Tecmed v. *Mexico* concerned a hazardous waste facility. The investor held a licence to operate the facility for one year, which was renewable annually. In response to community opposition to the facility, the authorities and the investor agreed that the facility should be moved to a different location. Within months of this agreement, the authorities declined to renew the annual licence that allowed the facility to operate at its original site.[173] The tribunal did not determine whether, prior to this decision, Tecmed had a right to continued operation of the facility in its existing location under Mexican law; it was enough that the investor had a reasonable expectation of continued operation.[174] On this basis, the tribunal found that the investor had been 'radically deprived of the economical use and enjoyment of its investment'.[175]

While agreeing that a measure's severe effect on the economic value of an investment was not sufficient to support a finding of indirect expropriation, the *Tecmed* Tribunal rejected a general exception to indirect expropriation for regulatory measures 'beneficial to society as a whole'.[176] Instead, it held that 'there must be a reasonable relationship of proportionality between the charge or weight imposed to the foreign investor and the aim sought to be realized' for a measure to fall outside the class of compensable indirect expropriation.[177] As authority for the requirement of overall proportionality, the tribunal cited four leading decisions of the ECtHR.[178] Applying this test, the tribunal observed that the interference with the investment was 'extreme' in light of the objective pursued and that, therefore, that it was not proportionate.[179]

The tribunal did not specifically require that a measure be the least investment-restrictive means of achieving a given objective to be proportionate.[180] However, it did observe that the environmental

---

[173] *Tecmed* v. *Mexico*, Award, para. 160.   [174] Ibid., paras. 149–50.   [175] Ibid., para. 115.
[176] Ibid., paras. 119–22.   [177] Ibid., para. 122.   [178] Ibid., para. 116, 122.
[179] Ibid., para. 148.
[180] Henckels, 'Indirect Expropriation and the Right to Regulate: Revisiting Proportionality Analysis and the Standard of Review in Investment Treaty Arbitration' (2012) 15 *Journal of International Economic Law*, p. 233.

and health issues relating to the operation of the site could have been addressed through financial penalties on the investor. This observation played an important role in justifying the tribunal's conclusion that the measure was not proportionate.[181] Thus, as with the proportionality approach to substantive review under the FET standard, the fact that other equally effective measures involving lesser interference with the investment were available was relevant, but not conclusive, to the question of whether the challenged measure was proportionate.[182]

Azurix v. *Argentina* concerned the alleged expropriation of a water concession contract. In discussing the effect required for a measure to amount to expropriation the tribunal agreed with *Tecmed* that: indirect expropriation does not require an interference with the investor's legal entitlements; and that a state could indirectly expropriate an investment by breaching prior unilateral statements in a way that deprives the investor of the 'reasonably-to-be-expected economic benefit of its investment.'[183] The tribunal also accepted that a finding of expropriation would require a further judgement that the interference with the value of the investment was not proportionate. 'This proportionality will not be found if the person concerned bears "an individual and excessive burden".'[184] On the facts, the tribunal found that disputes over tariffs and payment of bills under the concession did not have a sufficient effect on the value of the investment to amount to expropriation.[185]

The tribunal in *LG&E* v. *Argentina* relied on the same understanding of indirect expropriation. It cited *Tecmed* as authority for the proposition that

> it can generally be said that the State has the right to adopt measures having a social or general welfare purpose. In such a case, the measure must be accepted without any imposition of liability, except in cases where the State's action is obviously disproportionate to the need being addressed.[186]

The tribunal did not consider whether the measures in question were proportionate because they lacked sufficient effect on the investment to amount to indirect expropriation – they had not caused 'severe deprivation of LG&E's rights with regards to its investment or almost complete deprivation of the value of LG&E's investment.'[187]

---

[181] *Tecmed* v. *Mexico*, Award, para. 148.
[182] See Section 4.7.5.   [183] *Azurix* v. *Argentina*, Award, para. 316.   [184] Ibid., para. 311.
[185] Ibid., para. 322.
[186] *LG&E Energy* v. *Argentina*, Decision on Liability, para. 195.   [187] Ibid., para. 200.

5.6.1.1 Restatement of the *Tecmed* approach

The *Tecmed* approach is a clearly defined interpretation of indirect expropriation within the balancing structure. More recent cases that adopt this approach to indirect expropriation cite the *Tecmed* decision as authority for their conclusions. Under the *Tecmed* approach, a finding of indirect expropriation requires the following:

1. A 'radical deprivation' or 'near complete deprivation' of the value of the investment. Like the *Metalclad* approach, a measure that affects the reasonably expected economic value of the investment can amount to indirect expropriation, even if it does not interfere with property interests in the investment. However, the *Tecmed* approach seems to require a more severe decrease in economic value than the *Metalclad* approach.
2. A measure that exceeds this threshold of impact on economic value will only amount to an expropriation if there is a lack of proportionality between the loss to the claimant and the public interest pursued by the measure.
3. In examining whether the measure is proportionate, it is relevant, but not conclusive, that there are other means of achieving the public interest objective that involve lesser interference with the investment.

5.6.2 *The US annex approach: characterisation as a technique for balancing*

The most common balancing approach applied by tribunals involves characterisation of the impugned measure. The clearest statement of the approach is from *Feldman* v. *Mexico*: 'the essential determination is whether the actions . . . constitute an expropriation or nationalization, or are valid governmental activity'.[188] The language of characterisation is sometimes invoked by tribunals using effects or exception structures of inquiry.[189] Within the balancing structure, characterisation refers to a more specific method of reasoning. Tribunals that adopt this approach regard a wide range of effects on the investor and characteristics of the measure as potentially relevant. All these factors are weighed against each other, and the tribunal then makes a fact-specific conclusion. The interpretative annexes of recent US and Canadian BITs codify this approach. They require

---

[188] *Feldman* v. *Mexico*, Award, para. 98.
[189] *Biloune* v. *Ghana*, Award on Jurisdiction and Liability, para. 603; *Saluka* v. *Czech Republic*, Partial Award, para. 264.

tribunals to identify indirect expropriation through a 'case-by-case, fact-based inquiry'[190] and specify some of the factors that must be taken into account in this process of balancing.

5.6.2.1 The origins of an approach based on characterisation

The brief decision of SD Myers v. Canada laid out a basic framework for an approach based on characterisation. SD Myers challenged Canada's temporary export ban on polychlorinated biphenyl. The tribunal determined that 'expropriation' should be interpreted consistently with 'the whole body of state practice, treaties and judicial interpretations of that term'.[191] This approach contrasts with decisions applying both the effects and exception models, which tend to cite narrowly from the line of authority that supports their approach. In SD Myers, the tribunal positioned a measure's effect on the investment at the centre of characterisation, saying 'expropriations tend to involve the deprivation of ownership rights; regulations a lesser interference.'[192] Beyond this initial assessment 'international law makes it appropriate to consider both the purpose and effect of governmental measures'.[193] The decision did not refer to any 'purpose' elements because the facts fell short of establishing the effect necessary for expropriation.

In Feldman, the tribunal balanced the effects of a measure against its characteristics in a more even way. The claimant operated a business which exported cigarettes. After a number of years of inconsistent statements, the Mexican authorities decided that Feldman was no longer entitled to the tax rebates he had previously received.[194] Although the claimant alleged an 'agreement' with the authorities, the tribunal found that the claimant had no right to the rebates under Mexican law. In formulating the legal standard, the tribunal 'sought guidance' from both Metalclad and the Third Restatement. It recognised that regulations could amount to expropriation[195] but held that expropriation should be distinguished from noncompensable regulation 'in light of all the circumstances'.[196]

The tribunal identified four relevant factors in the case in question.[197] Two concerned the characteristics of the measure: the general character of the tax and the fact that the regime had a 'rational public purpose'.[198]

---

190 US 2012 Model BIT, annex B, art. 4(a).
191 SD Myers v. Canada, Partial Award, para. 280.   192 Ibid., para. 282.   193 Ibid., para. 281.
194 Feldman v. Mexico, Award, para. 109.   195 Ibid., para.110.   196 Ibid., paras. 106, 102.
197 Ibid., para. 111.   198 Ibid., paras. 112–6, 136–7.

The other two factors concerned the effects of the measure: the fact that the claimant was not deprived of any legal right and the fact that the investor retained control of the investment.[199] All four factors pointed against indirect expropriation. The tribunal's approach – a relatively open balancing of various factors – was most explicit in its conclusion: 'while none of these factors alone is necessarily conclusive, in the tribunal's view, taken together they tip the expropriation/regulation balance away from a finding of expropriation'. *Feldman* was cited and followed in *Generation Ukraine* v. *Ukraine*.[200]

The most comprehensive expression of an approach based on characterisation was made in *Fireman's Fund* v. *Mexico*. The tribunal said that

[t]o distinguish between a compensable expropriation and a noncompensable regulation by a host state, the following factors (usually in combination) may be taken into account: whether the measure is within the recognized police powers of the host State; the (public) purpose and effect of the measure; whether the measure is discriminatory; the proportionality between the means employed and the aim sought to be realized; the bona fide nature of the measure.[201]

The tribunal added that the effect on an investor's 'investment backed expectations' could also be considered.[202]

The concept of investment backed expectations is derived from jurisprudence on the US Fifth Amendment and is incorporated in the interpretative annexes of recent US and Canadian BITs.[203] A lengthy footnote in the *Fireman's Fund* decision explained that the concept of 'investment backed expectations' means that

interference with the investor's enterprise [should be] considered in light of the investor's chosen business model, the nature of the enterprise, the regulatory regime in place at the time of investment, and associated expectations.[204]

This much is consistent with the *Pope & Talbot* approach's focus on protection of property interests, which would include the protection of expectations that are based in the legal entitlements of the investor under prevailing regulatory arrangements.

---

[199] Ibid., paras. 111, 117–34.
[200] *Generation Ukraine* v. *Ukraine*, Award, para. 20.34.
[201] *Fireman's Fund* v. *Mexico*, Award, para. 176.   [202] Ibid., para. 176.
[203] See Section 5.6.2.2.
[204] Coe and Rubins, Regulatory Expropriation and the *Tecmed* Case: Context and Contributions' in Weiler (ed), *International Investment Law and Arbitration: Leading Cases from the ICSID, NAFTA, Bilateral Treaties and Customary International Law* (2005), cited in *Fireman's Fund* v. *Mexico*, Award, para. 176.

The application of the law to the facts in *Fireman's Fund* did not clarify the balancing or weighing process to be applied in characterisation. However, it did clarify the structure of the inquiry by requiring an initial threshold of effect before moving to the balancing process. Fireman's Fund challenged five separate regulatory measures in the recapitalization of a Mexican bank in which it was a major investor. The measure which came closest to expropriation was the repurchase of debentures by the state, which discriminated between peso-denominated debentures, held by Mexican nationals, and dollar-denominated debentures, held by Fireman's Fund.[205] The tribunal dismissed the indirect expropriation claim, saying, 'a discriminatory lack of effort by a host State to rescue an investment that has become virtually worthless, is not a taking of that investment.'[206] *Fireman's Fund* was cited and applied in *Corn Products* v. *Mexico* and followed, without citation, by *Arthur Daniel Midlands* v. *Mexico*.[207]

5.6.2.2 Codification of the characterisation approach in model BITs

Unlike most investment treaties, the 2004 Canadian Model BIT and the 2004 and 2012 US Model BITs provide some guidance as to the criteria by which indirect expropriation should be identified. This guidance is contained in annexes to the model treaties, which document 'understandings' on the interpretation of expropriation. The 2004 and 2012 US Models state:

The determination of whether an action or series of actions by a Party, in a specific fact situation, constitutes an indirect expropriation, requires a case-by case, fact-based inquiry that considers, among other factors:

i)   the economic impact of the government action, although the fact that an action or series of actions by a Party has an adverse effect on the economic value of an investment,
     standing alone, does not establish that an indirect expropriation has occurred;
ii) the extent to which the government action interferes with distinct, reasonable investment-backed expectations; and
iii) the character of the government action.[208]

---

[205] *Fireman's Fund* v. *Mexico*, Award, para. 202.   [206] Ibid., Award, para. 207.
[207] *Corn Products International* v. *Mexico*, Decision on Responsibility, para. 87; *Archer Daniel Midlands* v. *Mexico*, Award, para. 250.
[208] US 2012 Model BIT, annex B, art. 4(a).

The Canadian Model BIT articulates the same three factors and is worded almost identically.[209] Both annexes are 'integral parts' of their respective treaties.[210] They require indirect expropriation to be identified within a balancing structure; criteria i) and ii) refer to the effect of a measure, whereas criterion iii) refers to its characteristics.

Both model BITs include a further paragraph, clarifying that regulatory measures do not normally amount to indirect expropriation. The US Model reads:

> Except in rare circumstances, non-discriminatory regulatory actions by a Party that are designed and applied to protect legitimate public welfare objectives, such as public health, safety, and the environment, do not constitute indirect expropriations.[211]

The Canadian Model identifies the situation 'when a measure or series of measures are so severe in the light of their purpose that they cannot be reasonably viewed as having been adopted and applied in good faith' as an example of the 'rare circumstances' in which a non-discriminatory regulatory action could amount to indirect expropriation.[212] In addition to the three factors enumerated above, these further paragraphs require a tribunal to consider whether a measure is a 'non-discriminatory regulatory action' that protects a 'legitimate public welfare objective'.

Recent US and Canadian BITs incorporate these model provisions.[213] These interpretative annexes have also proved influential beyond North America. For example, the 2012 Japan-Korea-China Trilateral Investment Treaty contains a near-identical Protocol on indirect expropriation.[214] Other recent treaties contain annexes similar to the interpretative annexes of US and Canadian BITs, with the final paragraph modified to so as to carve out an exception: 'non-discriminatory regulatory action . . . designed and applied to achieve legitimate public welfare objectives *do not* constitute [indirect] expropriation'.[215] Provisions of the latter sort are better understood as falling within the exception structure of inquiry.

---

[209] Canada Model FIPA, annex B.13(1).
[210] Canada Model FIPA, art. 52(1); US 2012 Model BIT, art. 35.
[211] US 2012 Model BIT, annex B, art. 4(b).   [212] Canada Model FIPA, annex B.13(1), art. c).
[213] E.g. US-Uruguay BIT (4 November 2005), annex B; Canada-Peru BIT (14 November 2006), annex B.13(1).
[214] Japan-Korea-China Trilateral Investment Treaty (13 May 2012), protocol.
[215] Agreement Establishing the ASEAN-Australia-New Zealand Free Trade Area (27 February 2009), chp. 11, annex, emphasis added.

The first three criteria contained in US and Canadian annexes – economic impact, interference with investment backed expectations and the character of the measure – have their origin US Supreme Court jurisprudence on 'regulatory takings'.[216] Notwithstanding these domestic origins, the approach to indirect expropriation that these annexes require is remarkably similar to the characterisation approach of the decision considered in Section 5.6.2.1. As with *Feldman*, *Fireman's Fund* and their progeny, the annexes require a 'case-by-case' analysis that takes several factors into account, including a measure's characteristics and its effects.[217] Moreover, the particular factors to be considered in this process of balancing – the economic impact of a measure, the extent of interference with investment-backed expectations and the character of government action, specifically whether a measure is non-discriminatory and regulatory in character and designed to protect a legitimate welfare objective – are the same factors identified as relevant in decisions such as *Fireman's Fund*.[218] For both reasons, the approach to indirect expropriation laid down in these interpretative annexes can be understood as a development of an approach based on characterisation.[219]

So far, only one tribunal has interpreted and applied a treaty contain an annex on indirect expropriation based on the US model BIT. The case is *Railroad Development* v. *Guatemala*, a claim decided under CAFTA. (At least two other decisions – *Continental Casualty* v. *Argentina* and *Glamis Gold* v. *US* – have discussed the interpretative annex of the 2004 US model BIT in the course of interpreting treaties that did not contain such text.)[220] The dispute arose out of a railway concession owned and operated the claimant. In addition to the claimant's right to use the track, the

---

[216] *Kaiser Aetna* v. *United States* 444 US 164 (1979) 175; Newcombe, 'Canada's New Model Foreign Protection Agreement' (2004) [online], p. 6; Porterfield, 'International Expropriation Rules and Federalism' (2004) 23 *Stanford Environmental Law Journal*, p. 43.
[217] E.g., *Feldman* v. *Mexico*, Award, paras. 106, 102.
[218] *Fireman's Fund* v. *Mexico*, Award, para. 176.
[219] Other commentators have also noticed the similarities between the approach required by the interpretative annexes and the characterisation approach adopted by some tribunals. Yannaca-Small argues that the annexes require an approach similar to that used in existing arbitral jurisprudence. She understands existing jurisprudence to endorse an approach based on characterisation: Yannaca-Small, 'Indirect Expropriation and the Right to Regulate: How to Draw the Line', p. 460. Paparinskis argues that the annexes require a different approach to the *Tecmed* and *Methanex* approaches: Paparinskis, 'Regulatory Expropriation and Sustainable Development', p. 321.
[220] *Continental Casualty* v. *Argentina*, Award, para. 276; *Glamis Gold* v. *United States*, Award, para. 356.

claimant and the Guatemalan railway authority signed a lease contract allowing the claimant to use the authority's rolling stock. Two years later, the Guatemalan government declared that that the lease contract was void on the grounds that the authority had not followed procedures required by Guatemalan law in executing the contract.[221] The claimant contended that both the contract and its investment as a whole had been expropriated.

In assessing the investor's claim, the tribunal organised its analysis according to the criteria identified in the interpretative annex. It sequentially reviewed the character of the Guatemala's action, its purpose, the extent to which it interfered with investment-backed expectations and its impact on the claimant's investment. The tribunal's assessment of the character of the measure focused on whether the government's conduct was legal under Guatemalan law; its assessment on the purpose of the measure focused on whether the measure was specifically designed to deprive the investor of its investment. The tribunal did not make findings on either point.[222] In its analysis of the investor's investment backed expectations, the tribunal noted that it would normally be reasonable for an investor to assume that a government's internal requirements relating to the validity of contracts had been satisfied, and observed that both parties had proceeded for two years on this basis.[223] However, the tribunal's findings on the impact of the measure were ultimately decisive. It examined both the impact of the measure on the claimant's revenue and its impact on the claimant's rights of use and possession, concluding that the claimant had not been 'deprived substantially of the use and benefits of the investment'.[224] Thus, the measure was not capable of amounting to indirect expropriation.[225] This finding is consistent with the decision in *Fireman's Fund*, where an initial threshold of effect was required before any balancing process became necessary.[226]

Perhaps the most interesting part of the *Railroad Development* Tribunal's reasoning was its examination of the effect of the measure on the claimant's investment. In this section of the award, the tribunal gave as much attention to the measure's impact on the claimant's *legal entitlements* of possession and control of the investment as it gave to the measure's impact on the investment's *value*. While the CAFTA annex directs

---

[221] *Railroad Development Corporation* v. *Guatemala*, Award, paras. 30–37.
[222] Ibid., paras. 92, 110.   [223] Ibid., paras. 120–3.   [224] Ibid., paras. 151–2.
[225] Ibid., para. 151.   [226] *Fireman's Fund*, Award, paras. 202–7.

an arbitral tribunal to focus on 'the economic impact of the government action',[227] it immediately qualifies this direction by noting that 'the fact that an action . . . has an adverse effect on the economic value of an investment, standing alone, does not establish that an indirect expropriation has occurred'.[228] This qualification could be interpreted as requiring the impact on an investment's value to be considered in light of the extent of interference investor's property interests in the investment. The *Railroad Development* Tribunal did not discuss these intricacies in the drafting of the CAFTA annex. It seems to have regarded the CAFTA annex as codifying, rather than departing from, existing case law on the magnitude and type of effect on an investment required for a measure to be potentially expropriatory.[229] It remains to be seen how other tribunals will deal with this issue.

5.6.2.3 Restatement of the US annex approach

The interpretative annexes of the US and Canadian model BITs require a tribunal to identify indirect expropriation through a 'case-by-case' inquiry in which a non-exhaustive list of specified factors are considered. This process of characterisation is remarkably similar to the approach adopted by tribunals such as *Feldman* and *Fireman's Fund* in indirect expropriation claims brought under treaties that do not contain such interpretative annexes. The US annex approach can be restated as follows:

1. A minimum threshold of effect of substantial deprivation of the use and benefits of an investment is required for an indirect expropriation.[230] Determining whether a sufficiently serious interference has occurred seems to involve both a consideration of the economic impact of a measure on the investment and, because an adverse economic impact is not sufficient for an expropriation to have occurred, consideration of the extent to which the measure interferes with the investor's property interests in the investment.

2. Beyond this minimum threshold, the characteristics of the measure – whether it is discriminatory, of general application, and pursues a legitimate public purpose – are all potentially relevant in the indirect expropriation inquiry.

3. The extent to which the measure interferes with the investor's investment-backed expectations is also relevant, particularly

---

[227] CAFTA, annex 10-C, art. 4a)i).   [228] Ibid.

[229] *Railroad Development Corporation* v. *Guatemala*, Award, para. 151.

[230] Ibid., para. 151; similarly, *Fireman's Fund* v. *Mexico*, Award, para. 176.

expectations relating to the continuation of existing patterns of use of the investment.[231]

4. Tribunals applying this approach balance all the relevant considerations on the specific facts of the case and then characterise the measure as either expropriation or legitimate noncompensable government action.

5.7 Conclusion

This chapter examined the way in which arbitral tribunals interpret the concept of indirect expropriation under investment treaties. Section 5.2 reviewed the expropriation provisions of investment treaties and argued that arbitral tribunals treat differently worded expropriation provisions as if they all embody a common concept of indirect expropriation. Section 5.3 proposed a basic taxonomy of the structures of inquiry that tribunals use to distinguish indirect expropriation from legitimate, non-compensable government measures: those that look exclusively to the effects of the measure on the protected investment (the effects structure); those that define expropriation by its effects, subject to exceptions for measures with certain characteristics (the exception structure); and those that balance the effects on the investment and the characteristics of the impugned measure in determining whether an expropriation has occurred (the balancing structure).

Section 5.4 examined decisions within the effects structure. It identified two alternative interpretations of indirect expropriation within this structure: one, originating from *Metalclad*, which looks to the effect of the measure on the economic value of the investment; the other, originating from *Pope & Talbot*, which looks to the effect of the measure on the investor's property interests in the investment. Section 5.5 considered decisions within the exception structure. It identified one interpretation within this structure, involving the carve-out for legitimate regulatory conduct articulated in *Methanex*. Section 5.6 explored decisions within the balancing structure. It identified two interpretations within this structure: one involving proportionality review as articulated in *Tecmed*; the other involving characterisation of a measure as either expropriatory or noncompensable based on criteria that are now codified in the annex to the US model BIT. Although many of these approaches have their roots

---

[231] *Railroad Development Corporation* v. *Guatemala*, Award, paras. 120–3; *Fireman's Fund* v. *Mexico*, Award, para. 176.

in earlier decisions, they have been developed, clarified and endorsed in subsequent decisions.

This doctrinal analysis is, in itself, a contribution to scholarship on indirect expropriation. In the context of this book, the analysis in this chapter also performs a more specific function. Each interpretation identified in this chapter constitutes a different level of protection, which might be explicitly adopted in future investment treaties or through the amendment of existing treaties. Indeed, the US annex approach has already being adopted in several investment treaties concluded since 2004. Chapter 6 applies the framework developed in Chapter 3 to evaluate these different levels of protection. This evaluation leads to a set of conclusions about the level of protection that investment treaties should provide to foreign investors.

6 Application of the framework and conclusions

6.1 Introduction

In this chapter, I apply the framework developed in Chapter 3 to evaluate the differing levels of protection implied by different interpretations of each element of the fair and equitable treatment (FET) standard, as identified in Chapter 4, and different interpretations of indirect expropriation, as identified in Chapter 5. These different levels of protection are evaluated from a general, impartial perspective, in which the interests of all affected constituencies are weighted equally. This perspective was explained and justified in Section 1.2.4. It corresponds to the perspective of an individual state that is both a source and destination of foreign investment and that is seeking to determine the level of protection that should be provided through its investment treaties. Both the analysis contained in this chapter and the conclusions that emerge from it contribute to existing academic and policy debates about the level of substantive protection that investment treaties should provide to foreign investment. In Chapter 7, I explore the implications of these conclusions for the drafting and interpretation of investment treaties.

The analysis in this chapter also serves a wider purpose. While this chapter evaluates different levels of protection derived from existing arbitral jurisprudence, there is a greater range of options available to states when considering the level of protection that future investment treaties should provide. States could, for example, elect to entirely omit protections commonly found in existing treaties, or to include new protections with no basis in existing treaty practice, or to radically confine existing protections in ways that go beyond any interpretation of those protections found in existing arbitral awards.[1] The framework developed in Chapter 3 would

---

[1] E.g., ASEAN-China Agreement on Investment (15 August 2009), art. 7(2)(a), limiting the FET provision of that treaty to the doctrine of denial of justice, thereby excluding the

be equally useful in evaluating such options. The analysis in this chapter serves both as demonstration of the framework's utility in practice and as model of how the framework could be applied to evaluate a range of options beyond those considered here.

This chapter comprises six substantive sections. Section 6.2 briefly reintroduces the framework and explains the mechanics of its application. Sections 6.3, 6.4 and 6.5 apply the framework to evaluate differing levels of protection implied by different interpretations of each element of the FET standard. Section 6.6 applies the framework to evaluate differing levels of protection implied by different interpretations of indirect expropriation. In light of this analysis, Section 6.7 draws some broader, overall conclusions.

6.2 The framework: a brief recapitulation

In Chapter 2, I argued that the evaluation of alternative levels of protection that could be provided by investment treaties should be based on a comparison of the likely consequences of each level of protection, if it were adopted. In Chapter 3, I argued that the likely consequences of adopting a given level of protection should be divided into its effect on efficiency, the distribution of economic costs and benefits, flows of FDI into host states, the realisation of human rights and environmental conservation in host states and respect for the rule of law in host states. Chapter 3 drew a number of inferences relating to the likely consequences of various levels of investment treaty protection, which were stated in the form of propositions. It also articulated the normative criteria by which these consequences should be evaluated. Sections 6.3 to 6.6 of this chapter rely on these propositions, and the analysis underpinning them, to predict and evaluate the likely consequences of adopting each level of protection under consideration.

The methodology used in this section involves comparison of the likely consequences of adopting a range of different levels of protection. For this reason, the evaluation in Sections 6.3 to 6.6 is structured to focus on the points of difference between the various options under consideration – points of similarity being equally (un)desirable in each of the compared alternatives. To avoid the assessment of differences between alternatives

possibility that FET provision should be interpreted as providing any protection to investors' legitimate expectations or any possibility of substantive review of government conduct.

becoming unwieldy, Sections 6.3 to 6.6 are organised as a series of paired comparisons – and, in one case, a three-way comparison – between levels of protection. This simplifies the application of the framework and allows more precise focus on particular points of difference and the consequences likely to flow from these differences.

6.3 To what extent should the FET standard protect investors' legitimate expectations?

Chapter 4 argued that tribunals have understood the FET standard as comprising different 'elements', each of which operates as a quasi-independent liability rule. It then examined arbitral decisions interpreting and applying three of the most important elements of the FET standard: the protection of investors' legitimate expectations, procedural review of government conduct and substantive review of government conduct. I identified a number of alternative interpretations of each of these elements of the FET standard in the reasoning of arbitral awards.

This section applies the framework developed in Chapter 3 to evaluate the four distinct levels of protection of investors' legitimate expectations implied by different interpretations of the FET standard, as identified in Chapter 4. They are as follows:

   i)   The legal rights approach, in which legitimate expectations can only be based on legal rights vested in the investor.
   ii) The representations approach, in which legitimate expectations can be based on clear and specific unilateral statements made by the host state.
   iii) The stability approach, in which legitimate expectations can be based on general regulations in force at the time that the investment was made.
   iv) The business plan approach, in which legitimate expectations can be based on an investor's business plans, if the host state knew of those plans.

This section infers and evaluates the likely consequences of each approach if it were adopted prospectively. It begins by comparing the likely consequences of the business plan approach to the stability approach. It then compares the likely consequences of the stability approach to the representations approach and, finally, the likely consequences of the representations approach to the legal rights approach.

6.3.1 The business plan approach versus the stability approach

The essential difference between the business plan approach and the stability approach is that the former allows legitimate expectations to be derived solely from the business plans of a foreign investor. Therefore, evaluation of the two approaches turns on an examination of the consequences of extending a state's liability to actions that interfere with an investor's business plans, when such interference does not breach the investor's legal rights, breach unilateral assurances made by the host state or alter the regulatory regime that existed at the time of the investment.

6.3.1.1 Efficiency

One foundational causal proposition articulated in Chapter 3 is that legal rules that place some investors in a better legal position than other investors tend to reduce efficiency.[2] According to neo-classical economic theory, markets' ability to allocate capital efficiently depends on competitive equality among investors. This effect concerns relative levels of legal protection. A state's additional liability under the business plan approach does not turn on an examination of whether equivalent protections are provided to other investors. Rather, this approach would protect foreign investors' business plans, notwithstanding the fact that other investors were not entitled to equivalent protection under the domestic law of the host state. On this basis, the business plan approach is likely to lead to less efficient organisation of production than the stability approach.

Economic theory also suggests that, if certain empirical conditions exist, investment treaty protections may be able to improve the efficiency of government and investment decisions by solving hold-up problems. This effect concerns absolute levels of legal protection. To the extent that hold-up problems exist, investment treaty protections that require a state to pay compensation for conduct that is designed to extract a benefit from the investor *and* is not efficiency-improving on an *ex post* assessment can increase efficiency. However, investment treaty protections that require compensation beyond this narrow range of circumstances are likely to reduce efficiency by inducing moral hazard on the part of investors.[3] Because a number of legal substitutes are available to foreign investors to partially solve hold-up problems (internationalised contracts, for example), under-protection of foreign investment is likely to cause less efficiency loss than over-protection.[4]

---

[2] See Section 3.4.4.   [3] See Section 3.4.5.2.   [4] See Section 3.4.5.3.

Under the business plan approach, liability turns on an examination of the investor's business plans, not on an examination of whether the conduct that breached the investor's expectations was efficiency-improving or whether it was designed to extract a benefit from the investor. Determining whether the host state's conduct was efficient would require an assessment of the aggregate economic costs and benefits of the conduct. Because the business plan approach does not depend on an overall assessment of a state's conduct, it is highly unlikely that there would be any *de facto* correlation between a state's additional liability under the business plan approach and inefficient government conduct. Determining whether the host state's conduct was designed to extract a benefit from the investor would require examination of whether the state breached a bargain with the investor, whether sunk costs were present and whether the measure benefited the host state. None of these factors are relevant in the business plan approach.

For both reasons, even if hold-up problems did exist, the additional protection provided the business plan approach would be unnecessary to solve them. Accordingly, the business plan approach is likely to induce moral hazard on the part of investors. Indeed, an entitlement to compensation for interference with business plans is precisely the sort of liability rule that would discourage investors from internalising the risk to their business plans posed by future, efficiency-improving government conduct.

6.3.1.2 Distributive consequences

The previous section argued that preferring the business plan approach to the stability approach is likely to create net economic costs. Given that the business plan approach establishes a broader basis of state liability than the stability approach, any benefits to foreign investors of adopting this approach would entail greater corresponding costs in the territory of the host state. In democratic states this pattern of costs and benefits is likely to be regressive on egalitarian grounds.[5] Moreover, the benefit to investors cannot be justified by libertarian theory as the additional requirement to compensate for interference with investors' business plans is not linked to interference with investors' property rights.[6] Furthermore, the benefits to investors at the expense of other actors cannot be justified by political process theory

---

[5] See Section 3.5.6.   [6] See Section 3.5.5.

because they do not flow from situations in which a tribunal has judged that the investor was arbitrarily singled out to bear a loss.[7]

6.3.1.3 Foreign direct investment flows

Existing evidence suggests that differences in the level of protection provided by investment treaties are unlikely to have a significant impact on foreign direct investment (FDI) flows.[8] Moreover, neither of the two theories that speak to the relationship between investment treaties and FDI suggests that holding a state liable for interference with investors' business plans will increase FDI. Because liability for disruption of an investor's business plans does not concern the protection of agreements struck with the host state, commitment theory does not offer any reason to think that it will increase FDI.[9] Moreover, liability for disruption of an investor's business plans does not follow from an inquiry into the characteristics of a host state's legal regime, nor whether the state has acted legally or in accordance with principles of natural justice. As such, a state's additional liability under the business plan approach is highly unlikely to lead to greater FDI via the causal mechanism proposed by signalling theory.[10]

6.3.1.4 Respect for the rule of law

The primary mechanism by which investment treaty protections might affect the degree of respect for the rule of law in host states is through internalisation of these protections by decision-makers and law-makers. Assuming that investment treaty protections are internalised to some extent, the key issue is whether a state's additional liability under the business plan approach is linked to failure to respect the rule of law.[11] It is not. The Razian conception of the rule of law does not place substantive constraints on states' ability to enact laws that cause loss to individuals, regardless of whether the state knew of the potential for its action to cause such loss.

6.3.1.5 Realisation of human rights and environmental conservation

Both theory and evidence, to the extent it exists, suggest that states are less likely to maintain measures that give rise to liability under an investment treaty.[12] On this basis, investment treaty protections which

---

[7] See Section 3.5.8.   [8] See Section 3.6.3.   [9] See Section 3.6.4.
[10] See Section 3.6.4.   [11] See Section 3.8.4.   [12] See Section 3.7.4.3.

hold a state liable for loss cause by environmental or human rights–inspired measures are likely to lead to greater chilling of chilling of such measures. This translates to lesser realisation of these objectives in practice. In general terms, the business plan approach makes a state liable for a greater range of conduct than the stability approach. Furthermore, the scope of a state's additional liability turns on the impact of conduct on the investor's interests, without reference to whether the measure is effective in realising human rights or environmental conservation. As such, a greater range of environmental and human rights–inspired measures will trigger liability under the business plan approach. This is likely to lead to greater regulatory chill of environmental and human rights measures.

Theory also suggests that levels of protection which reduce a state's uncertainty about the extent of its liability tend to reduce the chilling of measures that would have been permissible under the level of protection in question.[13] Because it is difficult for a state to stay abreast of every foreign investor's business plans (and the potential impact of any contemplated conduct on any of these plans), the business plan approach entails a high degree of uncertainty about the extent of a state's prospective liability. This additional uncertainty constitutes a further reason why the business plan approach is likely to increase regulatory chill and diminish the realisation of human rights and environmental conservation.

6.3.1.6 Overall evaluation

There are no coherent arguments for preferring the business plan approach to the stability approach. Moreover, there are several reasons to conclude that the business plan approach is less desirable. It is highly likely that it will reduce economic efficiency by engendering moral hazard and that it will increase regulatory chill of human rights and environmental measures. In addition, it is likely to result in a pattern of costs and benefits that cannot be justified by any theory of distributive justice.

6.3.2 The stability approach versus the representations approach

Under the representations approach to the doctrine of legitimate expectations, expectations protected by the FET standard can be based on either clear and specific representations made to the investor by the host state

---

[13] See Section 3.7.4.4.

or on specific and enforceable legal rights of the investor. The key difference between the representations approach and the stability approach is that under the stability approach, legitimate expectations can also be based on the legal regime in force at the time the investment was made, even in the absence of specific representations that the regime would not be changed. Two further differences between the two approaches are that, insofar as expectations are based on unilateral representations, the stability approach requires the risk of ambiguity in such representations to be borne by the host state. Moreover, under the stability approach, when assessing whether a given expectation is legitimate, the perspective of the investor weighs more heavily in the balance than countervailing factors such as the political, social and cultural conditions in the host state.

6.3.2.1 Efficiency

The broader scope of state liability for change to the regulatory framework under the stability approach is likely to increase moral hazard.[14] This is because, under the stability approach, the assessment of whether a state is liable for regulatory change turns on the question of whether the changed regulation was 'basic' to the investment decision, not whether the regulatory change was an opportunistic attempt to extract a benefit from the investor nor whether the change itself was efficient on an *ex post* economy-wide assessment. Similarly, under the stability approach, liability for breach of unilateral statements arises independently of whether it would be efficient for a state to reverse its previously stated position. Economy-wide judgements – for example, whether the expectation was reasonable given the political and economic situation in the host state – weigh less heavily in the determination of whether an expectation was legitimate than under the representations approach. For all these reasons, the stability approach is less likely to encourage investors to assess adequately the risk to their projects posed by efficient changes in regulation.

Moreover, the additional protection provided by the stability approach is not concerned with establishing competitive equality between investors. On the contrary, this approach is especially likely to create an uneven playing field between investors. This is because the stability approach protects foreign investors from changes to laws of general application; such laws usually affect a range of investors, including domestic

---

[14] See Section 3.4.5.2.

and foreign investors not protected by an investment treaty. This discriminatory overprotection of some foreign investors is likely to be associated with further inefficiency.

6.3.2.2 Distributive consequences

The previous section argued that preferring the stability approach to the representations approach is likely to entail net economic costs. Given that the broader protection of the stability approach benefits foreign investors, these costs would be borne by actors within the host state. In states that are broadly democratic, this pattern of costs and benefits is likely to be regressive on egalitarian grounds. Moreover, the benefits of the stability approach to foreign investors cannot be justified by political process theory, as liability is not contingent on the exclusion of a foreign investor from the decision-making process that leads to a breach of expectations, nor on the arbitrary 'singling out' of a foreign investor from among similarly situated investors.[15]

Evaluation of the additional distributive transfers associated with the stability approach according to libertarian theory is more difficult. Libertarianism cannot justify the broader protection of investors from losses caused by breach of unilateral representations. On the other hand, libertarianism demands compensation for changes to the investor's legal entitlements to use, enjoy and dispose of property. This is consistent with the protection provided to expectations based on the regulatory framework at the time the investment was made under the stability approach.

6.3.2.3 Realisation of human rights and environmental conservation

Unlike the representations approach, liability under the stability approach can arise from changes to regulations. This increases the risk that new measures of general application that are effective in realising human rights and environmental conservation will be chilled. Moreover, under the stability approach, the assessment of whether a state is liable for regulatory change turns primarily on the impact of conduct on the investor's interests, rather than broader assessments of whether the measure is effective in realising human rights or environmental conservation.

In addition, the broader scope of liability under the stability approach creates greater uncertainty for host state regulators than an approach

---

[15] See Section 3.5.8.

where legitimate expectations only arise from enforceable legal rights and clear and specific representations made to the investor. For both reasons, it is likely to cause greater regulatory chill than the representations approach.

6.3.2.4 FDI flows

Commitment theory suggests that investment treaties could increase FDI they allow foreign investors to enforce bargains made with the host state. This theory provides no reason to think that the stability approach would stimulate greater flows of FDI than the representations approach. The stability approach provides greater protection to foreign investors than the representations approach in two relevant respects: a state may be liable for breach of ambiguous representations, and a state may be liable for changes to the legal framework in force at the time the investment was made. However, an ambiguous unilateral statement is not akin to a term of a negotiated bargain, nor does the fact that a given regulatory framework was in place at the time an investment was made constitute, of itself, an agreement to maintain the framework. Thus, commitment theory does not justify the stability approach, in which the risk of liability for the investor's reliance on ambiguous unilateral statements lies with the state.

6.3.2.5 Respect for the rule of law

Even assuming host states do internalise investment treaty protections to some extent, it is unlikely that the stability approach would lead to improvements in respect for the rule of law. Under the stability approach, liability does not turn on whether any change to the legal regime governing the investment complies with the rule of law. It does not depend, for example, on whether the conduct is lawful under domestic law, whether the change is prospective or whether the new law are open, clear and of general application. Moreover, a state's greater scope of liability for breach of unilateral statements under the stability approach does not depend on whether an agency's discretion under law to take a new position was 'guided by open, clear and stable general rules.'[16] Such criteria of liability might arguably encourage respect for the rule of law in host states, but they find no place in the stability approach.

---

[16] Raz, 'The Rule of Law and Its Virtue' (1977) 93 *The Law Quarterly Review*, p. 200; cf. *International Thunderbird Gaming* v. *Mexico*, Separate Opinion, para. 88.

The Razian conception of the rule of law does require that laws be relatively stable, so that people can be guided by their knowledge of the content of the law.[17] This principle provides some justification for the stability approach. However, liability for change to the regulatory framework under the stability approach turns on analysis of whether the change in question is to the substantive detriment of an investor, not an analysis of whether changes were repeated or erratic. Thus, while the stability approach may encourage greater stability in the law, this effect would be an indirect and limited consequence of discouraging particular *substantive* legal changes.

6.3.2.6 Overall Evaluation

The only justifications for the stability approach are the partial justification provided by libertarian theory and the limited and indirect justification based on the principle of stability – one sub-principle within the Razian conception of the rule of law. On the other hand there are good reasons to believe that preferring the representations approach to the stability approach would lead to net economic benefits, to distributional effects that are more consistent with both egalitarian theories of distributive justice and political process theory and to lesser interference with the realisation of human rights and environmental conservation. These are sufficient grounds for a clear preference for the representations approach.

6.3.3 *The representations approach versus the legal rights approach*

The essential distinction between the representations and the legal rights approaches is whether a protected expectation can be based on a specific and clear unilateral statement made by the host state. Some such expectations fall within the scope of the representations approach; none are protected under the legal rights approach. This difference aside, the two approaches are doctrinally similar. Both agree that only reasonable expectations are protected by the doctrine; that the determination of whether an expectation is reasonable must be made in light of the political, socioeconomic, cultural and historical conditions in the host state, as well as the host state's prerogative to alter regulations. Both agree that to recover for breach of a legitimate expectation, an investor must have relied on the expectation in making the investment.

---

[17] Raz, 'The Rule of Law and Its Virtue', p. 199.

6.3.3.1 Efficiency

The comparison of the two approaches' consequences for economic efficiency raises complex issues. A state's liability does not, under either approach, turn on a comparison of the foreign investor's treatment with the treatment of domestic investors. Greater legal protection of the expectations of foreign investors than is available to domestic investors disturbs competitive equality between investors. At least in some states, the representations approach goes beyond the protections that domestic law provide to investors from departure from unilateral assurances.[18] On this basis, the representations approach is likely to be less efficient than the legal rights approach.

There are further issues with the absolute level of protection provided by each approach – particularly its effect on the efficiency of foreign investors' decisions. To the extent that hold-up problems exist, investment treaty protections that require a state to pay compensation for conduct that is designed to extract a benefit from the investor *and* is not efficiency-improving on an *ex post* assessment can increase efficiency. However, investment treaty protections that require compensation beyond this narrow range of circumstances are likely to reduce efficiency by inducing moral hazard on the part of investors.[19] Thus, the two key issues are whether, under each approach, liability turns on an examination of whether the government conduct in question was efficient and whether the government conduct was opportunistic.

Liability does not turn on an explicit examination of whether a state's conduct is efficient under either approach. However, under both approaches, tribunals have developed principles that govern the determination of whether an expectation is legitimate. The assessment of whether expectations are reasonable in all the circumstances may involve the tribunals in limited, *de facto* review of the economic costs and benefits of the government's change of position – the factors which determine the efficiency of the government's action. However, under the representations approach, the question of whether an expectation based on a unilateral representation was legitimate turns on the circumstances in which

---

[18] Marboe, 'State Responsibility and Comparative State Liability for Administrative and Legislative Harm to Economic Interests' in Schill (ed), *International Investment Law and Comparative Public Law* (2010), p. 409; Mairal, 'Legitimate Expectations and Informal Administrative Representations' in Schill (ed), *International Investment Law and Comparative Public Law* (2010), p. 450.

[19] See Section 3.4.5.2.

the expectation formed, not on analysis of the conduct that allegedly breached the expectation or its economic consequences.[20] Accordingly, a state's additional liability under the representations approach does not reflect the inefficiency of government conduct. On the other hand, insofar as the representations approach protects expectations based on 'quasi-contractual' promises,[21] it may provide some protection against opportunistic breach of implicit bargains made between the investor and the host state at the time of the investment.

Thus, we have three interim conclusions that form part of the overall efficiency assessment. On the one hand, the representations approach provides additional protection against breach of quasi-contractual promises. This may assist in solving hold-up problems, insofar as they exist, by disciplining opportunistic conduct by the host state. On the other hand, liability under the representations approach does not turn on whether the breach of representation was justified on account of being *ex post* efficient. Accordingly, the representations approach would encourage moral hazard. Furthermore, the representations approach is associated with a greater risk of discriminatory overprotection of some foreign investors by granting them rights that are not available to other investors. In reconciling these three competing factors, it is useful to recall one of the important conclusions of Section 3.4.7. Insofar as there is a tension between offering unduly broad protection to foreign investment and unduly narrow protection, it is likely to be more efficient to err on the side of under-protection on account of the availability of other tools to foreign investors to solve hold-up problems. For this reason, the legal rights approach, with its narrower scope of liability, is likely to be more efficient.

6.3.3.2 Distributive consequences

The previous section argued that preferring the representations approach to the legal rights approach is, on balance, likely to entail net economic costs. Given that the broader protection of the representations approach benefits foreign investors, these costs would be borne by actors within the host state. In states that are broadly democratic, this pattern of costs and benefits is likely to be regressive on egalitarian grounds. Moreover, the additional benefit to foreign investors at the expense of other actors associated with the representations approach cannot be justified by political process theory. Liability for breach of an investor's expectations under

---

[20] See *CMS Gas* v. *Argentina*, Final Award, para. 175.
[21] *Glamis Gold* v. *United States*, Award, para. 767; similarly, *Cargill* v. *Mexico*, Award, para. 293.

the representations approach is independent of whether the investor was singled out to bear a loss caused by a state's change in position.[22]

Furthermore, the protection of expectations based on unilateral statements cannot be justified by libertarianism. Expectations based on unilateral statements are neither rights nor entitlements owned by the investor under domestic law. (If expectations were so protected, an investment treaty claim could rely on a specific legal right vested under the domestic legal system when a state makes a unilateral statement, without having to rely on the statement itself as the basis for liability under the FET standard.) This is an important point of contrast with the legal rights approach. The protection of legal rights vested in the investor can be justified – indeed, is required – by libertarian theories of justice.

6.3.3.3 Realisation of human rights and environmental conservation

Both approaches provide similar levels of certainty to government decision-makers about the contours of liability under the FET standard for interference with an investor's legitimate expectations. Therefore, any difference between the chilling effect of the representations and the legal rights approach could only stem from the greater scope of liability under the representations approach. Government measures that give rise to liability are more likely to be chilled than those that do not and, under the representations approach, more new measures and changes in policy will give rise to liability than under the legal rights approach. That said, the difference in chilling may be relatively small. To the extent that liability for effective environmental and human rights measures is excluded by the balancing tests built into the representations approach,[23] it would decrease the additional chilling caused by extension of the scope of the doctrine to departures from unilateral statements.

6.3.3.4 Respect for the rule of law

Assessment of the consequences of the two approaches for respect for the rule of law in host states is more speculative. Assuming that host states do internalise investment treaty protections to some extent, the key issue is whether liability for breach of a unilateral statement under the representations approach turns on the degree of a state's compliance

---

[22] *National Grid* v. *Argentina*, Award, paras. 176–9.

[23] *Duke Energy* v. *Ecuador*, Award, para. 340; *Biwater* v. *Tanzania*, Award, para. 601; *Saluka* v. *Czech Republic*, Partial Award, para. 305.

with the rule of law. If disregard of the rule of law made liability more likely (and respect for it made liability less likely), it would be arguable that the representations approach encouraged respect for the rule of law.

A government's departure from a clear and specific unilateral statement may, but does not necessarily, offend Razian principles. The primary question is whether the domestic legal regime has open, prospective, clear and relatively stable rules concerning the legal (in)significance of unilateral statements. If it is clear that a unilateral statement is legally insignificant, then breach of such a statement is entirely consistent with the principle that the law should be knowable.[24] Razian concerns only arise if domestic law is uncertain as to the legal significance of statements or if the departure from a previous statement is an exercise of discretion under law that is not controlled by open, stable, clear and general rules. Under the representations approach, the determination of liability may be somewhat sensitive to these issues. The legal position of the investor is one factor that weighs in the determination of whether an expectation is reasonable.[25] On the other hand, under this approach, a state may still be liable for breach of a unilateral statement in a context where the legal insignificance of the statement is clear, obvious and undisputed.[26] Penalising a state for the breach of such statements does not establish an incentive structure that could plausibly encourage respect for the rule of law.

6.3.3.5 FDI flows

Existing evidence suggests that differences in the level of protection provided by investment treaties are unlikely to have a significant impact on FDI flows.[27] However, it is still useful to consider the implications of theories that link investment treaties to FDI. Commitment theory implies that investment treaty protections that allow investors to enforce the terms of bargains they have made with the host state are likely to increase flows of FDI. Depending on the circumstances, specific and clear unilateral statements made by host states could be conceived of as components of an overall bargain negotiated and agreed between prospective investors and the host state. To the extent that the unilateral statements protected by the representations approach do emerge from informal bargaining processes, this approach could plausibly lead to greater FDI flows.

---

[24] Raz, 'The Rule of Law and Its Virtue', p. 198.
[25] *Biwater* v. *Tanzania*, Award, para. 601.
[26] See *National Grid* v. *Argentina*, Award, para. 177.   [27] See Section 3.6.3.

6.3.3.6 Overall evaluation

Compared with the legal rights approach, the representations approach is likely to result in marginally increased FDI and have an equivocal impact on the degree of respect for the rule of law. Both these conclusions are tentative in that they are premised on assumptions about the operation of complex causal mechanisms that link the content of investment treaty protections to particular consequences. In contrast, it is likely that the representations approach would, on balance, decrease economic efficiency, both on account of giving foreign investors greater legal rights than domestic investors and by virtue of inducing moral hazard on the part of foreign investors. This would entail net costs within the territory of the host state and benefits to foreign investors – a pattern of distributive consequences that cannot be justified by any theory of justice considered in this book. Furthermore, it would involve a minor increase in regulatory chill, implying reduced realisation of human rights and environmental conservation. These are sufficient grounds to conclude that the legal rights approach is the more desirable level of protection of foreign investors' legitimate expectations.

6.3.4 Conclusion: the most desirable level of protection of legitimate expectations

On the basis of the foregoing analysis, I conclude that, of the four options considered, the legal rights approach is the most desirable level of protection of investors' legitimate expectations. The legal rights approach is preferable to the representations approach on the grounds that it is likely to lead to greater economic efficiency, a distribution of income that is more desirable according to all the theories of distributive justice considered in this book and greater realisation of human rights and environmental conservation. This section has also argued that increasingly expansive options for protecting investors' legitimate expectations are progressively less desirable. There are few grounds for preferring the stability approach to the representations approach and no coherent justifications for preferring the business plan approach to the stability approach.

6.4 To what extent should the FET standard provide for procedural review of government conduct?

Chapter 4 identified three interpretations of the procedural element of the FET standard:

i)   A narrow approach, based on *Genin*, in which procedural unfairness must be aggravated either by being intentional or by having led to an outcome that cannot be justified on substantive grounds for it to breach the FET standard;

ii) An intermediate approach, based on *Chemtura*, in which procedural unfairness is sufficient to breach the FET standard if it is 'both serious itself and material to the outcome' of an administrative process; and

iii) An exacting approach, based on the detailed set of procedural and transparency requirements outlined in *Tecmed*.

Relying on the framework developed in Chapter 3, this section infers and evaluates the likely consequences of each approach if it were adopted prospectively. This section begins by comparing the narrow approach to the intermediate approach. It then compares the intermediate approach to the exacting approach.

6.4.1 *The narrow approach versus the intermediate approach*

The key difference between the narrow and the intermediate approaches is the threshold of liability. Under the narrow approach, only 'extreme' procedural unfairness can breach the FET standard and, even then, only when aggravated by being intentional or by having led to an outcome that cannot be justified on substantive grounds. Under the intermediate approach, procedural unfairness would entail liability if it were 'both serious itself and material to the outcome' of an administrative process.[28] In the narrow approach, procedural fairness seems to be tied closely to notions of good faith in the conduct of domestic procedure. Under the intermediate approach, procedural fairness refers to a more specific set of characteristics of domestic procedures: notice, hearing, timeliness, objectivity and lawfulness in administrative decision-making; a similar standard of conduct in contractual negotiations; and a requirement of transparency – that is, that legal rules be capable of being known. This section examines whether the lower threshold and broader grounds of liability imposed by the intermediate approach would be desirable.

6.4.1.1 Efficiency

Neither the narrow nor the intermediate approach determines the extent of procedural fairness to which a foreign investor is entitled by reference to the treatment of domestic investors. Thus, there is a risk that both approaches would confer greater rights on foreign investors and, there-fore, cause economic inefficiency. This risk can be safely discounted so

---

[28] *Chemtura* v. *Canada*, Award, para. 148.

far as the narrow approach is concerned; its minimal protections would not go beyond what is provided in the domestic law of the majority of host states. An analysis of the intermediate approach is less clear-cut and is complicated by potential variations in the degree of procedural fairness to which individuals are entitled in different national legal systems. Although it seems unlikely that the intermediate approach confers significantly greater protection than domestic investors would be entitled to in Western legal systems,[29] no study has yet compared the procedural element of the FET standard to Chinese or Islamic legal systems. In any case, the remedial provisions associated with the intermediate approach – a right to compensation for procedural unfairness – may place foreign investors in a better position than domestic investors even in Western states.[30] On this basis, the intermediate approach is likely to reduce efficiency.

The question of whether the additional protection provided by the intermediate approach is capable of improving efficiency by solving hold-up problems is more difficult to answer. Under the intermediate approach, serious unfairness can result from proceedings where decision-making is fundamentally biased, lacks an evidentiary basis or fails to consider the interests of the investor (when the investor is directly and substantially affected by the decision). Such procedures are more likely to lead to conduct that is substantively inefficient because the decision-maker has failed to reflect on the full array of costs and benefits of the decision. Moreover, in many circumstances, opportunistic conduct would violate the procedural protections of the intermediate approach relating to the lawfulness and procedural fairness of executive action. To extent that the additional scope of liability under the intermediate approach correlates with both inefficient and opportunistic conduct by the host state, it may increase efficiency by helping to resolve hold-up problems (to the extent they exist). It is not possible to predict whether this effect would outweigh any efficiency loss due to discriminatory overprotection of foreign investors.

6.4.1.2 Distributive consequences

The previous section argued that it is difficult to predict whether the intermediate approach would create net economic benefits. Therefore, while

---

[29] della Cananea, 'Equivalent Standards under Domestic Administrative Law' in Ortino et al. (eds), *Investment Treaty Law: Current Issues II* (2007), p. 155.
[30] Van Harten, *Investment Treaty Arbitration and Public Law* (2007), p. 106.

it is clear that the intermediate approach would benefit foreign investors on account of providing greater protection, it is unclear whether it would entail net costs for host states. Political process theory provides a limited justification for the benefits that would accrue to investors under the intermediate approach. In Chapter 3, I argued that there is no evidence that foreign investors are a *general* class of actor that suffers practical disadvantage in host state decision-making processes.[31] Accordingly, the non-contingent protections provided by the intermediate approach cannot be seen as redress for systematic exclusion of foreign investors. However, foreign investors may suffer specific instances of practical disadvantage. Although liability under the intermediate approach does not turn on an assessment of whether the foreign investor was denied the opportunity to participate in a domestic decision-making process that was available to other affected constituencies, it is arguable that findings of serious unfairness by a non-contingent standard will correlate with such situations.

6.4.1.3 Realisation of human rights and environmental conservation

Liability under the procedural element of FET does not turn on the substantive content of government conduct. The procedural element of the FET standard would permit a host state to introduce any human rights or environmental measure, so long as the procedures by which the measure was introduced were fair. As such, there is unlikely to be any direct regulatory chill caused by any level of protection from procedural unfairness. Chilling could only occur indirectly, to the extent that the risk of liability for procedural shortcomings in the introduction of new measures were so acute that it had the effect of dissuading decision-makers from adopting particular substantive measures. This is clearly not a risk under the narrow approach. Nor is it a significant risk under the intermediate approach. The standard under the intermediate approach is 'not procedural perfection',[32] it would impose liability only for serious unfairness.[33] This approach would also allow the host state flexibility in the way it provides this minimum standard of fairness because liability only arises if a procedure is unfair overall, allowing for mechanisms of review and correction under domestic law. It is unlikely that decision-makers who

---

[31] See Section 3.5.8.   [32] *AES Summit Generation* v. *Hungary*, Award, para. 9.3.40.
[33] *Chemtura* v. *Canada*, Award, para. 148.

were aware of the procedural requirements of the intermediate approach would be discouraged from introducing particular substantive measures.

6.4.1.4 FDI flows

Neither the narrow nor the intermediate approach deals with the enforceability of agreements between the host state and foreign investors. Hence, commitment theory does not provide a reason to think that either approach will affect FDI flows. Signalling theory raises more challenging issues. To the extent that a given level of protection places greater costs on states with 'bad governance', it may discourage such states from remaining parties to investment treaties, which – in turn – would allow foreign investors to infer that a state has 'good governance' from the fact it has become (and remains) party to an investment treaty. Chapter 3 noted reasons to doubt that such indirect causal mechanisms operate in practice.[34] Nevertheless, for the sake of completeness, it should be noted that signalling theory may give some tentative support to an association between the intermediate approach and increased FDI flows. The existence of such an effect would depend on the ability of this approach to place additional costs on states that do not respect the rule of law.

6.4.1.5 Respect for the rule of law

The primary mechanism by which investment treaty protections might affect the degree of respect for the rule of law in host states is through internalisation of these protections by decision-makers and law-makers. Assuming that both approaches are internalised to some extent, the intermediate approach would be likely to lead to greater respect for the rule of law. Liability under the intermediate approach is closely linked to a basic level of compliance with Razian principles. Raz's conception of the rule of law includes the requirement that a state act according to law and that a state observe principles of natural justice – '[o]pen and fair hearing, absence of bias and the like'.[35] Liability under the intermediate approach turns on whether a state's conduct was a serious departure from similar principles, particularly principles of lawfulness, notice and fair hearing in administrative proceedings. Transparency, in the sense that laws are capable of being known, is also fundamental to the Razian conception the rule of law. The intermediate approach places an obligation of transparency, understood in this sense, on host states. As a state would be able

---

[34] See Section 3.6.4.   [35] Raz, 'The Rule of Law and Its Virtue', p. 201.

to avoid liability under the intermediate approach by showing that it has acted consistently with the foregoing principles, this approach provides a structure of liability that is more likely to encourage respect for the rule of law.

6.4.1.6 Overall evaluation

There is little to distinguish the expected consequences of the narrow and intermediate approaches for the realisation of human rights and environmental conservation, economic efficiency and FDI flows. And, relying on political process theories of justice, there are only marginal grounds for preferring the distributive impacts of the intermediate approach. Accordingly, the overall evaluation turns on their impact on respect for the rule of law. The extent of this impact depends on a set of further assumptions regarding the extent of internalisation of investment treaty protections by host states' decision-makers and law-makers. If investment treaty protections are internalised to some extent, the intermediate approach is likely to lead to greater respect for the rule of law. The greater the degree of internalised compliance, the more significant these consequences would be. These potential impacts on the degree of respect for the rule of law justify a marginal preference for the intermediate approach. That said, this conclusion should be refined if future evidence relevant to assumptions about the degree of internalisation of investment treaty protections comes to light.

6.4.2 The intermediate approach versus the exacting approach

There is a marked difference between the threshold of liability under the intermediate and exacting approaches. Under the exacting approach, any procedural unfairness would require compensation. The fact that a domestic legal system provides mechanisms to redress such unfairness would not appear to be relevant. Under the intermediate approach, procedural unfairness must be serious and material to require compensation, with this assessment made in light of any opportunities for correction of procedural unfairness within the legal system of the host state. The scope of host states' procedural obligations is also broader under the exacting approach. The exacting approach includes requirements to initiate fair proceedings to consider investors' contractual proposals and to provide certainty to investors about the way that existing laws will be applied in the future. This section examines whether the lower threshold and broader grounds of liability imposed by the exacting approach are desirable.

6.4.2.1 Efficiency

The exacting approach imposes liability for failure to comply with a set of procedural obligations on the state that are not defined by reference to the way similarly situated investors are treated under domestic law. Moreover, the exacting approach is likely to confer legal protection on foreign investors that goes well beyond the entitlements of other investors under domestic law. This discriminatory overprotection is, in itself, likely to reduce economic efficiency.

The additional protection provided by the exacting standard is also unlikely to assist in addressing hold-up problems. This is for two reasons. First, the lower threshold and broader grounds of liability mean that a much broader range of procedural misconduct is caught by the exacting approach, diluting any correlation between opportunistic conduct and liability. Second, the obligation to provide certainty about the way that existing laws will be applied in future does not distinguish between efficient and inefficient exercises of future discretion and is, therefore, likely to encourage moral hazard on the part of foreign investors.

An investor's entitlement under the exacting approach to force a state to enter contractual negotiations is particularly concerning from an efficiency standpoint. Absent externalities, bargaining between two parties that leads to mutually beneficial agreement increases economic efficiency. If a mutually beneficial agreement cannot be reached – that is, if there is no possible agreed course of conduct that is mutually beneficial – the most efficient outcome is for *no* agreement to be reached. Thus, an important procedural prerequisite for maximising efficiency through bargaining is the ability of each party to reject proposals that are to its obvious detriment, without providing a full administrative hearing. The ability to reject proposals prevents waste of resources when no efficient bargain is possible and focuses the attention of both parties on those options that might be mutually beneficial. The requirement under the exacting approach that host states give serious and fair consideration to foreign investors' contractual proposals is likely to reduce economic efficiency.

6.4.2.2 Distributive consequences

The previous section argued that preferring the exacting approach to the intermediate approach is likely to entail net economic costs. Given that the broader protection of the exacting approach benefits foreign investors – the exacting approach demands a standard of 'perfect public regulation in a perfect world' that even diligent host states are likely to find difficult to satisfy[36] – these costs would be borne by actors within the host state. This pattern of costs and benefits is likely to be regressive on egalitarian grounds in states that are broadly democratic. The benefit to foreign investors cannot be justified by libertarian theory because it does not follow from the protection of property rights. Nor can the additional scope of liability under the exacting approach be justified by political process theory. The exacting approach is not concerned with equalising the influence of foreign and domestic constituencies over domestic decision-making. Under this approach, a state could incur liability in circumstances where a foreign investor has significantly greater influence over domestic decision-making than domestic constituencies.

6.4.2.3 Realisation of human rights and environmental conservation

Each of the three alternative levels of protection from procedural unfairness permit a host state to introduce human rights and environmental measures, so long as the procedures by which the measures are introduced are fair. As such, there is unlikely to be any direct regulatory chill caused by the procedural element. Chilling could only occur indirectly, to the extent that the risk of liability for procedural shortcomings in the introduction of new measures were so acute that it had the effect of dissuading decision-makers from adopting particular substantive measures. This risk is far more serious under the exacting approach than the intermediate approach. The exacting approach imposes a requirement that, at the time it makes its investment, an investor should be able to determine the laws that will govern its investment for the entire length of the project.[37] Although this is phrased as a procedural obligation, it is one that would foreclose a host states' ability to make *substantive* legal and policy changes, so far as they affect an existing foreign investment. Any new environmental or human rights measure would entail the liability of the host state to the extent it caused loss to an investment. Because host states are more likely to abandon measures that give rise to liability than those that do not, the exacting approach is likely to be associated with greater regulatory chill.

---

[36] Douglas, 'Nothing If Not Critical for Investment Treaty Arbitration: Occidental, Eureko and Methanex' (2006) 22 *Arbitration International*, p. 28.

[37] *Tecmed* v. *Mexico*, Award, para. 154.

6.4.2.4 FDI flows

Neither the intermediate nor the exacting approach deals with the enforceability of agreements between the host state and foreign investors. Hence, commitment theory does not provide a reason to think that either approach would affect FDI flows. Signalling theory raises more challenging issues. Any possibility that the exacting approach would increase FDI would depend on its ability to penalise states that do not respect the rule of law.[38]

6.4.2.5 Respect for the rule of law

Neither approach would affect the degree of respect for the rule of law in host states unless it were internalised by decision-makers and law-makers. Assuming that both approaches were internalised to some extent, a key issue is whether a state's additional liability under the exacting approach – namely, liability for *any* procedural unfairness – is likely to encourage greater respect for the rule of law. It is doubtful that it would. If internalised, the exacting approach may encourage primary decision-makers to respect Razian principles, yet discourage the development of a legal system based on the rule of law. Unlike the exacting approach, liability under the intermediate approach turns on a complete assessment of the investor's treatment, including whether domestic law provides complementary mechanisms that give the investor an opportunity to be heard and to ensure that decision-making is lawful, evidence-based and unbiased. As such, it seems that the intermediate approach would be more likely to act as a complement to, rather than a substitute for, the development of the rule of law in host states.[39]

Moreover, in important respects, liability under the exacting approach does not turn on whether a state has complied with the rule of law. The requirement under the exacting approach that a state correct an investor's misunderstanding of the law imposes an obligation greater in scope and different in character to the Razain principle that laws should be clear and capable of being known.[40] The requirement that it should be possible for an investor to know the way in which laws will be applied in the future

---

[38]   See Section 3.6.4.
[39]   See Ginsburg, 'International Substitutes for Domestic Institutions: Bilateral Investment Treaties and Governance' (2005) 25 *International Review of Law and Economics*, p. 119, arguing, in a different context, that investment treaties may either complement or substitute for the development of respect for the rule of law in host states.
[40]   *Metalclad* v. *Mexico*, Award, para. 76.

goes well beyond the principle of certainty embodied in the rule of law. Raz is surely right that '[i]t is humanly inconceivable that law can consist only of general rules and very undesirable that it should.'[41] Governance by law requires 'particular legal orders' – conferrals of discretionary power on decision-makers to address particular problems. Respect for the rule of law requires that discretionary power should only be exercised to the extent that it is conferred by law and that it be constrained by open, stable and general rules governing its exercise. The fact that a foreign investor does not know how a future discretion will be exercised is entirely consistent with the rule of law, so long as the investor is capable of knowing the rules and procedures that will govern its exercise. That a state may act consistently with the rule of law and still incur liability under the exacting approach makes it unlikely that the exacting approach will encourage greater respect for the rule of law than the intermediate approach.

6.4.2.6 Overall evaluation

There are no reasons to prefer the exacting approach to the intermediate approach. It is unlikely to lead to greater FDI, likely to lead to a distribution of costs and benefits that cannot be justified by any of the theories of justice that I have considered in this book and would, if anything, reduce respect for the rule of law in host states. Moreover, there are strong grounds for preferring the intermediate approach. It is likely to lead to greater economic efficiency and less chilling of effective human rights and environmental regulations. Overall, it is clearly a more desirable level of protection from procedural unfairness than the exacting approach.

6.4.3 Conclusion: the most desirable level of protection from procedural unfairness

This section has argued that the intermediate approach is the most desirable level of protection from procedural unfairness. It has identified strong grounds for preferring the intermediate approach to the exacting approach. The comparison of the intermediate to the narrow approach was more finely balanced. The overall preference for the intermediate approach to the narrow approach was based on the assumption that the

---

[41] Raz, 'The Rule of Law and Its Virtue', p. 197.

procedural element of the FET standard is internalised in host states to some extent.

6.5 To what extent should the FET standard provide for substantive review of government conduct?

Chapter 4 identified four interpretations of the substantive element of the FET standard, one of which is the view that the FET standard does not provide for substantive review of government conduct. The four interpretations are as follows:

i) The 'no substantive review' approach, in which the FET standard does not provide for review of government conduct on substantive grounds.

ii) The margin of appreciation approach, in which government conduct must be reasonable to comply with the FET standard and a state is entitled to a margin of appreciation in its choice of policy objectives.

iii) The politics-as-irrationality approach, in which government conduct must be reasonable to comply with the FET standard and politically motivated conduct is presumptively irrational.

iv) The proportionality approach, in which government conduct must be proportionate to comply with the FET standard.

This section applies the framework developed in Chapter 3 to evaluate the level of protection implied by each of these four approaches. I begin by comparing the two different approaches that are broadly based on the principle of reasonableness – the margin of appreciation approach and the politics-as-irrationality approach. I then compare the margin of appreciation approach to the proportionality approach and, finally, the margin of appreciation approach to the 'no substantive review' approach.

6.5.1 The margin of appreciation approach versus the politics-as-irrationality approach

Both the margin of appreciation approach and the politics-as-irrationality approach are based on the principle of reasonableness. According to both approaches, conduct must be capable of justification by a rational policy and be a reasonable attempt to achieve that policy in order to be consistent with the FET standard. Neither approach is fully doctrinally developed, in that neither has developed a comprehensive theory of the objectives that are 'rational', nor a precise articulation of the standard of review demanded by the requirement of a reasonable connection between means and ends. However, each approach is sufficiently developed to be adopted in future investment treaties and to allow comparison of key points of difference between the approaches.

The main difference between these two approaches is the degree of deference shown to a state's choice of policy objective. Under the margin of appreciation approach, a state is entitled to a margin of appreciation in its choice of policy objectives, and the politicisation of government conduct does not imply that it fails to pursue a rational objective. In contrast, under the politics-as-irrationality approach, tribunals scrutinise states choice of policy objective more closely and the politicisation of government conduct implies that it fails to pursue a rational objective. This difference between the approaches, while apparently minor, is of considerable practical significance. In most arbitral decisions involving substantive review – notably, *AES* v. *Hungary*, *Biwater* v. *Tanzania*, *Eastern Sugar* v. *Czech Republic*, *Glamis Gold* v. *US*, *Merrill & Ring* v. *Canada*, *Metalpar* v. *Argentina*, *Occidental* v. *Ecuador (II)* and *Tecmed* v. *Mexico* – the impugned conduct was partially motivated by political pressures on the host state. These decisions are likely to be broadly representative of future scenarios in which the substantive element of the FET standard is applicable. The significance of politicisation, thereby, becomes central to the extent of a state's liability.

6.5.1.1 Efficiency

The additional scope of liability under the politics-as-irrationality approach does not turn on an assessment of whether domestic investors are protected from politically motivated conduct under domestic law. Moreover, contrary to the assumption made by some commentators,[42] there is no evidence for the general proposition that foreign investors are more vulnerable to politically motivated conduct than their domestic counterparts.[43] For both reasons, granting foreign investors additional

---

[42] Ratner, 'Regulatory Takings in Institutional Context: Beyond the Fear of Fragmented International Law' (2008) 102 *American Journal of International Law*, p. 483; Paulsson, 'Indirect Expropriation: Is the Right to Regulate at Risk?' (2005) [online], p. 4; Wälde and Weiler, 'Investment Arbitration under the Energy Charter Treaty in the Light of New NAFTA Precedents: Towards a Global Code of Conduct for Economic Regulation' (2004) 1 *Transnational Dispute Management*, fn. 119; Choi, 'The Present and Future of the Investor-State Dispute Settlement Paradigm' (2007) 10 *Journal of International Economic Law*, p. 735; *Tecmed* v. *Mexico*, Award, para. 122; *Gallo* v. *Canada*, Award, para. 335.

[43] Desbordes and Vauday, 'The Political Influence of Foreign Firms in Developing Countries' (2007) 19 *Economics & Politics*, p. 447; Aisbett and McAusland, 'Firm Characteristics and Influence on Government Rule-Making: Theory and Evidence' (2013)

protection against politically motivated conduct places them in a better legal position than their competitors and, therefore, is likely to lead to allocative inefficiency.

The question of whether additional protection against politically motivated conduct can increase the efficiency of government and investor decision-making raises more difficult questions. In Chapter 3, I argued that, to the extent that hold-up problems exist, investment treaty protections that require a state to pay compensation for conduct that is designed to extract a benefit from the investor *and* is not efficiency-improving on an *ex post* assessment can increase efficiency. However, I also noted that investment treaty protections that require compensation beyond this narrow range of circumstances are likely to reduce efficiency by inducing moral hazard on the part of investors.[44] As such, the key question is whether a state's additional liability for politically motivated conduct under the politics-as-irrationality approach protects foreign investors from conduct that is both inefficient and opportunistic.

The politicisation of government conduct is unlikely to correlate with whether it is efficient. This point is best illustrated by distinguishing two situations that might both be described as 'politicised'. In the first, the influence of a well-connected and politically powerful minority motivates government conduct; in the second a broad-based or populist campaign motivates government conduct. The former sort of politicisation is more likely to lead to inefficient decisions as it encourages decision-makers to overvalue the costs and benefits of a decision that accrue to the particular minority. In contrast, the latter sort of politicisation is likely to be associated with more efficient decisions, as populist and majoritarian movements provide a means of aggregating costs and benefits that are spread thinly over a wide range of individuals and encourage decision-makers to properly value those costs.[45] Liability under the politics-as-irrationality approach is not sensitive to this distinction, or any other proxy for the efficiency of government conduct.

---

29 *European Journal of Political Economy*, p. 226; Huang, 'Are Foreign Firms Privileged by Their Host Governments? Evidence from the 2000 World Business Environment Survey' (2005) [online].

[44] See Section 3.4.5.2.

[45] There is an extensive literature arguing that government decision-makers tend to undervalue diffuse costs, compared with those with costs that fall on organized minorities; see Stigler, 'The Theory of Economic Regulation' (1971) 2 *Bell Journal of Economics and Management Science*; Peltzman, 'Toward a More General Theory of Regulation' (1976) 19 *Journal of Law and Economics* 211.

The politicisation of government conduct may be more sensitive to whether government conduct is opportunistic because there is likely to be some overlap between what tribunals have described as 'political' motivations and conduct designed to extract a benefit from the investor. However, the presence of political motivations is an inadequate proxy for the presence of opportunism. It is not sensitive to other indicia of opportunism, such as the presence of sunk costs or whether the host state has reneged on a bargain with an investor.[46] For this reason, and because the presence of political motivations is unlikely to correlate with the efficiency of government conduct, the politics-as-irrationality approach significantly overprotects investors against risks of government conduct that should be factored into the investor's decision-making. In other words, this approach is likely to be inefficient on account of inducing moral hazard on the part of foreign investors.

6.5.1.2 Distributive consequences

Compared with the margin of appreciation approach, the politics-as-irrationality approach benefits foreign investors, as it provides a broader entitlement to compensation. Without needing to determine whether such benefits entail correlative costs to the host state, it is clear that these benefits to the foreign investor would not be justified by libertarian theory, as the extent of the state's liability is unrelated to the question of whether the state has interfered with the investor's property rights.

An evaluation of the distributive consequences of the two approaches from the perspective of political process theory is more nuanced. Political process theory suggests that it is unfair for states to impose losses on minorities who were at a practical disadvantage in decision-making processes and that it is unfair for government decisions to arbitrarily single-out particular minorities to bear losses. Politicisation is, at most, an imperfect proxy for the former. The existence of political controversy or activism surrounding government conduct is not direct evidence that a foreign investor was at a disadvantage, as compared to other affected constituencies, in the decision-making process that led to such conduct. Such exclusion could only be identified by an inquiry into whether an investor had been precluded from making representations or lobbying against the impugned measure.

The second distributive norm derived from political process theory – that individuals should not be arbitrarily singled out to bear losses – is

---

[46] See Section 3.4.5.2.

not concerned with the objectives that motivate government conduct as such. Rather, it is concerned with the allocation of losses associated with the achievement of particular policy objectives. It requires that losses be allocated on a rational basis and provides a fairness justification for compensation when there is no reasoned basis for the allocation of loss associated with a measure (that may well pursue a rational objective). Liability under the politics-as-irrationality approach does not turn on an assessment of whether a foreign investor has been arbitrarily singled out because it does not focus on the allocation of loss associated with a measure. Moreover, politicisation of decision-making is an unreliable proxy for arbitrary allocation of loss. Consider, for example, an admittedly politically motivated ban on the dumping of cyanide in rivers. Such a measure would not *arbitrarily* single out a foreign-owned gold mine that is the only actor currently dumping cyanide in rivers. The investment bears the full burden of loss associated with the measure, but this allocation of loss is rational in light of the objective of the measure. The loss could not equally have been allocated to other mines that do not dump cyanide in rivers. Accordingly, political process theory would not require compensation. Overall, it is difficult to justify the *general* scepticism of politically motivated conduct under the politics-as-irrationality approach by reference to the specific concerns about horizontal discrimination that underpin political process theory.

6.5.1.3 Realisation of human rights and environmental conservation

The politics-as-irrationality approach is likely to cause significantly more regulatory chill than the margin of appreciation approach. In Chapter 3, I argued that regulatory chill is most likely to occur in situations in which investors initiate, or threaten to initiate, arbitration in response to new government measures.[47] In these situations, measures that would give rise to liability under investment treaties are more likely to be chilled than measures that would not. The decisive question, then, is whether the politics-as-irrationality approach extends a state's liability to measures effective in realising human rights or environmental conservation objectives that would not incur liability under the margin of appreciation approach. There can be little doubt that it does.

---

[47] See Section 3.7.4.3.

Political activism and controversy is one mechanism by which human rights and environmental concerns are brought to the attention of lawmakers. The realisation of these objectives through public policy typically relies on political, as opposed to economic, persuasion or pressure.[48] This observation is sufficient to show that some measures that are, subjectively, politically motivated will be, objectively, concerned with the realisation of human rights or environmental conservation. There is no reason to think that such populist or politically motivated measures would be ineffective in realising environmental conservation or human rights. The link between the subjective motivation (political or otherwise) of government conduct and its effectiveness in achieving desirable consequences raises complex questions about decision-making, the answers to which are likely to vary among decision-makers within and between countries. However, for the purpose of evaluating alternative liability rules, the issue is not whether political pressure always leads to the most effective measures for realising human rights and achieving environmental conservation but whether political pressure sometimes encourages decision-makers to introduce somewhat effective measures. There are strong grounds for concluding that it does. The presumption that politically motivated conduct is irrational is, therefore, likely to entail increased regulatory chill.

6.5.1.4 Respect for the rule of law

Under both the margin of appreciation and politics-as-irrationality approaches a host state's liability arises from the review of government conduct on substantive grounds. A state's liability does not turn on the formal and procedural characteristics of the impugned conduct under either approach. Specifically, a state's additional liability for politically motivated conduct under the politics-as-irrationality approach does not depend on whether a politically motivated measure was introduced lawfully, embodied in a form that is prospective, open and clear and applied consistently with principles of natural justice. As such, this additional scope of liability is unlikely to increase respect for the rule of law in host states.

6.5.1.5 FDI flows

Neither the margin of appreciation approach nor the politics-as-irrationality approach concerns the enforcement of agreements made

---

[48] Sen, *Development as Freedom* (1999), p. 182.

between the host state and foreign investors. Accordingly, commitment theory suggests that neither will affect the flow of FDI into host states. Signalling theory posits an indirect causal link between investment treaties and FDI, which relies on the ability of investment treaty protections to place greater liability on states with 'bad governance' than those with 'good governance'. The foregoing analysis shows that imposing liability for politically motivated conduct does not correlate with liability for economically inefficient conduct nor with liability for disregard of the rule of law. There are no grounds to think that extending liability to politically motivated conduct allows investment treaties to better operate as good governance signals.

6.5.1.6 Overall evaluation

Compared with the margin of appreciation approach, a state's additional liability under the politics-as-irrationality approach would be likely to significantly increase the chilling effect of desirable human rights and environmental measures and, if anything, to decrease economic efficiency. It is likely to lead to a complex pattern of costs and benefits that cannot be justified by libertarian theory and is difficult to justify by political process theory. The additional scope of liability under the politics-as-irrationality approach is unlikely to affect FDI flows or the degree of respect for the rule of law in host states in either direction. On this basis, I conclude that the margin of appreciation approach is the more desirable of the two approaches based on the principle of reasonableness.

6.5.2 The margin of appreciation approach versus the proportionality approach

The margin of appreciation approach and the proportionality approach share important similarities. Under both approaches, in order to be consistent with the FET standard government conduct must be capable of justification by a rational policy objective and must have some means-ends connection with the achievement of that policy objective. The difference between the two approaches lies in the way that tribunals scrutinise the effectiveness of the conduct in question in achieving its objective. Under the margin of appreciation approach, it is enough that the conduct in question has a rational connection with the objective pursued. The question of whether other, more effective or less intrusive means of achieving the objective does not arise. In contrast, under the proportionality approach, the interference with the claimant's investment must be proportionate in light of the objective pursued. In this assessment, it is relevant, but not conclusive, that there are other means of achieving the public interest objective that involve lesser interference with the investment.

6.5.2.1 Efficiency

A state's additional liability under the proportionality approach is not defined by reference to the way that similarly situated investors are treated by the host state. As such, there is a risk that this approach confers rights on foreign investors that go beyond the rights of their competitors. Moreover, the proportionality approach to substantive review confers rights on foreign investors that are likely to go beyond their entitlements under the domestic law of most host states. This is because the proportionality approach grants foreign investors a *general* right to challenge government conduct on the grounds that it is disproportionate, in contrast to the significantly more confined operation of proportionality review in most legal systems. For example, in common law systems, an innocent counter-party is not required to exercise a right to terminate a contract proportionately. If the guilty party breaches a contract and that breach creates a right to terminate, the innocent party is entitled to exercise the right to terminate at its discretion.[49] In contrast, applying the proportionality approach to substantive review under the FET standard, the tribunal in *Occidental v. Ecuador (II)* held that a state must act proportionately in the exercise of a right to terminate a contract following an investor's breach.[50] Because the proportionality approach confers protections on foreign investors that go beyond domestic law in many states and because these protections are not defined by reference to the treatment of similarly situated investors, it is likely to reduce efficiency compared with the margin of appreciation approach.

Furthermore, the additional protection provided by the proportionality approach is unlikely to assist in solving hold-up problems, to the extent that they exist. A state's additional liability for disproportionate conduct is unlikely to correlate with situations in which the state has acted opportunistically or situations in which it has acted inefficiently. The assessment of whether a measure is proportionate turns largely on its effectiveness in achieving the desired objective, considered in light of the extent of interference with the investment. This assessment may correspond with whether a measure is efficient to a limited extent, in that

---

[49] *Union Eagle Ltd* v. *Golden Achievement Ltd* [1997] AC 514, per Lord Hoffmann.
[50] *Occidental* v. *Ecuador (II)*, Award, para. 427.

it requires consideration of some of the costs and benefits of the conduct in question. However, under the proportionality approach, the focus is on the extent of interference with the investment,[51] rather than the costs and benefits for the full range of affected actors. Thus, the determination of liability under the proportionality approach gives a greater weight to the interests of the investor than would an overall assessment of the costs and benefits of the conduct in question.

Moreover, the determination of liability under the proportionality approach is unlikely to correlate with the presence of opportunism on the part of the host state. The proportionality approach to substantive review does not take into account any of the obvious indicia of opportunism – for example, whether the investment involves sunk costs, whether the state had reneged on a bargain with the investor or whether the state extracts a benefit from the investor by means of the challenged conduct. Because a state's additional liability under the proportionality approach does not turn on whether government conduct is inefficient or opportunistic, it is likely to reduce the efficiency of investor conduct by inducing moral hazard.

6.5.2.2 Distributive consequences

The previous section argued that a state's additional liability under the proportionality approach is likely to entail net economic costs. Coupled with the broader scope of liability under the proportionality approach, this net economic cost means that any benefit to foreign investors accrues at the expense of a greater loss in the territory of host states. In democratic states, this pattern of costs and benefits is likely to be regressive on egalitarian grounds. Moreover, the benefit to foreign investors under the proportionality approach cannot be justified by libertarian theory. This is because the additional requirement to compensate for conduct that is substantively disproportionate is not linked to interference with investors' property rights.

6.5.2.3 Realisation of human rights and environmental conservation

Section 3.7.7 concluded that investment treaty protections which hold a state liable for a greater range of loss caused by environmental or human rights–inspired measures are likely to lead to greater chilling of such

---

[51] E.g., *Occidental v. Ecuador (II)*, Award, para. 450.

measures. Under the margin of appreciation approach, environmental and human rights–inspired conduct would not breach the substantive element of the FET standard so long as there was a rational connection between the host state's conduct and the objective pursued. In contrast, under the proportionality approach, a government could be liable for conduct that advanced an environmental or human rights objective if it imposed a disproportionate burden on the investment in question in light of the objective pursued. On this basis, the proportionality approach is likely to lead to greater chilling of somewhat effective environmental and human right measures on account of their significant impact on particular foreign investors.

One argument that might be made in favour of the proportionality approach is that it would discourage governments from adopting measures that are somewhat effective in realising human right and environmental objectives and encourage them, instead, to pursue more effective alternatives that entail less interference with foreign investment. If this were the case, it would constitute an important argument in favour of the proportionality approach. However, there is, as yet, no evidence to suggest that attaching a potential cost (i.e., the risk of liability under an investment treaty) to the adoption of somewhat effective environmental and human rights measures encourages primary decisions-makers to adopt more effective measures.[52] Because investment treaty protections are unlikely to be deeply internalised by primary decision-makers at the time when original regulatory decisions are made,[53] it is highly unlikely that they would encourage 'better' regulatory decisions at first instance. Holding a state liable for conduct that is somewhat effective in achieving environmental and human rights objectives is more likely to result simply in the abandonment of these somewhat effective measures.

The extent of additional regulatory chill under the proportionality approach may, however, be small; it will depend, in part, on doctrinal questions which are not fully specified within that approach. In particular, the significance that tribunals give to the availability of other courses of conduct that would have involved lesser interference with the investment is likely to bear on the extent of regulatory chill associated with the proportionality approach. The more willing the tribunals are to find liability on the grounds that other less restrictive courses of conduct were available to a state, the greater the likely chilling of somewhat effective

---

[52] See Section 3.7.5.   [53] See Section 3.7.4.2.

measures. On the other hand, if greater deference were shown by tribunals to primary decision-makers' findings of fact and judgements about the desirability of various courses of conduct, any chilling effects would likely be reduced.

A further chilling effect could arise from the fact that the proportionality approach provides less certainty to states about the scope of their prospective liability under the FET standard. Under the margin of appreciation, a state can be confident that a measure taken in good faith which has a rational connection with the objective pursued will not give rise to liability under the substantive element of the FET standard. The fact that a state may not be able to predict in advance precisely how effective a given policy will be would not give rise to a risk of liability. In contrast, liability under the proportionality approach turns on *ex post* judgements about the balance struck between the investor's interests and the objective pursued, which will be more difficult to predict in advance. This provides further grounds to conclude that proportionality approach is likely to lead to greater regulatory chill.

6.5.2.4 Respect for the rule of law

Under both the margin of appreciation and proportionality approaches, a host state's liability arises from the review of government conduct on substantive grounds. A state's liability does not turn on the formal and procedural characteristics of the impugned conduct under either approach. Specifically, a state's additional liability for disproportionate conduct under the proportionality approach does not depend on whether that conduct was introduced lawfully, embodied in a form that is prospective, open and clear and applied consistently with principles of natural justice. As such, this additional scope of liability is unlikely to increase respect for the rule of law in host states.

6.5.2.5 FDI flows

Neither the margin of appreciation approach nor the proportionality approach concerns the enforcement of agreements made between the host state and foreign investors. Accordingly, commitment theory suggests that neither will affect the flow of FDI into host states. Signalling theory posits an indirect causal link between investment treaties and FDI, which relies on the ability of investment treaty protections to place greater liability on states with 'bad governance' than those with 'good governance'. The foregoing analysis shows that imposing liability for disproportionate conduct does not correlate with liability for economically inefficient conduct or liability for disregard of the rule of law. There are no grounds to think that extending liability to disproportionate conduct allows investment treaties to better operate as good governance signals.

6.5.2.6 Overall evaluation

The additional scope of liability under the proportionality approach is unlikely to affect FDI flows or the degree of respect for the rule of law in host states in either direction. The proportionality approach is, however, likely to be less efficient than the margin of appreciation approach, both on account of granting foreign investors rights that go beyond those available to other investors under domestic law and on account of inducing moral hazard. Because the proportionality approach is likely to lead to net economic costs, the benefits of the additional protection it provides to foreign investors accrue at the expense of host states. These distributive effects cannot be justified by any theory of distributive justice considered in this book. Moreover, the proportionality approach is, if anything, likely to lead to greater regulatory chill of somewhat effective human rights and environmental measures. On this basis, there are no grounds for preferring the proportionality approach to the margin of appreciation approach and clear grounds for preferring the latter to the former.

6.5.3 The margin of appreciation approach versus the 'no substantive review' approach

In the previous sections I argued that, of the three interpretations that allow the possibility of substantive review under the FET standard, the margin of appreciation approach should be preferred. Of these three approaches, the margin appreciation approach is the most deferent to host states. A question, therefore, arises as to whether the possibility of substantive review of government conduct should be entirely excluded under the FET standard. In comparing the 'no substantive review' approach to the margin of appreciation approach, I avoid making any assumptions about the other protections that might be included in an investment treaty that adopts either of these approaches. This allows comparison of the two approaches on their own terms. However, as I explain in the Section 6.5.4, structuring the comparison in this way may understate the attractiveness of 'no substantive review' approach.

6.5.3.1 Efficiency

Liability under the margin of appreciation approach arises if government conduct that affects a foreign investment does not pursue a rational public policy or if such conduct pursues a rational public policy but does not have a rational connection with the realisation of that policy. Because liability does not depend on how similarly situated investors are treated, this approach risks granting foreign investors better legal rights than their competitors, thereby reducing allocative efficiency. However, this risk may be small in practice. The extent of any inefficiency due to discriminatory overprotection of foreign investors would depend on whether the margin of appreciation approach goes beyond the protection otherwise provided by the domestic law of the states in question.

The margin of appreciation approach could also improve the efficiency of investor and host state conduct if it helps redress hold-up problems (to the extent that such problems exist). In assessing this possibility, the key question is whether liability under the margin of appreciation approach is limited to measures that are both inefficient and opportunistically designed to extract a benefit from the foreign investor. The margin of appreciation approach does not involve direct consideration of whether government conduct is efficient. However, in the case of both government conduct that does not pursue a rational public policy and government conduct that has no rational connection with the policy it pursues the benefits are likely to be negligible and outweighed by the attendant costs. In the same way, although liability under the margin of appreciation approach does not turn on whether government conduct is opportunistic, there is likely to be a close correlation between the two. One reason why a government might treat an investment in a way that cannot be justified by *any* rational public policy is because the purpose of the government's conduct is simply to appropriate an investor's assets. On this basis, the margin of appreciation approach is likely to increase efficiency.

Thus, there are two potentially countervailing effects to be considered. The first is the risk of inefficiency due to the grant of rights to foreign investors under the margin of appreciation approach that are not available to other investors nor defined by reference to the treatment of other investors; the second is the potential for efficiency gains through the ability of the margin of appreciation approach to solve hold up problems. The balance of these two effects will depend on the empirical conditions in the states in question. In states where foreign investors do suffer from hold-up problems in practice – for example, states in which opportunistic conduct by the executive is not effectively constrained by domestic law – the efficiency gains from solving hold-up problems are more likely to outweigh any inefficiency caused by the discriminatory effect of the margin of appreciation approach.

6.5.3.2 Distributive consequences

The previous section concluded that, compared with the 'no substantive review' approach, the net economic effect of the margin of appreciation approach is equivocal. It suggested that, if anything, this approach is likely to increase efficiency, at least in some states. For levels of protection that generate net economic benefits, the benefits to foreign investors that result from broader substantive protection do not necessarily entail any corresponding costs in the territory of host states. As such, concerns under theories of distributive justice, particularly egalitarian concerns, are unlikely to arise.

That said, none of the theories of justice considered in this book provides clear justifications for the economic benefits that the margin of appreciation approach confers on foreign investors. Libertarian theories are equivocal because liability under the margin of appreciation approach does not turn on whether the host state has interfered with the investor's property rights; political process theories are inapt because liability does not turn on whether foreign investors were excluded from political participation or arbitrarily singled-out to bear loses. Overall, there are no strong grounds for preferring the distributive consequences of either the margin of appreciation approach or the 'no substantive review' approach.

6.5.3.3 Realisation of human rights and environmental conservation

The protection provided by the margin of appreciation approach is unlikely to lead to chilling of any measures that are effective in realising human right or environmental conservation. Under this approach, it is clear that the realisation of human rights and the protection of the environment are rational public policies. And tribunals within this approach have clarified that politicisation of conduct that pursues these objectives does not call the legitimacy of such measures into question. The margin of appreciation approach also requires that there be a rational connection the conduct in question and the objective pursued. Only measures that are deeply misguided or that are not, in fact, motivated by the cited objective would fail to satisfy this standard. On this basis, there is little risk of regulatory chill associated with the margin of appreciation approach compared with the no substantive review approach.

6.5.3.4 Respect for the rule of law

Under the margin of appreciation approach, a host state's liability arises from the review of government conduct on substantive grounds. Liability does not turn on the formal and procedural characteristics of the impugned conduct. Specifically, liability does not turn on whether the conduct was lawful, embodied in a form that is prospective, open and clear and applied consistently with principles of natural justice. As such, a host state's liability under the margin of appreciation approach is unlikely to increase respect for the rule of law in host states compared with the no substantive review approach.

6.5.3.5 FDI flows

The margin of appreciation approach is not concerned with the enforcement of agreements made between the host state and foreign investors. Accordingly, commitment theory suggests that it is unlikely to stimulate the flow of FDI into host states. Signalling theory posits an indirect causal link between investment treaties and FDI, which relies on the ability of investment treaty protections to place greater liability on states with 'bad governance' than those with 'good governance'. Under the margin of appreciation approach, government conduct that affects a foreign investment and does not pursue a rational public policy, or that pursues a rational public policy but does not have a rational connection with the realisation of the policy, would trigger state liability. In these circumstances, liability would not arise under the 'no substantive review' approach. On any conception of 'good governance', liability for irrational conduct is likely to arise more often in badly governed state than a well-governed state. Thus, the margin of appreciation approach would allow investment treaties to operate more effectively as signals of good governance and may, thereby, indirectly lead to an increase in FDI.

6.5.3.6 Overall evaluation

The overall evaluation of the margin of appreciation approach and the 'no substantive review' approach is finely balanced. Neither approach is likely to affect the degree of the respect for the rule of law in host states, nor to lead to significant regulatory chill of desirable human rights and environmental measures. Any differences in the distributive impacts of the two approaches are likely to be relative minor, and the theories of distributive justice considered in this book do not provide grounds for preferring the pattern of costs and benefits associated with one approach to the other.

A preference between the two approaches turns on their impact on economic efficiency and FDI flows. The assessment favours the margin of appreciation on both counts. Insofar as investors face hold-up problems in practice, the margin of appreciation approach is likely to improve efficiency by providing compensation for irrational measures that have no purpose other than to extract a benefit from the investor. Insofar as lack information about the quality of the governance in host states, the margin of appreciation approach may improve the ability of investment treaties to act as signal by penalising states that are poorly governed. Signalling theory suggests that, by this mechanism, the margin of appreciation would lead to greater FDI flows. However, because both these conclusions are also finely balanced, they are likely to be sensitive to variation in the conditions in host states. The ability of the margin of appreciation approach to increase efficiency is likely to be specific to states where hold-up problems are endemic – for example, states where the executive is not subject to effective legal constraints under domestic law. The ability of the margin of appreciation approach to increase FDI is likely to specific to countries where domestic governance has recently improved, and the state lacks other tools to signal this improvement to foreign investors. In the case of developed countries with functioning legal systems, there is little reason to prefer the margin of appreciation approach to the 'no substantive review' approach.

6.5.4 Conclusion: the most desirable level of protection from substantive irrationality

This section has considered four interpretations of the substantive element of the FET standard. Three of these interpretations specify different level of protection against government conduct that lacks sufficient substantive justification, and a fourth entirely rejects the possibility of substantive review of government conduct. Of the three interpretations that envisage substantive review of government conduct under the FET standard, the margin of appreciation approach is clearly the most desirable. Sections 6.5.1 and 6.5.2 concluded that there were no grounds to prefer either the politics-as-irrationality approach or the proportionality approach to the margin of appreciation approach. The margin of appreciation is likely to lead to greater economic benefits *and* less regulatory chill of desirable environmental and human rights measures than either of these two alternatives.

The comparison of the margin of appreciation approach to the 'no substantive review' approach is more finely balanced. On balance, I concluded that the margin of appreciation approach is, if anything, likely to lead to greater net economic benefits and FDI flows than the 'no substantive review' approach. However, I also noted that these conclusions are sensitive to the assumptions about the circumstances in the states that are party to the investment treaty in question and, specifically, that the justifications for the margin of appreciation approach are less relevant to investment treaties between developed states with well-functioning legal systems.

In the comparison of the 'no substantive review' approach to the margin of appreciation approach, I avoided making any assumptions about the other protections that might be present in an investment treaty that adopts either of these approaches. This allowed comparison of the two approaches on their own terms. In practice, regardless of whether the margin of appreciation or the 'no substantive review' approach to the FET standard were preferred, an investment treaty would contain other substantive protections – for example, provisions dealing with expropriation. Given that the overall evaluation of these two approaches to substantive review under the FET standard is finely balanced, it is relevant to consider how the presence of other provisions within the treaty bears on the analysis.

The strongest argument for favouring the margin of appreciation approach is its ability to increase economic efficiency by solving hold-up problems. This is because the contours of liability under the margin of appreciation approach correlate roughly with conduct that gives rise to hold-up problems. However, hold-up problems are better addressed by appropriately drafted indirect expropriation provisions in which the crux of the inquiry is whether property owned by the investor has been acquired for the benefit of the host state.[54] If an investment treaty contains a well-drafted indirect expropriation, any additional ground of liability for conduct that is substantively irrational would be unnecessary to solve hold-up problems, largely removing the justification for preferring the margin of appreciation approach to the complete 'no substantive review' approach.

---

[54] See Section 3.4.5.2.

6.6 Which of the five levels of protection against indirect expropriation is the most desirable?

Chapter 5 identified five alternative interpretations of the concept of indirect expropriation in arbitral decisions under investment treaties. They are as follows:

i) The *Metalclad* approach: that indirect expropriation is defined by its effect on the economic value of the investment.

ii) The *Pope & Talbot* approach: that indirect expropriation is defined by a substantial deprivation of the investor's property interests in the investment.

iii) The *Methanex* approach: that indirect expropriation is subject to an exception for measures with certain characteristics.

iv) The US annex approach: that identifying indirect expropriation requires a tribunal to balance an assessment of the effects of the measure with consideration of a range of the measures' characteristics.

v) The *Tecmed* approach: that indirect expropriation is defined by severe loss of economic value of the investment, subject to proportionality review.

This section applies the framework developed in Chapter 3 to evaluate the five distinct levels of protection implied by these different interpretations of the concept of indirect expropriation.

Organising the evaluation of these five alternatives poses certain challenges. Unlike the levels of protection derived from the FET standard these five options do not fit neatly along a scale ranging from narrower to broader liability of the host state. As such, it is not possible to evaluate each level of protection in a paired comparison against incrementally more (or less) expansive alternatives. I address these challenges by first evaluating the relative desirability of protections within each of the three structures of inquiry identified in Chapter 5 – the effects, exception and balancing structures. This narrows the set of alternatives to the most desirable level of protection within each structure of inquiry. These levels of protection are then evaluated against each other.

Accordingly, I begin, in Section 6.6.1, by comparing the *Metalclad* and *Pope & Talbot* approaches, both of which rely on the effect structure. This evaluation concludes that the *Pope & Talbot* approach is clearly the more desirable. In Section 6.6.2, I compare the US annex and *Tecmed* approaches, both of which rely on the balancing structure. This evaluation suggests that the US annex approach is the more desirable. Finally, in Section 6.6.3, I compare the *Methanex* approach with the *Pope & Talbot* and US annex approaches in a three-way comparison. This evaluation concludes that the US annex and the *Methanex* approaches are more desirable than the *Pope & Talbot* approach, but I am not able to come to a final preference between the two.

6.6.1 *The* Metalclad *approach versus the* Pope & Talbot *approach*

The *Metalclad* approach and the *Pope & Talbot* approach define indirect expropriation exclusively by its effect on an investment. The primary difference between the levels of protection is qualitative in character – the effect on which the inquiry focuses. The *Metalclad* approach looks to loss of economic value of the investment, whereas the *Pope & Talbot* approach examines the extent of interference with the investor's property interests in the investment. A secondary difference between the two levels of protection is the extent of effect required to constitute indirect expropriation. The *Pope & Talbot* approach requires 'substantial deprivation', a higher threshold than deprivation of a 'significant part' of the value of the investment under the *Metalclad* approach. The practical implication of this second difference is that, even when the qualitative distinction between property interests and loss of economic value is not relevant (that is, in situations in which an interference with property interests causes loss of economic value), some measures that amount to indirect expropriation under the *Metalclad* approach would not amount to indirect expropriation under the *Pope & Talbot* approach. The following comparison focuses on these two points of difference.

Readers may notice that liability under the business plan approach to the FET standard is triggered by state action that interferes with an investor's business plans, which is similar to the *Metalclad* approach's focus on denial of expected economic benefits, and that liability under the stability approach is triggered by changes to the investor's basic entitlements to use, enjoy and dispose of its investment under the regulatory arrangements at the time the investment, which is similar to the *Pope & Talbot* approach's understanding of deprivation of property interests. However, the *Metalclad* approach is not identical to the business plan approach to legitimate expectations under the FET standard, nor is the *Pope & Talbot* approach identical to the stability approach. One key difference is that the threshold of effect on an investment required for a finding of liability is significantly lower under each of the levels of protection derived from the FET standard than under the corresponding approaches derived from indirect expropriation decisions. This is evinced by the success of

FET claims in cases in which indirect expropriation claims argued on the same facts fail.[55]

6.6.1.1 Efficiency

A state's additional liability under the *Metalclad* approach is likely to reduce economic efficiency for two reasons. The first is that legal protections that place some foreign investors in a better position than other investors are likely to reduce efficiency by interfering with competitive equality. Liability under the *Metalclad* approach does not turn on an examination of whether the measure that caused economic loss to the foreign investor was discriminatory or whether equivalent legal protections are available to other investors under domestic law.

The second reason is that liability rules that compensate foreign investors for loss caused by government measures are likely to induce moral hazard on the part of foreign investors, save to the extent that they redress situations in which a state adopts measures that are not efficiency improving for the purpose of extracting a benefit from the investor. A state's additional liability under the *Metalclad* approach does not correlate with opportunism of this sort. The inquiry under the *Metalclad* approach focuses on whether an investor has been deprived of the economic benefits of an investment 'even if not necessarily to the obvious benefit of the state'.[56] In contrast, the hallmark of opportunistic conduct that can lead to hold-up problems is that it benefits the host state. Moreover, a state's liability under the *Metalclad* approach arises regardless of whether the measure that causes significant loss to the investor is efficient on an overall assessment. For both reasons, a state's additional liability under the *Metalclad* approach is highly likely to induce moral hazard on the part of foreign investors and, therefore, to reduce efficiency.

6.6.1.2 Distributive consequences

The previous section argued that preferring the *Metalclad* approach to the *Pope & Talbot* approach is likely to entail net economic costs. Given that the broader protection of the *Metalclad* approach benefits foreign investors, these costs would be borne by actors within the host state. This pattern

---

[55] E.g., *Occidental v. Ecuador (I)*, Final Award; *Walter Bau v. Thailand*, Award; *MTD v. Chile*, Award. For discussion: Fietta, 'Expropriation and the "Fair and Equitable Treatment" Standard' in Ortino et al. (eds), *Investment Treaty Law: Current Issues II* (British Institute of International and Comparative Law 2007), p. 183.

[56] *Metalclad v. Mexico*, Award, para. 103.

of costs and benefits is likely to be regressive on egalitarian grounds in states that are broadly democratic. Furthermore, this pattern of distributive consequences cannot be justified by any other theory of distributive justice. The *Metalclad* approach extends the obligation to compensate beyond interferences with property interests to interferences with the expected economic benefits of an investment. This expanded scope of liability cannot be justified by libertarianism's concern for the protection of the bundle of legal entitlements validly acquired by the investor. Moreover, because the *Metalclad* approach does not look to whether the decline of economic value emerged from a political process from which the investor was excluded or whether the investor was arbitrarily singled out to bear the costs of a measure, these distributive transfers cannot be justified by political process theory.

6.6.1.3 FDI flows

The greater scope of liability under the *Metalclad* approach is unlikely to increase FDI flows. Existing evidence suggests that the level of substantive protection provided by investment treaties is unlikely to have a significant impact on the magnitude and destination of FDI flows. Even if the adoption of different levels of protection did influence FDI flows, existing theories that purport to explain the causal connection between FDI and investment treaties provide no reason to think that the *Metalclad* approach would be associated with greater FDI than the *Pope & Talbot* approach. Commitment theory suggests that protections that allow an investor to enforce bargains it has made with the host state would increase FDI flows. However, the *Metalclad* approach protects the economic value of investment, rather than interests arising out of agreements with the host state.

6.6.1.4 Realisation of human rights and environmental conservation

Both theory and current evidence suggest that states are less likely to maintain environmental and human rights measures that give rise to liability under an investment treaty. Under both the *Metalclad* and *Pope & Talbot* approaches, liability turns on the effect of a measure on an investment, without reference to whether the measure is effective in realising human rights or environmental conservation. On this basis, both approaches are likely to cause some regulatory chill. A state's liability under the *Metalclad* approach is broader – in both qualitative and quantitative terms – than under the *Pope & Talbot* approach. Thus, it is likely to be associated with greater regulatory chill of measures that are desirable on human rights and environmental grounds.

Chapter 3 also argued that investment treaty protections that reduce uncertainty about the extent of states' liability would tend to reduce regulatory chill, with concomitant improvements in the realisation of human rights and environmental conservation.[57] It is undoubtedly easier for a state to ascertain the extent of investors' property interests under existing legal arrangements, and whether a proposed measure would interfere with those interests, than it is for a state to determine whether a proposed measure interferes with the expected economic benefits of an investment. To make a prospective determination about whether a measure would significantly affect the value of an investment, the state would require access to private commercial information about the investment held by the investor. As such, the *Pope & Talbot* approach provides a host state with greater certainty about the extent of its liability than the *Metalclad* approach and is likely to be associated with lower levels of regulatory chill.

6.6.1.5 Respect for the rule of law

The primary mechanism by which investment treaty protections might affect the degree of respect for the rule of law in host states is through internalisation of these protections by decision-makers and law-makers. Assuming that both approaches are internalised to some extent, the key issue is whether a state's additional liability under the *Metalclad* approach is linked to failure to respect the rule of law. Overall, it is not. Liability under the *Metalclad* approach turns primarily on the extent of economic loss caused by the measure. The determination of whether a state has interfered with a reasonably expected economic benefit does not turn on whether the measure was consistent with the requirements of open, clear and prospective law, nor on whether the state observed the principles of natural justice. Moreover, the *Metalclad* approach would not encourage greater stability in domestic legal systems than the *Pope & Talbot* approach; under the *Metalclad* approach liability stems from interference with expectations of value that are not grounded in the law of the host state. This contrasts with the *Pope & Talbot* approach, in which liability can only arise from changes in the investor's legal entitlements under the law of the host state.

---

[57] See Section 3.7.4.4.

6.6.1.6 Overall evaluation

There are strong grounds for preferring the *Pope & Talbot* approach to the *Metalclad* approach. The former is likely to be more efficient than the *Metalclad* approach, to entail a pattern of distributive consequences that is more consistent with libertarian and political process theories, and, by virtue of causing less regulatory chill, to lead to greater realisation of human rights and environment conservation. On the other hand, there are no coherent justifications for preferring the *Metalclad* approach to the *Pope & Talbot* approach.

6.6.2 *The US annex approach versus the* Tecmed *approach*

Both the US annex approach and the *Tecmed* approach fall within the balancing structure of inquiry. There are many similarities between the two approaches, yet they differ in meaningful ways. The first difference is the nature of the effect that defines a measure as potentially expropriatory. The *Tecmed* approach follows the *Metalclad* approach in focusing on the impact on the economic value of the investment. (However, it should be noted that the *Tecmed* approach demands a higher threshold of economic impact for a measure to be expropriatory than the *Metalclad* approach: 'radical deprivation' of economic value, rather than deprivation 'of a significant part' of an investment's value.) Although the US annex approach also turns partly on the 'economic impact' of a measure, an adverse economic impact cannot, of itself, establish than an indirect expropriation has occurred.[58] It seems that a substantial deprivation of property interests is also required.[59] A subsidiary similarity between the *Tecmed* and US annex approaches is that both agree that the effect of a measure should be assessed in light of an investor's expectations.[60]

The second difference between the approaches concerns the range of characteristics of a measure that are relevant in the balancing process that occurs when a measure exceeds the threshold of effect necessary for expropriation. The *Tecmed* approach considers only the purpose of the measure, which is balanced against its effect on the investment according to the principle of proportionality. The US annex approach considers, among other factors, whether the measure is non-discriminatory, regulatory in

---

[58] US 2012 Model BIT, annex B, art. 4(a)i.

[59] *Railroad Development Corporation* v. *Guatemala*, Award, paras. 151–2; similarly, *Fireman's Fund* v. *Mexico*, Award, para. 176.

[60] *Tecmed* v. *Mexico*, Award, para. 122; US 2012 Model BIT, annex B, art. 4(a)ii); *Fireman's Fund* v. *Mexico*, Award, para. 176.

character and applied to protect a legitimate public welfare objective. The evaluation of these levels of protection concentrates on these points of difference. In the context of this evaluation, it is important to emphasise that neither approach is self-evidently more favourable to the investor or to the host state. It is possible to imagine measures that might require compensation under the US annex approach but not under the *Tecmed* approach and vice versa.

6.6.2.1 Efficiency

The US annex approach is likely to lead to more efficient economic outcomes. Liability under this approach is at least somewhat sensitive to whether a measure is non-discriminatory. Making liability referable to the treatment of domestic investors reduces the disturbance to conditions of competitive equality engendered by investment treaty protections. In contrast, the *Tecmed* approach establishes a pattern of liability that is more likely to put foreign investors in a better position than other investors.

The US annex approach is also better designed to address hold-up problems. Although neither approach seeks to determine whether a measure that affects an investment was opportunistic or inefficient, the inquiry under the US annex approach better reflects both concerns. With respect to the efficiency of the measure, the US annex approach invites a broader weighing of the benefits and costs of a measure that do not accrue to an investor. In contrast, the means-ends proportionality review under the *Tecmed* approach seeks only to ascertain whether the investor has been forced to bear 'an individual and excessive burden.'[61] With respect to whether the measure was designed to extract a benefit from the foreign investor, the *Tecmed* approach focuses on the loss of value to the foreign investor, rather than the question of whether the host state reneged on a bargain with the investor or sought to appropriate the sunk capital of the investor. Within the US annex approach, the greater relevance of interference with an investor's property interests means that liability is sensitive to at least one indicia of opportunism. For both reasons, the US annex approach is likely to be more efficient that the *Tecmed* approach.

6.6.2.2 Distributive consequences

The previous section argued that preferring the US annex approach is likely to entail net economic benefits. Regardless of whether this is true,

---

[61] *Azurix* v. *Argentina*, Award, para. 311.

the US annex approach better accords with the prescriptions of libertarianism. Liability under the US annex approach requires interference with an investor's property interests, while liability under the *Tecmed* approach requires severe economic loss. Protection of property interests can be justified by libertarian theory, whereas protection of economic value cannot.

An evaluation of the distributive impacts of the approaches in light of political process theory is more intricate. On one hand, under the US annex approach, a finding of liability is sensitive to the determination of whether a measure is non-discriminatory and of general application in a way that means-ends proportionality of the *Tecmed* approach is not. Under the US annex approach, a state is more likely to be found liable for a measure that discriminatorily singles out a foreign investor and less likely to be held liable for a non-discriminatory measure of general application that severely affects an investor. On the other hand, liability under the *Tecmed* approach is sensitive to the question of whether a particular investor bears 'an individual and excessive burden.'[62] Thus, in different ways, the grounds for liability in both approaches reflect political process theory's concern with protecting investors from being arbitrarily singled out to bear the costs of a measure.

6.6.2.3 Respect for the rule of law

Neither the US annex approach nor the *Tecmed* approach makes the finding of liability sensitive to whether a measure was consistent with the requirements of open, clear and prospective law, nor on whether principles of natural justice were observed in its introduction. If there is any difference in the consequences of the two approaches for the degree of respect for the rule of law, they are likely to marginally favour the US annex approach. The US annex approach requires interference with property interests, whereas, under the *Tecmed* approach, liability can arise from severe loss of economic value that does not result from any interference with an investor's legal entitlements. Because the former approach protects legal interests, it is, if anything, more likely to encourage stability and certainty in the domestic legal system.

6.6.2.4 FDI flows

Little can be said about the consequences of the two approaches for the attraction of FDI. Both approaches are equally concerned with the

---

[62] Ibid., para. 311.

protection of 'investment-backed expectations', which may provide some protection against the host state reneging on bargain made with the foreign investor. Neither approach enables investment treaties to act as signals of strong legal institutions. As such, neither commitment theory nor signalling theory offers reasons to think one approach would be associated with greater FDI flows than the other.

6.6.2.5 Realisation of human rights and environmental conservation

Chapter 3 argued that states are less likely to maintain measures that give rise to liability under investment treaties than those that do not.[63] As such, the key question is the extent to which each approach holds a state liable for loss cause by environmental or human rights–inspired measures. Both the US annex approach and the *Tecmed* approach take the purpose of a measure into account in determining whether it amounts to indirect expropriation. Under both approaches a measure's human rights or environmental purpose would weigh against a finding of liability. In this way, both approaches would result in less regulatory chill than approaches within which liability turns exclusively on a measure's effects.

Beyond these basic similarities, the comparison of the two approaches' likely impacts on the realisation of human rights and environmental conservation is more nuanced. The proportionality approach may result in the chilling of somewhat effective environmental and human rights measures because of the risk of tribunals imposing liability on the basis of *ex post* determinations that less restrictive measures were available to the host state.[64] Under the US annex approach, somewhat effective human rights and environmental measures adopted in good faith are less likely to give rise to liability; liability would only arise 'in rare circumstances'.[65] Accordingly, the US annex approach is likely to cause marginally less regulatory chill.

Further differences between the approaches' consequences for regulatory chill could flow from the degree of certainty each approach provides to decision-makers. On one hand, the US annex approach focuses on the property interests of the investor, which is likely to give regulators greater clarity about the extent of liability under investment treaties than the *Tecmed* approach's focus on loss of economic value. It is easier for regulators to determine a foreign investor's legal entitlements under

---

[63] See Section 3.7.4.3.   [64] See Section 6.5.2.3.   [65] US 2012 Model BIT, annex B, art. 4(b).

domestic law than to identify the underpinnings of the economic value of a private investment project. On the other hand, means-ends proportionality under the *Tecmed* approach is a more structured, and arguably more certain, criterion of liability than the ad hoc balancing of a number of a measure's characteristics under the US annex approach. Given these differences between the approaches, it is difficult to determine which provides government decision-makers with more certainty and, therefore, which approach would be associated with greater 'uncertainty' chill.

6.6.2.6 Overall evaluation

There is no basis to distinguish the impact of the US annex and *Tecmed* approaches on FDI flows. There are only weak and empirically tenuous grounds for distinguishing their consequences for respect for the rule of law in host states – a comparison which, if anything, favours the US annex approach. The comparison of the two approaches consequences for the realisation of human rights and environmental conservation also marginally favours the US annex approach. The comparison of economic costs and benefits and distributive impacts is more clear-cut. The pattern of liability associated with the US annex approach better accords with the tenets of libertarianism than the *Tecmed* approach. The US annex approach is also more consistent with the principle of competitive equality among investors and less likely to induce moral hazard, both characteristics that are associated with net economic benefits. With no clear reasons to prefer the *Tecmed* approach and good reasons to prefer the US annex approach, I conclude that the latter should be preferred.

6.6.3 *The* Methanex *approach versus the US annex approach versus the* Pope & Talbot *approach*

The previous sections concluded that the *Pope & Talbot* approach was the more desirable of the two levels of protection that look exclusively to a measure's effects and that the US annex approach was the more desirable of the two levels of protection that balance a measure's effects against its characteristics. It remains to compare these two approaches to each other and to compare them both to the *Methanex* approach, which adopts an exception structure of inquiry.

This potentially complex three-way comparison is simplified by the fact that assessment of a measure's effects in all three approaches is based on the *Pope & Talbot* approach. Under the *Pope & Talbot* approach itself, a measure amounts to indirect expropriation if it substantially deprives an investor of its property interests in the investment. Under the *Methanex* approach, a substantial deprivation of property interests also seems to be required.[66] In the US annex approach, the focus is on the 'economic impact' of the measure; however, tribunals have interpreted this to mean that a measure must cause both a loss of value and a substantial deprivation of property interests to be potentially expropriatory.[67]

Given their similar views on the relevance of a measure's effects, the primary difference between the three approaches concerns the relevance of a measure's characteristics. Under the *Pope & Talbot* approach, a measure's characteristics are irrelevant. Under the US annex approach, a measure's characteristics – particularly, whether it is non-discriminatory, regulatory in character and pursues a legitimate public welfare objective – are weighed against its effect. Under the *Methanex* approach, a measure that satisfies the criteria of being 'non-discriminatory regulation for a public purpose … enacted in accordance with due process' and that does not breach specific commitments made to the investor does not constitute indirect expropriation.[68] The evaluation that follows examines the consequences of these different views of the relevance of a measure's characteristics in the indirect expropriation inquiry.

6.6.3.1 Efficiency

Differences in the consequences of the three approaches for economic efficiency stem, above all, from the extent to which they place foreign investors in a position of competitive equality with domestic investors. Some states do provide investors with protection against indirect expropriation through domestic law. However, the scope of liability imposed by the *Pope & Talbot* approach is not affected by the degree of protection provided by domestic law or the way in which other investors are treated by the host state. The US annex and *Methanex* approaches fare better in the latter respect because they make it less likely that a state will be held liable for interference with property rights caused by non-discriminatory measures that are non-compensable as a matter of domestic law.

The different levels of protection could also affect economic efficiency to the extent they solve hold-up problems. A key issue is how well each liability rule conforms to the principle that investors should only be compensated for loss caused by government conduct that is both inefficient and

---

[66] *Suez and Vivendi; AWG Group* v. *Argentina*, Decision on Liability, para. 140; *Chemtura* v. *Canada*, Award, para. 249.

[67] *Railroad Development Corporation* v. *Guatemala*, Award, paras 151–2; similarly, *Fireman's Fund* v. *Mexico*, Award, para. 176.

[68] *Methanex* v. *United States* Final Award, pt IV, chp. D, para. 7.

designed to extract a benefit from the investor. The *Pope & Talbot* approach, again, is the least desirable. It focuses the indirect expropriation inquiry exclusively on the effect of a measure on the investment, rather than requiring an economy-wide reckoning of a measure's costs and benefits or consideration of whether the adverse impact on the investor resulted in a commensurate benefit to the host state.

The *Methanex* approach is more desirable because determining whether a measure satisfies the criteria of the carve-out to indirect expropriation would entail at least some *de facto* assessment of the benefits of a measure that do not accrue to the investor.[69] The condition that a measure not 'breach a specific commitment' also restrains opportunistic use of the carve-out. But this condition is over-inclusive, because there are situations when breach of a commitment will not be opportunistic – for example, when a government, in light of new information about the costs and benefits of a given activity, introduces new regulations in breach of a previous commitment.[70]

The US annex approach best avoids problems of inefficiency stemming from moral hazard on the part of investors. Under this approach, interference with reasonable investment-backed expectations is one factor that is taken into account in the overall characterisation of a measure, but it is not a strict condition that a measure must satisfy in order to fall within a carve-out to indirect expropriation. Instead, the extent of interference with investment-backed expectation is one factor than enters the overall balancing exercise and could be outweighed by other factors that suggest that the measure is a legitimate regulation and is not designed to extract a benefit from the investor. This means that liability under the US annex approach better correlates with opportunistic conduct by the host state. Moreover, in determining whether a measure amounts to indirect expropriation, the US annex approach requires a tribunal to make a broad assessment of a measure taking into account many factors. This broader inquiry invites at least some consideration of a measure's costs and benefits to actors other than investor, which reduces the risk of a tribunal finding that an efficient measure triggers liability.

---

[69] This argument has been made in detail in Aisbett, Karp and McAusland, Police Powers, Regulatory Taking and the Efficient Compensation of Domestic and Foreign Investors' (2010) 86 *The Economic Record*, p. 381.

[70] Aisbett, 'ISDS through the lens of welfare economics', conference paper presented at 21st Investment Treaty Forum Public Meeting: The Economic and Financial Aspects of Investor-State Arbitration, British Institute of International and Comparative Law, 24 October 2013 (copy on file with the author).

6.6.3.2 Distributive consequences

The previous section argued that preferring the *Pope & Talbot* approach to either of the other alternatives is likely to entail net economic costs. Because the *Pope & Talbot* approach also benefits foreign investors through broader protection, this approach entails a net loss to be borne by actors within the host state. In states that are broadly democratic, this pattern of costs and benefits is likely to be regressive on egalitarian grounds. Moreover, this pattern of costs and benefits cannot be justified by political process theory. The *Pope & Talbot* approach does not seek to ascertain whether the investor has been excluded from political processes or whether it has been arbitrarily singled out to bear the expense of a measure. This is a notable point of contrast with the US annex and *Methanex* approaches. Under both these approaches, the determination of liability is sensitive to assessment of whether the measure in question is non-discriminatory and general in application (the requirement under the *Methanex* and US annex approaches that a measure be a 'regulation' should be understood as a requirement that the measure be of general application). On the other hand, the uncompromising imposition of liability for measures that interfere with property interests under the *Pope & Talbot* approach conforms better to libertarian theory than the other two approaches.

6.6.3.3 FDI flows

Existing evidence suggests that the level of substantive protection provided by investment treaties is unlikely to have a significant impact on FDI flows. The theories that purport to link investment treaties with FDI flows provide only a tentative basis for preferring any one of the three approaches to the others. While none of the approaches purports to protect bargains struck between the host state and foreign investors, the *Methanex* approach does condition the availability of the carve-out to indirect expropriation on the requirement that a state has not acted in breach of specific commitments made to the investor. The same liability for substantial deprivation in breach of specific commitment is provided by the *Pope & Talbot* approach (in the less targeted sense that a substantial deprivation necessarily amounts to indirect expropriation, regardless of whether a specific commitment has been breached). In contrast, under the US annex approach, a measure that amounts to a substantial deprivation and breaches 'reasonable investment-backed expectations' will not necessarily amount to indirect expropriation. In practice, there are likely to be few situations in which such measures are found not amount to indirect expropriation (one example could be a non-discriminatory regulatory measure designed to protect a legitimate public welfare objective that, nevertheless, had a severe effect on the investment). However, the possibility that such measures might not amount to indirect expropriation implies, in principle, that the US annex approach would be marginally less effective at attracting FDI.

6.6.3.4 Realisation of human rights and environmental conservation

Examination of the consequences of the three approaches for realisation of human rights and environmental conservation is equally challenging. The question of regulatory chill turns principally on the extent to which each approach would impose liability for measures that are effective in realising human rights or achieving environmental conservation. It is clear that the *Pope & Talbot* approach is least desirable on these grounds. Unlike the other two approaches, a state is not able to avoid liability for a measure that causes substantial deprivation by showing that it had a human rights or environmental purpose.

The *Methanex* approach is probably more desirable than US annex because it provides a clear exception to measures with certain public purposes – which appear to include environmental and human rights purposes – provided they satisfy other criteria. One caveat to this conclusion arises from the criterion that a measure must not be inconsistent with a specific commitment made to the investor if it is to fall within the *Methanex* exception. The consequence of this condition is that effective human rights and environmental measures would still incur liability if they cause substantial deprivation and breach a specific commitment to an investor. However, in light of references in US annex decisions to 'investment-backed expectations', this is not a major point of difference between the approaches.

A further question is the extent to which uncertainty associated with the contours of liability under each level of protection could be expected to cause additional chilling of measures that may have been permitted under the level of protection in question. In this respect, the *Pope & Talbot* and *Methanex* approaches fare better than the US annex approach. Both provide definitions of the contours of a state's liability for indirect expropriation that are clear in principle. The US annex approach differs. It requires an ad hoc inquiry in which a number of factors are relevant. The outcome of such an inquiry may be very difficult for decision-makers to predict in advance.

Thus, the US annex approach is likely to lead to greater regulatory chill resulting from uncertainty.

6.6.3.5 Respect for the rule of law

The final ground for comparison of the approaches is their consequences for the degree of respect for the rule of law in host states. The primary mechanism by which investment treaty protections might affect the degree of respect for the rule of law in host states is through internalisation of these protections by decision-makers and law-makers. Assuming that all three approaches are internalised to some extent, levels of protection under which liability depends on an assessment of whether the host state has complied with Razian principles are more likely to encourage respect for those same principles. Because liability under the *Pope & Talbot* approach is indifferent to whether a measure that has caused substantial deprivation is consistent with the rule of law, this approach is least likely to advance its realisation. Liability in both the US annex approach and the *Methanex* approach is somewhat sensitive to Razian concerns. This is more so under the *Methanex* approach than under US annex. The US annex approach involves consideration of the procedures by which a measure was adopted only so far as this is incidental to determination of whether a measure was 'designed and applied to protect a legitimate public welfare objective'. In contrast, measures adopted in accordance with due process will not incur liability under the *Methanex* approach, provided other criteria are satisfied. Although none of the decisions within the *Methanex* approach elaborates on the meaning of 'due process', it presumably embodies minimum requirements of legality and natural justice.

6.6.3.6 Overall evaluation

Overall evaluation of these three alternatives requires qualitative judgement about the relative desirability of a set of incommensurable consequences. In my judgement, the *Pope & Talbot* is the least desirable of the three overall. It is the least desirable in terms of its net economic benefits, respect for the rule of law and realisation of human rights and environmental conservation. The only coherent argument for preferring the *Pope & Talbot* approach to either of the other alternatives is that it better accords with the prescriptions of libertarian theory.

Comparison of the US annex approach and the *Methanex* approach is more finely balanced. This section has argued that the US annex approach is likely to lead to greater economic benefits, whereas the *Methanex* approach is likely to be associated with realisation of human rights and environmental conservation and, perhaps, greater FDI flows and respect for the rule of law. These points of difference are all relatively minor and – particularly in the case of consequences for the rule of law – depend on causal inferences about investment treaty protections for which there is little empirical evidence. In my view, there are insufficient grounds to express an overall preference for one approach.

This is all the more so given that the *Methanex* and US annex approaches are both underspecified in important respects. The precise level of protection provided by the *Methanex* approach depends on the meaning of legal concepts internal to the approach, such as 'public purpose' and 'due process', that are not yet fully articulated. The precise level of protection provided by the US annex approach depends on the correctness of the assumption that tribunals applying the approach will continue to take the view that a severe loss of economic value is insufficient to amount to an expropriation in the absence of substantial deprivation of property interests.[71]

6.6.4 Conclusion: the most desirable level of protection from indirect expropriation

Section 6.6.3 concluded that the US annex approach and the *Methanex* approach are the most desirable level of protections against indirect expropriation, although it was been unable to justify a preference between these two approaches. The previous sections compare the *Metalclad* approach to the *Pope & Talbot* approach and the *Tecmed* approach to the US annex approach. This set of comparison is not sufficient to determine a complete rank-ordering of the remaining levels of protection. However, Section 6.6.1's conclusion that there is no consequence-based rationale for preferring the *Metalclad* approach to the *Pope & Talbot* approach – the *Pope & Talbot* approach itself not being one of the most desirable approaches – strongly suggests that the *Metalclad* approach would emerge as the least desirable if a full set of comparisons were performed.

6.7 Overall conclusions

The previous sections applied the framework developed in Chapter 3 to evaluate various levels of protection derived from interpretations of existing investment treaty provisions. In this section, I draw out some of

[71] See Section 5.6.2.2.

the broader conclusions that emerge from the application of the framework. Many of these conclusions concern the extent to which the various desirable objectives that constitute the framework are, in fact, in tension with one another. These conclusions are relevant to academic and policy debates that go beyond the desirability of particular levels of protection.

The first and most important conclusion to emerge from the framework's application is that, even when taken on their own terms, 'economic' arguments do not provide unconditional justification for higher levels of investment treaty protection. Indeed, in many cases, lower levels of protection would deliver greater economic benefits. It follows that 'economic' objectives – efficiency and the attraction of FDI – are not fundamentally in tension with 'non-economic' objectives; tension between the two may arise in certain situations but not in others.[72]

This conclusion is immanent in the analysis of economic theory and evidence in Chapter 3, but the evaluation of alternative levels of protection in this chapter showed that it is of great practical importance. I argued that many of the more expansive interpretations of existing investment treaty protections are *less* desirable on economic grounds. For example, the proportionality approach to the substantive element of FET is likely to entail net economic costs compared with the margin of appreciation approach. The margin of appreciation approach is also likely to result in less regulatory chill of desirable human rights and environmental conservation measures than the proportionality approach. In several of the other comparisons conducted in this chapter, 'economic' and 'non-economic' objectives point in the same direction.

This conclusion has implications for the way that debate about investment treaties is framed. A common view in the existing scholarly literature is that the protection of foreign investment under investment treaties involves a tension between economic benefits and sovereignty costs for host states.[73] This view is also implicit in commentary that frames debate about investment treaties as a balance between investors' rights and states' regulatory autonomy.[74] One important contribution of this

---

[72] See McCrudden, *Buying Social Justice* (2007), p. 577, reaching a similar conclusion in the context of international regulation of public procurement.

[73] Sornarajah, *The International Law on Foreign Investment* (3rd edn, 2010), p. 186; cf. Vandevelde, 'The Political Economy of a Bilateral Investment Treaty' (1998) 92 *American Journal of International Law*, p. 622.

[74] Kingsbury and Schill, 'Public Law Concepts to Balance Investors' Rights with State Regulatory Actions in the Public Interest – The Concept of Proportionality' in Schill (ed),

book is to suggest that this way of framing existing academic and policy debate should be abandoned.

A second conclusion is that, of the various alternatives considered, lower levels of protection are, in general, more desirable than higher levels of protection. For example, I concluded that the legal rights approach – the least protective interpretation of the doctrine of legitimate expectations – was the most desirable. The evaluation of various approaches to the substantive element of the FET standard and the concept of indirect expropriation also found less protective approaches to be more desirable. It is important to formulate this conclusion carefully. Narrower protections are not, self-evidently, more desirable. And it is not always possible to say which of two qualitatively different levels of protections is 'narrower'. In some areas, notably the procedural element of the FET standard, arbitral jurisprudence seems to be converging around a level of protection that is the most desirable of the options considered. However, on an overall assessment, existing arbitral jurisprudence errs on the side of providing greater protection to foreign investment than can be justified.

One practical implication of the first two conclusions, taken together, concerns the use of exceptions clauses in future investment treaties. Kurtz, among others, has argued that states should address concerns that existing investment treaty protections confer overly generous protection by inserting exceptions clauses in future investment treaties.[75] Such clauses could ensure that a state is not required to pay compensation to foreign investors when it adopts legitimate human rights or environmental regulations. The analysis in this chapter supports the view that the inclusion of appropriately drafted exceptions clause can be a significant improvement compared with the status quo.[76] However, exceptions clauses presume a tension between competing objectives. The policy case for the inclusion of exceptions clauses assumes that there are clear rationales for the 'core' protection, yet also a need to

---

International Investment Law and Comparative Public Law (2010), p. 103; Mann H, 'The Right of States to Regulate and International Investment Law' (2002) [online], p. 5; Spears, 'The Quest for Policy Space in a New Generation of International Investment Agreements' (2010) 13 Journal of International Economic Law, p. 1042.

[75] Kurtz, 'Australia's Rejection of Investor-State Arbitration': Causation, Omission and Implication' (2012) 27 ICSID Review, p. 81.

[76] E.g., Section 6.6.4, which concluded that the Methanex approach (which establishes a carve-out to the concept of indirect expropriation) is more desirable than the Pope & Talbot approach.

safeguard competing objectives through exceptions. In contrast, I have argued that, in many cases, there is no coherent justification for the levels of protection implied by existing arbitral jurisprudence. In these circumstances, policy-makers should reflect on whether the core protection in question – for example, the protection of expectations based on laws of general application[77] or the review of government conduct on substantive grounds[78] – is justified before moving to secondary questions relating to the appropriate drafting of exceptions clauses.

A third conclusion concerns the distinction between the impact of government conduct on the legal entitlements of an investor and the impact of conduct on the economic value of the investment. Insofar as liability turns on the impact of a state's conduct on the investor's interests, investment treaty protections that focus on interference with legal entitlements are preferable to protections that focus on loss of economic value. For example, the comparison of the representations approach and the legal rights approach to legitimate expectations raised doubts about the desirability of protecting the expectations of foreign investors that have no basis in the legal system of the host state, even when such expectations rest on specific unilateral representations made by the host state. There are far more serious concerns about the business plan approach to legitimate expectations and the *Metalclad* approach to indirect expropriation, within which loss of economic value of an investment is sufficient to trigger a state's liability without any additional requirement of breach of a unilateral representation.

A fourth conclusion concerns the desirability of arbitral deference to policy judgements made by host states. Public law critiques of investment treaties tend to argue that protections that entail greater deference to domestic policy judgements would be desirable. The comparison of margin-of-appreciation and politics-as-irrationality approaches suggests that deference to a host state's choice of policy objectives is likely to be highly desirable so far as substantive review of the justifications for government conduct is concerned. Indeed, debates about deference aside, there are real questions about whether investment treaties should grant tribunals a general jurisdiction to review the substantive justifications of any government conduct that affects a foreign investor. A respectable case can be made for excluding the possibility of substantive review under

---

[77] See Section 6.3.2.   [78] See Section 6.5.3.

the FET standard altogether, leaving the standard focused on questions of procedural fairness and the protection of enforceable and specific rights validly acquired under domestic law.[79] In contrast, determining the appropriate degree of deference to policy choices that entail interference with foreign investors' legal rights raises more challenging questions, which normally involve the balancing of competing objectives. In such situations, greater deference to host states is not, self-evidently, more desirable.

A fifth conclusion concerns the impact of various levels of protection on the degree of respect for the rule of law. Although the argument that investment treaty protections promote respect for the rule of law is one of the most common justifications for the existence of investment treaties, the analysis in the preceding sections showed that determining the impact of investment treaty protections on respect for the Razian understanding of that concept is complex. As the comparison of the intermediate and exacting approaches to the procedural element of the FET standard shows, levels of protection that impose more demanding obligations on host states relating to the conduct of domestic administration are not necessarily associated with improvements in respect for the rule of law.

A final conclusion is that a significant minority of arbitral tribunals have interpreted common provisions of existing investment treaties as entailing a level of protection for which there is *no* coherent justification. This is a powerful conclusion. It is a stronger claim than the claim that tribunals have disregarded particular relevant interests or the claim that tribunals have not struck the right balance between competing objectives. It is a claim that some arbitral tribunals have understood existing provisions in a way that is profoundly misguided. Such indefensibly broad understandings of existing treaty protections are not confined to earlier cases. The *Metalclad* Tribunal's interpretation of indirect expropriation, for example, is still cited and applied in modern awards. This conclusion suggests that states should seek to draft the provisions of future investment treaties more precisely to reduce the scope of interpretative discretion that they confer on arbitral tribunals. This conclusion raises further questions, which I have not sought to address in this monograph, about whether arbitral tribunals are an appropriate institution for the resolution of investor-state disputes.

[79] See Sections 6.5.3.6 and 6.5.4.

6.8 Summary

In this chapter, I examined the level of protection that investment treaties should provide to foreign investment. The chapter considered differing levels of protection implied by different interpretations of each element of the FET standard, as identified in Chapter 4, and different interpretations of indirect expropriation, as identified in Chapter 5. I applied the framework developed in Chapter 3 to compare and evaluate the likely consequences of adopting each level of protection prospectively. On this basis, I concluded that the legal rights approach is the most desirable level of protection of investors' legitimate expectations; that the intermediate approach is the most desirable level of protection from procedural unfairness; that, depending on the circumstance of the states in question, the margin of appreciation approach is probably the most desirable level of protection against substantive irrationality; and that the US annex and *Methanex* approaches are the two most desirable levels of protection against indirect expropriation. While the evaluation in this chapter focused on differing levels of protection implied by existing arbitral jurisprudence, the analysis in this chapter demonstrates how the framework developed in Chapter 3 could be used to evaluate a wider range of drafting options for future investment treaties.

In Section 6.7, I drew a number of more general conclusions. The most important of these is that, insofar as the drafting and interpretation of investment treaties is concerned, 'economic' and 'non-economic' objectives are not necessarily in tension. This is because economic justifications for protecting foreign investment are much weaker than is generally supposed. This conclusion calls into question the way that both critics and proponents of investment treaties frame existing debate about investment treaties. Much existing debate assumes that the essential challenge in drafting and interpreting investment treaty protections is to balance the need for investment protection with other, competing public interests.[80] In this chapter, I have shown that, in many situations, the justifications for protecting foreign investment are *not* in tension with 'public interest' objectives, so no questions of balance arise. The conclusions drawn in this chapter also have implications for states and arbitral tribunals. These implications are the subject of Chapter 7.

---

[80] E.g., Schill, 'Fair and Equitable Treatment, the Rule of Law, and Comparative Public Law', p. 154.

7   Implications of the conclusions

7.1 Introduction

In Chapter 6, I applied the framework developed in Chapter 3 to evaluate various levels of protection implied by different interpretations of the fair and equitable treatment (FET) and indirect expropriation provisions of investment treaties. In this chapter, the focus shifts to the practical implications of the conclusions for states and arbitral tribunals. In light of the conclusions of Chapter 6, Section 7.2 argues that states should consider revising their drafting practice for future investment treaties and clarifying the level of protection provided by existing investment treaties. It reviews three possible courses of action for states, which might be adopted individually or in combination: changes to the drafting of substantive protections of new investment treaties; amendments to the substantive protections of existing investment treaties; and interpretative statements relating to the interpretation of existing investment treaties.

Section 7.3 considers the implications of the analysis for arbitral tribunals and practitioners. In 7.3.1, I argue that, even on a strictly formalist understanding of Article 31 of the Vienna Convention of the Law of Treaties (VCLT), the analysis presented in previous chapters is relevant to doctrinal debates about the characterisation of investment treaties' object and purpose and to debates about how a treaty's object and purpose should influence the interpretative exercise. In 7.3.2, I take the argument one step further and suggest that the interpretation of legal texts inevitably requires an adjudicator to make policy choices. The analysis presented in this book provides a basis for more informed interpretative choices.

7.2 The implications for states: drafting, amendment and clarification of investment treaties

This book is relevant to states in that it provides an informed basis for addressing a controversial question of public policy. Recent reviews of investment treaty practice in Australia and the United States and ongoing policy reviews in the European Union (EU) demonstrate that the level of substantive protection provided by investment treaties is a subject of active policy debate.[1] Although there are other resources available to government policy-makers considering the drafting of investment treaties – notably, publications by the UN Conference on Trade and Development (UNCTAD) and the Commonwealth Secretariat – these resources are limited to articulating a range of alternative levels of protection that policy-makers might adopt.[2] They do not seek to provide grounds for choosing between these options. The analysis contained in this book contributes to the existing policy literature by providing a framework to determine and evaluate the costs and benefits of providing different levels of investment treaty protection.

7.2.1 The case for reconsidering existing treaty practice

The analysis in this book is also relevant to state in more specific ways. The conclusions of Chapters 4, 5 and 6 suggest that states should reconsider the way that investment treaty protections are drafted. The case for drafting future treaties more precisely and for amending or clarifying existing treaties rests on two propositions. The first is that tribunals have interpreted given provisions of existing investment treaties as entailing very different levels of protection. The second is that some of these interpretations are profoundly undesirable.

---

[1] All these policy reviews considered the level of substantive protection provided by investment treaties: Productivity Commission, 'Bilateral and Regional Trade Agreements: Productivity Commission Research Report'; Advisory Committee on International Economic Policy, 'Report of the Advisory Committee on International Economic Policy Regarding the Model Bilateral Investment treaty' (2009), annex B. Compare the position of: European Commission, 'Proposal for Regulation on financial responsibility for investor-state dispute settlement tribunals' (21 June 2012), with European Parliament 'Amendments on proposal for Regulation on financial responsibility for investor-state dispute settlement tribunals' (23 May 2013).

[2] VanDuzer, Simons and Mayeda, *Integrating Sustainable Development into International Investment Agreements: A Guide for Developing Countries* (Commonwealth Secretariat 2012), pp. 147–52; UNCTAD, *Fair and Equitable Treatment: A Sequel*, sec. IV.

Chapters 4 and 5 constitute a detailed and sustained argument for the first proposition. I showed that arbitral tribunals have interpreted FET and indirect expropriation provisions of existing treaties in a number of distinct ways. It is sometimes suggested that these interpretative disagreements were confined to earlier cases and that a more consistent approach has since emerged.[3] This is not so. Chapters 4 and 5 show that tribunals continue to interpret investment treaty protections as entailing markedly different levels of protection. All sixteen approaches identified in this book (eleven approaches to different elements of the FET standard and five approaches to indirect expropriation) have been applied in decisions rendered since 2007. Indeed, in some areas – specifically, the extent to which the FET standard protects an investor's legitimate expectations and the extent to which it provides for substantive review of government conduct – the range of doctrinal disagreement between tribunals has significantly *increased* since 2007.

Chapter 6 constitutes a detailed and sustained argument for the second proposition. I contended that some tribunals have interpreted common investment treaty protections as providing a level of protection for which there is *no* coherent justification. This conclusion constitutes a strong case for drafting investment treaty protections more precisely. Better drafted provisions would reduce the scope of interpretative discretion conferred on arbitral tribunals and clarify how much protection the state parties to a treaty intend provide.[4]

7.2.2 The range of options available to states

In this book, I have evaluated a range of differing levels of protection derived from interpretations of existing investment treaty provisions. However, there is a broader range of options available to states in redrafting investment treaty protections, including the abandonment of existing provisions, the invention of entirely new provisions and the tying of existing levels of protection to doctrines of national law. These options could be adopted individually or in some combination. I do not intend to foreclose debate about the desirability of levels of protection that are not evaluated here.

---

[3] Schill, 'W(h)ither Fragmentation: On the Literature and Sociology of International Investment Law' (2011) 22 *European Journal of International Law*, pp. 890–4.
[4] Similarly, Ortino, 'Refining the Content and Role of Investment "Rules" and "Standards": A New Approach to International Investment Treaty Making' (2013) 28 *ICSID Review*, p. 167.

Indeed, in some respects, the conclusions of Chapter 6 point toward the need to consider more radical alternatives than those based on existing case law. For example, in Section 6.3.4, I argued that the least protective approach to the legitimate expectations element of the FET standard should be preferred. This raises the possibility that even less protective alternatives, which have no basis in current arbitral practice, would be still more desirable. The framework developed in Chapter 3 could be applied to evaluate such options. Rather than limiting the options available to states, I submit that the evaluation of various levels of protection implied by existing arbitral awards offers a useful starting point for states that are reconsidering the level of protection that their investment treaties provide.

7.2.3 The perspective of a single state

The evaluation thus far has been conducted from a general, impartial perspective, in which the consequences for all affected actors are weighted equally. This perspective is explained and justified in Section 1.2.4. It corresponds to the collective interest of states in the drafting of multilateral investment treaties. For example, assuming that negotiations are ultimately successful, the investment chapter of the Trans-Pacific Partnership will apply to a range of developed and developing states that have very different systems of government. In determining the level of protection to be adopted in a treaty of this sort, states will need to agree to a shared view about the level of protection that should be provided to foreign investment.

The perspective of a single state may (but will not necessarily) depart from the general, impartial perspective presented in this book. This is because any state seeking to negotiate an investment treaty will be particularly concerned to maximise the benefits and minimise the costs that accrue to that state itself. The most important factor in determining whether the perspective of a single state departs from the impartial perspective is whether that state is a net recipient or a net source of foreign investment. A state that is almost exclusively a source of investment would have an interest in higher levels of protection than a state that is almost exclusively a destination for investment. These distributive effects are considered in detail in Section 3.5.2. There are other points at which the framework flags the way in which country-specific concerns would feed into the analysis. For example, Section 3.7.4.2 argues that developing countries are likely to be more susceptible to regulatory chill resulting from 'threat' effects.

However, in the drafting of model investment treaties, the self-interest of any single state will tend to converge toward the general, impartial perspective presented here. There are several reasons for this, which are presented in Section 1.2.4. To summarise: first, most states are both importers and exporters of capital, at least to some extent. Second, through investment treaties, states bind themselves with respect to an uncertain range of regulatory actions that may affect an uncertain set of future investments. Third, a model investment treaty, by its nature, embodies a level of protection that a given state is prepared to offer to differently situated states. Recent consultations on the new US and EU model investment treaties illustrate the importance of general concerns in determining the level of protection that should be provided in a model investment treaty.[5]

Nevertheless, in principle, it would be possible for states to tailor the level of protection they provide in each treaty to the particular characteristics of the partner state in question. Historically, this practice has been unusual. Such a practice would complicate enormously states' efforts to negotiate and comply with investment treaties and would risk being circumvented by the structuring of foreign investment or the use of most-favoured nation (MFN) clauses.

Assuming, for the purposes of argument, that some states do wish to individually calibrate the level of protection that they provide in each investment treaty, the analysis in this book would still offer a useful point of departure. The framework developed in Chapter 3 contains a range of disaggregated insights about the extent to which the impacts of a given level of protection are likely to vary with the characteristics of the state in question. It would also be possible to map additional evidence of the circumstances of the relevant states on to the framework. For example, evidence may be available about the extent to which the institutions of government in a particular state internalise international law. This could lead to more refined predictions about the likely impact of a given level of protection on government decision-making that are specific to the state in question.[6]

---

[5] Advisory Committee on International Economic Policy, 'Report of the Advisory Committee on International Economic Policy Regarding the Model Bilateral Investment Treaty'; European Commission, 'Proposal for Regulation on Financial Responsibility for Investor-State Dispute Settlement Tribunals' (21 June 2012); with European Parliament 'Amendments on Proposal for Regulation on Financial Responsibility for Investor-State Dispute Settlement Tribunals' (23 May 2013).

[6] See Sections 3.4.5.1 and 3.7.4.3.

7.2.3.1 Ideology and the policy preferences of states

International law governing the protection of foreign property was, historically, highly controversial.[7] The broad spread of investment treaties that confer remarkably similar levels of substantive protection on foreign investment suggests that much of this fundamental ideological conflict has abated.[8] Nevertheless, it remains clear that states disagree about the appropriate balance between the 'market', property rights and the regulatory prerogatives of the state.[9] One of the most important conclusions of this book is that, in determining the level of substantive protection that investment treaties should provide, the objectives of protecting property rights and maximising net economic benefits (stereotypically 'capitalist' concerns) do not necessarily conflict with other objectives of distributive justice, human rights and environmental protection (stereotypically concerns of the New International Economic Order).[10] On this basis, the conclusions of this book are offered to all states as a set of insights about the likely consequences of adopting different levels of protection.

Nonetheless, in some situations, there is a tension between different objectives. In such circumstances, states may reasonably come to different views about the appropriate balance between competing objectives, views that reflect their own policy preferences. For example, a state that is ideologically committed to the inviolability of property rights may sensibly prefer the *Pope & Talbot* approach to indirect expropriation, even though alternative approaches could be expected to entail greater net economic benefits and lead to greater realisation of human rights and environmental protection. On the other hand, neither an ideological commitment to the inviolability of property rights nor a commitment to the economic benefits of free markets can plausibly justify preferring the *Metalclad* approach to the *Pope & Talbot* approach.

7.2.4 Drafting the substantive protections of new investment treaties

The simplest way for states to adopt a preferred level of protection is to incorporate the new level of protection in new investment treaties when they are signed. There are few legal constraints on states' ability to define the level of protection to be provided to foreign investment in future investment treaties. One potential complication could arise if

---

[7] Lowenfeld, *International Economic Law* (2nd edn, 2008), pp. 491–2.
[8] Schill, *The Multilateralization of International Investment Law* (2009), p. 6.
[9] UNCTAD, *Development Implications of International Investment Agreements* (2007), p. 4.
[10] See UNGA Res 3281 (XXIX) (9 December 1974).

states sought to specify a level of protection in an investment treaty below that required by customary international law. Chapters 4 and 5 observed that tribunals have taken different views of the extent of states' obligations under customary international law.[11] Academic commentary also recognises that this is a subject of considerable disagreement.[12] All the levels of protection considered in this book are consistent with arguable views of what custom requires. Even tribunals endorsing the least protective interpretations considered in this book have justified their views as being consistent with customary international law.[13]

Even assuming, for the purpose of argument, that a state's preferred level of protection fell below the requirements of customary international law, there would be no obstacle to its inclusion in an investment treaty. Within the context of the relationship between the parties to the treaty in question, states are free to agree to derogate from general customary international law (subject to constraints of *jus cogens*).[14] Moreover, it is clear that a state may limit its consent to jurisdiction to investor-state arbitration to the violation of particular protections defined in a treaty.[15]

More practical problem could arise if a state adopted a lower level of protection in new investment treaties than it had in previous treaties, only to find that investors were able to rely on more expansive protections in earlier investment treaties via an MFN clause in the new treaty. This risk could be avoided in several ways – for example, by excluding earlier treaties from the scope of coverage of the MFN clause or by excluding particular substantive provisions of the new treaty from the scope

---

[11] See Sections 4.2.2.1 and 5.2.2.

[12] McLachlan, Shore and Weiniger, *International Investment Arbitration: Substantive Principles* (2007), p. 17; Schwebel, 'The United States 2004 Model Bilateral Investment Treaty: An Exercise in the Regressive Development of International Law' (2006) 3(2) *Transnational Dispute Management*, p. 4.

[13] E.g., *Glamis Gold* v. *United States*, Award, para. 627, endorsing the narrow approach to procedural review; *Methanex* v. *United States* Final Award, pt. IV, chp. D, para. 7, arguing for a 'police powers' carve-out to indirect expropriation.

[14] Condorelli, 'Custom' in Bedjaoui (ed), *International Law: Achievements and Prospects* (1991), p. 184; McLachlan, 'Investment Treaties and General International Law' (2008) 57 *International and Comparative Law Quarterly*, p. 374.

[15] *Case Concerning Oil Platforms (Iran v. United States)* Preliminary Objection, Judgment of 12 December 1996, ICJ Rep 803, para. 38, holding that the United States had not consented to the Court's jurisdiction to decide claims relating to the breach of customary international law on the use of armed force and that the submission to jurisdiction was limited to the scope of the treaty; similarly, *Case Concerning Oil Platforms (Iran v. United States)* Judgment of 6 November 2003, Separate Opinion of Judge Higgins ICJ Rep 225, para. 52.

of application of the MFN clause. Another, more far-reaching, solution would be to omit an MFN clause from the new treaty. States will need to consider the drafting of MFN clauses if the specification of a given level of protection in a particular treaty is to be effective.

7.2.4.1 New protections or redrafting of existing provision

An important practical question in translating the preferred level of protection into treaty language is whether to redraft existing provisions or to discard them entirely. The latter approach could, for example, involve omitting FET provisions from new investment treaties and substituting a set of specific provisions that deal with the investor's legitimate expectations, procedural unfairness, substantive irrationality and other elements of the FET standard. Until now, states have preferred an evolutionary approach, involving the redrafting and clarification of existing provisions.[16] Because the different levels of protection evaluated in this book are derived from arbitral interpretations of existing provisions, it makes sense to redraft, rather than replace, those provisions. Linking the preferred approach to a given understanding of an existing standard is also likely to provide greater clarity about the intended level of protection to arbitral tribunals.

7.2.4.2 The redrafting of existing provisions to adopt the preferred level of protection

It would be relatively simple to redraft existing provisions to adopt a desired level of protection. Consider, for example, a state that decided to specify that the level of protection provided to an investor's legitimate expectations by a particular investment treaty was that defined by the legal rights approach. The protection of legitimate expectations is just one element of the FET standard, and thus the clarifying text is best drafted in the negative. One possible formulation is as follows:

The obligation to provide fair and equitable to foreign investment does not require a state to act consistently with an investor's legitimate expectations, except insofar as those expectations are:

- based on a specific and enforceable legal right validly acquired by the investor; and

---

[16] E.g., US 2012 Model BIT, art. 5; COMESA Investment Agreement, art. 14; ASEAN Comprehensive Investment Agreement, art. 11.

- legitimate and reasonable in the circumstances, considered in light of normal business risks, regulatory patterns in the industry and any specific representations made by the state to the investor; and
- relied upon by the investor in making the decision to invest.[17]

A clause of this sort could be inserted immediately after the statement of the state parties' FET obligation, or it could be incorporated in an interpretative annex to the treaty. The other levels of protection evaluated in this book are equally amenable to being translated into treaty language in this way.

7.2.5 Amendment of existing treaties

A second way for states to adopt the desired level of protection is to amend existing investment treaties. The same issues that arise in the context of drafting new investment treaties – the choice between replacing and redrafting existing provisions and the practicalities of drafting – also arise in the context of treaty amendment. These issues were addressed in the previous section. This section considers two additional issues that arise in the context of treaty amendment.

7.2.5.1 The extent of states' power to amend existing treaties

The basic rule defined by Article 39 VCLT is that 'a treaty may be amended by the agreement of the parties.'[18] This formulation places few limits on the form an 'agreement' to amend a treaty may take. In the absence of further requirements that a treaty defines for its own amendment, a treaty may be amended 'by an agreement which does not itself constitute a treaty, or by an oral agreement'.[19] For prudential reasons, states seeking to specify the level of protection provided by existing investment treaties should do so by agreement in writing.

Some commentators have argued that any distinction between agreements 'amending' an existing treaty and agreements 'interpreting' an existing treaty is only a matter of degree.[20] For example, in 2002, the Czech and Dutch governments agreed to a 'common position' on certain issues relating to the interpretation and application of the Czech-Netherlands bilateral investment treaty (BIT).[21] At least one commentator

---

[17] Derived from restatement of the legal rights approach, Section 4.5.1.3.
[18] VCLT, art. 39.   [19] Aust, *Modern Treaty Law and Practice* (2000), p. 213.
[20] Roberts, 'Power and Persuasion in Investment Treaty Interpretation: The Dual Role of States' (2010) 104 *American Journal of International Law*, p. 201.
[21] *CME* v. *Czech Republic*, Final Award, paras. 87–93.

characterised this common position as an amendment,[22] notwithstanding the fact that it did not purport to modify the treaty. One of the few differences between 'interpretations' and 'amendments' is that an agreement that purports to amend an existing treaty will be presumed to operate prospectively.[23] I return to this issue in the examination of interpretative statements in Section 7.2.6.

7.2.5.2 The impact on the amendment of existing treaties on investors' rights

In this section, I address the concern that states are subject to limitations in the extent to which they can amend investors' rights under a treaty. In examining this argument, an important threshold question is whether investment treaties confer legal rights on foreign investors. The prevailing view in academic commentary and arbitral awards is that they do.[24] However, a minority view is that investment treaties grant substantive legal rights exclusively to states, with foreign investors granted only a procedural right to enforce the substantive rights of their home state through investor-state arbitration.[25] If investment treaties did not grant substantive legal rights to foreign investors, no issue would arise concerning the impact of amendment of substantive protections on investors' rights. On the other hand, an issue could arise if, consistently with the mainstream view, investment treaties do confer substantive rights on foreign investors. It is unnecessary to resolve this debate; the answer may well depend on the way in which the investment treaty in question is drafted. The following paragraphs proceed on the assumption that investment treaties do confer substantive rights on foreign investors. I argue that, even on this assumption, those rights are subject to prospective alteration by agreement between the state parties to the investment treaty that created the rights in question.

Any discussion about the impact of amendments on investor rights inevitably takes place in the shadow of academic debate about the legitimacy of the Free Trade Commission's (FTC) binding interpretation of NAFTA's Article 1105(1).[26] This interpretation was issued after the *Pope &*

---

[22] Salacuse, *The Law of Investment Treaties* (2010), p. 350.

[23] Roberts, 'Power and Persuasion in Investment Treaty Interpretation', p. 201.

[24] Douglas, *The International Law of Investment Claims* (2009), para. 65; *Corn Products International* v. *Mexico*, Decision on Responsibility, paras. 165–9; *Cargill* v. *Mexico*, Award, para. 422.

[25] *Archer Daniel Midlands* v. *Mexico*, Award, paras. 178–9.

[26] Notes of Interpretation of Certain Chapter 11 Provisions (31 July 2001).

Talbot Tribunal's decision on the merits had been rendered, while the tribunal was determining the damages to be awarded. The *Pope & Talbot* Tribunal was evidently displeased by this intervention and indicated that it perceived the FTC's statement to constitute an 'amendment' rather than an 'interpretation' of art 1105(1).[27] Although this has proved a minority view among tribunals and commentators, it retains some support.[28] If the statement had constituted an amendment, two legal consequences would have followed: the amendment would not have entered into force because amendments to NAFTA require ratification to enter into force;[29] and, even when the amendment did enter into force, it would be presumed to operate prospectively.[30] For both reasons, characterising the state parties' intervention as an 'amendment' would have entailed the result that the tribunal was bound to apply the original, unamended provision as the applicable law in the dispute in question.

This controversy should not be understood as casting doubt on the ability of states to prospectively alter the rights conferred on investors by investment treaties. Investors' rights under an investment treaty are created by agreement between states, and they may be withdrawn, terminated or modified in the same way.[31] Articles 36 and 37 of the VCLT deal with treaties that grant rights to other states. Even in this situation – a situation in which the justification for protecting the reliance interest of the third party beneficiary is significantly more compelling[32] – the rights of the third party states may be amended unless 'it is established that the right was intended not to be revocable or subject to modification without the consent of the third State.'[33] It is clear from the text of Articles 36 and 37 of the VCLT that the central issue in determining whether the parties to a treaty may amend the rights of a third state is the *intention* of the treaty parties.[34]

Assuming, for the purpose of argument, that states are constrained by Articles 36 and 37 of the VCLT in their ability to alter investors' rights, it

---

[27] *Pope & Talbot* v. *Canada*, Award in Respect of Damages, para. 47.

[28] Brower CH, 'Why the FTC Notes of Interpretation Constitute a Partial Amendment of NAFTA Article 1105' (2006) 46 *Virginia Journal of International Law*, p. 358.

[29] NAFTA, art. 2202.

[30] Roberts, 'Power and Persuasion in Investment Treaty Interpretation', p. 201.

[31] Ibid., p. 210.

[32] The European Court of Human Rights appears to accept that 'an established practice within the member States could give rise to an amendment to the Convention' notwithstanding that the European Convention on Human Rights confers rights directly on individuals, *Ocalan* v. *Turkey* (2005) 41 EHRR 985, para. 163; cf. *Corn Products International* v. *Mexico*, Decision on Responsibility, paras. 163–5.

[33] VCLT, art. 37(2).   [34] Cf. Aust, *Modern Treaty Law and Practice*, p. 210.

would be necessary to determine whether the parties to an investment treaty intended the rights of investors to be incapable of modification or revocation. This question can only be answered definitively through a treaty-by-treaty analysis. However, considering the text of typical investment treaties, it is difficult to infer any intention by the state parties to depart from the normal presumption in favour of the possibility of amendment.[35] Although some investment treaties do specify that the provisions of the treaty will continue to apply to established investments for a certain period if the treaty is terminated,[36] such provisions address the continued operation of the treaty in the event of unilateral termination by one party. They do not evince an intention to limit the treaty parties' powers to agree to amendments that alter the rights of investors. On this basis, I conclude that it is highly unlikely that states are subject to limitations in their ability to amend any particular investment treaty prospectively by agreement.

For the sake of completeness, I also consider the implications of the principle of estoppel. While the doctrine of estoppel has been recognised as a general principle of international law,[37] commentators have urged caution in the application of the principle.[38] In cases in which the International Court of Justice (ICJ) has recognised the principle of estoppel, it has been applied to prevent a state from denying the validity of past legal acts previously accepted by the state in question as valid. For example, the ICJ has prevented Nicaragua from denying the validity of an arbitral award it previously accepted as valid[39] and precluded Thailand for arguing that a treaty with Cambodia, which it had previously accepted as valid, was concluded in error.[40] Such controversies concerning the legal validity of past acts are distinct from questions concerning limitations on the power of states to amend existing legal rights by future, valid legal acts. The principle of estoppel does not prevent prospective amendment of the rights an investment treaty confers on an investor, even if the investor has invested on the assumption that a right to a given standard of treatment will subsist for the entire duration of the investment.

---

[35] Roberts, 'Power and Persuasion in Investment Treaty Interpretation', p. 211.

[36] Australia-Mexico BIT (23 August 2005), art. 24 (3).

[37] Cheng, *General Principles of Law as Applied by International Courts and Tribunals* (1987), p. 141.

[38] Crawford, *Brownlie's Principles of Public International Law* (8th edn, 2012), pp. 420–1.

[39] *Arbitral Award by the King of Spain (Honduras v. Nicaragua)* Judgment of 18 November 1960, ICJ Reports 192, 213.

[40] *Temple Case (Cambodia v. Thailand)* Judgment of 15 June 1962, ICJ Reports 6, 32.

7.2.6 Interpretative statements clarifying the meaning of existing investment treaties

An alternative to amending existing investment treaties would be for the state parties to a given investment treaty to issue an agreed interpretative statement, clarifying that an existing provision of the investment treaty entails the desired level of protection. All the levels of protection considered in this book are based on interpretations of existing investment treaty provisions by arbitral tribunals. On this basis, each level of protection constitutes a plausible interpretation of common treaty provisions. Although I argue that it would almost certainly be permissible for states to adopt the preferred level of protection by making joint interpretative statements, I conclude that changes in the extent of investors' rights are best made through amendments, for prudential reasons.

7.2.6.1 The extent of states' explicit and implicit authority to clarify a treaty provision through interpretative statements

Some investment treaties, such as NAFTA, establish specific procedures that provide for the adoption of interpretative statements setting out the parties' joint understanding of the meaning of existing provisions. However, even in the absence of explicit authorisation, there is an abundance of authority for the proposition that, acting jointly, the state parties to a treaty have the authority to interpret it.[41] Articles 31 and 32 of the VCLT have been accepted as constituting customary international law on the interpretation of treaties.[42] Article 31(3)(a) provides:

> 3. There shall be taken into account, together with the context:
>
> (a) any subsequent agreement between the parties regarding the interpretation of the treaty or the application of its provisions;

The ICJ has given this principle broad application:

> [A]n agreement as to the interpretation of a provision reached after the conclusion of the treaty represents an authentic interpretation by the parties which must be read into the treaty for purposes of its interpretation.[43]

---

[41] Sinclair, *The Vienna Convention on the Law of Treaties* (2nd edn, 1984), p. 136; Gardiner, *Treaty Interpretation* (2008), p. 32.

[42] *Avena and Other Mexican Nationals (Mexico v. United States)* Judgment of 31 March 2004, ICJ Reports 12, 37–38.

[43] *Kasikili/Sedudu Island (Botswana v. Namibia)* Judgment of 13 December 1999, ICJ Reports 1045, 1075.

As with an amendment to a treaty, the form of a subsequent agreement relating to the interpretation of a treaty is unimportant.[44]

7.2.6.2 The impact of interpretative statements on investors' rights

Following the FTC's interpretative statement, NAFTA tribunals have recognised a wide discretion for states to interpret provisions conferring rights on foreign investors. In response to the argument that the FTC's interpretative statement was illegitimate amendment, the *ADF* Tribunal noted that

we have the Parties themselves – all the Parties – speaking to the Tribunal. No more authentic and authoritative source of instruction on what the Parties intended to convey in a particular provision of NAFTA, is possible.[45]

The tribunal in *Methanex* expressed a similar view:

If a legislature, having enacted a statute, feels that the courts implementing it have misconstrued the legislature's intention, it is perfectly proper for the legislature to clarify its intention. In a democratic and representative system in which legislation expresses the will of the people, legislative clarification in this sort of case would appear to be obligatory. The Tribunal sees no reason why the same analysis should not apply to international law.[46]

The fact that such interpretative statements may have the effect, in practice, of modifying the extent of investors' rights under NAFTA does not seem to have caused either tribunal particular concern.

Roberts has examined in detail the question of whether there are any limits to states' discretion to alter the scope of investors' rights through the exercise of interpretative authority. She identifies two important dimensions to states' exercise of interpretative authority. The first is whether the agreed interpretation is a 'reasonable' interpretation of the provision in question; the second is the timing of the interpretation. She argues that states are only constrained from adopting binding interpretations that are both unreasonable and late (in the sense of being adopted after a claim has been brought).[47] Even in extreme situations involving unreasonable and late interpretative agreement, the legal basis of the constraint on the powers of states to interpret the instrument that they have created is unclear. The constraint Roberts identifies seems to have its

[44] Gardiner, *Treaty Interpretation*, p. 216.   [45] *ADF Group* v. *United States*, Award, para. 177.
[46] *Methanex* v. *United States* Final Award, pt. IV, chp. C, para. 22.
[47] Roberts, 'Power and Persuasion in Investment Treaty Interpretation' p. 213.

origins in prudential concerns about preserving 'the credibility of invest-ment treaty commitments'[48] and a legal realist assumption that tribunals will be inclined to resist such blatant interventions in the adjudicatory process by finding some justification to refuse to give effect to them.[49] Arguably, some constraint is also implied by the structure of Article 31 of the VCLT, in which a 'subsequent agreement... regarding the interpre-tation of the treaty' is only one, albeit a highly significant, element that must be 'taken into account' in the interpretative exercise.[50]

For present purposes, it is unnecessary to define the outer limit on states' authority to define the level of protection provided by invest-ment treaties through interpretative statements. Throughout this book, I have made the case for adopting given levels of protection in invest-ment treaties on the basis that the preferred rule would be applied prospectively. As Roberts argues, there are strong prudential grounds to avoid altering investors' rights retrospectively and even more com-pelling grounds to avoid creating the impression of interfering in the adjudication claims that have been already been brought. It is for these reasons that I conclude that any agreement between states about the level of protection provided by investment treaties is better presented as a prospective 'amendment' clarifying the level of protection provided by investment treaties than as a retrospective 'interpretation'.[51]

7.3 The implications for arbitrators and practitioners: the interpretation of existing treaties

The analysis in this book also has implications for practitioners and arbi-trators faced with the task of interpreting the substantive protections of investment treaties, as they are currently drafted. My argument proceeds in two stages. In Section 7.3.1, I argue that Article 31 of the VCLT requires a tribunal to interpret the substantive protections of an investment treaty in light of the treaty's object and purpose. As such, the VCLT requires a tri-bunal to come to a view about the objectives of the treaty and to consider the extent to which various plausible interpretations of the treaty text

---

[48] Ibid., p. 213.   [49] Ibid., p. 214.

[50] Similarly, Study Group of the International Law Commission, *Fragmentation of International Law: Difficulties Arising from the Diversification and Expansion of International Law* (2006), paras. 473–74.

[51] Cf. van Aaken, 'International Investment Law between Commitment and Flexibility: A Contract Theory Analysis' (2009) 12 *Journal of International Economic Law*, p. 536.

advance these objectives. The analysis presented in this book is relevant to both questions.

In Section 7.3.2, I argue that, the application of the VCLT aside, there is ample evidence that arbitrators' underlying normative and causal assumptions influence the way in which they interpret investment treaties *in practice*. This is not necessarily problematic. On the contrary, the interpretation of legal texts inevitably involves the making of policy choices. Practitioners should, however, be conscious of the underlying assumptions that they bring to the task of treaty interpretation. The analysis presented in this book calls into question many of the underlying assumptions that currently inform the interpretation of investment treaties.

7.3.1 The characterisation and significance of a treaty's 'object and purpose'

Article 31(1) of the VCLT requires that:

[a] treaty shall be interpreted in good faith in accordance with the ordinary meaning to be given to the terms of the treaty in their context and in the light of its object and purpose.

This provision has been accepted as reflecting customary international law on the interpretation of treaties, including by investment treaty tribunals.[52] It requires a treaty interpreter to consider a treaty's 'object and purpose' – a phrase that has been understood as broadly equivalent to a treaty's 'aims' or 'objectives'.[53] Thus, even if one adopts a strictly formalist view of treaty interpretation, the interpreter must engage with questions about the objectives pursued by that treaty.

Three more specific observations can be made about Article 31(1) of the VCLT. First, it directs the treaty interpreter to consider the shared purpose of the state parties embodied in the treaty, as opposed to the individual objectives of any one state party. As such, Article 31(1) requires the treaty interpreter to adopt an impartial perspective akin to the one adopted in this book. Second, it directs the interpreter to consider *the treaty's* object and purpose, as opposed to the purpose of the particular provision of the treaty in question. This means that the object and purpose should be

---

[52] *Avena and other Mexican Nationals (Mexico v. United States)* Judgment of 31 March 2004, ICJ Reports 12, 37–38; *Suez and Vivendi; AWG Group v. Argentina*, Decision on Liability, para. 262; *Burlington Resources v. Republic of Ecuador*, Decision on Jurisdiction, para. 104; *Noble Ventures v. Romania*, Award, paras. 50, 55.

[53] Weeramantry, *Treaty Interpretation in Investment Arbitration* (2012), para. 3.78.

characterised at an appropriate level of generality. Third, a treaty's object and purpose is 'a means of shedding light on the ordinary meaning' of the terms in question.[54] As such, the relevance of a treaty's 'object and purpose' in the interpretative exercise will vary with the clarity and specificity of the terms in question. Where the ordinary meaning of the terms in their context is relatively clear, the treaty's object and purpose will have less of a role to play. In contrast, for provisions drafted in vague and highly indeterminate language – for example, the FET provisions of investment treaties – the object and purpose will be more important in shedding light on the 'ordinary meaning'.[55]

There may be differences between the objects and purposes of different investment treaties. I do not attempt to provide a complete account of the object and purpose of particular investment treaties or to develop a full theory of treaty interpretation that defines the relative weight of the 'object and purpose' in the interpretative exercise compared to other relevant factors, such as the 'context'. My aim is more modest – to show the way in which the analysis provided in this book can and should inform the interpretative process required by Article 31(1) of the VCLT.

7.3.1.1 The characterisation of a treaty's object and purpose

Some investment treaties contain provisions that specifically identify their purpose, notably the Energy Charter Treaty (ECT).[56] However, the vast majority of investment treaties do not specifically state their purpose. In these situations, the task of characterising the treaty's object and purpose falls on the interpreter. Most commentators agree that a treaty's preamble is an important source of guidance in this process of characterisation.[57] Investment treaties often identify a range of aims and objectives in their preamble. For example, the preamble of the US-Argentina BIT includes the following recitals:

Recognizing that agreement upon the treatment to be accorded such investment will stimulate the flow of private capital and the economic development of the Parties;

---

[54] Gardiner, *Treaty Interpretation*, p. 190.
[55] Ortino, 'The Investment Treaty System as Judicial Review: Some Remarks on Its Nature, Scope and Standards' (2012), p. 3.
[56] ECT, art. 2.
[57] E.g., Fitzmaurice, 'The Law and Procedure of the International Court of Justice 1951–54: Treaty Interpretation and Other Treaty Points' (1957) 33 *British Yearbook of International Law*, p. 228; *Aguas del Tunari* v. *Bolivia*, Award on Jurisdiction, para. 241.

Agreeing that fair and equitable treatment of investment is desirable in order to maintain stable framework for investment and maximum effective use of economic resources.[58]

In light of these recitals, questions arise as to how a tribunal should characterise the treaty's object and purpose. The analysis contained in this book, which clarifies the normative underpinnings of existing debate about investment treaties, is relevant to this process of characterisation in several ways. It suffices to point out two of these, using the US-Argentina BIT as an example.

First, the analysis contained in this book suggests that it would be unlikely for states to conclude a treaty for the purpose of attracting FDI per se. Section 3.6.1 considered the reasons why states may wish to promote the flow of private capital and concluded that additional FDI has no normative value in itself. The argument implies that attracting FDI should be understood as a means of achieving economic benefits. On this basis, the promotion of FDI should *not* be characterised as an element of the 'object and purpose' of the US-Argentina BIT but rather as a means to achieve economic development, which is an element of the treaty's object and purpose.[59]

Second, there is the question of whether 'maintaining a stable legal framework' should be characterised as an element of the treaty's overall object and purpose. The significance of this preambular text – which is unique to US BITs dating from the 1980s and 1990s – has been controversial in practice. On the basis of this recital, some tribunals seem to have concluded that stability is the over-riding object and purpose of the US-Argentina BIT. For example, the tribunal in *CMS Gas* v. *Argentina* referred to this *purpose* as the justification for interpreting the FET standard as entailing a substantive *obligation* to maintain a stable legal framework.[60] Other tribunals have rejected the view that the maintenance of a stable legal framework is an element of the treaty's object and purpose. For example, the tribunal in *Continental Casualty* v. *Argentina*, concluded that it was merely 'a precondition for one of the two basic objects of the treaty, namely the promotion of the investment flow.'[61] The analysis in this book supports a third view, which differs from both of these. Consistently with the view expressed in *Continental Casualty* v. *Argentina*, the maintenance

---

[58] US-Argentina BIT (14 November 1991).
[59] van Aaken has made a similar argument: van Aaken, 'Opportunities for and Limits to an Economic Analysis of International Law' (2011) 3 *Transnational Corporations Review*, p. 38.
[60] *CMS Gas* v. *Argentina*, Final Award, para. 274.
[61] *Continental Casualty* v. *Argentina*, Award, para. 258.

of a stable legal framework could be a means of achieving the treaty's economic objectives, but only to the limited extent articulated in Section 3.4.5. In addition (and contrary to the view expressed in *Continental Casualty v. Argentina*) the maintenance of a stable legal framework could be among the objects of the treaty itself, as a component of the rule of law. However, insofar as it is an element of the treaty's object and purpose, the objective of 'maintaining a stable legal framework' should be understood in a particular sense – namely, preventing repeated or erratic changes to national law, as opposed to preventing changes to national laws that are to foreign investors' detriment.[62]

The analysis in this book is particularly important to doctrinal debates about the characterisation of investment treaties' 'object and purpose' because the reasoning of existing arbitral awards on point is often impressionistic and lacking in justification. In an empirical study of the interpretation of investment treaties, Fauchald found that arbitral tribunals regularly referred to a treaty's object and purpose in the course of their reasoning. However, among such decisions, 'a clear majority of decisions ... did not refer to any source for their statements concerning the object and purpose.'[63] For example, in *Sempra v. Argentina*, the tribunal ignored references to economic objectives in the preamble to the US-Argentina BIT and, without explaining its reasoning, concluded that 'object and purpose' of the BIT included ensuring the 'stability of the law', 'the observance of legal obligations' and an unspecified conception of 'justice'.[64] Only the first of these three objectives could plausibly have been derived from terms and preamble of the BIT itself; it is not possible to discern why the tribunal regarded the latter objectives as forming part of the treaty's object and purpose. The analysis in this book can contribute to a more satisfactory approach.

7.3.1.2 The relevance of the analysis in determining whether plausible interpretations advance a treaty's object and purpose

When faced with competing plausible interpretations of the terms of an investment treaty, the VCLT requires an arbitral tribunal to consider the extent to which these interpretations accord with the treaty's object and purpose. In other words, the VCLT requires a tribunal to consider

---

[62] See, Raz, 'The Rule of Law and Its Virtue' (1977) 93 *The Law Quarterly Review*, p. 199.
[63] Fauchald, 'The Legal Reasoning of ICSID Tribunals: An Empirical Analysis' (2008) 19 *European Journal of International Law*, p. 322.
[64] *Sempra Energy v. Argentina*, Award, para. 300.

the consequences of adopting various interpretations, with these consequences evaluated through the lens of the treaty's 'object and purpose'.[65]
(To be the clear, the question under Article 31 is whether a given interpretation of the treaty text will realise the treaty's object and purpose. In
other words, consistent with the analysis in the book, Article 31 requires
the consequentialist inquiry to examine alternative *legal rules*, as defined
through the process of interpretation. Questions relating to the consequences of resolving a particular dispute in favour of the investor or in
favour of the host state do not arise as such.) In their preambles, the vast
majority investment treaties refer, among other objectives, to the goal of
promoting mutual economic prosperity or economic development.[66] The
consequentialist analysis presented in this book is directly relevant to the
question of whether various plausible interpretations of an investment
treaty advance these objectives.

Some commentators have cautioned against using arguments about
a treaty's purpose to justify a decision to ignore or override the terms of the
treaty in question.[67] Strictly speaking, this is correct – under the VCLT,
the inquiry is ultimately directed towards ascertaining the meaning of the
treaty text. However, this stricture imposes less of a constraint on the use
of consequentialist arguments in treaty interpretation than might first
appear. Language is inherently ambiguous and imprecise, so the text of a
treaty can never fully define its own meaning.[68] Moreover, the text of the
substantive protections of investment treaties is unusually vague. A close
examination of the ordinary meaning of the words 'fair' and 'equitable'
sheds little light on the question of whether a legitimate expectation
(a principle which, itself, lacks any textual basis) can be based on an
ambiguous unilateral representation made by a host state.[69] In practice,

---

[65] Cf. Sinclair, *The Vienna Convention on the Law of Treaties*, p. 121, arguing that the
consideration of consequences of a given interpretation is, in any case, inherent in the
concept of 'ordinary meaning'.

[66] References to the objectives of 'economic development', 'prosperity' or similar appear
in the preambles of US, Canadian, French, German, Dutch, Chinese, Australian and UK
investment treaties, among others.

[67] Gardiner, *Treaty Interpretation*, p. 190.

[68] Hart, *The Concept of Law* (2nd edn, 1994), p. 126; Kolb, *Interprétation et création du droit
international: Esquisses d'une herméneutique juridique moderne pour le droit international public*
(2006), p. 457.

[69] Similarly, Lowe, 'The Politics of Law-Making: Are the Method and Character of Norm
Creation Changing?' in Byers (ed), *The Role of Law in International Politics: Essays in
International Relations and International Law* (2000), p. 221, arguing that 'non-legal' factors
are more likely to be relevant when the primary legal norms in question do not dictate
clear solutions.

arbitral tribunals have been regularly justified their interpretations of investment treaties' substantive protections on the grounds that they advance the treaty's object and purpose.[70]

Finally, I address some potential objections to the use of consequentialist arguments in the interpretation of treaties. Douglas has argued against interpreting investment treaties in light of their policy goals, even if such objectives are reflected in a treaty's preamble. He suggests that investment treaties often identify several competing objectives and that arbitral tribunals are not in a position to assess whether particular interpretations of an investment treaty provision are likely to achieve such objectives.[71] Five observations can be made by way of response to this claim. First, it is not clear that the objects and purposes identified through an analysis of investment treaties' preambles are as elusive as Douglas implies. On the contrary, many treaties envisage a chain of causation in which the protection of foreign investment is a means to increasing foreign investment for the purpose of creating economic benefits.[72] Second, insofar as investment treaties do identify multiple objectives, the analysis in this book has shown that these objectives – for example, economic benefits and the promotion of the rule of law – are not necessarily in tension. Third, basic forms of consequentialist reasoning do not seem to be beyond the capabilities of tribunals. Causal models like the hold-up model are relatively easy to grasp and clear in their implications. Arbitral tribunals already rely on causal arguments and assumptions when interpreting investment treaties.[73] Fourth, given the vague terms in which investment treaties are drafted, it is not clear that alternative interpretative methods that exclude consequentialist argument entirely are particularly attractive. Douglas suggests that tribunals should instead draw on 'principles' from beyond the treaty in question. But the difficulty with existing arbitral jurisprudence is not that it is unprincipled; it is that tribunals disagree about which principles should control – for example, whether substantive review should be guided by the principle of reasonableness or proportionality – and on how agreed principles should be understood – for example, the level of protection implied by the principle of legitimate expectations.[74] Discouraging the use of well-founded

---

[70] E.g., *MTD* v. *Chile*, Award, para. 113.
[71] Douglas, *The International Law of Investment Claims*, para. 146.
[72] van Aaken, 'Opportunities for and Limits to an Economic Analysis of International Law', p. 38.
[73] E.g., *MTD* v. *Chile*, Award, para. 113.
[74] Douglas, *The International Law of Investment Claims*, para. 148.

consequentialist arguments is more likely to cause tribunals to fall back on unexamined assumptions. Fifth and finally, given the express terms of the VCLT, it is not clear that the option of ignoring a treaty's object and purpose is a choice that is open to an arbitral tribunal in any event.

7.3.2 The influence of 'extra-legal' factors on interpretation in practice

In practice, arbitral tribunals rely on a range of normative and causal assumptions when interpreting the substantive protections of investment treaties. In this section, I advance a theory of interpretation based on the 'soft positivism' of Hart and Kelsen, which suggests that this practice is, to some extent, both inevitable and justifiable. I then review some of the ways in which 'extra-legal' factors influence the interpretation of investment treaties. I argue that the analysis in this book can contribute to a more informed and better reasoned jurisprudence.

7.3.2.1 Treaty interpretation inevitably involves 'policy' choices

Hart and Kelsen are among the most important figures in twentieth-century jurisprudence. Both propose positivist theories of law in which the validity of individual legal rules depends on the validity of higher-order rules that govern rule creation.[75] Although there are some differences between their overarching jurisprudential theories (particularly in relation to the nature of the ultimate foundation on which this hierarchical conception of legal validity depends),[76] both offer similar accounts of the interpretation of legal rules. For present purposes, there are two important propositions common to their theories of interpretation.

The first is that the meaning of legal rules, such as investment treaty protections, is inherently indeterminate to some extent.[77] Their theories do not suggest that legal rules are radically indeterminate – 'not every rule is open to doubt on all points'.[78] Rather, their theories posit a degree of indeterminacy – a range of situations in which the rule in question will not provide a single answer 'which is clearly right or wrong.'[79] In such cases, interpretation of a rule involves a *choice* between competing plausible interpretations by the person or institution exercising interpretative authority.[80] The second proposition common to the theories of both is that, in making interpretative choices, interpreters necessarily rely on

---

[75] Kelsen, 'On the Theory of Interpretation' (1990) 10 *Legal Studies*, p. 127; Hart, *The Concept of Law*, pp. 100–10.
[76] Hart, *The Concept of Law*, p. 246.   [77] Kelsen, 'On the Theory of Interpretation', p. 128.
[78] Hart, *The Concept of Law*, p. 150.   [79] Ibid., p. 150.   [80] Ibid., p. 150.

'extra-legal' or 'policy' considerations.[81] This follows from the proposition that sources and principles internal to a legal system do not fully determine the meaning of legal rules.

Other scholars and practitioners of international investment law have proposed similar theories of interpretation. For example, invoking Kelsen, Stern has argued:

When arbitrating a case, an arbitrator has to make political choices even if... the question submitted to his or her judgment is not a political question.[82]

To be sure, Hart and Kelsen's theories do not imply that arbitral tribunals should abandon the interpretative methodology required by Article 31 VCLT. Rather, they imply that the proper application of this interpretative methodology will not always lead to 'one right answer'.[83] *Within* the interpretative methodology required by Article 31, choices between plausible, alternative interpretations will sometimes be required. In making such choices, one of the factors a tribunal should consider is the extent to which the various interpretations under consideration are likely to produce desirable consequences.[84] By contributing to our understanding of the consequences of investment treaty protections, this book offers a basis for more informed interpretative choices.

7.3.2.2 The role of normative and causal assumptions in investment treaty interpretation in practice

In practice, 'extra-legal' normative and causal assumptions frequently influence arbitral tribunals' interpretation of investment treaties. This influence can be seen both in the reasoning of individual decisions and in the evolving patterns of investment treaty jurisprudence. I begin by providing some examples of the former. This discussion is not intended to be exhaustive; documenting the extent to which various normative and causal assumptions influence the way that tribunals interpret investment treaties could be the subject of an entire monograph of its own.

One of the most obvious ways in which unarticulated assumptions enter the interpretative exercise is through arguments that a given interpretation of a treaty provision would lead to an undesirably high or

---

[81] Kelsen, *Introduction to the Problems of Legal Theory* (1992), p. 463.

[82] Stern, 'Are Some Issues Too Political to Be Arbitrable?' (2009) 24 *ICSID Review – Foreign Investment Law Journal*, p. 93.

[83] Cf. Dworkin, *Taking Rights Seriously* (2013), p. 336.

[84] Lowe, 'The Politics of Law-Making: Are the Method and Character of Norm Creation Changing?' in Byers (ed), *The Role of Law in International Politics: Essays in International Relations and International Law* (Oxford University Press 2000), p. 216.

undesirably low level of protection. For example, in *Vivendi* v. *Argentina (II)*, the respondent argued that the FET standard should be interpreted as co-extensive with the doctrine of denial of justice. The tribunal rejected this argument on the grounds that it would

eviscerate the fair and equitable treatment standard. Although the standard is commonly understood to include a prohibition on denial of justice, it would be significantly diminished if it were limited to claims for denial of justice.[85]

In contrast, in *Paushok* v. *Mongolia*, the claimant argued that the FET standard required the tribunal to review the substantive justifications for tax legislation passed by the Mongolian Parliament. In concluding that liability under the FET standard did not arise from the implementation of poorly designed measures, the tribunal argued:

[T]he fact that a democratically elected legislature has passed legislation that may be considered as ill-conceived, counter-productive and excessively burdensome does not automatically allow to conclude that a breach of an investment treaty has occurred. If such were the case, the number of investment treaty claims would increase by a very large number.[86]

Without taking a view on the correctness of either decision, it is clear that the arguments of both tribunals depend on unarticulated assumptions about the appropriate level of protection that investment treaties should provide. The argument that a given interpretation would 'significantly diminish' the level of protection provided by an investment treaty is meaningless unless it is based on an underlying assumption of this sort. Similarly, arguments that adopting a given interpretation would dramatically increase the number of investment treaty claims depend on underlying assumptions about the appropriate number of claims that a substantive protection should allow.

Unarticulated assumptions enter tribunals' reasoning in other ways. For example, in *EDF* v. *Argentina*, the tribunal held that a state's decision to abrogate express contractual commitments made to a foreign investor was inherently unfair and, therefore, in breach of the FET standard:

Even if such specific commitments might be temporarily suspended during a state of emergency, fairness requires the host state to repair the economic balance within a reasonable time after the state of emergency has ended.[87]

---

[85] *Compañia de Aguas del Aconquija and Vivendi* v. *Argentina (II)*, Award, para. 7.4.11.
[86] *Sergei Paushok* v. *Mongolia*, Award on Jurisdiction and Liability, para. 299.
[87] *EDF* v. *Argentina*, Award, para. 1002.

However, this argument relies on a particular conception of fairness – one that links fairness to the observance of promises – which the tribunal neither explains nor justifies. Relying on other conceptions of fairness might have led the tribunal to quite different conclusions. For example, perhaps the most influential political philosopher of the twentieth century, John Rawls, has proposed a theory of 'justice as fairness'. Unlike the tribunal's reasoning, Rawls' conception of fairness is based on egalitarian norms.[88]

A further example can be found in arbitral awards that adopt the politics-as-irrationality approach to the substantive element of the FET standard. None of the decisions adopting this approach explain why government conduct that is politically motivated is incompatible with the requirement that government conduct bear 'a reasonable relationship to some rational policy'.[89] Presumably, the argument relies on both normative assumptions about the appropriate role of 'politics' in public decision-making and causal assumptions about the impact of 'politics' on the making of effective public policy.

Empirical and causal assumptions also play an important role in arbitral reasoning. For example, in the interpretation of the jurisdictional provisions of NAFTA, the *Gallo* v. *Canada* tribunal stated that

[f]oreigners are more exposed than domestic investors to the sovereign risk attached to the investment and to arbitrary actions of the host State, and may thus, as a matter of legitimate policy, be granted a wider scope of protection.[90]

This is an assumption for which there is little evidence.[91] The tribunal in *Tecmed* v. *Mexico* justified its famously expansive interpretation on the FET standard partly on the grounds that it was necessary for 'maximizing the use of the economic resources of each Contracting Party by facilitating the economic contributions of their economic operators.'[92] In doing so, it assumed that higher levels of protection are associated with more efficient use of economic resources. I have shown that this assumption does not withstand scrutiny.[93]

The foregoing examples illustrate some of the ways that 'extra-legal' factors enter into arbitral reasoning in individual decisions. The influence of extra-legal factors on the interpretation of investment treaties is also evident in trends in arbitral jurisprudence as whole. Both critics and supporters of investment treaties have observed that the

---

[88] Rawls, *Justice as Fairness: A Restatement* (2001); see Section 3.5.6.
[89] *Biwater* v. *Tanzania*, Award, para. 693.   [90] *Gallo* v. *Canada*, Award, para. 335.
[91] See Section 3.2.2.   [92] *Tecmed* v. *Mexico*, Award, para. 156.   [93] See Section 3.4.

system of investment treaty arbitration exhibits a degree of 'reflexivity', with arbitral jurisprudence responding both to academic commentary and state practice.[94] This is unsurprising. Many arbitrators also perform a range of other roles within the investment treaty system – notably, as counsel for parties to investment treaty disputes and as academics that study investment treaties.[95] In these roles, they are likely to be exposed to ongoing debates about the objectives and impacts of investment treaties. In this way, academic and policy debates influence the set of concepts and assumptions that arbitrators bring to their interpretative and adjudicative tasks.[96]

The fact that the interpretation of the substantive protections of investment treaties is influenced by 'extra-legal' factors is not, in itself, a problem. On the contrary, the interpretative theories of Hart and Kelsen suggest that 'policy' considerations – assumptions about the objectives investment treaties are designed to achieve and the extent to which various possible interpretations of the treaty text would achieve these objectives – have a legitimate role to play in the interpretative process. The problem is that such assumptions are often left unarticulated. While these assumptions remain implicit, they can escape reflection and scrutiny. As a result, the way that some tribunals have interpreted investment treaties' substantive protections is based on assumptions for which there is little theoretical or evidentiary justification.[97]

Rather than seeking to exclude 'extra-legal' factors from influencing the interpretation of investment treaties, my view is that arbitrators' background assumptions should be acknowledged and debated more openly. In the words of Hart:

Judges should not seek to bootleg silently into the law their own conceptions of the law's aims or justice or social policy or other extra-legal element required for decision but should openly identify and discuss them.[98]

---

[94] Schneiderman, 'Legitimacy and Reflexivity in International Investment Arbitration: A New Self-Restraint?' (2011) 2 *Journal of International Dispute Settlement*, p. 494; Roberts, 'Power and Persuasion in Investment Treaty Interpretation' p. 198; Brower CH, 'Corporations as Plaintiffs under International Law: Three Narratives about Investment Treaties' (2009) 9 *Santa Clara Journal of International Law*, p. 211.

[95] The multiple roles of the most regularly appointed arbitrators are documented in Corporate Observatory Europe and the Transnational Institute, *Profiting from Injustice*, pp. 35–50. However, I do not intend to endorse the argument, made in *Profiting from Injustice*, that this practice is necessarily improper.

[96] Similarly, Lowe, 'The Politics of Law-Making', p. 221.

[97] E.g., *Tecmed* v. *Mexico*, Award, para. 156.

[98] Hart, 'American Jurisprudence through English Eyes: The Nightmare and the Noble Dream' (1977) 11 *Georgia Law Review*, p. 978.

The analysis provided in this book affords a basis for a more informed debate about the policy objectives to which investment treaties are directed and for a more rigorous assessment of the extent to which particular interpretations of investment treaties' substantive protections are likely to achieve these objectives.

7.4 Conclusion

The analysis presented in the first six chapters of this book has important implications for states and practitioners. In Section 7.2, I argued that states should consider revising their drafting practice for future investment treaties and clarifying the level of protection provided by existing investment treaties. In particular, states should reconsider the way in which they draft the substantive protections of new investment treaties and consider amending the substantive protections of existing investment treaties, in order to clarify more precisely the level of protection that they provide.

Section 7.3 examined the implications of the analysis for the interpretation of investment treaties as they are currently drafted. Section 7.3.1 showed that the analysis is relevant to the interpretation of investment treaties, even on a strictly formalist application of Article 31 of the VCLT. Relying on the jurisprudential theories of Hart and Kelsen, Section 7.3.2 argued that the interpretation of investment treaties inevitably requires consideration of 'policy' factors. Consistent with these jurisprudential theories, normative and causal assumptions play an important role in existing arbitral jurisprudence. However, the particular assumptions on which existing jurisprudence is based are not always well-founded. The analysis in this book can contribute to a more informed and better reasoned jurisprudence on the interpretation of the substantive protections of investment treaties.

8　The future of debate about investment treaties

Investment treaties grant a range of generous substantive rights to foreign investors. In particular, they normally grant foreign investors the right to be treated 'fairly and equitably' and the right to be compensated for the expropriation of their investments. However, arbitral tribunals have disagreed about the level of protection that such provisions confer on foreign investment. In Chapters 4 and 5, I identified a range of different interpretations of investment treaties' FET and indirect expropriation provisions. In Chapter 6, I evaluated the level of protection implied by each of these interpretations. This evaluation was nuanced, but it led to some clear conclusions. I argued that there were strong grounds for preferring the level of protection articulated by some tribunals to the level of protection articulated by others. Chapter 7 explored the implications of these conclusions for states, in the drafting and amendment of investment treaties, and for arbitral tribunals, in the interpretation of existing investment treaties.

In addition to these practical conclusions, this book makes a number of contributions to wider academic debates about investment treaties. In Chapter 2, I showed that disagreement about the level of protection that investment treaties should provide seldom stems from fundamental disagreement about which objectives are desirable. Rather, disagreement stems primarily from embedded causal assumptions about the likely consequences of differing levels of protection and, to a lesser extent, disagreement about how competing objectives should be prioritised. This is an important insight. It implies that scholarship about investment treaties should pay greater attention to articulating underlying causal assumptions, examining whether they are theoretically coherent and testing them against available evidence. In other words, consequentialist reasoning should play a greater role in academic debate.

The framework developed in Chapter 3 provides a structure for conceptualising, identifying and evaluating the consequences of providing differing levels of protection in investment treaties. Within this structure, I offered a detailed assessment of explanatory theory and empirical evidence relating to the consequences of investment treaty protections. The analysis contained in Chapter 3 constitutes an informed basis for predicting the likely consequences of adopting various levels of protection and for determining the extent to which different objectives are in tension with one another. On this basis, I conclude that the 'economic' objectives of investment treaties – efficiency and the attraction of FDI – are not necessarily in tension with 'non-economic' objectives, such as the realisation of human rights. This conclusion calls into question the premise on which much existing debate about investment treaties is based.

In this book, I applied the framework developed in Chapter 3 to evaluate differing levels of protection implied by competing interpretations of investment treaty protections. However, the framework has a much wider range of potential application. It could be used by policy-makers to evaluate a range of differing levels of protection that are not considered here, including the abandonment of existing substantive protections, the invention of entirely new provisions and the greater use of exceptions clauses. It also offers a point of departure for policy-makers considering the desirability of other features of investment treaties – for example, the extent to which they grant foreign investors procedural rights to bring claims directly to investor-state arbitration.

We are still in the early stages of understanding investment treaties. Over time, new evidence will continue to emerge about the consequences of investment treaties and the substantive protections that they provide. The analysis of theory and evidence in Chapter 3 will need to be updated as new evidence comes to light. But the framework will continue to provide a useful structure within which to assess and evaluate such evidence. In this way, the framework can bring greater rigour and clarity to ongoing debate about investment treaties.

Bibliography

Abs H and Shawcross H, 'Draft Convention on Investments Abroad, April 1959' (1960) 9 *Journal of Public Law* 116

Advisory Committee on International Economic Policy, 'Report of the Advisory Committee on International Economic Policy Regarding the Model Bilateral Investment Treaty' (2009), www.uschamber.com/sites/default/files/grc/ BITReviewReportandAnnexFinalVersion.pdf. Accessed 30 January 2012

Ahlborn C and Berg C, 'Can State Aid Control Learn from Antitrust? The Need for a Greater Role for Competition Analysis under State Aid Rules' in Biondi A, Eeckhout P and Flynn J (eds), *The Law of State Aid in the European Union* (Oxford University Press 2004)

Aisbett E, 'Bilateral Investment Treaties and Foreign Direct Investment: Correlation versus Causation' in Sauvant K and Sachs L (eds), *The Effect of Treaties on Foreign Direct Investment: Bilateral Investment Treaties, Double Taxation Treaties and Investment Flows* (Oxford University Press 2009)

'ISDS through the Lens of Welfare Economics', conference paper presented at 21st Investment Treaty Forum Public Meeting: The Economic and Financial Aspects of Investor-State Arbitration, British Institute of International and Comparative Law, 24 October 2013

Aisbett E, Karp L and McAusland C, 'Compensation for Regulatory Taking in International Investment Agreements: Implications of National Treatment and Rights to Invest' (2010) 1 *Journal of Globalization and Development* 1

'Police Powers, Regulatory Taking and the Efficient Compensation of Domestic and Foreign Investors' (2010) 86 *The Economic Record* 367

Aisbett E and McAusland C, 'Firm Characteristics and Influence on Government Rule-Making: Theory and Evidence' (2013) 29 *European Journal of Political Economy* 214

Alvarez J, 'Critical Theory and the North American Free Trade Agreements Chapter Eleven' (1997) 28 *University of Miami Inter-American Law Review* 303

'Review: *Investment Treaty Arbitration and Public Law* by Gus van Harten' (2008) 102 *American Journal of International Law* 909

'The Once and Future Foreign Investment Regime' in Arsanjani M et al. (eds), *Looking to the Future: Essays in Honor of Michael Reisman* (Martinus Nijhoff 2010)

Alvarez J and Khamsi K, 'The Argentine Crisis and Foreign Investors' in Sauvant K (ed), *Yearbook on International Investment Law and Policy 2008–2009* (Oxford University Press 2009)

American Law Institute, *Restatement of the Law Third – The Foreign Relations Law of the United States*, Volume 2 (American Law Institute Publishers 1987)

Anderson S and Grusky S, 'Challenging Corporate Investor Rule' (2007), www.ipsdc.org/reports/070430-challengingcorporateinvestorrule.pdf. Accessed 30 January 2012

Appleton B, 'Regulatory Takings: The International Law Perspective' (2002) 11 *New York University Environmental Law Journal* 35

Arai-Takahashi Y, *The Margin of Appreciation Doctrine and the Principle of Proportionality* (Intersentia Uitgevers 2002)

Aranguri C, 'The Effect of BITs on Regulatory Quality and the Rule of Law in Developing Countries' (2010), www.iilj.org/research/documents/IF2010-11. Aranguri.1.pdf. Accessed 20 April 2011

Atik J, 'Repenser NAFTA Chapter 11: A Catalogue of Legitimacy Critiques' (2003) 3 *Asper Review of International Business and Trade Law* 215

Aust A, *Modern Treaty Law and Practice* (Cambridge University Press 2000)

Australian Government, 'OBPR Guidance Note – Best-Practice Regulation' (2013), www.finance.gov.au/obpr/docs/CBA_guidance_note.pdf. Accessed 24 October 2013

Bachand R and Rousseau S, 'International Investment and Human Rights: Political and Legal Issues' (2003), www.ichrdd.ca/site/_PDF/publications/globalization/bachandRousseauEng.pdf. Accessed 10 June 2010

Bagwell K and Staiger R, 'An Economic Theory of GATT' (1999) 89 *The American Economic Review* 215

Banga R, 'Impact of Government Policies and Investment Agreements on FDI Inflows', (2003), www.icrier.org/pdf/WP116.PDF. Accessed 5 May 2010

BBC, 'Government Rejects Labour's "Cigarette U-Turn" Claim' (2013), www.bbc.co.uk/news/health-23281804. Accessed 26 October 2013

Beauvais J, 'Regulatory Expropriations under NAFTA: Emerging Principles and Lingering Doubts' (2002) 10 *New York University Environmental Law Journal* 245

Been V and Beauvais J, 'The Global Fifth Amendment? NAFTA's Investment Protections and the Misguided Quest for an International "Regulatory Takings" Doctrine' (2003) 78 *New York University Law Review* 30

Berger A, Busse M, Nunnenkamp P and Roy M, 'More Stringent BITs, Less Ambiguous Effects on FDI? Not a Bit!' (2011) 112 *Economics Letters* 227

Bernasconi-Osterwalder N and Hoffmann R, 'The German Nuclear Phase-Out Put to the Test in International Investment Arbitration? Background to the New Dispute Vattenfall v Germany (II)' (2012), www.iisd.org/pdf/2012/german_nuclear_phase_out.pdf. Accessed 27 October 2013

Bingham T, *The Rule of Law* (Allen Lane 2010)

Bishop D, 'Toward a More Flexible Approach to the International Legal Consequences of Corruption' (2010) 25 *ICSID Review* 63

Bjorklund A, 'Investment Treaty Arbitral Decisions as Jurisprudence Constante' in Picker C, Bunn I and Arner D (eds), *International Economic Law: The State and Future of the Discipline* (Hart Publishing 2008)

Blackwood E and McBride S, 'Investment as the Achilles Heel of Globalisation?: The Ongoing Conflict between the Rights of Capital and the Rights of States' (2006) 25 *Policy and Society* 43

Blaug M, *The Methodology of Economics or How Economists Explain* (Cambridge University Press 1992)

Blume L and Rubinfeld D, 'Compensation for Takings: An Economic Analysis' (1984) 72 *California Law Review* 569

Blume L, Rubinfeld D and Shapiro P, 'The Taking of Land: When Should Compensation Be Paid?' (1984) 99 *The Quarterly Journal of Economics* 71

Bonilla S and Castro R, 'A Law-and-Economics Analysis of International Investment Agreements: Latin America' (2006), http://papers.ssrn.com/sol3/Papers.cfm?abstract_id=1007684. Accessed 24 June 2010

Bonnitcha J and Aisbett E, 'An Economic Analysis of the Substantive Protections Provided by Investment Treaties' in Sauvant K (ed), *Yearbook on International Investment Law & Policy 2011–2012* (Oxford University Press 2013)

Booth C and Squires D, *The Negligence Liability of Public Authorities* (Oxford University Press 2006)

Brower CH, 'Structure, Legitimacy, and NAFTA's Investment Chapter' (2003) 36 *Vanderbilt Journal of Transnational Law* 37
'NAFTA's Investment Chapter: Initial Thoughts about Second-Generation Rights' (2003) 36 *Vanderbilt Journal of Transnational Law* 1533
'Why the FTC Notes of Interpretation Constitute a Partial Amendment of NAFTA Article 1105' (2006) 46 *Virginia Journal of International Law* 347
'Corporations as Plaintiffs under International Law: Three Narratives about Investment Treaties' (2009) 9 *Santa Clara Journal of International Law* 179
'Obstacles and Pathways to Consideration of the Public Interest in Investment Treaty Disputes' in Sauvant K (ed), *Yearbook on International Investment Law & Policy* (Oxford University Press 2009)

Brower CN, Ottolenghi M and Prows P, 'The Saga of CMS: Res Judicata, Precedent, and the Legitimacy of ICSID Arbitration' in Binder C et al. (eds), *International Investment Law for the 21st Century* (Oxford University Press 2009)

Brower CN and Schill S, 'Is Arbitration a Threat or a Boon to the Legitimacy of International Investment Law?' (2009) 50 *Chicago Journal of International Law* 471

Brower CN and Steven L, 'Who Then Should Judge?: Developing the International Rule of Law under NAFTA Chapter 11' (2001) 2 *Chicago Journal of International Law* 193

Bubb R and Rose-Ackerman S, 'BITs and Bargains: Strategic Aspects of Bilateral and Multilateral Regulation of Foreign Investment' (2007) 27 *International Review of Law and Economics* 291

Burke-White W and von Staden A, 'Private Litigation in a Public Sphere: The Standard of Review in Investor-State Arbitrations' (2010) 35 *Yale Journal of International Law* 283

Burns JH, 'Happiness and Utility: Jeremy Bentham's Equation' (2005) 17 *Utilitas* 46

Busse M, Königer J and Nunnenkamp P, 'FDI Promotion through Bilateral Investment Treaties: More Than a Bit?' (2010) 146 *Review of World Economics* 147

Buthe T and Milner HV, 'Bilateral Investment Treaties and Foreign Direct Investment: A Political Analysis' in Sauvant K and Sachs L (eds), *The Effect of Treaties on Foreign Direct Investment: Bilateral Investment Treaties, Double Taxation Treaties and Investment Flows* (Oxford University Press 2009)

Calabresi G, *The Costs of Accidents: A Legal and Economic Analysis* (Yale University Press 1970)

'The Pointlessness of Pareto' (1991) 100 *Yale Law Journal* 1211

Calabresi G and Klevorick A, 'Four Tests for Liability in Torts' (1985) 14 *Journal of Legal Studies* 585

Calabresi G and Melamed AD, 'Property Rules, Liability Rules, and Inalienability: One View of the Cathedral' (1972) 85 *Harvard Law Review* 1089

Caruso D, 'Private Law and State-Making in the Age of Globalization' (2006) 39 *New York University Journal of International Law and Politics* 1

Cheng B, *General Principles of Law as Applied by International Courts and Tribunals* (Grotius Publications 1987)

Cheng T-H, 'Power, Authority and International Investment Law' (2005) 20 *American University International Law Review* 465

Choi W-M, 'The Present and Future of the Investor-State Dispute Settlement Paradigm' (2007) 10 *Journal of International Economic Law* 725

Choudhury B, 'Defining Fair and Equitable Treatment in International Investment Law' (2005) 6 *The Journal of World Investment and Trade* 297

'Recapturing Public Power: Is Investment Arbitration's Engagement of the Public Interest Contributing to the Democratic Deficit?' (2008) 41 *Vanderbilt Journal of Transnational Law* 775

Chung O, 'The Lopsided International Investment Law Regime and Its Effect on the Future of Investor-State Arbitration' (2007) 47 *Virginia Journal of International Law* 953

Claussen K, 'The Casualty of Investor Protection in Times of Economic Crisis' (2009) 118 *Yale Law Journal* 1545

Coase R, 'The Problem of Social Cost' (1960) 3 *Journal of Law and Economics* 1

'Nobel Prize Lecture' (1991), http://nobelprize.org/nobel_prizes/economics/laureates/1991/coase-lecture.html. Accessed 25 April 2011

Coe J and Rubins N, 'Regulatory Expropriation and the *Tecmed* Case: Context and Contributions' in Weiler T (ed), *International Investment Law and Arbitration: Leading Cases from the ICSID, NAFTA, Bilateral Treaties and Customary International Law* (Cameron May 2005)

Cohen GA, *Rescuing Justice and Equality* (Harvard University Press 2008)

Coleman J, *Risks and Wrongs* (Oxford University Press 1992)

Colen L and Guariso A, 'What Type of FDI Is Attracted by BITs', in de Schutter O, Swinnen J and Wouters J (eds), *Foreign Direct Investment and Human Development: The Law and Economics of International Investment Agreements* (Routledge 2013)

Colen L, Maertens M and Swinnen J, 'Foreign Direct Investment as an Engine of Economic Growth and Human Development', in de Schutter O, Swinnen J and Wouters J (eds), *Foreign Direct Investment and Human Development: The Law and Economics of International Investment Agreements* (Routledge 2013)

Collier P and Goderis B, 'Commodity Prices, Growth, and the Natural Resources Curse: Reconciling a Conundrum' (2007), http://economics.ouls.ox.ac.uk/13218/1/2007-15text.pdf. Accessed 5 December 2011

Commission J, 'Precedent in Investment Treaty Arbitration: A Citation Analysis of Developing Jurisprudence' (2007) 24 *Journal of International Arbitration* 129

Condorelli L, 'Custom' in Bedjaoui M (ed), *International Law: Achievements and Prospects* (Martinus Nijhoff 1991)

Cooter R, 'Unity in Tort, Contract and Property: The Model of Precaution' (1985) 73 *California Law Review* 1

Cooter R, Marks S and Mnookin R 'Bargaining in the Shadow of Law: A Testable Model of Strategic Behavior' (1982) 11 *Journal of Legal Studies* 225

Cooter R and Ulen T, *Law & Economics* (5th edn, Pearson Addison-Wesley 2008)

Cordonier Segger M-C and Kent A, 'Promoting Sustainable Investment through International Law' in Cordonier Segger M-C, Gehring M and Newcombe A (eds), *Sustainable Development in World Investment Law* (Kluwer Law International 2011)

Cordonier Segger M-C and Newcombe A, 'An Integrated Agenda for Sustainable Development in International Investment Law' in Cordonier Segger M-C, Gehring M and Newcombe A (eds), *Sustainable Development in World Investment Law* (Kluwer Law International 2011)

Corporate Observatory Europe and the Transnational Institute, *Profiting from Injustice,* www.tni.org/profitingfrominjustice.pdf. Accessed 17 October 2013

Coupé T, Orlova I and Skiba A, 'The Effect of Tax and Investment Treaties on Bilateral FDI Flows to Transition Economies' in Sauvant K and Sachs L (eds), *The Effect of Treaties on Foreign Direct Investment: Bilateral Investment Treaties, Double Taxation Treaties and Investment Flows* (Oxford University Press 2009)

Craig P, 'Formal and Substantive Conceptions of the Rule of Law: An Analytical Framework' (1997) Public Law 467

Crawford J, 'International Law and the Rule of Law' (2003) 24 *Adelaide Law Review* 1
'Treaty and Contract in Investment Arbitration' (2008) 24 *Arbitration International* 351
'Continuity and Discontinuity in International Dispute Settlement' in Binder C et al. (eds), *International Investment Law for the 21st Century* (Oxford University Press 2009)
Brownlie's Principles of Public International Law (8th edn, Oxford University Press 2012)

de Schutter O, Swinnen J and Wouters J, 'Foreign Direct Investment and Human Development' in de Schutter O, Swinnen J and Wouters J (eds), *Foreign Direct Investment and Human Development: The Law and Economics of International Investment Agreements* (Routledge 2013)

della Cananea G, 'Equivalent Standards under Domestic Administrative Law' in Ortino F et al. (eds), *Investment Treaty Law: Current Issues II* (British Institute of International and Comparative Law 2007)

Desbordes R and Vauday J, 'The Political Influence of Foreign Firms in Developing Countries' (2007) 19 *Economics & Politics* 421

Diehl A, *The Core Standard in International Investment Protection: Fair and Equitable Treatment* (Kluwer 2012)

Dolzer R, 'Indirect Expropriation of Alien Property' (1986) 1 *ICSID Review – Foreign Investment Law Journal* 41

'Indirect Expropriations: New Developments?' (2002) 11 *New York University Environmental Law Journal* 64

'Fair and Equitable Treatment: A Key Standard in Investment Treaties' (2005) 39 *The International Lawyer* 87

'The Impact of International Investment Treaties on Domestic Administrative Law' (2006) 37 *International Law and Politics* 952

Dolzer R and Bloch F, 'Indirect Expropriation: Conceptual Realignments?' (2003) 5 *International Law FORUM du droit international* 155

Dolzer R and Schreuer C, *Principles of International Investment Law* (Oxford University Press 2008)

Principles of International Investment Law (2nd edn, Oxford University Press 2012)

Dolzer R and von Walter A, 'Fair and Equitable Treatment – Lines of Jurisprudence on Customary Law' in Ortino F, Sheppard A and Warner H (eds), *Investment Treaty Law: Current Issues, Volume 1* (British Institute of International and Comparative Law 2006)

Douglas Z, 'The Hybrid Foundations of Investment Treaty Arbitration' (2003) 74 *British Yearbook of International Law* 151

'Nothing If Not Critical for Investment Treaty Arbitration: Occidental, Eureko and Methanex' (2006) 22 *Arbitration International* 27

The International Law of Investment Claims (Cambridge University Press 2009)

'The ICSID Regime of State Responsibility' in Crawford J, Pellet A and Olleson S (eds), *The Law of International Responsibility* (Oxford University Press 2010)

Doyle C and Van Wijnbergen S, 'Taxation of Foreign Multinationals: A Sequential Bargaining Approach to Tax Holidays' (1994) 1 *International Tax and Public Finance* 211

Dunoff J and Trachtman J, 'Economic Analysis of International Law' (1999) 24 *Yale Journal of International Law* 1

Dworkin R, 'Hard Cases' (1975) 88 *Harvard Law Review* 1057

Law's Empire (Hart 1998)

Taking Rights Seriously (Bloomsbury Academic 2013)

Dyzenhaus D, 'The Politics of Deference: Judicial Review and Democracy' in Taggart M (ed), *The Province of Administrative Law* (Hart Publishing 1997)

Eagle S, *Regulatory Takings* (Michie 1996)

Echandi R, 'What Do Developing Countries Expect from the International Investment Regime', Alvarez J, Sauvant K, Ahmed K, and Vizcaino G (eds), *The Evolving International Investment Regime* (Oxford University Press 2011)

Edley C, *Administrative Law* (Yale University Press 1990)

Egger P and Merlo V, 'The Impact of Bilateral Investment Treaties on FDI Dynamics' (2007) 30 *The World Economy* 1536

Egger P and Pfaffermayr M, 'The Impact of Bilateral Investment Treaties on Foreign Direct Investment' in Sauvant K and Sachs L (eds), *The Effect of Treaties on Foreign Direct Investment: Bilateral Investment Treaties, Double Taxation Treaties and Investment Flows* (Oxford University Press 2009)

Eisenberg T and Schwab S, 'The Reality of Constitutional Tort Litigation' (1987) 72 *Cornell Law Review* 641

Elkins Z, Guzman A and Simmons B, 'Competing for Capital: The Diffusion of Bilateral Investment Treaties, 1960–2000' (2006) 60 *International Organization* 811

Ellickson R, *Order without Law* (Harvard University Press 1991)

Ely JH, *Democracy and Distrust: A Theory of Judicial Review* (Harvard University Press 1980)

Endicott M, 'Remedies in Investor-State Arbitration: Restitution, Specific Performance and Declaratory Awards' in Kahn P and Wälde T (eds), *New Aspects of International Investment Law* (Martinus Nijhoff Publishers 2007)

Englard I, 'The System Builders: A Critical Appraisal of Modern American Tort Theory' (1980) 9 *Journal of Legal Studies* 27

Epstein R, *Takings: Private Property and the Power of Eminent Domain* (Harvard University Press 1985)

'One Step beyond Nozick's Minimal State: The Role of Forced Exchanges in Political Theory' (2005) 21 *Social Philosophy and Policy* 286

European Commission, 'Towards a Comprehensive European International Investment Policy' (2010), http://italaw.com/documents/CommissionPolicyCommunication.pdf. Accessed 30 January 2012

'Proposal for a Regulation of the European Parliament and of the Council establishing a framework for managing financial responsibility linked to investor-state dispute settlement tribunals established by international agreements to which the European Union is a party' (21 June 2012), COM(2012) 335 final, 2012/0163 (COD), http://trade.ec.europa.eu/doclib/docs/2012/june/tradoc_149567.pdf. Accessed 20 November 2013

European Parliament, 'Amendments adopted by the European Parliament on 23 May 2013 on the proposal for a regulation of the European Parliament and of the Council establishing a framework for managing financial responsibility linked to investor-state dispute settlement tribunals established by international agreements to which the European Union is party' (23 May 2013), Procedure 2012/0163(COD), P7_TA-PROV(2013)0219, www.europarl.europa.eu/sides/getDoc.do?pubRef=-//EP//TEXT+TA+P7-TA-2013-0219+0+DOC+XML+V0//EN. Accessed 20 November 2013

Farber D, 'Economic Analysis and Just Compensation' (1992) 12 *International Review of Law and Economics* 125

Fauchald O, 'The Legal Reasoning of ICSID Tribunals: An Empirical Analysis'
(2008) 19 *European Journal of International Law* 301

Fietta S, 'Expropriation and the "Fair and Equitable Treatment" Standard' in
Ortino F et al. (eds), *Investment Treaty Law: Current Issues II* (British Institute of
International and Comparative Law 2007)

Finnis J, *Natural Law and Natural Rights* (Clarendon Press 1980)
  'Natural Law and Legal Reasoning' (1990) 38 *Cleveland State Law Review* 1
  'The Truth in Legal Positivism' in George R (ed), *The Autonomy of Law* (Clarendon
  Press 1996)

Fischel W, 'Exploring the Kozinski Paradox: Why Is More Efficient Regulation a
Taking of Property?' (1991) 67 *Chicago-Kent Law Review* 865
  Regulatory Takings: Law, Economics and Politics (Harvard University Press 1995)

Fischel W and Shapiro P, 'Takings, Insurance, and Michelman: Comments on
Economic Interpretations of "Just Compensation" Law' [1988] 17 *Journal of
Legal Studies* 269

Fitzmaurice G, 'The Law and Procedure of the International Court of Justice
1951–54: Treaty Interpretation and Other Treaty Points' (1957) 33 *British
Yearbook of International Law* 203

Fortier LY and Drymer S, 'Indirect Expropriation in the Law of International
Investment: I Know It When I See It, or *Caveat Investor*' (2004) 19 *ICSID Review –
Foreign Investment Law Journal* 293

Franck S, 'The Legitimacy Crisis in Investment Treaty Arbitration: Privatizing
Public International Law through Inconsistent Decisions' (2005) 73 *Fordham
Law Review* 1521
  'Empirically Evaluating Claims about Investment Treaty Arbitration' (2007) 86
  North Carolina Law Review 1
  'Foreign Direct Investment, Investment Treaty Arbitration, and the Rule of
  Law' (2007) 19 *Global Business and Development Law Journal* 337
  'Empiricism and International Law: Insights for Investment Treaty Dispute
  Resolution' (2008) 48 *Virginia Journal of International Law* 767

Freeman A, 'Recent Aspects of the Calvo Doctrine and the Challenge to
International Law' (1946) 40 *American Journal of International Law* 121

Freidman D, *Law's Order: What Economics Has to Do with Law and Why It Matters*
(Princeton University Press 2000)

Friedman M, *Essays in Positive Economics* (University of Chicago Press 1953)

Fry J, 'International Human Rights Law in Investment Arbitration: Evidence of
International Law's Unity' (2007) 18 *Duke Journal of Comparative and
International Law* 77

Gallagher K and Birch M, 'Do Investment Agreements Attract Investment?
Evidence from Latin America' in Sauvant K and Sachs L (eds), *The Effect of
Treaties on Foreign Direct Investment: Bilateral Investment Treaties, Double Taxation
Treaties and Investment Flows* (Oxford University Press 2009)

Gallus N, 'The Influence of the Host State's Level of Development on
International Investment Treaty Standards of Protection' (2005) 6 *Journal of
World Investment and Trade* 711

Gantz D, 'Potential Conflict between Investor Rights and Environmental Regulation under NAFTA's Chapter 11' (2001) 33 *George Washington International Law Review* 651

Gardiner R, *Treaty Interpreation* (Oxford University Press 2008)

Garner B (ed), *Black's Law Dictionary* (8th edn, West Group 2004)

Gehring M, 'Impact Assessments of Investment Treaties' in Cordonier Segger M-C, Gehring M and Newcombe A (eds), *Sustainable Development in World Investment Law* (Kluwer Law International 2011)

Gibbard A and Varian H, 'Economic Models' (1978) 75 *Journal of Philosophy* 664

Ginsburg T, 'International Substitutes for Domestic Institutions: Bilateral Investment Treaties and Governance' (2005) 25 *International Review of Law and Economics* 107

Graham E, 'Regulatory Takings, Supernational Treatment, and the Multilateral Agreement on Investment: Issues Raised by Nongovernmental Organizations' (1998) 31 *Cornell International Law Journal* 599

Grierson-Weiler T and Laird I, 'Standards of Treatment' in Muchlinski P, Ortino F and Schreuer C (eds), *The Oxford Handbook of International Investment Law* (Oxford University Press 2008)

Gross S, 'Inordinate Chill: BITs Non-NAFTA MITs and Host State Regulatory Freedom – an Indonesian Case Study' (2003) 24 *Michigan Journal of International Law* 893

Grosse R and Trevino L, 'New Institutional Economics and FDI Location in Central and Eastern Europe' in Sauvant K and Sachs L (eds), *The Effect of Treaties on Foreign Direct Investment: Bilateral Investment Treaties, Double Taxation Treaties and Investment Flows* (Oxford University Press 2009)

Grossman G and Lai E, 'International Protection of Intellectual Property' (2004) 94 *American Economic Review* 635

Guzman A, 'Why LDCs Sign Treaties That Hurt Them: Explaining the Popularity of Bilateral Investment Treaties' (1998) 38 *Virginia Journal of International Law* 639

'Explaining the Popularity of Bilateral Investment Treaties' in Sauvant K and Sachs L (eds), *The Effect of Treaties on Foreign Direct Investment: Bilateral Investment Treaties, Double Taxation Treaties and Investment Flows* (Oxford University Press 2009)

Halabi S, 'Efficient Contracting between Foreign Investors and Host States: Evidence from Stabilization Clauses' (2011) 31 *Northwestern Journal of International Law and Business* 261

Hallward-Driemeier M, 'Do Bilateral Investment Treaties Attract FDI? Only a Bit . . . and They Could Bite' in Sauvant K and Sachs L (eds), *The Effect of Treaties on Foreign Direct Investment: Bilateral Investment Treaties, Double Taxation Treaties and Investment Flows* (Oxford University Press 2009)

Hamilton C and Rochwerger P, 'Trade and Investment: Foreign Direct Investment through Bilateral and Multilateral Treaties' (2005) 18 *New York International Law Review* 1

Harris D, O'Boyle M and Warbrick C, *Law of the European Convention on Human Rights* (Butterworths 1995)

Harrison J, 'Human Rights Arguments in Amicus Curiae Submissions: Promoting Social Justice?' in Dupuy P-M, Francioni F and Petersmann E-U (eds), *Human Rights in International Investment Law and Arbitration* (Oxford University Press 2009)

Harsanyi JC, 'Cardinal Welfare, Individualistic Ethics, and Interpersonal Comparisons of Utility' (1955) 63 *The Journal of Political Economy* 309

Hart HLA, 'American Jurisprudence through English Eyes: The Nightmare and the Noble Dream' (1977) 11 *Georgia Law Review* 969

The Concept of Law (2nd edn, Oxford University Press 1994)

Hart HLA and Honoré T, *Causation in the Law* (2nd edn, The Clarendon Press 1985)

Heckman J and Vytlacil E, 'Econometric Evaluation of Social Programs, Part I: Causal Models, Structural Models and Econometric Policy Evaluation' in Griliches Z and Intriligator M (North-Holland 2008)

Helfer L and Slaughter A-M, 'Why States Create International Tribunals: A Response to Professors Posner and Yoo' (2005) 93 *California Law Review* 899

Henckels C, 'Indirect Expropriation and the Right to Regulate: Revisiting Proportionality Analysis and the Standard of Review in Investment Treaty Arbitration' (2012) 15 *Journal of International Economic Law* 223

'Balancing Investment Protection and the Public Interest: The Role of the Standard of Review and the Importance of Deference in Investor-State Arbitration' (2013) 4 *Journal of International Dispute Settlement* 197

Hepburn J, 'The Duty to Give Reasons for Administrative Decisions in International Law' (2012) 61 *International and Comparative Law Quarterly* 641

Hepburn J and Peterson LE, 'Cuba Prevails in Rare State-to-State Investment Treaty Arbitration Initiated by Italy on behalf of Italian Nationals' (2011) *IA Reporter*, http://ezproxy.ouls.ox.ac.uk:4998/articles/20110704_3. Accessed 11 January 2012

US-Ecuador Inter-State Investment Treaty Award Released to Parties; Tribunal Member Part Ways on Key Issues' (2012) *IA Reporter*, www.iareporter.com. virtual.anu.edu.au/articles/20121030_1. Accessed 12 October 2013

Hepple B, 'Book Reviews: *The Costs of Accidents*' (1970) 28 *Cambridge Law Journal* 350

Hertier H, 'Causal Explanation' in della Porta D and Keating M (eds), *Approaches and Methodologies in the Social Sciences* (Cambridge University Press 2008)

Hickman T, 'The Reasonableness Principle: Reassessing Its Place in the Public Sphere' (2004) 63 *Cambridge Law Journal* 166

Higgins R, 'The Taking of Property by the State: Recent Developments in International Law' (1982) 176 *Recueil des Cours de l'Académie de Droit International* 259

High Commissioner for Human Rights, *Economic, Social and Cultural Rights: Human Rights, Trade and Investment* (United Nations 2003)

Hirsch M, 'Interactions between Investment and Non-Investment Obligations' in Muchlinski P, Ortino F and Schreuer C (eds), *The Oxford Handbook of International Investment Law* (Oxford University Press 2008)

'Investment Tribunals and Human Rights: Divergent Paths' in Dupuy P-M, Francioni F and Petersmann E-U (eds), *Human Rights in International Investment Law and Arbitration* (Oxford University Press 2009

Hobér K, 'Remedies in Investment Disputes' in Bjorklund A, Laird I and Ripinsky S (eds), *Investment Treaty Law: Current Issues III* (British Institute of International and Comparative Law 2009)

Hoffmann A, 'Indirect Expropriation' in Reinisch A (ed), *Standards of Investment Protection* (Oxford University Press 2008)

Howse R, 'Sovereignty, Lost and Found' in Shan W, Simons P and Singh D (eds), *Redefining Sovereignty in International Economic Law* (Hart 2008)

Huang Y, 'Are Foreign Firms Privileged by Their Host Governments? Evidence from the 2000 World Business Environment Survey' (2005), http://dspace. mit.edu/bitstream/handle/1721.1/18075/4538-04.pdf?sequence=1. Accessed 20 April 2011

Innes R, 'Takings, Compensation, and Equal Treatment for Owners of Developed and Undeveloped Property' (1997) 40 *Journal of Law and Economics* 403

International Centre for Settlement of Investment Disputes, 'Ecuador Submits a Notice under Article 71 of the ICSID Convention' (2009), http://icsid. worldbank.org/ICSID/FrontServlet?requestType=CasesRH&actionVal=Open Page&PageType=AnnouncementsFrame&FromPage=NewsReleases&page Name=Announcement20. Accessed 23 January 2012

International Law Commission, *Draft Articles of the International Law Commission* (Yearbook of the International Law Commission, Volume II, Part Two, 2001)

Jackson JH, 'Sovereignty-Modern: A New Approach to an Outdated Concept' (2003) 97 *American Journal of International Law* 782

Jarvin S, 'Non-Pecuniary Remedies: The Practice of Declaratory Relief and Specific Performance in International Commercial Arbitration' in Rovine A (ed), *Contemporary Issues in International Arbitration and Mediation: The Fordham Papers 2007* (Martinus Nijhoff 2008)

Kantor M, 'Fair and Equitable Treatment: Echoes of FDR's Court-packing Plan in the International Law Approach Towards Regulatory Expropriation' (2006) 5 *The Law and Practice of International Courts and Tribunals* 231

Kaplow L, 'An Economic Analysis of Legal Transactions' (1986) 99 *Harvard Law Review* 515

'Horizontal Equity: New Measures, Unclear Principles' (2000), www.nber.org/ papers/w7649.pdf. Accessed 25 April 2011

Karl J, 'International Investment Arbitration: A Threat to State Sovereignty?' in Shan W, Simons P and Singh D (eds), *Redefining Sovereignty in International Economic Law* (Hart 2008)

Kaufmann D, Kraay A and Mastruzzi M, 'Governance Matters VIII: Aggregate and Individual Governance Indicators 1996–2008' (2009), http://papers.ssrn.com/ sol3/papers.cfm?abstract_id=1424591. Accessed 26 July 2010

Kaufmann-Kohler G, 'Arbitral Precedent: Dream, Necessity or Excuse? The 2006 Freshfields Lecture' (2007) 23 *Arbitration International* 357

Kelsen H, 'On the Theory of Interpretation' (1990) 10 *Legal Studies* 127

Introduction to the Problems of Legal Theory (Oxford University Press 1992)

Kennedy D, 'Cost Benefit Analysis of Entitlement Problems: A Critique' (1984) 33 *Stanford Law Review* 387

Kerner A, 'Why Should I Believe You? The Costs and Consequences of Bilateral Investment Treaties' (2009) 53 *International Studies Quarterly* 73

Kim S, 'Bilateral Investment Treaties, Political Risk and Foreign Direct Investment' (2007) 11 *Asia Pacific Journal of Economics & Business* 6

King J, *Judging Social Rights* (Cambridge University Press 2012)

Kingsbury B and Schill S, 'Public Law Concepts to Balance Investors' Rights with State Regulatory Actions in the Public Interest – The Concept of Proportionality' in Schill S (ed), *International Investment Law and Comparative Public Law* (Oxford University Press 2010)

Kinnear M, 'The Continuing Development of the Fair and Equitable Treatment Standard' in Bjorklund A, Laird I and Ripinsky S (eds), *Investment Treaty Law: Current Issues III* (British Institute of International and Comparative Law 2009)

Kläger R, 'Fair and Equitable Treatment' and Sustainable Development' in Cordonier Segger M-C, Gehring M and Newcombe A (eds), *Sustainable Development in World Investment Law* (Kluwer Law International 2011)
'Fair and Equitable Treatment' in International Investment Law (Cambridge University Press 2011)

Knahr C, 'Indirect Expropriation in Recent Investment Arbitration' (2009) 6 *Transnational Dispute Management* 1

Kolb R, *Interprétation et création du droit international: Esquisses d'une herméneutique juridique moderne pour le droit international public* (Bruylant 2006)

Koskenniemi M, *From Apology to Utopia: The Structure of International Legal Argument* (Cambridge University Press 2006)

Kreindler R, 'Fair and Equitable Treatment – A Comparative International Law Approach' (2006) 3 *Transnational Dispute Management* 1

Kriebaum U, 'Privatizing Human Rights: The Interface between International Investment Protection and Human Rights' (2006) 3 *Transnational Dispute Management* 1
'Partial Expropriation' (2007) 8 *Journal of World Investment and Trade* 69
'Regulatory Takings: Balancing the Interests of the Investor and the State' (2007) 8 *Journal of World Investment and Trade* 717
'Local Remedies and the Standards for the Protection of Foreign Investment' in Binder C et al. (eds), *International Investment Law for the 21st Century* (Oxford University Press 2009)

Kriebaum U and Schreuer C, 'The Concept of Property in Human Rights Law and International Investment Law' in Breitenmoser S (ed), *Human Rights, Democracy and the Rule of Law* (Nomos 2007)

Krommendijk J and Morijn J, 'Proportional by What Measure(s)? Balancing Investor Interests and Human Rights by Way of Applying the Proportionality Principle in Investor-State Arbitration' in Dupuy P-M, Francioni F and Petersmann E-U (eds), *Human Rights in International Investment Law and Arbitration* (Oxford University Press 2009)

Kronman A, *The Lost Lawyer: Failing Ideals of the Legal Profession* (Belknap Press 1993)

Kulick A, *Global Public Interest in International Investment Law* (Cambridge University Press 2012)

Kurtz J, 'The Use and Abuse of WTO Law in Investor-State Arbitration: Competition and Its Discontents' (2009) 20 *European Journal of International Law* 749

  'Australia's Rejection of Investor-State Arbitration: Causation, Omission and Implication' (2012) 27 *ICSID Review* 65

Lall S and Narula R, 'Foreign Direct Investment and Its Role in Economic Development: Do We Need a New Agenda?' (2004) 16 *The European Journal of Development Research* 447

Leeks A, 'The Relationship between Bilateral Investment Treaty Arbitration and the Wider Corpus of International Law: The ICSID Approach' (2007) 65 *University of Toronto Faculty of Law Review* 1

Lerner A, *The Economics of Control: Principles of Welfare Economics* (Macmillan 1944)

Lester S, 'Liberalization or Litigation? Time to Rethink the International Investment Regime' (2013) *Policy Analysis*, www.cato.org/publications/policy-analysis/liberalization-or-litigation-time-rethink-international-investment. Accessed 17 October 2013

Levinson D, 'Making Government Pay: Markets, Politics, and the Allocation of Constitutional Costs' (2000) 67 *University of Chicago Law Review* 345

Levmore S, 'Just Compensation and Just Politics' (1990) 22 *Connecticut Law Review* 285

Lipsey R and Lancaster K, 'The General Theory of the Second Best' (1956) 24 *The Review of Economic Studies* 11

Louthan S, 'A Brave New Lochner Era? The Constitutionality of NAFTA Chapter 11' (2001) 34 *Vanderbilt Journal of Transnational Law* 1443

Lowe V, 'Sustainable Development and Unsustainable Arguments' in Boyle A and Freestone D (eds), *International Law and Sustainable Development: Past Achievements and Future Challenges* (Clarendon Press 1999)

  'The Politics of Law-Making: Are the Method and Character of Norm Creation Changing?' in Byers M (ed), *The Role of Law in International Politics: Essays in International Relations and International Law* (Oxford University Press 2000)

  'Regulation or Expropriation?' (2002) 55 *Current Legal Problems* 447

  'Changing Dimensions of International Investment Law' (2007), http://papers.ssrn.com/sol3/papers.cfm?abstract_id=970727. Accessed 28 November 2013

  'Sovereignty and International Economic Law' in Shan W, Simons P and Singh D (eds), *Redefining Sovereignty in International Economic Law* (Hart 2008)

Lowenfeld A, *International Economic Law* (2nd edn, Oxford University Press 2008)

Lunney GS, 'Takings, Efficiency, and Distributive Justice: A Response to Professor Dagan' (1990) 99 *Michigan Law Review* 157

MacDougall GDA, 'The Benefits and Costs of Private Investment from Abroad' (1960) 36 *Economic Record* 13

Mairal H, 'Legitimate Expectations and Informal Administrative Representations' in Schill S (ed), *International Investment Law and Comparative Public Law* (Oxford University Press 2010)

Malik M, 'Fair and Equitable Treatment' (2009), www.iisd.org/pdf/2009/best_practices_bulletin_3.pdf. Accessed 27 October 2010

Mann FA, 'British Treaties for the Promotion and Protection of Investments' (1981) 52 *British Yearbook of International Law* 241

Mann H, 'The Right of States to Regulate and International Investment Law' (2002), www.iisd.org/pdf/2003/investment_right_to_regulate.pdf. Accessed 26 November 2009

'Investment Agreements and the Regulatory State: Can Exceptions Clauses Create a Safe Haven for Governments?' (2007), www.iisd.org/pdf/2007/inv_agreements_reg_state.pdf. Accessed 5 June 2010

'International Investment Agreements, Business and Human Rights: Key Issues and Opportunities' (2008), www.iisd.org/pdf/2008/iia_business_human_rights.pdf. Accessed 27 November 2009

Marboe I, *Calculation of Compensation and Damages in International Investment Law* (Oxford University Press 2009)

'State Responsibility and Comparative State Liability for Administrative and Legislative Harm to Economic Interests' in Schill S (ed), *International Investment Law and Comparative Public Law* (Oxford University Press 2010)

Margolis J, 'Comment on Niskanen "Bureaucrats and Politicians"' (1975) 18 *Journal of Law and Economics* 645

Marjosola H, 'Public/Private Conflict in Investment Treaty Arbitration – A Study on Umbrella Clauses' (2009) *Helsinki Law Review* 103

Markesinis B and Fedtke J, 'Damages for the Negligence of Statutory Bodies: The Empirical and Comparative Dimension to an Unending Debate' (2007) *Public Law* 229

Markusen J, 'Commitment to Rules on Investment: The Developing Countries' Stake' (2001) 9 *Review of International Economics* 287

Marsh A, 'The Impact of Liability on Public Bodies: Lessons from the Literature' (2008), www.bristol.ac.uk/sps/aboutus/sps-staff-details/marsh. Accessed 18 February 2011

Marshall A, *Principles of Economics* (9th edn, MacMillan 1920)

Maupin J, 'Public and Private in International Investment Law' (2014) 54 *Virginia Journal of International Law* (forthcoming)

Mayeda G, 'Sustainable International Investment Agreements: Challenges and Solutions for Developing Countries' in Cordonier Segger M-C, Gehring M and Newcombe A (eds), *Sustainable Development in World Investment Law* (Kluwer Law International 2011)

McCrudden C, *Buying Social Justice* (Oxford University Press 2007)

McLachlan C, 'The Principle of Systemic Integration and Article 31(3)(c) of the Vienna Convention' (2005) 54 *International and Comparative Law Quarterly* 279

'Investment Treaties and General International Law' (2008) 57 *International and Comparative Law Quarterly* 361

McLachlan C, Shore L and Weiniger M, *International Investment Arbitration: Substantive Principles* (Oxford University Press 2007)

Mercuro N and Medema S, *Economics and the Law; From Posner to Post-Modernism and Beyond* (2nd edn, Princeton University Press 2006)

Miceli T, *The Economic Theory of Eminent Domain: Private Property, Public Use* (Cambridge University Press 2011)

Miceli T and Segerson K, 'Regulatory Takings: When Should Compensation Be Paid?' (1994) 23 *Journal of Legal Studies* 749

Michelman F, 'Property, Utility, and Fairness: Comments on the Ethical Foundation of "Just Compensation" Law' (1967) 80 *Harvard Law Review* 1165

Miles K, *The Origins of International Investment Law: Empire, the Environment and the Safeguarding of Capital* (Cambridge University Press 2013)

Mina W, 'External Commitment Mechanisms, Institutions, and FDI in GCC Countries' (2009) 19 *International Financial Markets, Institutions and Money* 371

Montt S, *State Liability in Investment Treaty Arbitration* (Hart 2009)

Moran T, Graham E and Blomström M, 'Introduction and Overview' in Moran T, Graham E and Blomström M (eds), *Does Foreign Direct Investment Promote Development?* (Institute for International Economics 2005)

Morin J-F and Gagné G, 'What Can Best Explain the Prevalance of Bilateralism in the Investment Regime?' (2007) 36 *Journal of International Political Economy* 53

Morita S and Zaelke D, 'Rule of Law, Good Governance and Sustainable Development' (2005), http://www.inece.org/conference/7/vol1/05_Sachiko_Zaelke.pdf. Accessed 26 July 2010

Mountfield H, 'Regulatory Expropriations in Europe: The Approach of the European Court of Human Rights' (2002) 11 *New York University Environmental Law Journal* 136

Mourra MH, 'The Conflicts and Controversies in Latin American Treaty-Based Disputes' in Mourra MH (ed), *Latin American Investment Treaty Arbitration* (Kluwer Law International 2007)

Muchlinski P, 'The Rise and Fall of the Multilateral Agreement on Investment: Where Now?' (2000) 34 *The International Lawyer* 1033

Multinational Enterprises and the Law (2nd edn, Oxford University Press 2007)

'Policy Issues' in Muchlinski P, Ortino F and Schreuer C (eds), *The Oxford Handbook of International Investment Law* (Oxford University Press 2008)

Neumayer E, *Greening Trade and Investment* (Earthscan 2001)

Neumayer E and Spess L, 'Do Bilateral Investment Treaties Increase Foreign Direct Investment to Developing Countries' in Sauvant K and Sachs L (eds), *The Effect of Treaties on Foreign Direct Investment: Bilateral Investment Treaties, Double Taxation Treaties and Investment Flows* (Oxford University Press 2009)

Newcombe A, 'Canada's New Model Foreign Protection Agreement' (2004), http://ita.law.uvic.ca/documents/CanadianFIPA.pdf. Accessed 7 May 2008

'The Boundaries of Regulatory Expropriation in International Law' (2005) 20 *ICSID Review – Foreign Investment Law Journal* 1

'Sustainable Development and Investment Treaty Law' (2007) 8 *Journal of World Investment and Trade* 357

'General Exceptions in International Investment Agreements' in Cordonier
    Segger M-C, Gehring M and Newcombe A (eds), *Sustainable Development in
    World Investment Law* (Kluwer Law International 2011)
Newcombe A and Paradell L, *Law and Practice of Investment Treaties: Standards of
    Treatment* (Kluwer Law International 2009)
Nottage L, 'What Future for Investor-State Arbitration Provisions in Asia Pacific
    Treaties?' (2011) *East Asia Forum*, www.eastasiaforum.org/2011/04/26/
    what-future-for-investor-state-arbitration-provisions-in-asia-pacific-treaties.
    Accessed 30 January 2012.
Nozick R, *Anarchy, State and Utopia* (Basil Blackwell 1974)
Office for National Statistics, 'Share of the Wealth' (2006), www.statistics.gov.uk/
    cci/nugget.asp?id=2. Accessed 28 May 2010
Office of the United States Trade Representative, 'Outlines of the Trans-Pacific
    Partnership Agreement' (2011), www.ustr.gov/about-us/press-office/
    fact-sheets/2011/november/outlines-trans-pacific-partnership-agreement.
    Accessed 22 February 2012
Oh CH and Fratianni M, 'Do Additional Bilateral Investment Treaties Boost
    Foreign Direct Investment?' (2010), http://mofir.univpm.it/files/working%
    20paper/Mofir_43.pdf. Accessed 8 August 2010
Omalu M, *NAFTA and the Energy Charter Treaty* (Kluwer Law International
    1999)
Ortino F, 'From 'Non-discrimination' to 'Reasonableness': A Paradigm Shift in
    International Economic Law?' (2005), http://centers.law.nyu.edu/
    jeanmonnet/papers/05/050101.html. Accessed 28 October 2009
'The Social Dimension of International Investment Agreements: Drafting a
    New BIT/MIT Model?' (2005) 7 *International Law FORUM du droit international*
    243
'Non-Discriminatory Treatment in Investment Disputes' in Dupuy P-M,
    Francioni F and Petersmann E-U (eds), *Human Rights in International Investment
    Law and Arbitration* (Oxford University Press 2009)
'The Investment Treaty System as Judicial Review: Some Remarks on Its
    Nature, Scope and Standards' (2012), http://papers.ssrn.com/sol3/papers.cfm?
    abstract_id=2181103. Accessed 27 November 2013
'Refining the Content and Role of Investment "Rules" and "Standards": A New
    Approach to International Investment Treaty Making' (2013) 28 *ICSID Review*
    152
Osmani S, 'The Sen System of Social Evaluation' in Basu K and Kanbur R (eds),
    *Arguments for a Better World: Essays in Honor of Amartya Sen – Volume I: Ethics,
    Welfare and Measurement* (Oxford University Press 2008)
Paparinskis M, 'Regulatory Expropriation and Sustainable Development' in
    Cordonier Segger M-C, Gehring M and Newcombe A (eds), *Sustainable
    Development in World Investment Law* (Kluwer Law International 2011)
The International Minimum Standard and Fair and Equitable Treatment (Oxford
    Univeristy Press 2013)

'Analogies and Other Regimes of International Law' in Douglas Z, Pauwely J and Viñuales J (eds), *The Foundations of International Investment Law: Bringing Theory into Practice* (Oxford University Press 2014)

Paradell L, 'The BIT Experience of the Fair and Equitable Treatment Standard' in Ortino F et al. (eds), *Investment Treaty Law: Current Issues II* (British Institute of International and Comparative Law 2007)

Paulsson J, 'Arbitration without Privity' (1995) 10 *ICSID Review – Foreign Investment Law Journal* 232

'Indirect Expropriation: Is the Right to Regulate at Risk?' (2005), www.oecd.org/dataoecd/5/52/36055332.pdf. Accessed 24 November 2009

Denial of Justice in International Law (Cambridge University Press 2005)

Paulsson J and Douglas Z, 'Indirect Expropriation in Investment Treaty Arbitrations' in Horn N (ed), *Arbitrating Foreign Investment Disputes: Procedural and Substantive Legal Aspects* (Kluwer Law International 2004)

Pavoni R, 'Environmental Rights, Sustainable Development, and Investor-State Case Law: A Critical Appraisal' in Dupuy P-M, Francioni F and Petersmann E-U (eds), *Human Rights in International Investment Law and Arbitration* (Oxford University Press 2009)

Peinhardt C and Allee T, 'Devil in the Details? The Investment Effects of Dispute Settlement Variation in BITs' in Sauvant K, *Yearbook on International Investment Law & Policy 2010–2011* (Oxford University Press 2012)

'Different Investment Treaties, Different Effects' (2012), www.vcc.columbia.edu/content/different-investment-treaties-different-effects. Accessed 21 February 2012

Peltzman S, 'Toward a More General Theory of Regulation' (1976) 19 *Journal of Law and Economics* 211

Petersmann E-U, 'Constitutional Theories of International Economic Adjudication and Investor-State Arbitration' in Dupuy P-M, Francioni F and Petersmann E-U (eds), *Human Rights in International Investment Law and Arbitration* (Oxford University Press 2009)

'Human Rights, Constitutionalism, and 'Public Reason' in Investor-State Arbitration' in Binder C et al. (eds), *International Investment Law for the 21st Century* (Oxford University Press 2009)

Peterson LE, *Human Rights and Bilateral Investment Treaties: Mapping the Role of Human Rights Law within Investor-State Arbitration* (Rights and Democracy 2009)

'Canada Settles NAFTA Claim by Pulp & Paper Company for $130 Million; Spotlight Turns to Federal Government's Being on Hook for Actions of Province' (2010) *IA Reporter*, http://ezproxy.ouls.ox.ac.uk:4998/articles/20100830_1. Accessed 23 January 2012

'Hungary Prevails in First of Three Energy Charter Treaty (ECT) Arbitrations over Power Pricing Disputes; Arbitrators Affirm That "Politics" Is Not a Dirty Word' (2010) *IA Reporter*, www.iareporter.com/articles/20100928_7. Accessed 27 January 2011

'Parties in *Vattenfall* v *Germany* Case Suspend Proceedings' (2010), *IA Reporter*, http://ezproxy.ouls.ox.ac.uk:4998/articles/20100319_6. Accessed 30 January 2010

'Analysis: Australian Defense Strategy Puts Emphasis on Timing of Philip Morris's Corporate Structuring Moves, Claims "Abuse" of Investment Treaty' (2011) *IA Reporter*, http://ezproxy.ouls.ox.ac.uk:4998/articles/20111231_8. Accessed 24 January 2012

'Ecuador Initiates Unusual State-to-State Arbitration against United States in Bid to Clarify Scope of Investment Treaty Obligation' (2011) *IA Reporter*, http://ezproxy.ouls.ox.ac.uk:4998/articles/20110704_4. Accessed 11 January 2012

'ICSID Panels Convened in Disputes over Uruguay's Tobacco Policies, Venezuelan Airport Concession, Polish Health-Care Venture, and Hungarian Energy Investment' (2011) *IA Reporter*, www.iareporter.com/articles/20110330. Accessed 28 April 2011

Peterson LE and Gray K, *International Human Rights in Bilateral Investment Treaties and in Investment Treaty Arbitration* (International Institute of Sustainable Development 2003)

Pigou AC, *The Economics of Welfare* (Macmillan 1932)

Pogge T, *Realizing Rawls* (Cornell University Press 1989)

Poirier M, 'The NAFTA Chapter 11 Expropriation Debate through the Eyes of a Property Theorist' (2003) 33 *Environmental Law* 851

Polinsky M and Shavell S, 'Economic Analysis of Law' in Durlauf S and Blume L (eds), *The New Palgrave Dictionary of Economics* (2nd edn, Palgrave Macmillan 2008)

Porterfield M, 'International Expropriation Rules and Federalism' (2004) 23 *Stanford Environmental Law Journal* 3

Posner E and Yoo J, 'Judicial Independence in International Tribunals' (2005) 93 *California Law Review* 1

Posner R, 'Reviews: *The Costs of Accidents*' (1970) 37 *University of Chicago Law Review* 636

The Economics of Justice (Harvard University Press 1981)

'Cost-Benefit Analysis: Definition, Justification and Comment on Conference Papers' (2000) 29 *Journal of Legal Studies* 1153

Economic Analysis of Law (Aspen Publishers 2007)

Potesta M, 'Legitimate Expectations in Investment Treaty Law' (2013) 28 *ICSID Review* 88

Poulsen L, 'The Importance of BITs for Foreign Direct Investment and Political Risk Insurance: Revisiting the Evidence', in Sauvant K (ed), *Yearbook on International Investment Law & Policy 2009/2010* (Oxford University Press 2010)

'Bounded Rationality and the Diffusion of Modern Investment Treaties' (2013) 57 *International Studies Quarterly* 1

Poulsen L and Aisbett E, 'When the Claim Hits: Bilateral Investment Treaties and Bounded Rational Learning' (2013) 65 *World Politics* 273

Price D, 'Private Party vs Government, Investor-State Dispute Settlement: Frankenstein or Safety Valve' (2000) 26 *Canada United States Law Journal* 107

Productivity Commission, 'Bilateral and Regional Trade Agreements: Productivity Commission Research Report' (2010), www.pc.gov.au/__data/assets/pdf_file/0010/104203/trade-agreements-report.pdf. Accessed 30 January 2012

Ratner S, 'Regulatory Takings in Institutional Context: Beyond the Fear of Fragmented International Law' (2008) 102 *American Journal of International Law* 475

Rawls J, *A Theory of Justice* (rev edn, Belknap Press 1999)

Justice as Fairness: A Restatement (Belknap Press 2001)

Raz J, 'The Rule of Law and Its Virtue' (1977) 93 *The Law Quarterly Review* 195

Reed L and Bray D, 'Fair and Equitable Treatment: Fairly and Equitably Applied in Lieu of Unlawful Indirect Expropriation?' in Rovine A (ed), *Contemporary Issues in International Arbitration and Mediation: The Fordham Papers 2007* (Martinus Nijhoff 2008)

Reiner C and Schreuer C, 'Human Rights and International Investment Arbitration' in Dupuy P-M, Francioni F and Petersmann E-U (eds), *Human Rights in International Investment Law and Arbitration* (Oxford University Press 2009)

Reinisch A, 'Expropriation' in Muchlinski P, Ortino F and Schreuer C (eds), *The Oxford Handbook of International Investment Law* (Oxford University Press 2008)

'Legality of Expropriations' in Reinisch A (ed), *Standards of Investment Protection* (Oxford University Press 2008)

Reisman WM, 'The View from the New Haven School of International Law' (1992) 86 *American Society of International Law Proceedings* 118

Reisman WM and Arsanjani M, 'The Question of Unilateral Governmental Statements as Applicable Law in Investment Disputes' (2004) 19 *ICSID Review – FILJ* 328

Reisman WM and Sloane R, 'Indirect Expropriation and Its Valuation in the BIT Generation' (2003) 74 *British Yearbook of International Law* 115

Robbins J, 'The Emergence of Positive Obligations in Bilateral Investment Treaties' (2006) 13 *University of Miami International and Comparative Law Review* 403

'Robertson on Utility and Scope' (1953) 20 *Economica* 99

Roberts A, 'Power and Persuasion in Investment Treaty Interpretation: The Dual Role of States' (2010) 104 *American Journal of International Law* 179

'Clash of Paradigms: The Actors and Analogies Shaping the Investment Treaty System' (2013) 107 *American Journal of International Law* 45

'State-to-State Investment Treaty Arbitration: A Hybrid Theory of Interdependent Rights and Shared Interpretive Authority' (2014) 55 *Harvard International Law Journal* 1

Roemer J, *Theories of Distributive Justice* (Harvard University Press 1996)

Rose-Ackerman S and Rossi J, 'Disentangling Deregulatory Takings' (2000) 86 Virginia Law Review 1435

Ruiz Fabri H, 'The Approach Taken by the European Court of Human Rights to the Assessment of Compensation for "Regulatory Expropriations" of the

Property of Foreign Investors' (2002) 11 *New York University Environmental Law Journal* 148

Ryan C, 'Meeting Expectations: Assessing the Long-term Legitimacy and Stability of International Investment Law' (2008) 29 *University of Pennsylvania Journal of International Law* 725

Sachs J and Warner A, 'Natural Resources and Economic Development: The Curse of Natural Resources' (2001) 45 *European Economic Review* 827

Sachs L, 'Bilateral Investment Treaties and FDI Flows' (2009) *World Association of Investment Promotion Agencies (WAIPA) Newsletter* 5

Sachs L and Sauvant K, 'BITs, DTTs and FDI Flows: An Overview' in Sauvant K and Sachs L (eds), *The Effect of Treaties on Foreign Direct Investment: Bilateral Investment Treaties, Double Taxation Treaties and Investment Flows* (Oxford University Press 2009)

Salacuse J, *The Law of Investment Treaties* (Oxford University Press 2010)

Salacuse J and Sullivan N, 'Do BITs Really Work?: An Evaluation of Bilateral Investment Treaties and Their Grand Bargain' in Sauvant K and Sachs L (eds), *The Effect of Treaties on Foreign Direct Investment: Bilateral Investment Treaties, Double Taxation Treaties and Investment Flows* (Oxford University Press 2009)

Salvatore D, *International Economics* (9th edn, John Wiley & Sons 2007)

Sampliner G, 'Arbitration of Expropriation Cases under U.S. Investment Treaties – A Threat to Democracy of the Dog That Didn't Bark' (2003) 18 *ICSID Review – FILJ* 1

Sanders A, 'Of All Things Made in America Why Are We Exporting the *Penn Central* Test?' (2010) 30 *Northwestern Journal of International Law and Business* 339

Sarooshi D, 'The Essentially Contested Nature of the Concept of Sovereignty: Implications for the Exercise by International Organizations of Delegated Powers of Government' (2004) 25 *Michigan Journal of International Law* 1107

Sasson M, *Substantive Law in Investment Treaty Arbitration: The Unsettled Relationship between International and Municipal Law* (Kluwer 2010)

Scanlon T, *What We Owe Each Other* (Belknap Press 1998)

Schill S, 'Fair and Equitable Treatment under Investment Treaties as an Embodiment of the Rule of Law' (2006), www.iilj.org/publications/2006-6Schill.asp. Accessed 11 June 2010

'Do Investment Treaties Chill Unilateral State Regulation to Mitigate Climate Change?' (2007) 24 *Journal of International Arbitration* 469

'Book Reviews' (2009) 20 *European Journal of International Law* 229

The Multilateralization of International Investment Law (Cambridge University Press 2009)

'Multilateralizing Investment Treaties through Most-Favored-Nation Clauses' (2009) 27 *Berkley Journal of International Law* 496

'Fair and Equitable Treatment, the Rule of Law and Comparative Public Law' in Schill S (ed), *International Investment Law and Comparative Public Law* (Oxford University Press 2010)

'W(h)ither Fragmentation: On the Literature and Sociology of International Investment Law' (2011) 22 *European Journal of International Law* 875

'Deference in Investment Treaty Arbitration: Re-Conceptualising the Standard of Review' (2012) 3 *Journal of International Dispute Settlement* 1

Schneiderman D, *Constitutionalizing Economic Globalization: Investment Rules and Democracy's Promise* (Cambridge University Press 2008)

'Investing in Democracy? Political Process and International Investment Law' (2010) 60 *University of Toronto Law Journal* 909

'Legitimacy and Reflexivity in International Investment Arbitration: A New Self-Restraint?' (2011) 2 *Journal of International Dispute Settlement* 471

Schreiber W, 'Realizing the Right to Water in International Investment Law: An Interdisciplinary Approach to BIT Obligations' (2008) 48 *Natural Resources Journal* 431

Schreuer C, 'Non-Pecuniary Remedies in ICSID Arbitration' (2004) 20 *Arbitration International* 325

'Fair and Equitable Treatment in Arbitral Practice' (2005) 6 *The Journal of World Investment and Trade* 357

'The Concept of Expropriation under the ECT and Other Investment Protection Treaties ' in Ribeiro C (ed), *Investment Arbitration and the Energy Charter Treaty* (JurisNet 2006)

Schreuer C and Kriebaum U, 'At What Time Must Legitimate Expectations Exist?' in Werner J and Ali AH (eds), *A Liber Amicorum: Thomas Wälde – Law beyond Conventional Thought* (Cameron May 2010)

Schwebel S, 'The United States 2004 Model Bilateral Investment Treaty: An Exercise in the Regressive Development of International Law' (2006) 3(2) *Transnational Dispute Management* 1

Scott R and Stephan P, *The Limits of Leviathan: Contract Theory and the Enforcement of International Law* (Cambridge University Press 2006)

Sen A, 'The Impossibility of a Paretian Liberal' (1970) 78 *Journal of Political Economy* 152

'Interpersonal Aggregation and Partial Comparability' (1970) 38 *Econometrica* 393

'Rational Fools: A Critique of the Behavioral Foundations of Economic Theory' (1977) 6 *Philosophy and Public Affairs* 317

Inequality Reexamined (Clarendon Press 1992)

'Maximization and the Act of Choice' (1997) 65 *Econometrica* 745

Development as Freedom (Oxford University Press 1999)

'Consequential Evaluation and Practical Reason' (2000) 97 *The Journal of Philosophy* 477

'The Discipline of Cost-Benefit Analysis' (2000) 29 *Journal of Legal Studies* 931

'Incompleteness and Reasoned Choice' (2004) 140 *Synthese* 43

Rationality and Freedom (Harvard University Press 2004)

The Idea of Justice (Allen Lane 2009)

Sethi D and Judge W, 'Reappraising Liabilities of Foreignness within an Integrated Perspective of the Costs and Benefits of Doing Business Abroad' (2009) 18 *International Business Review* 404

Shackelford S, 'Investment Treaty Arbitration and Public Law, by Gus van Harten' (2008) 44 *Stanford Journal of International Law* 215

Shan W, 'Calvo Doctrine, State Sovereignty and the Changing Landscape of International Law' in Shan W, Simons P and Singh D (eds), *Redefining Sovereignty in International Economic Law* (Hart 2008)

Shavell S, *Economic Analysis of Accident Law* (Harvard University Press 1987)

Shea D, *The Calvo Clause: A Problem of Inter-American and Internaional Law and Diplomacy* (University of Minnesota Press 1955)

Shenkman E, 'Could Principles of Fifth Amendment Takings Jurisprudence Be Helpful in Analyzing Regulatory Expropriation Claims under International Law?' (2002) 11 *New York University Environmental Law Journal* 174

Sheppard A, 'The Distinction between Lawful and Unlawful Expropriation' in Ribeiro C (ed), *Investment Arbitration and the Energy Charter Treaty* (JurisNet 2006)

Shihata I, 'Towards a Greater Depoliticization of Investment Disputes: The Roles Of ICSID and MIGA' (1986) 1 *ICSID Review – FILJ* 1

Shinkman M, 'The Investors' View: Economic Opportunities versus Political Risks in 2007–11' in Kekiz L and Sauvant K (eds), *World Investment Prospects to 2011* (2007), http://graphics.eiu.com/upload/WIP_2007_WEB.pdf. Accessed 20 January 2012

Simma B, 'Foreign Investment Arbitration: A Place for Human Rights?' (2011) 60 *International and Comparative Law Quarterly* 573

Simma B and Kill T, 'Harmonizing Investment Protection and International Human Rights: First Steps Towards a Methodology' in Binder C et al. (eds), *International Investment Law for the 21st Century* (Oxford University Press 2009)

Simon H, 'Rationality in Psychology and Economics' (1986) 59 *Journal of Business* 209

Sinclair I, *The Vienna Convention on the Law of Treaties* (2nd edn, Manchester University Press 1984)

Slaughter AM, *A New World Order* (Princeton University Press 2004)

Smith S, 'The Rights of Private Law' in Robertson R and Hang T (eds), *The Goals of Private Law* (Hart Publishing 2009)

Snodgrass E, 'Protecting Investors' Legitimate Expectations: Recognizing and Delimiting a General Principle' (2006) 21 *ICSID Review – Foreign Investment Law Journal* 1

Sornarajah M, 'Power and Justice: Third World Resistance in International Law' (2006) 10 *Singapore Year Book of International Law* 19

'The Neo-Liberal Agenda in Investment Arbitration: Its Rise, Retreat and Impact on State Sovereignty' in Shan W, Simons P and Singh D (eds), *Redefining Sovereignty in International Economic Law* (Hart 2008)

The International Law on Foreign Investment (3rd edn, Cambridge University Press 2010)

Spears S, 'The Quest for Policy Space in an New Generation of International Investment Agreements' (2010) 13 *Journal of International Economic Law* 1037

Spence M, 'Job Market Signaling' (1973) 87 *Quarterly Journal of Economics* 355

Spiermann O, 'Premature Treaty Claims' in Binder C and others (eds), *International Investment Law for the 21st Century* (Oxford University Press 2009)

Stanley J, 'Keeping Big Brother out of Our Backyard: Regulatory Takings as Defined in International Law and Compared to American Fifth Amendment Jurisprudence' (2001) 15 *Emory International Law Review* 349

Stern B, 'In Search of the Frontiers of Indirect Expropriation' in Rovine A (ed), *Contemporary Issues in International Arbitration and Mediation: The Fordham Papers 2007* (Martinus Nijhoff 2008)

'Are Some Issues Too Political to Be Arbitrable?' (2009) 24 *ICSID Review – Foreign Investment Law Journal* 90

Stigler GJ, 'The Economics of Information' (1961) 69 *Journal of Political Economy* 213

'The Theory of Economic Regulation' (1971) 2 *Bell Journal of Economics and Management Science* 13

Stigler GJ, 'Two Notes on the Coase Theorem' (1989) 99 *The Yale Law Journal* 631

Stiglitz J, 'Regulating Multinational Corporations: Towards Principles of Cross-Border Legal Frameworks in a Globalized World Balancing Rights with Responsibilities' (2008) 23 *American University International Law Review* 451

Stoehr J and Perkins J, 'Perspectives of Stakeholders' in Franck S and Joubin-Bret A (eds), *Investor State Disputes: Prevention and Alternatives to Arbitration II* (United Nations 2011)

Stokey M and Zeckhauser R, *A Primer for Policy Analysis* (Norton 1978)

Stone Sweet A and Mathews J, 'Proportionality Balancing and Global Constitutionalism' (2008) 47 *Columbia Journal of Transnational Law* 73

Study Group of the International Law Commission, *Fragmentation of International Law: Difficulties Arising from the Diversification and Expansion of International Law* (2006), UN Doc. A/CN.4/L.702, www.un.org/ga/search/view_doc.asp?symbol=A/CN.4/L.702. Accessed 25 April 2014

Subedi S, 'The Challenge of Reconciling the Competing Principles with the Law of Foreign Investment with Special Reference to the Recent Trend in the Interpretation of the Term "Expropriation"' (2006) 40 *The International Lawyer* 121

Suda R, 'The Effect of Bilateral Investment Treaties on Human Rights Enforcement and Realization' (2005), www.law.nyu.edu/global/workingpapers/2005/ECM_DLV_015787. Accessed 19 April 2010

Sunstein C, 'Incommensurability and Valuation in Law' (1994) 92 *Michigan Law Journal* 779

The Cost-Benefit State: The Future of Regulatory Protection (American Bar Association 2002)

Swenson D, 'Why Do Developing Countries Sign BITs?' in Sauvant K and Sachs L (eds), *The Effect of Treaties on Foreign Direct Investment: Bilateral Investment Treaties, Double Taxation Treaties and Investment Flows* (Oxford University Press 2009)

Sykes A, 'International Law' in Polinsky M and Shavell S (eds), *Handbook of Law and Economics* (North-Holland 2007)

Thirlway H, 'The Sources of International Law' in Evans M (ed), *International Law* (Oxford University Press 2003)

Tienhaara K, *The Expropriation of Environmental Governance: Protecting Foreign Investors at the Expense of Public Policy* (Cambridge University Press 2009)

'Regulatory Chill and the Threat of Arbitration: A View from Political Science' in Brown C, Miles K (eds), *Evolution in Investment Treaty Law and Arbitration* (Cambridge University Press 2011)

Tobin J and Rose-Ackerman S, 'Foreign Direct Investment and the Business Environment in Developing Countries: The Impact of Bilateral Investment Treaties' (2005) Yale Law and Economics Research Paper No 293

'When BITs Have Some Bite: The Political-economic Environment for Bilateral Investment Treaties' (2011) 6 *Review of International Organizations* 1

Trachtman J, 'International Economic Law Research: a Taxonomy' in Picker C, Bunn I and Arner D (eds), *International Economic Law: The State and Future of the Discipline* (Hart 2008)

Treanor WM, 'The Original Understanding of the Takings Clause and the Political Process' (1995) 95 *Columbia Law Review* 782

Tremblay L, 'The Legitimacy of Judicial Review: The Limits of Dialogue between Courts and Legislatures' (2005) 3 *International Journal of Constitutional Law* 617

Trepte P, *Regulating Procurement: Understanding the Means and Ends of Public Procurement Regulation* (Oxford University Press 2004)

Tudor I, *The Fair and Equitable Treatment Standard in the International Law of Foreign Investment* (Oxford University Press 2008)

Turia T, 'Government Moves Forward with Plain Packaging of Tobacco Products' (2013), www.beehive.govt.nz/release/government-moves-forward-plain-packaging-tobacco-products. Accessed 19 October 2013

UNCTAD, *International Investment Agreements: Key Issues, Volume 1* (United Nations 2004)

'Latest Developments in Investor-State Dispute Settlement' (2005) International Investment Agreements Monitor

'Investment Policy Review of Brazil' (2005), http://unctad.org/en/docs/iteipcmisc20051_en.pdf. Accessed 30 March 2014

South-South Investment Agreements Proliferating (United Nations 2006)

'The Entry into Force of Bilateral Investment Treaties (BITs)' (2006) International Investment Agreements Monitor

Bilateral Investment Treaties 1995–2006, Trends in Investment Rule-Making (United Nations 2007)

Development Implications of International Investment Agreements (UNCTAD 2007)

South-South Cooperation in International Investment Agreements (United Nations 2007)

'Recent Developments in International Investment Agreements (2007 – June 2008)' (2008) International Investment Agreements Monitor

Investor-State Dispute Settlement and Impact on Investment Rulemaking (United Nations 2008)

'The Impact on Foreign Direct Investment of BITs' in Sauvant K and Sachs L (eds), *The Effect of Treaties on Foreign Direct Investment: Bilateral Investment Treaties, Double Taxation Treaties and Investment Flows* (Oxford University Press 2009)

'Recent Developments in International Investment Agreements (July 2008–June 2009)' (2009) International Investment Agreements Monitor

The Role of International Investment Agreements in Attracting Foreign Direct Investment to Developing Countries (United Nations 2009)

Investor State Disputes: Prevention and Alternatives to Arbitration (United Nations 2010)

Fair and Equitable Treatment: A Sequel (United Nations 2012)

'The Rise of Regionalism in International Investment Policymaking: Consolidation or Complexity?' (2013) IIA Issues Notes

World Investment Report 2013 (United Nations 2013)

'Brazil: Total Number of Bilateral Investment Treaties Concluded, 1 June 2013' (2013), http://unctad.org/Sections/dite_pcbb/docs/bits_brazil.pdf. Accessed 30 March 2014

Vadi V, 'Reconciling Public Health and Investor Rights: The Case of Tobacco' in Dupuy P-M, Francioni F and Petersmann E-U (eds), *Human Rights in International Investment Law and Arbitration* (Oxford University Press 2009)

'Critical Comparisons: The Role of Comparative Law in Investment Treaty Arbitration' (2010) 39 *Denver Journal of International Law and Policy* 67

Vadi V and Gruszczynski L, 'Standards of Review in International Investment Law and Arbitration: Multilevel Governance and the Commonweal' (2013) 16 *Journal of International Economic Law* 613

van Aaken A, 'Perils of Success? The Case of International Investment Protection' (2008) 9 *European Business Organization Law Review* 1

'International Investment Law between Commitment and Flexibility: A Contract Theory Analysis' (2009) 12 *Journal of International Economic Law* 507

'The International Investment Protection Regime through the Lens of Economic Theory' in Waibel M et al. (eds), *The Backlash against Investment Arbitration: Perceptions and Reality* (Kluwer Law International 2010)

'Primary and Secondary Remedies in International Investment Law and National State Liability: A Functional and Comparative View' in Schill S (ed), *International Investment Law and Comparative Public Law* (Oxford University Press 2010)

'Opportunities for and Limits to an Economic Analysis of International Law' (2011) 3 *Transnational Corporations Review* 27

Van Harten G, 'Private Authority and Transnational Governance: The Contours of the International System of Investor Protection' (2005) 12 *Review of International Political Economy* 600

Investment Treaty Arbitration and Public Law (Oxford University Press 2007)

'Five Justifications for Investment Treaties: A Critical Discussion' (2010) 2 *Trade, Law and Development* 1

'Perceived Bias in Investment Treaty Arbitration' in Waibel M et al. (eds), *The Backlash against Investment Arbitration: Perceptions and Reality* (Kluwer Law International 2010)

Sovereign Choices and Sovereign Constraints: Judicial Restraint in Investment Treaty Arbitration (Oxford University Press 2013)

Van Harten G and Loughlin M, 'Investment Treaty Arbitration as a Species of Global Administrative Law' (2006) 17 *European Journal of International Law* 121 van Rijn A, 'Right to the Peaceful Enjoyment of One's Possessions' in van Dijk P et al. (eds), *Theory and Practice of the European Convention on Human Rights* (4th edn, Intersentia 2006)

Vandevelde K, 'The Bilateral Investment Treaty Program of the United States' (1988) 21 *Cornell International Law Journal* 201

'The BIT Program: A Fifteen Year Appraisal' (1992) 86 *American Society of International Law Proceedings* 532

'The Political Economy of a Bilateral Investment Treaty' (1998) 92 *American Journal of International Law* 621

'The Economics of Bilateral Investment Treaties' (2000) 41 *Harvard International Law Journal* 469

'A Unified Theory of Fair and Equitable Treatment' (2010) 43 *International Law and Politics* 43

Bilateral Investment Treaties: History, Policy and Interpretation (Oxford University Press 2010)

VanDuzer JA, Simons P and Mayeda G, *Integrating Sustainable Development into International Investment Agreements: A Guide for Developing Countries* (Commonwealth Secretariat 2012)

Vasciannie S, 'The Fair and Equitable Treatment Standard in International Investment Law and Practice' (1999) 70 *British Yearbook of International Law* 99

Vicuña FO, 'Regulatory Authority and Legitimate Expectations: Balancing the Rights of the State and the Individual under International Law in a Global Society' (2003) 5 *International Law FORUM du droit international* 188

Vis-Dunbar D and Peterson LE, 'Bolivian Water Dispute Settled, Bechtel Forgoes Compensation' (2006) *Investment Treaty News* 1

Vis-Dunbar D and Poulsen LS, 'Reflections on Pakistan's Investment-Treaty Program after 50 Years: An Interview with the Former Attorney General of Pakistan, Makhdoom Ali Khan' (2009), www.investmenttreatynews.org /cms/news/archive/2009/03/16/pakistans-standstill-in-investment-treaty-making-an-interview-with-the-former-attorney-general-of-pakistan-makhdoom-ali-khan.aspx. Accessed 27 November 2009

von Bernstorff J, *The Public International Law Theory of Hans Kelsen* (Cambridge University Press 2010)

von Walter A, 'The Investor's Expectations in International Investment Arbitration' in Reinisch A and Knahr C (eds), *International Investment Law in Context* (Eleven International Publishing 2008)

Wagner JM, 'International Investment, Expropriation and Environmental Protection' (1999) 29 *Golden Gate University Law Review* 465

Wai R, 'Transnational Liftoff and Juridical Touchdown: The Regulatory Function of Private International Law in an Era of Globalization' (2002) 40 *Columbia Journal of Transnational Law* 209

Waincymer J, 'Balancing Property Rights and Human Rights in Expropriation' in Dupuy P-M, Francioni F and Petersmann E-U (eds), *Human Rights in International Investment Law and Arbitration* (Oxford University Press 2009)

Wälde T, 'Energy Charter Treaty-based Investment Arbitration' (2004) 5 *Journal of World Investment and Trade* 373

    'Interpreting Investment Treaties: Experiences and Examples' in Binder C et al. (eds), *International Investment Law for the 21st Century* (Oxford University Press 2009)

Wälde T and Kolo A, 'Environmental Regulation, Investment Protection and 'Regulatory Taking' in International Law' (2001) 50 *International and Comparative Law Quarterly* 811

Wälde T and Weiler T, 'Investment Arbitration under the Energy Charter Treaty in the Light of New NAFTA Precedents: Towards a Global Code of Conduct for Economic Regulation' (2004) 1 *Transnational Dispute Management* 1

Waldron J, 'The Core of the Case against Judicial Review' (2006) 115 *The Yale Law Journal* 1346

    The Right to Private Property (Clarendon Press 1990)

Weeramantry R, *Treaty Interpretation in Investment Arbitration* (Oxford University Press 2012)

Weiler T, 'Balancing Human Rights and Investor Protection: A New Approach for a Different Legal Order' (2004) 27 *Boston College International and Comparative Law Review* 429

Weiner A, 'Indirect Expropriations: The Need for a Taxonomy of "Legitimate" Regulatory Purpose' (2003) 5 *International Law FORUM du droit international* 166

Weinrib E, *The Goals of Private Law* (Harvard University Press 1995)

Westcott S, 'Recent Practice on the Fair and Equitable Treatment' (2007) 8 *The Journal of World Investment and Trade* 409

Weston B, '"Constructive Takings" under International Law: A Modest Foray into the Problem of "Creeping Expropriation"' (1975) 16 *Virginia Journal of International Law* 103

Whitsitt E, 'Claimant Seeks Enforcement of Environmental Laws in Notice of Dispute Alleging Expropriation of Barbadian Nature Sanctuary' (2010) *Investment Treaty News* 4

Wierzbowski M and Gubrynowicz A, 'Conflict of Norms Stemming from Intra-EU BITs and EU Legal Obligations: Some Remarks on Possible Solutions' in Binder C et al. (eds), *International Investment Law for the 21st Century* (Oxford University Press 2009)

Wilson P, 'Plain Packaging Bill Passes First Reading' (2014), http://www.3news.co.nz/Plain-packaging-bill-passes-first-reading/tabid/1607/articleID/331831/Default.aspx. Accessed 12 February 2014

Winisdoerffer Y, 'Margin of Appreciation and Article 1 of Protocol No 1' (1998) 19 *Human Rights Law Journal* 18

Wouters J, Duquez S and Hachez N, 'International Investment Law: The Perpetual Search for Consensus' in de Schutter O, Swinnen J and Wouters J (eds), *Foreign Direct Investment and Human Development: The Law and Economics of International Investment Agreements* (Routledge 2013)

Yackee J, 'Are BITs Such a Bright Idea? Exploring the Ideational Basis of Investment Treaty Enthusiasm' (2005) 12 *University of California Davis Journal of International Law and Policy* 195

'Conceptual Difficulties in the Empirical Study of Bilateral Investment Treaties' (2008) 33 *Brooklyn Journal of International Law* 405

'Do We Really Need BITs? Toward a Return to Contract in International Investment Law' (2008) 3 *Asian Journal of WTO and Health Law* 121

'Do BITs Really Work? Revisiting the Empirical Link between Investment Treaties and Foreign Direct Investment' in Sauvant K and Sachs L (eds), *The Effect of Treaties on Foreign Direct Investment: Bilateral Investment Treaties, Double Taxation Treaties and Investment Flows* (Oxford University Press 2009)

'Do Bilateral Investment Treaties Promote Foreign Direct Investment? Some Hints from Alternative Evidence' (2011) 51 *Virginia Journal of International Law* 397

Yannaca-Small C, '"Indirect Expropriation" and the "Right to Regulate" in International Investment Law' (2004), www.oecd.org/investment/internationalinvestmentagreements/33776546.pdf. Accessed 28 November 2013.

'Fair and Equitable Treatment Standard in International Investment Law' (2004), www.oecd.org/investment/internationalinvestmentagreements/33776498.pdf. Accessed 28 November 2013

'Indirect Expropriation and the Right to Regulate: How to Draw the Line?' in Yannaca-Small K (ed), *Arbitration under International Investment Agreements* (Oxford University Press 2010)

Zarsky L, 'Stuck in the Mud? Nation States, Globalization and the Environment' in Gallagher K and Werksman J (eds), *International Trade & Sustainable Development* (Earthscan 2002)

Zahrnt V, 'Transparency of Complex Regulation: How Should WTO Trade Policy Reviews Deal with Sanitary and Phytosanitary Policies?' (2011) 10 *World Trade Review* 217

Zweigert K, Kotz H, *Introduction to Comparative Law* (2nd edn, Oxford University Press 1998)

Index

Money Laundering: A New International Law Enforcement Model
Guy Stessens

Good Faith in European Contract Law
Reinhard Zimmermann and Simon Whittaker

On Civil Procedure
J. A. Jolowicz

Trusts: A Comparative Study
Maurizio Lupoi

The Right to Property in Commonwealth Constitutions
Tom Allen

International Organizations Before National Courts
August Reinisch

The Changing International Law of High Seas Fisheries
Francisco Orrego Vicuña

Trade and the Environment: A Comparative Study of EC and US Law
Damien Geradin

Unjust Enrichment: A Study of Private Law and Public Values
Hanoch Dagan

Religious Liberty and International Law in Europe
Malcolm D. Evans

Ethics and Authority in International Law
Alfred P. Rubin

Sovereignty Over Natural Resources: Balancing Rights and Duties
Nico Schrijver

The Polar Regions and the Development of International Law
Donald R. Rothwell

Fragmentation and the International Relations of Micro-States: Self-determination and Statehood
Jorri Duursma

Principles of the Institutional Law of International Organizations
C. F. Amerasinghe